Bermuda

Glenda Bendure
Ned Friary

LONELY PLANET PUBLICATIONS
Melbourne • Oakland • London • Paris

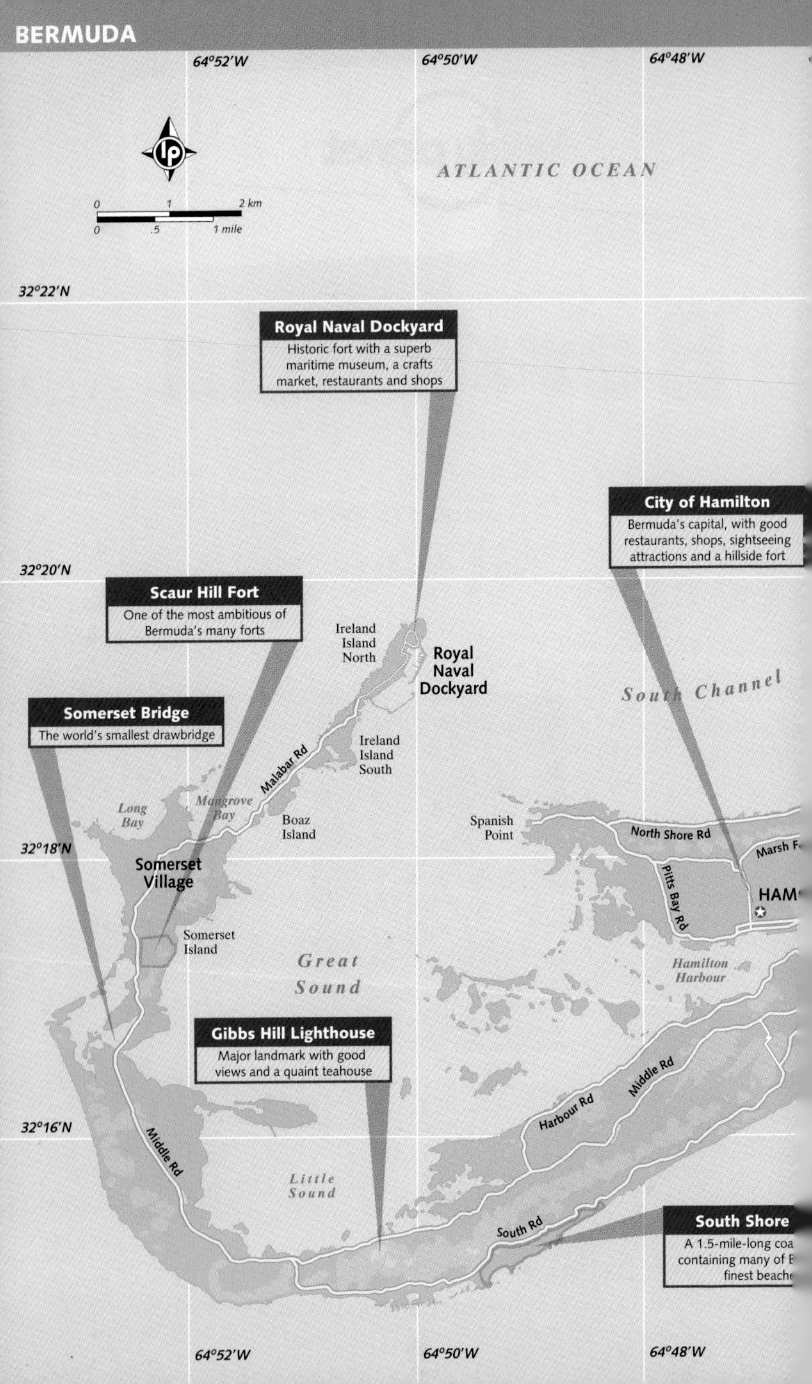

BERMUDA
64°52'W
64°50'W
64°48'W
0
1
2 km
0
.5
1 mile
ATLANTIC OCEAN
32°22'N
Royal Naval Dockyard
Historic fort with a superb maritime museum, a crafts market, restaurants and shops
City of Hamilton
Bermuda's capital, with good restaurants, shops, sightseeing attractions and a hillside fort
32°20'N
Scaur Hill Fort
One of the most ambitious of Bermuda's many forts
Ireland Island North
Royal Naval Dockyard
South Channel
Somerset Bridge
The world's smallest drawbridge
Ireland Island South
Malabar Rd
Long Bay
Mangrove Bay
Boaz Island
Spanish Point
North Shore Rd
32°18'N
Somerset Village
Pitts Bay Rd
HAM
Somerset Island
Great Sound
Hamilton Harbour
Gibbs Hill Lighthouse
Major landmark with good views and a quaint teahouse
Middle Rd
Harbour Rd
32°16'N
Middle Rd
Little Sound
South Rd
South Shore
64°52'W
64°50'W
64°48'W

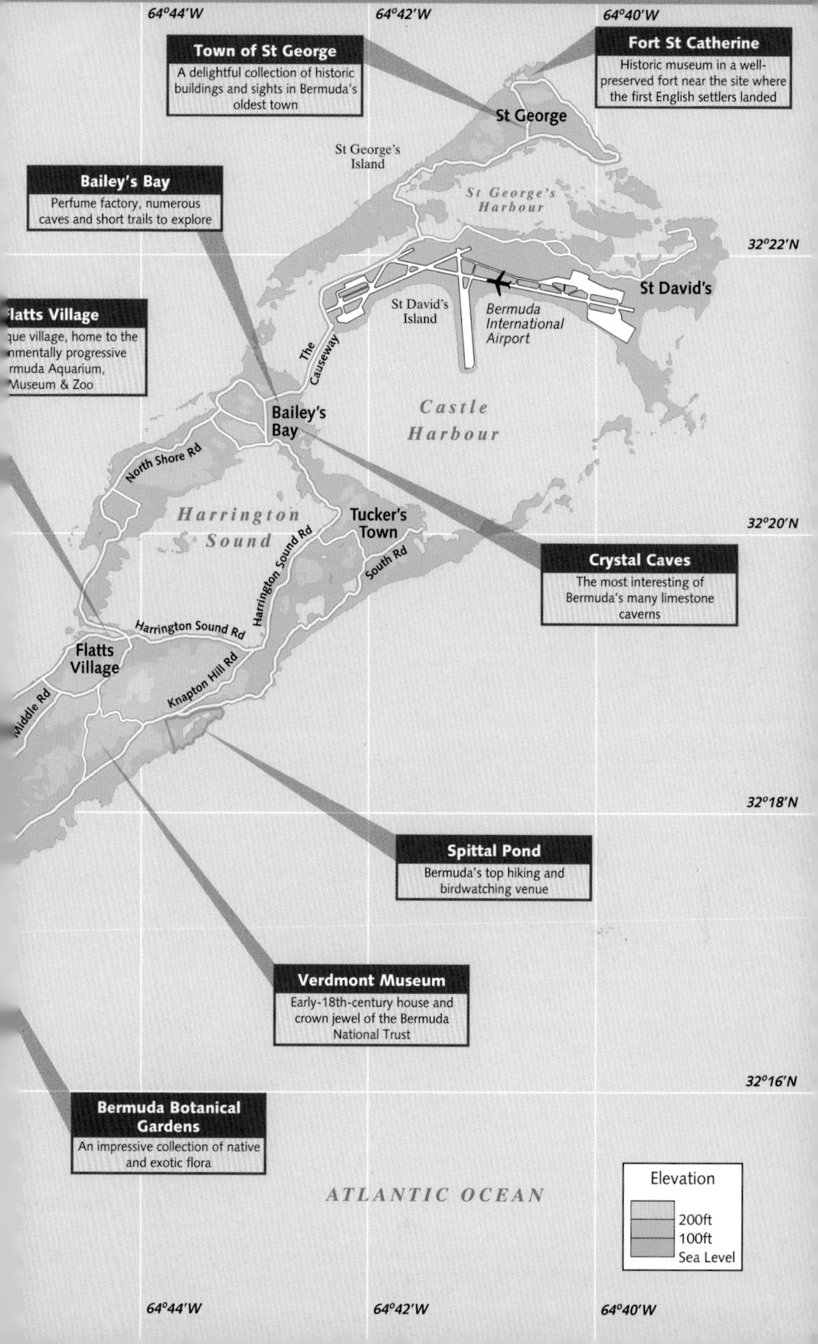

64°44′W 64°42′W 64°40′W

Town of St George

A delightful collection of historic buildings and sights in Bermuda's oldest town

Fort St Catherine

Historic museum in a well-preserved fort near the site where the first English settlers landed

Bailey's Bay

Perfume factory, numerous caves and short trails to explore

latts Village

que village, home to the
nmentally progressive
rmuda Aquarium,
Museum & Zoo

Crystal Caves

The most interesting of Bermuda's many limestone caverns

Spittal Pond

Bermuda's top hiking and birdwatching venue

Verdmont Museum

Early-18th-century house and crown jewel of the Bermuda National Trust

Bermuda Botanical Gardens

An impressive collection of native and exotic flora

St George
St George's Island
St George's Harbour
32°22′N
St David's
St David's Island
Bermuda International Airport
The Causeway
Bailey's Bay
Castle Harbour
North Shore Rd
Harrington Sound
Tucker's Town
32°20′N
Harrington Sound Rd
South Rd
Harrington Sound Rd
Flatts Village
Knapton Hill Rd
Middle Rd
32°18′N
32°16′N
ATLANTIC OCEAN

Elevation
200ft
100ft
Sea Level

64°44′W 64°42′W 64°40′W

Bermuda
2nd edition – September 2000
First published – March 1997

Published by
Lonely Planet Publications Pty Ltd ABN 36 005 607 983
90 Maribyrnong St, Footscray, Victoria 3011, Australia

Lonely Planet offices
Australia Locked Bag 1, Footscray, Victoria 3011
USA 150 Linden St, Oakland, CA 94607
UK 10a Spring Place, London NW5 3BH
France 1 rue du Dahomey, 75011 Paris

Photographs
Many of the images in this guide are available for licensing from Lonely Planet Images.
w www.lonelyplanetimages.com

Front cover photograph
Cup Match, St George (Scott Stallard/The Image Bank)

ISBN 1 86450 137 5

Printed by The Bookmaker International Ltd
Printed in China

ontents

RODUCTION 11

CITY OF HAMILTON

PEMBROKE PARISH

ST GEORGE'S PARISH

HAMILTON PARISH

SMITH'S PARISH

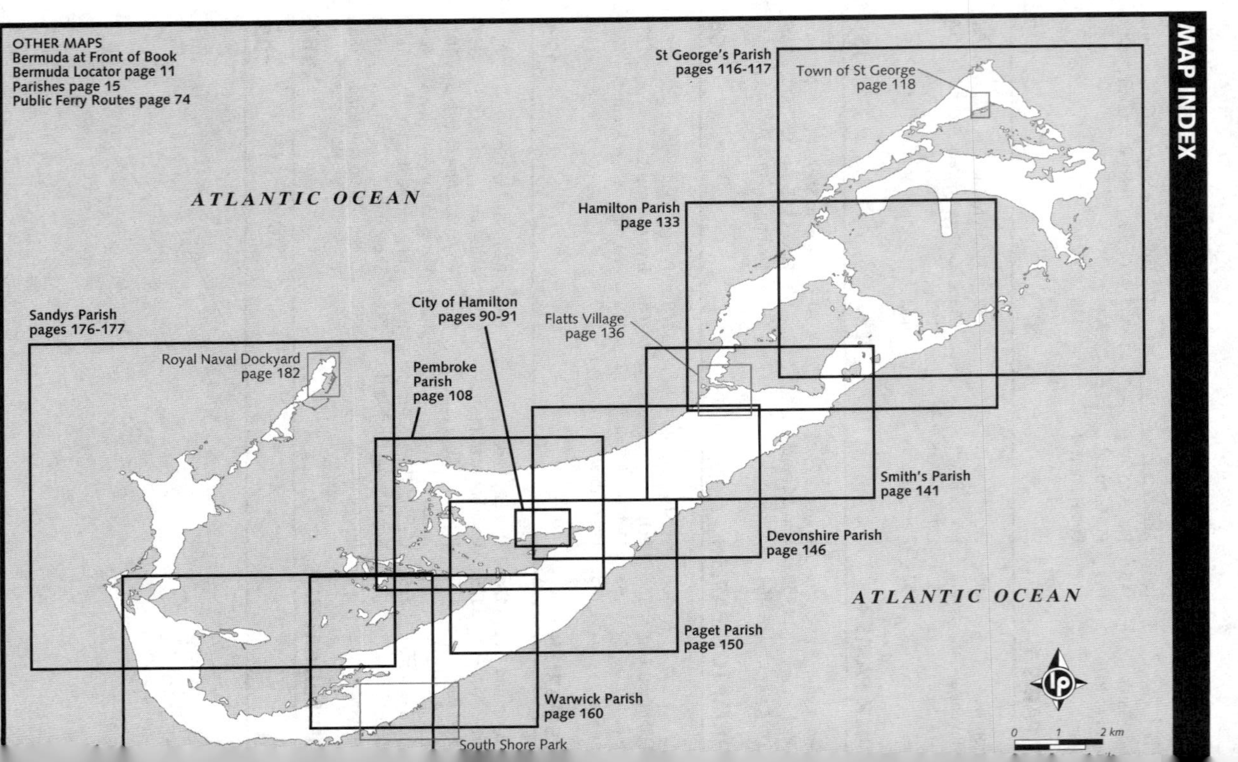
MAP INDEX
OTHER MAPS
Bermuda at Front of Book
Bermuda Locator page 11
Parishes page 15
Public Ferry Routes page 74
St George's Parish
pages 116-117
Town of St George
page 118
ATLANTIC OCEAN
Hamilton Parish
page 133
City of Hamilton
pages 90-91
Flatts Village
page 136
Sandys Parish
pages 176-177
Royal Naval Dockyard
page 182
Pembroke
Parish
page 108
Smith's Parish
page 141
Devonshire Parish
page 146
ATLANTIC OCEAN
Paget Parish
page 150
Warwick Parish
page 160
South Shore Park
0
1
2 km

The Authors

Glenda Bendure & Ned Friary

Glenda grew up in California's Mojave Desert and first traveled overseas as a high school AFS exchange student to India. Ned grew up near Boston and studied Social Thought & Political Economy at the University of Massachusetts in Amherst.

After meeting in Santa Cruz, California, where Glenda was finishing up her university studies, they took to the road and spent years traveling throughout Asia and the Pacific, including long-term stints in Japan, where Ned taught English and Glenda edited a monthly magazine. They eventually came back to the States, settled down on Cape Cod in Massachusetts and began to write for Lonely Planet.

In addition to this Bermuda book, Ned and Glenda are the authors of Lonely Planet's *Hawaii, Oahu, Eastern Caribbean* and *Denmark*, and they write the Norway and Denmark chapters of Lonely Planet's *Scandinavian & Baltic Europe on a shoestring*.

FROM THE AUTHORS

We'd like to thank the following people who answered questions, dug through their files or otherwise helped us with our research: Connie Dey and Sue Johnston of the Bermuda National Trust; Craig Burt at the Department of Agriculture, Fisheries & Parks; Lori Holland and Joy Sticca of the Bermuda Department of Tourism; Alison Outerbridge at the St George Visitors Service Bureau; and Jacqueline Horsfield at the Bermuda Underwater Exploration Institute.

Also thanks to Gilbert Darrell, Toni Daniels, Susan Moeller, Gene and Candy Ray, Rosemary LaPorte, and former Bermuda News Bureau chief Bill Breisky, and his wife, Barbara, who shared their stories of Bermuda and piled us high with reference materials.

This Book

FROM THE PUBLISHER

This 2nd edition of *Bermuda* is a product of the US office. It was edited by Christine Lee and David Zingarelli. Both David and Laura Harger served as senior editors, and David also proofread and generally dispensed wisdom throughout the project. Paul Sheridan and Susan Derby helped with proofreading. Maps were created by Patrick Phelan, with the assistance of Andrew Rebold and Guphy, and guidance from Monica Lepe and Tracey Croom Power. Ken DellaPenta indexed the book.

Henia Miedzinski designed this edition with guidance from Susan Rimerman. Illustrations were coordinated by Beca Lafore and created by Mark Butler, Hugh D'Andrade, John Fadeff, Hayden Foell, Rini Keagy, Beca Lafore, Justin Marler and Jennifer Steffey. Susan Rimerman designed the cover. Special thanks to David Rabin, Maren Lau, and the Bermuda Department of Tourism for producing additional photographs.

THANKS

Many thanks to the travelers who used the last edition and wrote to us with helpful hints, advic and interesting anecdotes. Your names appear in th back of this book.

Foreword

ABOUT LONELY PLANET GUIDEBOOKS

The story begins with a classic travel adventure: Tony and Maureen Wheeler's 1972 journey across Europe and Asia to Australia. Useful information about the overland trail did not exist at that time, so Tony and Maureen published the first Lonely Planet guidebook to meet a growing need.

From a kitchen table, then from a tiny office in Melbourne (Australia), Lonely Planet has become the largest independent travel publisher in the world, an international company with offices in Melbourne, Oakland (USA), London (UK) and Paris (France).

Today Lonely Planet guidebooks cover the globe. There is an ever-growing list of books, and there's information in a variety of forms and media. Some things haven't changed. The main aim is still to help make it possible for adventurous travelers to get out there – to explore and better understand the world.

At Lonely Planet we believe travelers can make a positive contribution to the countries they visit – if they respect their host communities and spend their money wisely. Since 1986 a percentage of the income from each book has been donated to aid projects and human-rights campaigns.

Updates Lonely Planet thoroughly updates each guidebook as often as possible. This usually means there are around two years between editions, although for more unusual or more stable destinations the gap can be longer. Check the imprint page (following the color map at the beginning of the book) for publication dates.

Between editions, up-to-date information is available in two free newsletters – the paper *Planet Talk* and email *Comet* (to subscribe, contact any Lonely Planet office) – and on our website at www.lonelyplanet.com. The *Upgrades* section of the website covers a number of important and volatile destinations and is regularly updated by Lonely Planet authors. *Scoop* covers news and current affairs relevant to travelers. And, lastly, the *Thorn Tree* bulletin board and *Postcards* section of the site carry unverified, but fascinating, reports from travelers.

Correspondence The process of creating new editions begins with the letters, postcards and emails received from travelers. This correspondence often includes suggestions, criticisms and comments about the current editions. Interesting excerpts are immediately passed on via newsletters and the website, and everything goes to our authors to be verified when they're researching on the road. We're keen to get more feedback from organizations or individuals who represent communities visited by travelers.

**/ Planet gathers
ıation for every-
ho's curious
the planet – and
ally for those
xplore it first-
Through
ooks, phrase-
activity guides,
literature,
tters, image
TV series and
e, we act as an
ation exchange
vorldwide com-
of travelers.**

Research Authors aim to gather sufficient practical information to enable travelers to make informed choices and to make the mechanics of a journey run smoothly. They also research historical and cultural background to help enrich the travel experience and allow travelers to understand and respond appropriately to cultural and environmental issues.

Authors don't stay in every hotel because that would mean spending a couple of months in each medium-size city and, no, they don't eat at every restaurant because that would mean stretching belts beyond capacity. They do visit hotels and restaurants to check standards and prices, but feedback based on readers' direct experiences can be very helpful.

Many of our authors work undercover; others aren't so secretive. None of them accept freebies in exchange for positive write-ups. And none of our guidebooks contain any advertising.

Production Authors submit their raw manuscripts and maps to offices in Australia, the USA, the UK or France. Editors and cartographers – all experienced travelers themselves – then begin the process of assembling the pieces. When the book finally hits the shops, some things are already out of date, we start getting feedback from readers and the process begins again....

WARNING & REQUEST

Things change – prices go up, schedules change, good places go bad and bad places go rupt – nothing stays the same. So, if you find things better or worse, recently opened c since closed, please tell us and help make the next edition even more accurate and usef genuinely value all the feedback we receive. Julie Young coordinates a well-traveled tea reads and acknowledges every letter, postcard and email and ensures that every morse formation finds its way to the appropriate authors, editors and cartographers for verifi

Everyone who writes to us will find their name in the next edition of the appropriate book. They will also receive the latest issue of *Planet Talk*, our quarterly printed new or *Comet*, our monthly email newsletter. Subscriptions to both newsletters are free. Th best contributions will be rewarded with a free guidebook.

Excerpts from your correspondence may appear in new editions of Lonely Planet books, the Lonely Planet website, *Planet Talk* or *Comet*, so please let us know if you want your letter published or your name acknowledged.

Send all correspondence to the Lonely Planet office closest to you:

Australia: PO Box 617, Hawthorn, Victoria 3122
USA: 150 Linden St, Oakland, CA 94607
UK: 10A Spring Place, London NW5 3BH
France: 1 rue du Dahomey, 75011 Paris

Or email us at: talk2us@lonelyplanet.com.au

For news, views and updates, see our website: www.lonelyplanet.com

HOW TO USE A LONELY PLANET GUIDEBOOK

The best way to use a Lonely Planet guidebook is any way you choose. At Lonely Planet, we believe the most memorable travel experiences are often those that are unexpected, and the finest discoveries are those you make yourself. Guidebooks are not intended to be used as if they provided a detailed set of infallible instructions!

Contents All Lonely Planet guidebooks follow the same format. The Facts about the Country chapters or sections give background information ranging from history to weather. Facts for the Visitor gives practical information on issues like visas and health. Getting There & Away gives a brief starting point for researching travel to and from the destination. Getting Around gives an overview of the transport options available when you arrive.

The peculiar demands of each destination determine how subsequent chapters are broken up, but some things remain constant. We always start with background, then proceed to sights, places to stay, places to eat, entertainment, getting there and away, and getting around information – in that order.

Heading Hierarchy Lonely Planet headings are used in a strict hierarchical structure that can be visualized as a set of Russian dolls. Each heading (and its following text) is encompassed by any preceding heading that is higher on the hierarchical ladder.

Entry Points We do not assume guidebooks will be read from beginning to end, but that people will dip into them. The traditional entry points are the list of contents and the index. In addition, however, some books have a complete list of maps and an index map illustrating map coverage.

There may also be a color map that shows highlights. These highlights are dealt with in greater detail later in the book, along with planning questions. Each chapter covering a geographical region usually begins with a locator map and another list of highlights. Once you find something of interest in a list of highlights, turn to the index.

Maps Maps play a crucial role in Lonely Planet guidebooks and include a huge amount of information. A legend is printed on the back page. We seek to have complete consistency between maps and text, and to have every important place in the text captured on a map. Map key numbers usually start in the top left corner.

gh inclusion in ebook usually s a recommen- , we cannot list good place. ion does not arily imply m. In fact, there umber of s why we might e a place – mes it is simply opriate to rage an influx elers.

troduction

pastel cottages, pink-sand beaches, essmen in Bermuda shorts, cricket ies and afternoon tea – Bermuda's types are its reality as well.

th just over 60,000 inhabitants and 21 sq of land, tiny Bermuda is one of the isolated island groups on earth. Far urban pollution, Bermuda enjoys clear and clean turquoise waters.

rmuda is sometimes associated with aribbean, which lies nearly 1000 miles south, but it shouldn't be. Bermuda is tropical island, but a subtropical one. eather is warm to hot from April to er, which is the main tourist season e time for swimming and water activ- t's much cooler in the 'winter' or 'low ,' with a mild climate similar to spring in temperate countries – a time when aches are best suited for strolling.

Bermuda is a getaway island, a hospitable place with a well-established tourism industry. The majority of visitors arrive from North America for short visits of three to seven days. Many are looking for nothing more than peace and quiet, which is easily found on tranquil Bermuda.

Yet there is plenty for active vacationers to do. Bermuda lays claim to the world's northernmost coral reefs, which not only harbor colorful fish but have been the cause of scores of shipwrecks over the centuries – all of which makes for exciting diving and snorkeling. There are also sailing opportunities, sightseeing cruises, hiking trails, world-class golf courses, deep-sea fishing, tennis and horseback riding.

With a British colonial history that dates back nearly four centuries, Bermuda offers numerous historic attractions. The coast is

rimmed with old forts, and the Town of St George, Bermuda's original 17th-century capital, exudes period charm.

Although Bermuda is made up of several islands, all the main ones are linked by bridges to form one continuous entity, and no place in Bermuda is more than an hour from the modern capital of Hamilton. Visitors can take advantage of the efficient public bus and ferry system or rent m to get around.

Despite the ties it has to Britain, Ber is geographically closer to the USA thus influenced by both countries. It's said that Bermuda seems very Brit American visitors, but America-like t ish visitors. Of course, it's both – but n all, it's uniquely Bermudian.

acts about Bermuda

TORY

its remote mid-Atlantic location, uda was well outside early migration s and remained unsettled prior to its very by European explorers.

rmuda takes its name from the Spanish ptain Juan de Bermúdez, who sighted ninhabited islands around 1503. The sh, in search of gold in the Americas, no interest in colonizing the sparse chain. In fact, there is no indication e Spanish ever deliberately landed on uda in the 16th century, although mis-tures at sea cast them ashore at least a mes.

ring the 16th century, Spanish galleons between Cuba and Spain commonly course that took them north along the a coast and then east out to sea. Al-h the extensive reefs surrounding ıda posed a potential hazard to their there were no other islands in the mid-tic that sea captains could use to take gs, so Bermuda became an important tional landmark. Once Bermuda was d, the ship's course could be reset ortheast to follow a straight line to the s and Spain.

long as the weather was fair, sailing Bermuda was generally uneventful. ver, the winds of hurricanes and other ful storms occasionally swept ships their intended course and onto Ber-s shallow reefs. Scores of Spanish their hulls loaded with gold bullion, completed the journey from the New to Spain. Just how many went down Bermuda remains unknown. Among rliest traces of Spanish presence in ıda is a rock that was found on the shore carved with the date 1543; this etching is speculated to have been the f a shipwrecked sailor.

treacherous reefs around the islands such a negative reputation among rs that by the mid-16th century, ıda was appearing on some Spanish charts with the nickname 'Islas Demonios,' or 'Isles of Devils.'

One well-documented shipwreck occurred in 1603, when a Spanish galleon, carried north by storm gales, struck a rock off Bermuda. The captain, Diego Ramirez, managed to navigate the damaged ship through the reef and into the Great Sound, the large body of water at the west end of Bermuda. Ramirez and his crew spent three weeks in Bermuda making repairs before returning to sea. The area where the Spanish sailors are believed to have camped, 2 miles northwest of present-day Hamilton, still bears the name Spanish Point.

Sir George Somers

On June 2, 1609, Admiral Sir George Somers, under the employ of the Virginia Company of London (which had been granted a charter by King James I to colonize America), set sail from England for North America with a fleet of nine ships carrying supplies and colonists to the recently established British settlement at Jamestown, Virginia.

En route, Somers, who was in command of the flagship *Sea Venture*, got caught in a fierce storm and lost contact with the rest of his fleet. The *Sea Venture*, badly damaged by the storm, eventually shipwrecked on a reef three-quarters of a mile off the eastern shore of Bermuda. Using skiffs, Somers was able to safely land all 150 people on board, coming ashore on the beach near the present-day Fort St Catherine.

The castaways salvaged much of the wreckage from the *Sea Venture* and almost immediately began construction of two new ships. Aware of the gloomy Spanish accounts of the island, the shipwrecked English colonists expected the worst, but instead found Bermuda to be surprisingly agreeable. The native cedar trees provided a suitable timber for the new ships, palmetto trees supplied thatch for shelters and the abundant nearshore fish proved easy to catch.

Much to their surprise, the colonists found the island rife with wild hogs. Some historians speculate that the hogs were accidentally released during an earlier shipwreck, but it's quite possible that early Spanish explorers had deliberately released the animals to provide a supply of fresh meat for Spanish ships that might pass by at a later date. However they got there, the hogs provided an easy source of food, and that allowed Somers to concentrate on his main goal – building replacement ships to carry the colonists to their original destination.

In 1610, the two new ships, the *Deliverance* and the *Patience*, set sail to continue the journey to Jamestown, their holds l with fresh supplies of dried fish and m couple of men were left behind on Ber in part to establish an English claim. that year, Somers returned to Bermud the intention of picking up more food supply the Jamestown colony, but he and died not long after landing. Alt the title failed to stick, the British of named the island chain the Somers Is in honor of the admiral.

The Pocahontas Connection

Pocahontas, the Powhatan Indian woman who befriended the English settlers in Jamestown, Virginia, has an interesting – if indirect – connection to Bermuda.

One of the men aboard the shipwrecked *Sea Venture*, which brought those first English settlers to Bermuda, was John Rolfe. His wife gave birth on the island to a baby girl, whom they named Bermuda. Little Bermuda Rolfe died soon after birth, however, and the baby's mother died not long after the Rolfes reached Jamestown, their original destination.

John Rolfe became a successful tobacco farmer in Virginia, and it was there that he first met Pocahontas. The two fell in love and married in April 1614, with the approval of both the Virginia governor and tribal chieftains, who hoped the marriage would help soothe tensions between Native Americans and English colonists.

Pocahontas

First Settlements

Back in England, the officers of the V Company took a keen interest in the ising reports they were given on the is suitability for colonization. The fac Bermuda was uninhabited weighed h in its favor, especially in light of the sieges and consequential famine that decimated the Jamestown settlemen Virginia Company decided to ame charter to include Bermuda as part New World holdings, and it organ party of 60 settlers to establish a pern colony there.

The new settlers landed on Berm 1612, under the leadership of Go Richard Moore, an able carpenter wh about building the village of St Geo 1620, the parliamentary Sessions which still stands in St George, be hold meetings of the colonial legis The only previous British possessio such a legislature was Jamestown makes Bermuda one of the self-governing colonies und British flag.

The colony of Bermuc divided into parishes, each for a major stockholder of t ginia Company. The parishe further divided into plots tha leased to settlers. Crops were plant the first slaves were brought to Be but agriculture was severely limited shallowness of the topsoil and the r upon rainwater. Bermuda's lack of ri it without a reliable water source t farmers through unexpected dry and prevented sugar cane, a water

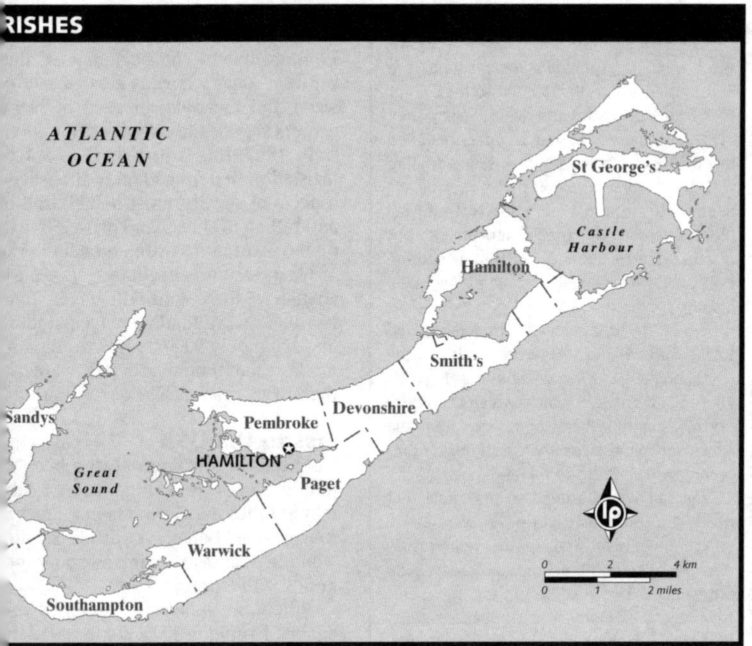

rom being successfully introduced. In d, Bermuda became reliant upon food s, mostly from the American colonies, nent its meager harvests.

many ways the Virginia Company Bermuda like a fiefdom: people were hat crops they could grow, trade was lled by the company and those who d the rules could be forced into in-ed servitude. Over time, the settlers e weary of all the restrictions that the ia Company and its successor, the da Company, placed upon them and eir case to London, where they suc-ly sued to have the charter rescinded . After that date, Bermuda was ruled itish crown colony in much the same the American colonies.

ry

st slaves were introduced to Bermuda . Although the vast majority came Africa, there were also American Indians, mainly Mahicans, taken from the American colonies. All came against their will, being captured and torn from their homelands and forcibly brought to the island. The Atlantic crossings were so brutally inhumane that many of the slaves, chained in the suffocating hulls of the ships, died en route.

For those who made it to Bermuda, the dehumanizing conditions continued after arrival, permeating every aspect of life. Slaves were buried in a separate part of the cemetery, away from whites, and as late as the early 19th century, island ministers could be imprisoned simply for preaching to blacks.

Degrading as the conditions may have been, they were not as hideous in Bermuda as they were elsewhere. Unlike slaves in other New World colonies, most of the slaves in Bermuda did not end up toiling in sweltering fields, but were put to work as servants, construction workers and sailors.

Turks Islands & the Salt Trade

After agriculture proved a meager option in Bermuda, many settlers turned to the sea for their hopes of wealth and riches. Sailing their own ships made of Bermuda cedar, they tried to notch out a place for themselves trading with the American colonies. The Bermudians needed to secure a commodity that was highly valued by the Americans – but resource-scarce Bermuda had little to offer. Eventually, the traders found what they were looking for in salt.

Around 1670, a party of Bermudians sailed to the Turks Islands, some 900 miles to the south, and began a lucrative business harvesting sea salt. The salt, which was shipped back north, brought a handsome price from the American colonists, as it was essential in preserving winter stores of fish and meat.

The salt works proved so profitable that nearly 1000 colonists and slaves were active on the Turks Islands raking, drying and shipping the salt. For a time, the salt traders even entertained the idea of turning the Turks Islands into a colony of Bermuda. However, that plan, which would have placed a colony (Turks Islands) under the domain of another colony (Bermuda), proved too unorthodox for British officials. Instead, by the beginning of the 19th century the British had incorporated the Turks Islands as part of the Bahamas colony, and Bermuda's role in the salt industry slipped into history.

Some of the slaves became skilled tradespeople and were able to pass their skills on to their children – a circumstance that would assure them opportunities in the trades long after the end of slavery.

By the early 1800s, slavery was being assailed by abolitionists in London, and the anti-slavery movement was gaining widespread support. Spurred by changing sentiments, the British Parliament finally took on the sugar barons who controlled vast estates in the British West Indies. Throughout the 18th century, the great wealth of these sugar barons had assured them a correspo degree of influence in affecting legislati London, but by the beginning of the century, sugar's heyday was clearly o wane and the political clout of plant owners significantly diminished.

In 1807, the British Parliament p legislation that immediately abolished aspects of slavery, most notably the b and selling of slaves, and phased out sl on the plantations over a broader peric 1834, slavery was no longer allowed i British colony, and all slaves livi Bermuda were finally emancipated. C approximately 9000 people residing ir muda at that time, nearly 5000 were list the census roles as black or 'coloured.'

Ties to the USA

Bermuda's history has always been c tied to that of the United States, a situ that at times put Bermuda in a squeez struggled to balance its trade relatic with the American mainland and its pc bonds with Britain.

When the American colonies re against Britain in 1775, some islanders sympathetic to the American caus Bermuda nonetheless remained lo the crown. After the Continental Co enacted a ban on trade with all B colonies that failed to support its st for independence, a Bermuda dele sailed to Philadelphia to request an e tion so that it could import America staples. The Congress made that exem conditional upon receiving the stores c powder held in the Bermuda magaz August 1775, in one of the more dar capades of the day, a group of Berm stole up to the St George arsenal, c away the gunpowder kegs and rowed out to a waiting Boston-bound ship.

During the War of 1812, Bermud again found itself, as a loyal British col odds with the United States. In Augus the British Navy used Bermuda as a b launch the Chesapeake Bay Campai was responsible for torching the US House and burning down much of Wa ton DC. The Americans, offended n attack, took revenge where they . Under the rules of war as they were ced during the period, American ships free to confiscate the cargo of any ship the British flag. As a result, Bermuda led lucrative booty for American pri-rs, who made an easy catch of much of uda's merchant fleet. The losses were tating for the Bermudian economy, was heavily dependent upon trade.

hough the War of 1812 spelled hard the US Civil War (1861-65) provided nomic boon for Bermuda, which was into the lucrative role of serving as a for blockade-runners. The Confeder- the southern states was heavily de-nt upon the sale of cotton to finance bellion against the northern states. President Lincoln imposed a block- southern ports in 1861, the south was to employ small, fast vessels to the gunboats of the northern navy. vessels were not capable of handling lantic shipping, however, and it be-necessary to use intermediate islands Bermuda and the Bahamas to trans-e cotton to England, where it pro- the raw material for hundreds of g mills. There was tremendous money nade, as the cotton, which was worth nts a pound in the south, fetched 10 that price on the English market. se, the guns and ammunition brought om England commanded a premium hern ports.

he height of the US Civil War, the f St George enjoyed unprecedented rity. The waterside warehouses over- with goods; stores and taverns d up to cater to mariners carrying fat f cash. The sea captains and traders ortunes. Then, in 1865, victories by thern forces ground the blockade- to a halt. As it had sided with the feated south, Bermuda's shipping in-reliant as it was upon trade with the ll but collapsed after the war.

nt of Tourism

s Louise, daughter of Queen Victoria wife of the Governor General of Canada, is credited with putting Bermuda on the map for North American tourists. Anxious to escape the long, cold Canadian winters, the princess paid an extended visit to Bermuda in 1883. The press took note of her stay, and journalists, including perennial traveler Mark Twain, followed in her wake. In 1884, Bermuda's first seaside resort – named, not surprisingly, The Princess Hotel – opened in Hamilton.

In his golden years, Twain himself became a frequent traveler to Bermuda, making annual journeys to the island. It was, in fact, the last place he ever visited; Twain set sail from Bermuda just nine days before his death in 1910.

By the early 20th century, Bermuda was well on the way to becoming a trendy winter destination for 'snow birds,' who flocked aboard steamers crossing regularly from New York to Hamilton. The crossing in winter, when stormy Atlantic seas are common, was rough enough that Twain compared his journey to 'going through hell' in order to reach paradise. Still, until the introduction of airplane service, winter – not summer – was the main tourist season in Bermuda.

World War II

Bermuda, with its strategic mid-Atlantic location, became a center for Allied military and intelligence operations during WWII.

Even though the war had ground tourism to a halt, island hotels were brimming with activity. The Princess Hotel, Bermuda's largest, was taken over by British intelligence agents, who turned the basement into an operations center. There, tucked out of view, scores of codebreakers interpreted correspondence passing between the USA and Europe, in an effort to uncover Axis espionage operations and decode secret messages. This effort involved painstakingly prying open suspected mail without damaging the seal, examining the letter and then quickly getting it back into circulation; it employed over 1000 people.

In addition to intelligence-gathering operations, Bermuda also served as a port for Britain's Royal Navy, which patrolled the North Atlantic for German submarines and

US Presence in Bermuda

At the outbreak of WWII, Britain was concerned with securing its shipping channels to the USA saw Bermuda as a strategic Atlantic station. Since Bermuda was much closer to the USA than it to Britain, it seemed inevitable to military planners that the USA would take over primary respo bility for developing military bases on the island.

In March 1941, US and British authorities met in London and signed a 99-year lease that han the US military a substantial chunk of Bermudian real estate, including the lion's share of St Da Island. The Bermudians, who were not given a voice in the negotiations, were so taken aback by lengthy terms of the lease and the magnitude of territory involved that rumors ran wild Bermuda was on the verge of being taken over as a US possession.

While the USA had no intention of laying claims to Bermuda, its presence there did bring r and permanent change to the sleepy colony. By the end of 1941, scores of Bermudians had fo work on military construction projects, including the building of Bermuda's first airport. The US itary introduced the widespread use of motor vehicles, which had previously been forbidden Bermuda's streets. In the postwar period, the airport opened to civilian traffic, giving islanders access to the US East Coast and opening Bermuda as a weekend getaway for American touris

With the end of the Cold War, the US bases in Bermuda – which included 1040 acres c David's Island and 250 acres in Southampton Parish – no longer filled any legitimate military n In the 1980s, US news programs took a fancy to exposing golf junkets to Bermuda by military b The bad press helped add Bermuda to the shortlist of base closures necessitated by post-Cold cutbacks in US military budgets. In September 1995, the USA ended its military presence in Bern by turning over 1330 acres, some 10% of Bermuda's total landmass, to the island governmen

battleships that threatened vital US-UK shipping lanes.

At the onset of the war, the USA also established a presence in Bermuda, most notably with the construction of an air base on St David's Island. The base, comprising some 1040 acres in all, was so large that it added another 1.25 sq miles to the island in the form of reclaimed land, thus boosting Bermuda's total landmass by more than 5%.

Postwar Changes

In the wake of WWII, many of the old colonial assumptions that prevailed in the British Empire were called into question. In Bermuda, the long-held political and economic preferences given to white males, at the expense of women and blacks, came under fire.

Although blacks had been granted the right to vote in the 19th century, franchise qualifications and other prejudices kept them from achieving any significant political power. Indeed, in the 100 years be emancipation and WWII, only a blacks had been elected to Parlia Women, on the other hand, had bee pletely blocked from the political aren 1944, when the right to vote was fina tended to them. Even after that, vote tration for both sexes was restric property owners, leaving fewer tha Bermudians eligible to vote.

Blacks in Bermuda faced policies regation that were not dissimilar to found in the USA – with the excepti Bermudian blacks were well entrenc the trades. In the 1950s, buoyed b clout in the trade movement, black I dians began to emerge as a politic social power to be reckoned with.

In 1959, intent on putting an end t gation, blacks boycotted movie theat restaurants, and were successful in those businesses to integrate. Unde sure, hotels and other businesses th iced discriminatory hiring practices n to open job opportunities to blacks.

1960, a grassroots movement called the mittee for Universal Suffrage sparked spread support with a drive to extend oting right to the 75% of the adult pop- on that didn't own 'qualifying property.' ervatives, unable to block the move- , were nonetheless able to amend the ation so that property owners were ed the right to cast two votes. Still, in 963 general election, every adult Ber- an age 25 and over could finally vote, ng the voting rolls fourfold to more 20,000.

fore universal suffrage was introduced, uda's political arena so narrowly rep- ted the interest of white landowners was free of political parties and rival rms. In 1963, the first political party rmuda, the Progressive Labour Party , was formed, in part to represent the sts of nonwhite Bermudians.

PLP, which advocated total inde- nce from Britain, won support from enfranchised voters and captured six seats in the 1963 general election. of the remaining independent mem- ary of the potential bloc vote that the ould cast, united to form a counter the United Bermuda Party (UBP), appealed to businesspeople and to sionals.

he years that followed, under encour- nt from Britain, the UBP, PLP and in- dent parliamentary members joined er to produce a constitution, which ffect in 1968. The new constitution ed for full internal self-government matters from health and finance to ation, while leaving control of secu- efense and diplomatic affairs to the

tion of Independence

gh Bermuda prides itself on the rela- rmony that exists between blacks and in the 1970s racial antagonisms mes flared into violent confronta- n March 1973, the Bermudian gover- Richard Sharples, was shot to death at the governor's mansion. His killers, two black Bermudian men, undertook the assassination in the misguided hope it would spark a black revolution. That never materialized. Instead, the vast majority of Bermudians, black and white, condemned the murder. However, when the two men were later convicted and sentenced to hang, many black Bermudians took to the streets to protest their executions, as they felt race was a factor in applying the death sentence. In 1977, responding to heightened unrest and race riots, the government moved to end de facto discrimination and to open talks on independence from Britain.

In the decade that followed, the independence movement became the dominant issue in Bermudian politics. Not only did the minority PLP support independence, but the more conservative UBP split on the issue after the premier, Sir John Swan, threw his support behind the independence campaign.

On August 16, 1995, in a referendum called by the premier, the issue of Bermudian independence from the crown finally came to a vote. With 16,369 votes cast against it and only 5714 votes in favor, the Independence Referendum was resoundingly defeated. Despite the years of fractious debate that the independence issue had evoked, just 25% of the electorate had voted in favor of breaking ties with Britain. In the wake of the election, Sir John Swan, who had made his political future contingent upon the passage of the referendum, announced his resignation after having led the government for 13 years.

The reasons behind the referendum defeat were varied, but in the end many Bermudians, regardless of their political affiliations, were apprehensive about the potential political and economic cost of independence. Certainly many had concerns about the financial strain that statehood would bring to an island of a mere 60,000 residents – everything from the need to maintain their own overseas diplomatic missions to the possible loss of commercial advantages with the UK.

Bermuda's long history of political and social conservatism undoubtedly played a significant role in the final vote. Employment

Distance from the Neighbors

Set in the isolated North Atlantic, Bermuda enjoys a wide berth from its neighbors. The nearest lies nearly 600 miles away at Cape Hatteras, North Carolina. And even though many people unfamiliar with Bermuda often mistakenly connect it with the Caribbean, nearly a thousand miles of ocean separate Bermuda from its tropical Caribbean neighbors to the south. In fact, Nova Scotia to the north is a bit closer!

As far as the motherland goes, London is a distant 3450 miles to the east. Not surprisingly, the places most frequently visited by Bermudians are not in the UK, but are New York and Boston, which are a cozy 750 and 775 miles, respectively, from sleepy Hamilton.

concerns also weighed into the decision to stick with the status quo, since many of the best-paying jobs rely on upscale tourism, which commonly plays up a genteel colonial image, and also upon offshore businesses. Indeed, many of the foreign companies operating in Bermuda, including British insurance firms and US financial services, let it be known that they found security in the current system of British law.

As a consequence of its defeat on the independence referendum, Bermuda has entered the 21st century as one of only a handful of remaining British colonies, in the company of scattered outposts such as the Falkland Islands off Argentina and volcano-ravaged Montserrat in the Eastern Caribbean.

GEOGRAPHY & GEOLOGY

Bermuda lies in the North Atlantic, 570 miles off the coast of North Carolina, the nearest landmass.

Bermuda is comprised of a cluster of some 150 small islands, which collectively total just 21 sq miles in area. The eight largest islands – St George's Island, St David's Island, Bermuda Island (or the 'main island'), Somerset Island, Watford Island, Boaz Island, Ireland Island North
and Ireland Island South – are connec
causeways and bridges to form a conti
fishhook-shaped land area that stretc
miles in length. In contrast, its width
ages less than a mile across, and at its
it barely reaches 2 miles. Together thes
nected principal islands contain mor
95% of Bermuda's landmass.

Bermudians tend to treat the con
islands as a single geographic entit
commonly refer to Bermuda simply
island.' Only about a dozen of the
islands are inhabited. Most of the un
ited islands are little more than rock
some are so small that there's not a g
agreement, even among government d
ments, as to the exact number of isla
the colony!

Formed about 100 million years ag
now extinct underwater volcano, the
are the uppermost tips of a pyramid-
mountain mass whose base extends
feet from the sea floor.

The islands have a limestone cap, w
comprised of coral deposits and the
of billions of shell-bearing creatur
gradually built up around the edges
submerged volcanic peaks. From a co
tion of accumulating deposits and lo
sea levels, the mountaintops eve
emerged as islands and gave rise
fringing coral reefs that surround
Over time the action of the su
pounded the limestone shells and co
grains of sand that have amassed in
merous bays and coves along the sh
giving Bermuda a generous str
pinkish-white-sand beaches.

Although some sections are fla
muda has a predominately hilly terr
highest point is a 259-foot hill cal
Peak, which is in Smith's Parish.

CLIMATE

Because of the warming effects of t
Stream, Bermuda enjoys a mild, ag
climate.

The average annual high temper
76°F, and the average annual low te
ture is 67°F. In the warmest months
September, the average high tempe

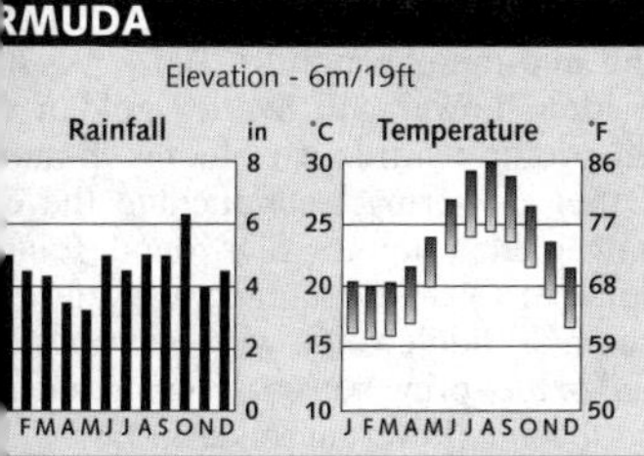

and the average low is 75°F. The coldest hs, January to March, have an average temperature of 68°F and an average f 60°F.

rmuda is frost-free; the lowest temper- on record is 44°F, which occurred in ary 1950. The highest temperature on d is 93°F, reached in August 1989.

lative humidity is high all year round, ng from an average of 75% in March to n August. The mean annual rainfall is 55 , which is distributed fairly evenly over ar with no identifiable rainy season.

hough Bermuda is not in the main ane belt that whips across the Carib- such storms do occasionally nip it if they back out to sea in a northerly direction.

a recorded two-day weather forecast, ed every four hours, dial ☎ 977. Call -1 for current weather, ☎ 977-2 for a e forecast and ☎ 977-3 for tropical warnings. From overseas, you can get ather information by calling ☎ 441-297- r by going online at www.weather.bm.

.OGY & ENVIRONMENT

ıda is a small island with limited re- s and a relatively high population y. Those conditions, along with the accommodate half a million visitors year, inevitably cause stress on the nment.

he waters surrounding Bermuda, hing practices have decimated nu- s reef-fish species, scallops and other marine life. The Nassau grouper, for le, which was once the mainstay of nd fishing industry, has been fished to rcial extinction. Turtle hunting, still nt until the 1960s, was responsible for wiping out Bermuda's entire nesting green sea turtle population.

In recent decades, Bermuda has made concentrated efforts to raise the level of environmental awareness, ranging from introducing natural history into the school curriculum to enacting strict regulations protecting marine life.

The 1966 Coral Reef Preserves Act set up marine preserves that protect plants and fish in substantial tracts of Bermuda's reef waters. Subsequent marine protection orders have extended coverage to other environmentally sensitive areas by restricting fishing, spear fishing and the taking of lobsters.

Other programs to restore native fauna are also making headway. The yellow-crowned night heron has been successfully brought back; turtle conservation projects are underway; and West Indian top shells, a type of mollusk, have been reintroduced. The cahow, an endemic seabird once thought to be extinct, is on the comeback, and a concerted effort to increase the number of nesting boxes has resulted in a growing number of eastern bluebirds.

In terms of environmental aesthetics, Bermuda has long been in the forefront – it is free of polluting heavy industry and does not allow billboards or neon signs. The use of public buses and ferries is encouraged, and the ownership of cars is strictly limited. Only one automobile is permitted per household – regardless of the number of drivers in the family! Bermudians have been known to concoct creative schemes to circumvent the spirit, if not the letter, of the law – such as dividing a home into two separate apartments – but that only stands as testimony to how effective the law actually is.

Recycling is encouraged, and there are drop-off centers for most household recyclables, including glass, aluminum, tin cans, newspaper, cardboard, motor oil and car batteries.

Although open space is at a premium, Bermuda nonetheless maintains a growing number of parks and nature reserves and is making efforts to restore some of the unpopulated islands, particularly Nonsuch Island, to their precolonial ecology.

FLORA & FAUNA

Flora

Bermuda, with its subtropical frost-free climate, is abloom with colorful flowers year-round. Since temperatures usually stay within the range of 50° to 90°F, tropical plants imported from the West Indies thrive here, and so do many of the flowers found in temperate climates.

In all, about a thousand different flowering plants can be found in Bermuda. Some of the more common are bougainvillea, hibiscus, oleander, morning glory (called 'bluebell' in Bermuda), poinsettia, freesia, nasturtium, chalice vine, garden geranium, night-blooming cereus, Mexican poppy, corallita (or chain-of-love, for its heart-shaped flowers), passion flower and bird-of-paradise. Easter lilies, introduced in 1853, are used locally to make perfume and are exported around Eastertime.

One of the few endemic flowers is the Bermudiana, a tiny blue-purple iris with a yellow center and grasslike leaves, which resembles the blue-eyed grass of North America. Its blooms begin in mid-April and last through May.

Old-style roses – including the multiflora, tea and bourbon varieties – have remained popular since the 1700s and can be seen in gardens around Bermuda.

Among the curiosities you'll find is the prickly pear cactus, which is common in St George's near the seaside forts and in other coastal areas. The prickly pear produces Bermuda's only native fruit.

Shrubs & Trees Bermuda's most whimsically named shrub is the match-me-if-you-can, so called because no two leaves – in mottled colors of red, yellow and green – have the same pattern. Other common shrubs are croton, shrimp plant, blue sage, red sage bush (lantana) and pittosporum, the latter boasting perfumed white flowers in winter and early spring. Fragrant rosemary, with tiny blue flowers, is prolific as a landscape planting.

The umbrella-shaped royal poinciana tree has gorgeous scarlet blossoms from late May through early October, and the smaller scarlet cordia tree has orange-red flow the midsummer months. The pink sh golden shower and Sydney golden w all produce attractive blooms in sun Other flowering trees include the c with golden flowers year-round; frang (plumeria), with fragrant waxy flow summer; fiddlewood, with leaves tha red in the spring before dropping; and with white flowering spikes in July.

The bay grape, abundant along the shore, has fruit that hangs in gra bunches at year's end and round leaves that turn red and gold before f Another easily identifiable tree is th danus, or screw pine, which has spiny l fruit that resembles pineapples and a that's anchored with multiple aerial r

Endemic trees include the Be cedar, which once covered vast tracts island; olivewood bark, an evergreen on rocky hillsides; and the Bermud metto, Bermuda's only native palm Early settlers made liquor from the the Bermuda palmetto and from the b of the Bermuda cedar.

Fast-growing casuarina (beefwood) native to Australia, were planted th out the island as a replacement f many Bermuda cedar trees that were en by cedar-scale infestation in the Prevalent in island parks, casuari long, needlelike leaves with a soft fe appearance.

For a close-up view of Bermuda's flora, the Bermuda Botanical Gard Paget is a great place to start – there find the widest variety of both native troduced species.

Food Crops Bermuda's soil is limes origin, so it tends to be strongly a Consequently, acidifiers such as sulf to be added before adding some cro depths are very shallow, seldom more to 3 feet in the relatively fertile vall as little as an inch elsewhere. Because shallowness the soil has a limited cap hold water, and droughts, which ca month or more in summer, create challenges for farmers.

e Onion Patch

ons were first planted in Bermuda in 1616 from seed brought from England. By the 17th ury, onions from Bermuda were being shipped to the West Indies, though large-scale cultivation not start until the 1830s. By this time, Bermuda onions were grown in both red and white vari-, using seed imported from the Madeira and Canary Islands. The climate and soil conditions ue to Bermuda helped produce ns that were notably tasty.

y the late 19th century, exported uda onions had become so well vn, particularly in New York markets, Bermuda was nicknamed 'The Onion n' and Bermudians themselves were times lightheartedly referred to as ons.'

rmuda no longer exports onions, ever. The major downfall was caused creased competition from 'Bermuda ns' grown commercially in Texas ng around 1900. In addition, protec-JS tariffs, crop damage from insects lisease, and a loss of Bermuda farm-to growing numbers of homes and s sealed the demise of onion exports. d, there are indications that as early 908, Bermuda was importing the d 'Bermuda onions' from Texas!

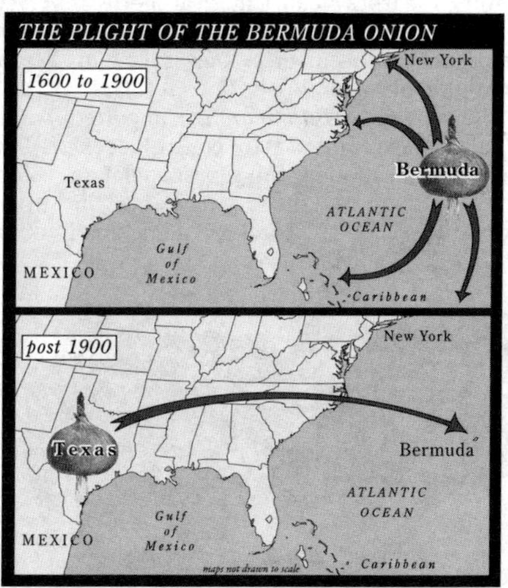

etheless, just about all of the major ole crops found in temperate climates 1 Bermuda, including lettuce, broc-uliflower, peas, potatoes, pumpkins, es, beets, cabbage, onions, carrots, cucumbers, corn, celery and kale.

ava, a root crop resembling sweet po-s also grown on the island and used e cassava pie, a local Christmastime .

s trees – orange, lemon, grapefruit, ngerine and tangelo – are popular in ardens. Another island favorite is the ree, the small yellow-orange fruit of used in pies, jams and liqueur.

r edible fruits grown in Bermuda are os, grapes, figs, papayas (locally called w), Surinam cherries, sugar apples p), guavas, strawberries and bananas.

Fauna

Bermuda has no native land mammals. The endemic Bermuda rock lizard *(Eumeces longirostris)*, a brown skink, was the only nonmarine land animal in Bermuda prior to human contact. Critically endangered, it fares poorly in altered environments and is now largely restricted to remote coastal cliffs and uninhabited islands.

Introduced lizards include the Jamaican anole *(Anolis grahami)*, which puffs out a showy orange throat sac as a territorial warning; the Warwick lizard (or *Anolis leachii)*, a foot-long lizard with golden eye rings; and the Somerset lizard (or *Anolis roquet)*, identifiable by its black eye patches. All of the lizard species are harmless, and there are no snakes, poisonous or otherwise, in Bermuda.

There are two kinds of whistling tree frogs: the *Eleutherodactylus johnstonei*, which is about 1 inch long, and the slightly larger but less common *Eleutherodactylus gossei*. Both are brown, nocturnal, live in trees close to the ground and were introduced to Bermuda near the end of the 19th century. The frogs create a musical chorus of loud, bell-like whistles that fill the night from April to November, as long as the temperature is above 68°F.

The giant toad *(Bufo marinus)*, imported from Guyana in 1875 to control cockroaches, is most often seen squashed flat on the road, hence its local nickname 'road toad.'

The road toad in its unsquished state

Butterfly species common to Bermuda include the monarch, cloudless sulphur, buckeye, gulf fritillary, red admiral and cabbage white. There's also a wide variety of nocturnal moths.

Birds Of the land birds that once inhabited Bermuda, only a single endemic species survives: chick of the village *(Vireo griseus)*, a subspecies of the white-eyed vireo. This small olive and yellowish bird that has spectacle-like circles around its eyes has shorter wings than its continental counterparts, having lost its need to fly long distances. The vireo can be spotted in parks and wooded areas.

A number of introduced species are now common to Bermuda. The most conspicuous is the kiskadee *(Pitangus sulphuratus)*, a noisy yellow-breasted flycatcher that is spotted on hotel grounds. The kiskade introduced from Trinidad in 1957 in hop bringing the lizard population down sc beetles introduced to prey on the c scale insects would have a better chan getting established.

Other common introduced land species include starlings, house sparrow ropean goldfinches, catbirds and mou doves. Two other birds, the northern ca and the eastern bluebird, were comm Bermuda until the 1950s, but the lo cedar habitat, coupled with increasing petition from kiskadees and sparrow brought drastic declines in their popula

Although Bermuda's resident sp may be limited, the island hosts a variety of migrant birds. The check some 350 birds includes three warblers, numerous shorebirds, h and ducks. Graceful white-tailed birds, more commonly called lo in Bermuda, can be seen swoopin gliding along the shore from Ma October. In addition, sandhill cran a number of other exotic birds, su the Pacific fairy tern, make the occa visit.

In spring, terns, storm petrels, jaege four species of shearwaters (greater, Manx and Cory's) pass by, often in that number in the thousands. The p the spring seabird migration occurs i and June.

Still, fall is the most varied time fo with the migrations reaching their p October. At that point, most of the birds and herons and some of the lan ducks and coots have arrived. Amo birds spotted during the fall migrati ospreys, ring-necked ducks, double- cormorants, eastern wood peewees, y bellied sapsuckers, scarlet tanagers breasted grosbeaks, gulls, thrushe sparrows.

Marine Life Because Bermuda is north, it may come as a surprise to so itors to learn that many tropical fis mon to the Caribbean can also be spo

ʼaters that surround Bermuda. Some of nore colorful fish include the clown ɜe, queen angelfish, rainbow parrotfish, beauty, spotted puffer, blue chromis, ·ye butterflyfish, blue tang, triggerfish ·range spotted filefish.

e key to all this marine life is Ber- ·'s coral formations, which grow in the shallow waters surrounding the islands. ɜ are the northernmost corals found in .tlantic and owe their existence to the ocean currents carried north by the Stream. In all, Bermuda has 24 species ·d coral, including brain coral and tree and another two dozen species of soft such as sea fans and sea rods.

ıddition to pretty fish, Bermuda's coral also harbor more menacing-looking ıres, including green moray eels that up to 10 feet long. Although moray ıay provide a bit of a shock to snorkel- ıo suddenly come upon them, they are ally nonaggressive, and the intimidat- ıouth-chomping motions that they are not meant for defense but to water across their gills, a breathing ınism. Three other species of eels are in Bermuda's waters: the speckled ·, brown moray and conger eel.

ch more dangerous than eels are the ·h-like Portuguese man-of-wars that metimes found in Bermuda's waters, ally from March to July. Waters where e been seen recently should be avoided (see Dangers & Annoyances in the Facts for the Visitor chapter).

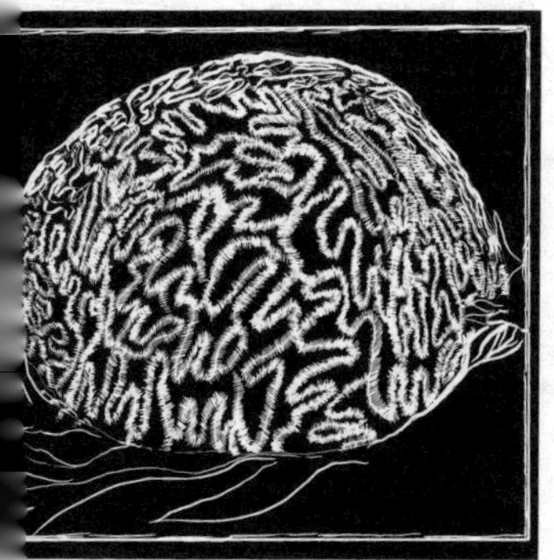

·ral flourishes in Bermuda's warm currents.

Bermuda's waters also hold brittle stars, sea horses, sea spiders, sea cucumbers, sea hares, sea anemones, sea urchins, squids, conchs, slipper lobsters and spiny lobsters.

Land crabs, active along the shoreline at night, make telltale burrows in dunes above the beach, particularly along the south shore. The females release their larvae into the ocean at least once each summer, often on nights following the full moon.

Humpback whales, migrating north from the Caribbean, can sometimes be seen off the south shore in March and April. Less common, but not unknown, are sightings of Cuvier's beaked whales and sperm whales. Various species of dolphins and porpoises are sometimes found in deeper waters as well. Green sea turtles, hawksbill turtles, loggerhead turtles and leatherback turtles can sometimes be seen near the reefs.

A great place to go for an introduction to Bermuda's marine life is the Bermuda Aquarium, Museum & Zoo in Flatts Village (see Flatts Village in the Hamilton Parish chapter), where you'll find tanks identifying nearly 200 species of fish and coral.

Endangered Species

Hundreds of miles from the nearest landmass, Bermuda's flora and fauna evolved in an isolated environment with limited competition and few predators. Consequently, when the first human settlers arrived on the scene 400 years ago they had a devastating impact.

Free-roaming pigs, believed to have been left by passing sailors in the 16th century, and rats, cats and dogs introduced by the first permanent settlers in the 17th century, spelled havoc for many species of endemic plants as well as ground-nesting birds. Other species met their demise through the direct action of humans.

One bird that offers a haunting testimony to species devastation is the Bermuda petrel, or cahow *(Pterodroma cahow)*. These quail-size seabirds were abundant when the first settlers landed, but they had no natural fear of people. Diego Ramirez, the Spanish captain who spent three weeks in Bermuda in 1603, noted that his men were able to make a ready catch of thousands of the plump little birds. When the English arrived six years later, they too developed an appetite for the cahow. The birds made such an easy catch – indeed, they would even land on the colonists' arms – that they all but disappeared within a few decades.

After three centuries without sightings, the cahow, which was officially listed as extinct, was rediscovered in 1951. Subsequent research identified 20 nesting pairs of the birds on four of the smaller uninhabited Castle Harbour islets. Although environmentalists were initially encouraged, the islands were found to be a marginal habitat for the ground-nesting birds, as rats preyed upon their eggs and the soil was so eroded that it was no longer sufficient for burrowing nests. The cahows had adapted by nesting in natural holes in the cliffs, but they had to compete for these nesting sites with the more aggressive longtails, a large tropic bird. Because the longtails nested later in the season, the cahows were sometimes forced to abandon their nests before they had a chance to rear their chicks.

To create more favorable odds for survival, special baffles were installed in the opening of the cahows' cliffside nesting holes, reducing the size of the entrance to prevent longtails from entering. In addition, naturalists created artificial nesting burrows, hollowed into the islands' rocky surfaces and roofed with concrete, in the hopes of returning the cahows to ground-level burrows and reducing competition with the longtails. In conjunction with these efforts, rats and other predatory mammals were eradicated from the four islets where the cahows nest.

The cahow, which lays but a single egg each year, is making a slow, precarious comeback. There are currently about 50 pairs of cahows, and they remain one of the rarest seabirds in the world.

National Parks

In 1986, legislation was enacted establishing a national parks system to protect, maintain and enhance the natural and historic character of environmentally sensitive Bermuda now has dozens of park nature reserves, collectively accounti nearly 1000 acres.

Although none of the parks is exten handful of properties – most notably S Pond Nature Reserve, the Bermuda B cal Gardens and South Shore Park – are enough to provide an hour or so of wa

GOVERNMENT & POLITICS

Bermuda is an internally self-gove British dependency with a bicameral p mentary government.

The official head of state is the I monarch. An appointed governor wh sponsible for external affairs, defense, and internal security represents the in Bermuda. Otherwise, the governor is largely symbolic, acting mainly c advice of the cabinet. The current go is Thorold Masefield, who has held th tion since 1997.

The premier, who is the leader of t jority party, heads the government a points the cabinet, which is 12-m ministerial body that's responsible fc ernment administration.

Parliament, which is responsible f acting legislation, is divided into two the House of Assembly, which has 40 e members, and the Senate, which members. Five of the Senate memb selected by the premier, and three ea selected by the leader of the oppositi the governor. Both branches of Parl sit for five-year terms. To be enacted, tion must be passed by the House, ap by the Senate and signed into law governor.

Bermuda has two major political the United Bermuda Party (UBP), promotes a conservative pro-busine form, and the Progressive Labour (PLP), which is supported by labor an largely black membership.

The PLP beat the UBP for the fi in the November 1998 elections. Al the UBP had a predominantly black ship at the time, it was unable to break ditional image as the party of conse s and won only 14 House seats. Hailed victory for working-class blacks, the swept the other 26 seats. The victory the UBP's reign as the majority party, tion it had held since Bermuda's Parnt divided into parties in the mid-1960s. e current premier is Jennifer Smith, as held the office since November 1998.

NOMY

uda has a gross domestic product ') of $2.2 billion and a workforce of people. The average income in Ber- is $34,600. The inflation rate is apnately 2.5% and the unemployment %.

the past century, tourism has been the stone of the economy; it accounts difor about 4000 jobs and indirectly for ps twice that number. Bermuda reabout 575,000 visitors per year, a third m arrive aboard cruise ships and have rage stay of three days. Visitors who by air have an average stay of six days. ically 84% of all visitors come from SA, followed by Canada with 7% and K with 5%. Of the remaining 4%, half come from Europe.

ecent years a growing number of inonal finance operations, attracted by sence of corporate and income taxes, et up offshore operations in Bermuda. are now some 300 international comwith a physical presence in Bermuda. include mutual funds services, investholding firms and insurance compaecializing in reinsurance, a type of ophic insurance that protects convennsurers against natural disasters.

ddition, there are more than 11,000 tional businesses that have no presn the island but are registered in Bermainly to shelter themselves from tax ities and other regulators elsewhere.

USA is the leading trade partner, acng for more than two-thirds of da's international trade. Most food thing are imported, and it is this situcompounded by high customs duties uda's leading tax source) that give da its unusually high cost of living.

To get a sense of the actual cost of living in Bermuda, consider the following: a pair of those snazzy Bermuda shorts will set you back around $50; add another $10 for a pair of socks to go with it and about $75 for a dress shirt and tie. In terms of larger expenses, a one-bedroom apartment costs around $1500 a month to rent, and a small car, such as a Ford Escort, costs around $20,000 to buy new.

POPULATION & PEOPLE

Bermuda's population is estimated at 61,000. About 25% of Bermudian citizens are under the age of 20, 65% are between the ages of 20 and 64 and the remainder are 65 years of age or older. The average life expectancy is 74 years for men and 78 years for women.

Nearly 75% of all islanders were born in Bermuda. Of those who are foreign-born, about 30% were born in the UK, 20% in the USA, 13% in the Azores or Portugal, 10% in Canada and 10% come from the Commonwealth Caribbean.

Most Bermudian blacks can trace their ancestry to slaves brought to the island in the 17th and 18th centuries. Blacks have been in the majority since colonial times and currently comprise about 61% of the population. Most of the remainder of the population is white, but there is also a small minority that is of American Indian descent.

EDUCATION

Bermuda has a literacy rate of 98%.

Education is free and compulsory for all children ages five through 16. The curriculum borrows from both British and US systems. The school year runs 40 weeks from September to June, with Christmas, spring and summer breaks that parallel those in the USA. Most schools are coed and all students are required to wear uniforms.

Postsecondary education is available at the Bermuda College, a two-year college that has an enrollment of approximately 600 students. In addition, an estimated 1200 Bermudians are enrolled as students overseas, predominately in the USA, Canada and the UK.

ARTS

Dance

Gombey dancing is an art form that is unique to Bermuda. Although it has roots in West African tribal music, Gombey dancing also incorporates influences from Christian missionaries, the British military and, most visibly, American Indians, from whom the Gombey dancers have adapted their colorful costumes.

A Gombey group traditionally consists of men and boys, referred to as a 'crowd.' The young boys are called 'warriors' and wear short capes and carry wooden tomahawks. The older boys are called 'Indians' and carry bows and arrows, and the head males, or 'chiefs,' wear long capes, carry whips and command the show. The capes of all the dancers are brightly colored and decorated with sequins, yarn fringe and trailing ribbons. Their tall headdresses are elaborately ornamented with glitter and peacock feathers, and long sleeves, gloves, scarves and masks keep their bodies covered from head to toe.

Military influence can be found in the use of a fife, which is customized from a beer bottle, and in whistles and snare drums. The beat is also carried by a goat-skin drum that has a billy goat skin on one side and a nanny goat skin on the other.

To the uninitiated, the Gombey dancers may just look like wildly costumed characters acrobatically jumping up and down to loud music, but in fact the dancing is carefully choreographed to specific rhythms. Pantomimes often portray stories from the Bible, such as fights between David and Goliath, or Daniel in the lion's den.

There are four main Gombey groups in Bermuda. To be part of one, you either have to be born into a family of dancers or have some other significant connection.

Gombey dancers traditionally take to the streets throughout Bermuda on Boxing Day and New Year's Day; when islanders hear their drums they come running out of their homes to watch the dances. If you're lucky enough to be in Bermuda during these holidays, you can catch the Gombeys dancing in the street. Otherwise, winter visitor watch a Gombey dancing performanc of charge every Tuesday afternoon fron vember to March in the main cruise shi senger terminal on Hamilton's waterfr

Painting, Sculpture & Crafts

Bermuda's pastel houses and gentle scapes have long inspired both local a ternational artists.

Among the more renowned artists have captured Bermuda scenes ove years are Americans Georgia O'K whose best-known island works d banana flowers and banyan trees in ch and pencil; Winslow Homer, who crea paintings on the island, concentrati seaside scenes; and Andrew Wyeth focused on the people of Bermuda. dian Jack Bush used watercolors to robust scenes with a tropical motif, a French cubist artist Albert Gleizes w in gouache and watercolors.

One of Bermuda's best-known co porary watercolorists is the late Birdsey, whose prolific art still fills ga both on the island and abroad. His da Joanne Birdsey Linberg, an artist h continues to maintain the family g Other well-known local painters wh their own galleries are Jill Amos Carole Holding, Michael Swan and Forbes.

Bermuda's most highly regarded co porary sculptor is Desmond Fountai casts graceful, life-size figures of p children and female nudes in bron sculptures can be seen at Hamilton hall and at several of the island's u hotels. Bermuda's other leading sc Chesley Trott, works in native cedar studio in the Bermuda Arts Centre Royal Naval Dockyard.

Bermuda Clayworks, a pottery s the Dockyard, handcrafts both orna and utilitarian pieces, such as vases, p and dishes, which are painted with isl signs. Dockyard Glassworks at the yard and the Bermuda Glassblowing in Bailey's Bay create colorful hand

ʳmuda Shorts

ıuda shorts are the closest things ıuda has to a national dress for Unlike other places around the d where this nearly knee-length of shorts is equated with casual , in Bermuda the namesake :s are an element of formal dress. ıe rest of the outfit consists of that reach just below the knee, a shirt, tie and jacket. The knees in exposed. As for coordinating ʼarious pieces, the shorts and t should be different colors, while ɔcks can complement either.

ıe shorts, incidentally, were ind by British soldiers in tropical ɔsts such as India, who took to ıing the lower half of the legs ıeir trousers to make their uni; more bearable in the heat. By arly 20th century, British soldiers ned in Bermuda were wearing shorts as standard uniform, and years that followed the more .le Bermudian version began to make an appearance. Today, Bermuda shorts are standard for male bankers, insurance executives and other conservatively dressed community leaders.

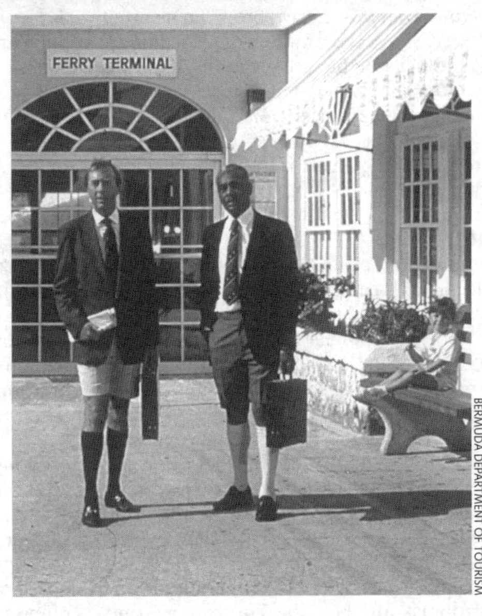

BERMUDA DEPARTMENT OF TOURISM

ems, from Christmas tree ornaments ɔerweights to elaborate tableware.

:e are dozens of other craftspeople in da, making jewelry, wall hangings, and-dipped candles, trinkets, toys and :. The largest variety of these handworks can be found at the Bermuda Iarket in the Royal Naval Dockyard.

tecture

the first things to strike visitors upon ; in Bermuda is the charming unifor: the homes on the island – quaint s painted in pastel hues with stepped ɔofs.

ough it may seem that the houses :signed solely for their pleasing aesthetics, their unique qualities are a consequence of local conditions, both in terms of available building material and the island's reliance upon rainwater.

The houses are built of locally quarried limestone. The roofs are cleverly designed to gather rainwater and direct it via angled stone gutters into a catchment tank that provides the residents with drinking water. The bleached-white color of the roofs is the result of their being painted with a limestone wash that acts as a water purifier. The appearance of these bright, textured roofs has earned them the nickname 'cake icing.'

The simplicity of the homes, free as they are of exterior embellishments, is necessitated by the smooth limestone surfaces.

Jalousied wooden window shutters provide the main ornamental feature. One decorative indulgence is the 'eyebrow,' an inverted letter V, above the windows of some homes.

Another notable architectural feature is the moongate, a round limestone gate often found at the entrance to Bermuda gardens. Thought to be of Chinese origin, passing through the moongate is traditionally said to bring good luck.

Literature

Bermuda can claim ties to a number of significant 20th-century writers who either vacationed or lived on the island.

Nobel prize winner Eugene O'Neill (1888-1953), who had a place in Warwick Parish, wrote a number of works while in Bermuda, including *Strange Interlude*. One of O'Neill's neighbors was the English playwright and composer Noel Coward (1899-1973).

American novelist, poet and biographer Hervey Allen (1889-1949) wrote the novel *Anthony Adverse* during his stay at Felicity Hall, a mansion in Somerset.

James Thurber (1894-1961), author and cartoonist for the *New Yorker* magazine, wrote the fairy tale *The 13 Clocks* and other stories during long stays on the island. He was a frequent contributor to *The Bermudian* magazine.

Munro Leaf (1905-76), an author and illustrator of books for children, had a home in Somerset. He wrote *The Story of Ferdinand*, about a Spanish bull, while living in Bermuda in the 1930s.

Peter Benchley, a frequent visitor to the island since the 1960s, wrote *Jaws* in Bermuda and found a setting for a second novel, *The Deep*, while diving in Bermuda. Benchley also used Bermuda for the setting of the suspense novel *Beast*, published in 1991.

SOCIETY & CONDUCT

Bermudian culture is a blend of British and African heritage. The British influence predominates in institutions, from the form of government to the educational system and legal framework. Politicians and judges still wear powdered wigs, bobbies direct traffic, afternoon tea is a ritual and a pint of the local pub is a common way to cap day's work. Cricket is Bermuda's popular sport. Fashion and manners r conservatively British.

The African influence is more subtl can be found in island music and dance notably in the rhythm of Gombey da Other African-related influences cor way of the West Indies, such as the po ity of reggae, steel drum and calypso m

Dos & Don'ts

For visitors, neatness in dress and poli in attitude go a long way. You should stop someone on the street for dire without first greeting them with ' morning' or 'Good afternoon'…a s 'Excuse me, could you tell me the way beach?' is considered abrupt and rude ordering a drink from a bar should b aced with a friendly 'hello.'

Dress is relatively formal, with b suits and skimpy beachwear conside appropriate in any place aside fro beach or the swimming pool. In fact, offense for men to appear in public w a shirt or for women to wear a bathi top in place of a blouse. Nude and p nude bathing are not permitted any in Bermuda.

RELIGION

The majority of islanders are Christi though the number of people affiliate the Anglican church has dropped to a 25% (from 45% in 1970), it remai largest denomination. This is follov Roman Catholic at 15%, African Me Episcopal at 12%, Seventh-Day Adve 6% and Methodist at 5%. Other ho worship in Bermuda include Jeh Witness, Baptist, Presbyterian, Ch Science and Muslim.

LANGUAGE

Bermudians speak English with a l and a predominantly British accent.

The use of Bermudian slang is m common today than in decades past,

› the pervasive influence of overseas , particularly American TV.

ıetheless, there are a few peculiarities. stance, the interchange of 'w' for 'v' is ıcommon, so that 'welcome' is often ınced as 'velcome.' Sometimes 'ing' is ned to 'in' ('wedding' thus becomes n') and the ending 'th' is sometimes ı as 'f' ('with' becomes 'vif').

Common island expressions include:

byes an gals – boys and girls
chinwag – chat
going tawhn – going to town (to Hamilton)
bailin – bathing suit
full hot – drunk
how you sound – what's wrong?
de rock – the rock (meaning Bermuda)

Facts for the Visitor

HIGHLIGHTS

The **Town of St George** is unique for its well-preserved period character. No trip to Bermuda would be complete without spending at least an afternoon strolling along its crooked streets and poking into its churches, museums and historic sites.

Although the **City of Hamilton** has a more modern, businesslike facade, it also has plenty to offer vacationers, including Bermuda's widest selection of restaurants and quality shops, interesting museums and a hilltop fort.

The **Royal Naval Dockyard** is the top sight at the western end of Bermuda. Its inner fort has been turned into the island's leading historic museum, the Bermuda Maritime Museum, and other buildings have been converted into craft shops and restaurants with atmosphere.

Pink-sand beaches are certainly a highlight in Bermuda. The most dazzling array is found at **South Shore Park**, and the turquoise waters and gentle, curving sands of Horseshoe Bay are often said to be the the most picturesque.

Other top places for viewing nature include the **Bermuda Botanical Gardens** in Paget, which displays hundreds of specimens of flora, and the **Crystal Caves** at Bailey's Bay, where you can walk deep into an underground cave and see impressive stalactites and stalagmites. The **Bermuda Aquarium, Museum & Zoo**, with its tanks of colorful fish, brilliant flamingos and an acclaimed endangered-species program, makes another interesting visit.

PLANNING

When to Go

Bermuda can be visited year-round, but the busiest tourist season, referred to as the 'summer season' or 'high season,' is from April through October. This is the time when Bermuda enjoys its warmest air and water temperatures and when the best conditions exist for water sports such as swimming, snorkeling and diving. It's al most vibrant time on the island, with lier hotel scene, greater entertainme tions and more visitors milling about

The winter is not quite warm eno most people to enjoy ocean swimmi many tourist-related activities, such a bottom boat cruises, suspend operati at least part of the season. Even a nur guesthouses and small hotels clos month or two, with January being the of least activity.

That doesn't necessarily mean that is a bad time to visit Bermuda – it d on what your interests are. Golfe tennis players will find temperature pleasant in the winter. Also on the p there are far fewer visitors to compe and getting a table at your favorite rant will be much easier. In addition visitors are treated to free 'Noven March' activities sponsored by the B Dept of Tourism; these include G dancing, guided walks in Hamilton George, and a skirling ceremony Hamilton by kilted bagpipers of t muda Islands Pipe Band.

Not surprisingly, most hotels drc rates in winter, and if you shop arou can find some good deals, even at the resorts. Likewise, airlines tend to c in winter.

For detailed climate information, Climate section in the precedin about Bermuda chapter. For specific taking place throughout the year, Public Holidays & Special Events later in this chapter. Also see the C Activities chapter for seasonal info on specific sports.

Maps

The Bermuda Dept of Tourism *Bermuda Handy Reference Map*, annually, is indeed handy and ma you'll need for a short visit or limite seeing. It shows major roads and l

BERMUDA DEPARTMENT OF TOURISM

an business suits

NED FRIARY

; in Bermuda!

GLENDA BENDURE

Gombey dancer's cape shows African heritage.

NED FRIARY

Monarch butterfly, a seasonal visitor

NED FRIARY

Frangipani

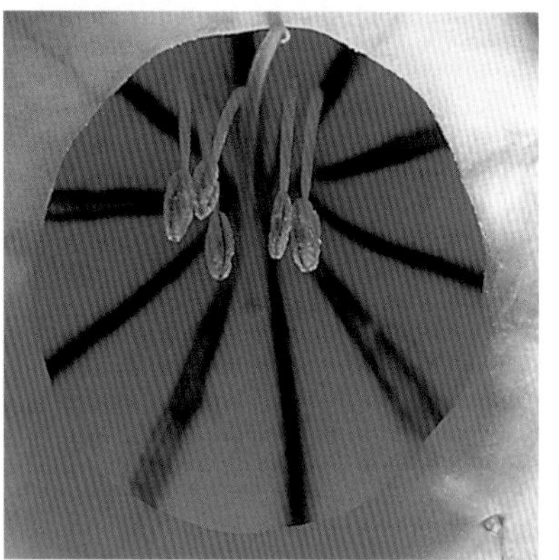
NED FRIARY

Honeycup

NED FRIARY

Kiskadee

PIERCE & NEWMAN

Sea turtles enjoy a peaceful moment.

tels, sightseeing attractions, beaches e like. You can obtain a copy from the of Tourism (see the Tourist Offices n, later in this chapter) in advance of rip, or pick it up at any one of the Viservice Bureaus in Bermuda after your .

most detailed foldout map, however, *Bermuda Islands*, by Island Maps). This authoritative map shows all the roads, parks, beaches, golf courses, ore shipwrecks, gas stations and the hotels, and can be purchased at tourist bookstores and hotel sundry shops.

to Bring

dians dress conservatively. Appropri- thing depends not only on the season sit, but also on where you stay and rt of dining you have in mind.

al sportswear is acceptable daytime nost anywhere in Bermuda, including me dining in restaurants. A number dining spots require dressing up for so men who plan on dining in fancy ants are best advised to bring along a and tie, and women are advised to nice dress or pantsuit. This also holds ou book into a hotel-dining package ludes fine dining.

rwise, particularly in the summer, ght clothing made of cotton or silk, reathe best in hot weather, is the itable. In winter, it's wise to pack an -weight jacket, a sweater and other olens as well.

u plan on renting a moped, you'll ap- having a windbreaker for cooler s and to offer protection in the event instorm. Another good thing for riders to bring is a bungee cord, so strap down a small bag in the basket moped, securing it from wind and ls of any potential drive-by thief.

od pair of walking shoes will be you decide to thoroughly explore ns of St George and Hamilton or of Bermuda's longer hikes, such as o Spittal Pond.

re to remember your swimsuit. hould bring their certification cards and logbooks. If you plan to do a lot of snorkeling, you might want to bring your own snorkel, mask and fins; of course, these can be rented in Bermuda, but the prices tend to be high. Likewise, tennis players can save rental fees by bringing their own racquets and tennis balls, and golfers by carting along their own clubs and golf balls. Keep in mind that some tennis courts insist on players wearing 'tennis whites.'

Birdwatchers will no doubt appreciate having a pair of binoculars. A Swiss Army knife, or similar knife with a corkscrew, can be handy for picnics. Bring a camera and film, as Bermuda is very picturesque.

Ziploc resealable plastic bags in a couple of sizes are indispensable for keeping things dry. You can use them to protect your film and camera equipment, to seal up airline tickets and passports, and to keep wet bathing suits away from the rest of your luggage.

Airlines do lose luggage from time to time, but you've got a better chance of recovering it if it's tagged with your name and address *inside* as well as outside – outside tags can always fall off or be removed. However, take heart: should you lose something or simply forget to pack it, you'll probably be able to find it after your arrival in Bermuda.

TOURIST OFFICES

Local Tourist Offices

The Bermuda Dept of Tourism (☎ 292-0023, fax 292-7537, email travel@bermudatourism .com) has its administrative office at Global House, 43 Church St, Hamilton. The mailing address is PO Box HM 465, Hamilton HM BX. Look for the tourism department's website at www.bermudatourism.com. As always when calling from outside Bermuda, prefix the 441 area code to the local number.

The chamber of commerce, in cooperation with the tourism department, staffs walk-in tourist offices (called Visitors Service Bureaus) year-round in the City of Hamilton, the Town of St George in St George's Parish and the Royal Naval Dockyard in Sandys Parish. See those regional chapters for details.

Tourist Offices Abroad

Before you visit Bermuda, you can contact the Bermuda Dept of Tourism to receive a standard packet of visitor information covering accommodations, activities and seasonal events. Upon request, the department will also send specific information on honeymoon packages, golf courses and yachting. In addition, if you have a fax machine, you can call the New York toll-free number listed below to receive fact sheets on a score of different topics via fax.

The Bermuda Dept of Tourism operates the following overseas offices:

Canada (☎ 416-923-9600, 800-387-1304, fax 416-923-4840) 1200 Bay St, Suite 1004, Toronto, Ontario M5R 2A5

UK (☎ 020-7771-7001, fax 020-7771-7037) 1 Battersea Church Rd, London SW11 3LY

USA *Head office* (☎ 212-818-9800, 800-223-6106, fax 212-983-5289) 205 E 42nd St, 16th floor, New York, NY 10017

USA *Regional offices* (☎ 404-524-1541, fax 404-586-9933) 245 Peachtree Center Ave NE, Suite 803, Atlanta, GA 30303

(☎ 617-742-0405, fax 617-723-7786) 44 School St, Suite 1010, Boston, MA 02108

(☎ 630-585-6918, fax 630-585-6948) 2835 Aurora Ave, Suite 115-315, Naperville, IL 60540

(☎ 630-585-6918, fax 630-585-6948) 268 S Beverly Dr, PMB 448, Beverly Hills, CA 90212

VISAS & DOCUMENTS

Passport

A passport is the preferred document for entry into Bermuda and is required of visitors from all countries that require a passport for re-entry purposes.

Your passport should remain valid until well after your trip. If it's about to expire, renew it before you go.

Applying for or renewing a passport can take from a few days to several months, so don't leave it till the last minute. Bureaucracy tends to grind faster if you do everything in person rather than rely on the mail or agents. Find out beforehand what is required: passport photos, birth certificate, exact payment in cash, whatever.

Australian citizens can apply at office or the passport office in thei capital; Britons can apply at majo offices; Canadians can apply at re passport offices; New Zealanders car at any district office of the Dept of I Affairs; and US citizens must ap person (but may usually renew by m either a US Passport Agency office o courthouses and post offices.

From the USA Visitors from the US present one of the following types of fication – note that if you're presentin tification that doesn't have a photo, s birth certificate, you'll need to also pr driver's license or similar photo ID dren 16 and under who are traveli their parents may present an offici certificate without a photo ID.)

- US passport – it needn't be valid, but expired, the photo should be recent enc it still resembles the bearer
- An official birth certificate with a raise a certified copy issued by a municipal
- US Naturalization Certificate
- US Alien Registration Card
- US Re-entry Permit

From Canada Visitors from Can need to present one of the following identification:

- A valid Canadian passport
- An official birth certificate or a certi along with a photo ID
- Canadian Certificate of Citizenship, official proof of Landed Immigrant st

From Other Countries Visito other countries, including the UK, European nations, Australia ar Zealand, must present a valid passp

Visas

Visas are not required of citizens countries, including the USA, Car UK, Australia, New Zealand and European countries.

ıs are required of citizens from the r Soviet Union, most countries in Africa and the Middle East (but not ɔr Egypt), Albania, Bosnia-Herzegov-ulgaria, Cambodia, China, Croatia, the Czech Republic, Haiti, Mongolia, ı, North Korea, Pakistan, Romania, Slovakia, Slovenia, Sri Lanka and m. Visitors from the above countries contact either a British embassy or ılate in their home country for visa ation.

igration authorities at the Bermuda ıtional Airport will determine your ted length of stay. They commonly stay of up to 21 days. Extensions can lied for at the Immigration Head-s (☎ 295-5151), 30 Parliament St, on.

rd Tickets

tors landing in Bermuda must be in ion of a return or onward ticket.

Insurance

l agent can sell you a travel insur-licy to cover losses you might incur you unexpectedly have to cancel p or change your itinerary. Keep in at many airlines, cruise lines, hotels kage tours have hefty penalties for ıtions or changes, and some are onrefundable.

od travel insurance policy will pro-verage for lost luggage as well as emergencies. There are a wide var-ɔolicies available, so check the fine r instance, some policies specifically 'dangerous activities,' which can common tourist activities such as ving or motorcycling. Also check to e policy covers an emergency flight the event of a medical crisis.

good idea to purchase travel insur-early as possible. If you buy it the fore you leave, you might find, for that you're not covered for delays departure caused by strikes or other l action that may have been in force ɔu took out the insurance.

Paying for your ticket with a credit card often provides limited travel accident insurance, and you may also be able to reclaim the payment if the operator doesn't deliver. Ask your credit card company what it will cover.

Other Documents

A driver's license can be useful as an ID, but you won't get much mileage out of it in Bermuda; the only vehicles that can be rented are mopeds, and no driver's license is required to rent them.

If you're a member of the National Trust in Australia, Barbados, Britain or another Commonwealth country, you'll get free entry into Bermuda National Trust sites by showing your membership card.

Divers should bring along their certification cards.

Photocopies

Before you leave home, you should photocopy all important documents (passport data page and visa page, credit cards, travel insurance policy, air tickets, driver's license etc). Leave one copy with someone at home and keep another with you, separate from the originals.

It's also a good idea to store details of your vital travel documents in Lonely Planet's free online Travel Vault in case you lose the photocopies or can't be bothered with them. Your password-protected Travel Vault is accessible online anywhere in the world – create it at www.ekno.lonelyplanet.com.

EMBASSIES & CONSULATES

Embassies Abroad

Bermuda's diplomatic representation is handled by British embassies and consulates around the world. British embassies abroad include the following:

Australia (☎ 02-6270-6666) British High Commission, Commonwealth Ave, Yarralumla, Canberra, ACT 2600

Canada (☎ 613-237-1530) British High Commission, 80 Elgin St, Ottawa K1P 5K7

Germany (☎ 30 201 840) British Embassy, Unter den Linden 32-34, D-10117 Berlin

France (☎ 01 44 51 31 00) British Embassy, 35 rue du Faubourg St Honor, 75383 Paris Cedex 08

New Zealand (☎ 04-472-6049) British High Commission, 44 Hill St, Wellington 1

USA (☎ 202-462-1340) British Embassy, 3100 Massachusetts Ave NW, Washington, DC 20008

Your Own Embassy

It's important to realize what your own embassy – the embassy of the country of which you are a citizen – can and can't do to help you if you get into trouble.

Generally speaking, it won't be much help in emergencies if the trouble you're in is remotely your own fault. Remember that you are bound by the laws of the country you are in. Your embassy will not be sympathetic if you end up in jail after committing a crime locally, even if such actions are legal in your own country.

In genuine emergencies, you might get some assistance, but only if other channels have been exhausted. If you need to get home urgently, a free ticket home is exceedingly unlikely – the embassy would expect you to have insurance. If all your money and documents are stolen, it might assist you with getting a new passport, but a loan for onward travel is out of the question.

Consulates in Bermuda

Bermuda has no embassies, but Portugal and the USA maintain consulates.

Portugal's consulate (☎ 292-1039) is in Melbourne House, 11 Parliament St, City of Hamilton.

The USA's consulate (☎ 295-1342) is at Crown Hill, 16 Middle Rd, Devonshire.

In addition, numerous countries have designated individuals as 'honorary consuls' in Bermuda. Keep in mind that these honorary consuls are often businesspeople, not permanent diplomats, and thus the list changes rather frequently. Currently it includes Austria, Belgium, Chile, Denmark, Finland, France, Germany, Italy, Jamaica, Luxembourg, the Netherlands, Norway, Philippines, Spain, Sweden and Switzerland.

See the blue pages of the Bermuda phone book for honorary consuls' contact details.

CUSTOMS

Visitors to Bermuda may bring in dut 200 cigarettes, 50 cigars, 1lb of toba quart of liquor and 1 quart of wine, as all clothing, sports equipment, came intended for personal use. Each vis also entitled to a $30 gift allowance.

Visitors are allowed to bring in up to meat and other food items per person fo own consumption, though these are to a 22% duty. Because of the high pric ported food, bringing in frozen meat an option worth considering if you are in a place with cooking facilities.

Bermuda restricts or prohibits the tation of animals, plants, fresh fruits a etables, pornography, firearms, spea offensive weapons and drugs. For in about customs laws, contact the C House at ☎ 295-4816.

MONEY

Currency

The legal tender is the Bermuda pegged at a 1:1 ratio with the US dol US dollar is generally accepted at fac in hotels, restaurants and shops.

The Bermuda dollar is divided i cents (¢). Coins come in denominatio (penny), 5¢ (nickel), 10¢ (dime), 25¢ (and one dollar. The coins have island there's a hog on the back of the penny, an angelfish on the nickel, a lily on the dime, a longtail tropic bir quarter and a sailboat on the bronze

Bills come in $2, $5, $10, $20, $50 a denominations.

Exchange Rates

At press time, exchange rates were as

country	unit		Bermu
Australia	A$1	=	
Canada	C$1	=	
EC	€1	=	
France	1FF	=	
Germany	DM1	=	
New Zealand	NZ$1	=	
USA	US$1	=	
UK	UK£1	=	

anging Money

est currency to take to Bermuda is the llar, as it can be used interchangeably he Bermudian dollar. US dollar trav- checks are also widely accepted. All foreign currencies, including the pound sterling, will need to be ex- ed at a bank.

Bank of Bermuda, which has bran- the airport as well as near the cruise ocks in Hamilton, St George and the Naval Dockyard, will cash traveler's worth up to a total of US$500 in US Canadian dollar or British pound de- ations, free of service charges. Expect a 1% commission if you cash more 500 in a single transaction. Although nk does not accept other foreign trav- hecks, it will exchange cash in most najor currencies.

ddition, the Bank of Bermuda has r ATMs in nearly two dozen loca- including the airport, Hamilton, St and Somerset – which will accept and Plus system ATM cards and Mas- l or Visa credit cards.

Bank of Butterfield also has a widely ed network of ATMs that accept the TM and credit cards as the Bank of da. Among the places you can find TMs are Bank of Butterfield branch Marketplace grocery stores and hopping centers.

r credit cards, such as Visa and Mas- , are accepted by most shops and ants, and the American Express card is accepted by many as well. and guesthouses are more fickle on ards; the larger resort hotels accept ut a number of the smaller places do ou intend to pay off your room bill redit card, be sure to inquire at the booking your reservation as to it will be honored – surprisingly, me of the high-end places don't hem.

no getting around it – Bermuda isn't And unlike many vacation destina- here airfare represents your most substantial expense, the largest slice of your travel costs in Bermuda is likely to be for accommodations.

Bermuda's high cost of living is reflected in the rates charged by island hotels – by the time service charges and taxes are added to the tariff, there are only a few places in Bermuda where you can squeak by for much less than $100 a day…and the average is easily twice that!

If you plan to stay seven days or less, look into package tours that include both airfare and hotel, as they will often work out more cheaply than buying the airfare and paying for the hotel separately. Although it's not heavily advertised, with many tour operators you can also create your own 'package tours' for stays of longer than seven days – so even if you're staying for a couple of weeks, this may be an option worth pursuing.

Eating in Bermuda can be a hefty expense as well. Most of the food consumed in Bermuda is imported, and prices are generally about 50% higher than those in the USA. Snacking on simple fare from grocery stores or getting a place with kitchen facilities and cooking some of your own meals can help keep costs relatively low.

In terms of dining out, some of the best-value meals can be found on weekdays in the City of Hamilton, where lunch deals for around $10 abound. However, dinner at these same restaurants might well run up a $25 tab. And if you stick with the resort restaurants, you can easily pay twice these amounts.

If you plan to eat meals in the place where you're staying, note that many guesthouses and hotels offer discounted meal plans that include breakfast and dinner. Some of the better plans offer a 'dine around' feature whereby guests are allowed to take their meals at a handful of affiliated restaurants.

Tipping & Bargaining

The usual restaurant tip is 15%, which most restaurants automatically add to the bill – if not, you should add the tip yourself. Hotels typically tag a 10% service charge onto your final room bill, which covers gratuities to hotel workers. For taxi drivers, a tip of about 10% is appropriate.

Bargaining is not a common practice in Bermuda.

Taxes

A 7.25% occupancy tax is added on to hotel bills upon check-out. Note that this tax is not included in hotel prices given throughout this book.

One other tax that affects visitors is the departure tax – $20 for air passengers and $60 for cruise ship passengers – but this is a hidden tax included in the ticket price and paid at the time of purchase.

Bermuda has no sales tax.

POST & COMMUNICATIONS

Postal Rates

Airmail letters cost 65¢ for the first 10 grams and 30¢ for each additional 10 grams when sent to the USA, Canada, Mexico, Central America, Venezuela, Colombia or the Caribbean. Postcards to these same destinations cost 60¢.

The cost is 80¢ for the first 10 grams, and 40¢ per additional 10 grams, for letters sent to the UK, Europe, North Africa and most of South America. Postcards to these destinations cost 75¢.

The cost is 90¢ for the first 10 grams, and 50¢ for additional 10 grams, to other destinations – including Australia, New Zealand, Asia and most of Africa. Postcards to these destinations cost 85¢.

Aerograms cost 60¢ to any international destination.

For mail sent within Bermuda for local delivery, the cost is 25¢ for a postcard and 30¢ for a letter of up to 20 grams.

Sending & Receiving Mail

There are post offices in every major village and town, from St George to Somerset. As a general rule, airmail posted by 9:30 am at the General Post Office in the City of Hamilton will leave the island the same day.

Most hotels will hold mail for their guests. In addition, mail can be received in your name, c/o General Delivery, General Post Office, 56 Church St, Hamilton HI Bermuda. Items not collected at the (Hamilton within 30 days will be retu the sender.

Aerial Sea Mail

The Bermuda postal system offers one o more unusual 'sea mail' services. What is culiar about it is that ships are not involve the service, but the mail is instead airl from Bermuda to the country of destina

To make sure people don't overuse discounted 'sea mail' rates, all surface m held in Bermuda until a closing date, wh equivalent to the scheduled date that imaginary ship would leave Bermuda, the additional time – typically three day mail to the USA, four days for mail tc UK – that it would normally take for a sh sail between Bermuda and the destinati

The Bermudians take it all quite seriou the closing date for sea mail is displayed post offices. If you manage to get some off shortly before the closing date, it ca tually be an efficient way to mail things the rates are roughly half those of re airmail.

Telephone

Local telephone numbers have seve All calls made in Bermuda to anothe in Bermuda are local calls and cost 2 a pay phone.

There are pay phones all arou island, including most shopping hotel lobbies, ferry terminals and the departure lounge. Most pay phones both Bermuda and US coins. For ma ternational calls, pay phones will Visa, MasterCard and American cards as well.

You can also purchase phone which can be convenient if you're be making a lot of calls or are maki seas calls, as you won't need a pock coins. Phone cards are available in and $50 denominations and can re ıased from tourist offices, drugstores ›ther shops around the island.

ɾou plan to use the phone in your hotel , check first for any surcharges – 75¢ is : average, but this varies by hotel.

al ☎ 411 for local directory assistance. irectory assistance for the USA, dial area code + 555-1212. For directory as-ce for other countries, dial ☎ 00 for the eas operator. For police, fire or ambu- emergencies, dial ☎ 911.

you're a cellular phone user, the uda Telephone Company has a mobile ›rk that supports North American ›g (AMPS) and Digital (TDMA) stan- ervice. Visitors can register for set-up e either before or after arriving in uda by calling ☎ 292-6032. It costs $10 vate the service, plus $5 a day to main- and a per-minute calling rate of 35¢ to epending on the time of day.

muda's country code is 1 and its inter- al access code is 011, the same as it is USA, Canada and some Caribbean ies.

to Bermuda Bermuda's area code is hich must be added to the seven-digit umber when calling from overseas.

can call Bermuda direct from the Canada and most Caribbean coun- y dialing ☎ 1 + 441 + seven-digit local r.

call Bermuda from anywhere else in rld, dial the international access code country you're calling from + 1 + 441 -digit local number. For instance, the cess code is 00, so from the UK dial 1 + 441 + local number.

rom Bermuda From Bermuda, you direct to the USA, Canada and most ean countries by dialing ☎ 1 + area local number.

all direct to other parts of the world, 011 + country code + area code + mber. For example, the country code UK is 44; hence: 011 + 44 + area code number. Other country codes are ia 61, France 33, Germany 49, Italy New Zealand 64.

Rates to the continental USA and Canada generally range from 75¢ to 95¢ per minute, and rates to most other countries are about $1.25 per minute. You can get current rates for any country by calling Cable & Wireless' 24-hour help line service at ☎ 297-7022.

In addition to placing direct-dial calls, you can also call home using the 'country direct system,' which will charge the call to your home phone bill or calling card. To make long-distance calls with AT&T's Direct Service, dial ☎ 1-800-872-2881. MCI WorldCom's WorldPhone service can be accessed by dialing ☎ 1-800-888-8000.

Fax

You can send or receive faxes at the Cable & Wireless office, on the corner of Church and Burnaby Sts in Hamilton. To send a fax, the cost is $2 for the first page and $1 for each additional page, plus the cost of the phone call. To receive a fax, the cost is $1 per page; faxes from overseas should be sent to ☎ 441-295-7909. The office is open 9 am to 5 pm weekdays.

Guests can usually send and receive faxes at their hotels, but it's wise to check the rate in advance.

Email & Internet Access

Traveling with a portable computer is a great way to stay in touch with home, but unless you know what you're doing, it's fraught with potential problems. If the power supply voltage in your home country is different from that in Bermuda (see Electricity, later in this chapter), bring a universal AC converter, which will enable you to plug it in without frying the innards. You may also need a plug adapter, which is often easiest to buy before you leave home.

Also, your PC-card modem may not work once you leave your home country – but you won't know for sure until you try. The safest option is to buy a reputable 'global' modem before you leave home. Keep in mind that the telephone socket may be different from that at home as well, so ensure that you have at least a US RJ-11 telephone adapter that works with your modem. You can almost always find an adapter that will convert from RJ-11 to the local variety. For more information on traveling with a portable computer, see www.teleadapt.com or www.warrior.com.

To use public access points to get your email, you'll need to know your incoming (POP or IMAP) mail server name, your account name and your password.

The simplest way to get online in Bermuda is through one of the cybercafes in Hamilton (see Email & Internet Access under Information in the City of Hamilton chapter). There are currently no international service providers with Bermuda dial-in nodes, but local provider Logic Communications (☎ 296-9600) can set up an account for short-term visitors for around $30 a week.

If you're carrying a laptop, you may want to check in advance with your hotel to see if the room has a phone jack that can accommodate modem hookups; these are becoming more common as hotels upgrade and renovate.

INTERNET RESOURCES

The World Wide Web is a rich resource for travelers. You can research your trip, hunt down bargain airfares, book hotels, check on weather conditions or chat with locals and other travelers about the best places to visit (or avoid!).

There's no better place to start your Web explorations than the Lonely Planet website (www.lonelyplanet.com). Here you'll find succinct summaries on traveling to most places on earth, postcards from other travelers and the Thorn Tree bulletin board, where

you can ask questions before you go c pense advice when you get back. Yo also find travel news and updates for m our most popular guidebooks, and th WWWay section links you to the most travel resources elsewhere on the Web

The Bermuda Dept of Tourism c reached at www.bermudatourism.co general tourist information. The *Ber Sun* website at www.bermudasun.br gold mine of information; it allows y access a wide array of information Bermuda, including weather, news, ar entertainment, sports and general t information.

BOOKS

There are numerous books about Ber both fiction and nonfiction, that can p insights to the island.

Keep in mind that some books ar lished in different editions by differer lishers in different countries. As a re book might be a hardcover rarity country but readily available in pap in another. Fortunately, bookstores braries can search by title or author, s local bookstore or library is best pla advise you on the availability of the ing recommendations.

If you aren't able to find any of books before your trip, you can pick th at bookstores in Bermuda after you a

History & Culture

The Story of Bermuda and Her People, by S Zuill, is the most comprehensive and tative history of the island available.

Another World – Bermuda and the Modern Tourism, by Duncan McDonal noteworthy. It tells not only the history ism but also how Bermuda came to be th is today.

Sea Venture, by Willoughby Patton, ap school-age children. It tells the story of th shipwreck from the perspective of a board the ship.

Held in Trust, by the Bermuda National Tr attractive book that details the histori nature reserves and other property u auspices of the Trust.

ıral History

ıda's Marine Life, by Wolfgang Sterrer, ıer director of the Bermuda Biological on, is an excellent 300-page book with color ography and detailed descriptions of fish, aceans and other local marine life.

ers of the Deep – Underwater Bermuda, by ael Burke, Stephen Kerr et al, is a hard- coffee-table book with lovely underwater os of Bermuda's fish, coral and anemones.

ide to the Reef, Shore and Game Fish of ıuda, by Louis S Mowbray, who was curator ermuda's aquarium for 25 years and a eer of game fishing in Bermuda, describes fish, complete with drawings.

da Shipwrecks, by Daniel and Denise Berg, vell-researched book detailing many of the recks found in Bermudian waters.

s of Bermuda is a compact book by Hans W ıau, with photos and text that feature some more common flowers found on the island. ough there are a number of books about bean flora that include some Bermudian rs, this one is specific to Bermuda.

da, Her Plants & Gardens (1609-1850), by ollett, gives a historic background on flora, ng and gardening on the island, for travelers sted in the origin of plants.

le to the Birds of Bermuda, by Eric Amos, best book for birdwatchers. It describes than 300 species of birds that have been n Bermuda and gives detailed information ding sites around the island.

& Snorkeling Bermuda, by Lawson Wood ely Planet/Pisces Books), gives in-depth s on the best underwater sites. It includes photos of wrecks, corals and fish and has a l section on underwater photography.

ral

eter Benchley's best-known novel, was n in Bermuda. His diving outings inspired later write ***The Deep***, an adventure novel Bermuda. It incorporates an interesting island life and fiction and makes a good side read.

la Abstracts, by photographer Graeme oridge, is an artistic book that captures the of Bermuda's unique architecture.

a in Full Color, by Hans W Hannau, gives l background on the people and places of ıda, complete with color photographs.

Peter Benchley wrote *Jaws* while in Bermuda.

Images of Bermuda, by Roger A LaBrucherie, and ***The Beauty of Bermuda***, by Scott Stallard, are both handsome coffee-table books with notable photography.

Bermuda Triangle Mystery Solved, by Lawrence David Kusche, is one of several books about the Bermuda Triangle that will provide interesting reading for those fascinated with the mysteries of vanished ships and planes.

The Last Pink Bits, by Harry Ritchie, is an enjoyable account of the author's travels in Bermuda and a handful of other scattered island outposts that comprise the last remnants of the once-formidable British empire.

Outerbridge's Original Cookbook, by Alexis Outerbridge, has 160 pages of recipes for drinks, soups and various other dishes that use sherry peppers sauce. ***Bermudian Cookery***, a 190-page spiral-bound book published by the Bermuda Junior Service League, has recipes for a variety of favorite island foods.

FILMS

Several videos available may be of interest to tourists. Among the most popular are the videotapes in the 'Island of Bermuda' series, which includes such titles as *Bermuda*

Highlights, *Dive Bermuda* and *Bermuda Bound Paradise Found*. Priced at $30 each, tapes can be purchased at island bookstores or ordered for postal delivery from Panatel VDS (☎ 296-4333), PO Box HM 1997, Hamilton HM HX.

A few Hollywood movies have been shot in Bermuda, including *The Deep* (1977), based on Peter Benchley's novel of the same name, starring Jacqueline Bisset and Nick Nolte; *Chapter Two* (1979), an autobiographical comedy by Neil Simon, starring Marsha Mason and James Caan; and *That Touch of Mink* (1962), starring Cary Grant and Doris Day.

NEWSPAPERS & MAGAZINES

The *Royal Gazette*, the leading Bermuda newspaper, has both local and international news and is published Monday to Saturday. You can find a scaled-down version online at www.accessbda.bm.

The *Bermuda Sun*, published on Wednesday and Friday, focuses almost solely on island issues and is a good source for entertainment happenings. It has an excellent website at www.bermudasun.bm.

A handy item to pick up as soon as you arrive is *This Week in Bermuda*, a free weekly publication loaded with visitor-related information, including an events schedule, sightseeing details and ads aplenty. If you don't find one at the airport, the publication can be readily found around the island at hotels and other businesses that cater to tourists.

Also worth picking up is *Destination Bermuda*, a free full-color magazine that is published annually and written with both tourists and business visitors in mind. It has sections on activities, shopping and restaurants as well as feature articles on topics ranging from real estate to the arts. Look for it at tourist offices and island hotels.

Bermuda, a full-color magazine published quarterly and geared to visitors, has an interesting range of feature articles about Bermuda. Annual subscription rates are $20 in the USA and $28 in other countries, including postage, from Bermuda Magazine (☎ 292-7279, 800-247-3620), PO Box 5061, Brentwood, Tennessee 37024.

The Bermudian, a full-color mo magazine in its sixth decade of public is geared more to Bermudians, with ar on business, local personalities and h and gardens. An annual subscription i country outside Bermuda costs $40, po included, from The Bermudian Publi Company (☎ 295-0695), PO Box HM Hamilton HM AX.

You can also find a range of internat newspapers, such as the *New York T* the *Boston Globe*, the *Wall Street Jo* the *Globe & Mail*, the *Guardian* and tain's *Sunday Times*.

RADIO & TV

Bermuda has cable TV, which include US networks ABC, CBS, CNN, Fox, NBC, PBS and numerous other cha Local news is shown at 7 pm on chan (ZBM) and channel 4 (VSB), and foll at 7:30 pm with CBS network nev channel 3 and NBC news on channel 4 muda weather service broadcasts co ous weather and tide forecasts on ch 11. Ongoing international news service CNN is broadcast on channel 15 and BBC World on channel 8.

Bermuda has two radio broadc companies. The Bermuda Broadc Company plays mixed music at AM and 1340, and plays rock and contemp music at FM 89. DeFontes Broadcasti erates at AM 1160, with BBC World S and local public affairs; AM 1280, wit gious programming; AM 1450, with c and western music; and FM 106.1, wit temporary music.

VIDEO SYSTEMS

Bermuda uses the same NTSC video as in the USA and Canada, which is patible with the PAL system used in E and Australia. If you want to buy a vi play back at home, check to verify t recorded in the same system you use.

PHOTOGRAPHY & VIDEO

Print film is readily available in Berm though slide film can be a bit more d to find. As with most items in Bermu s are on the high side: a 36-exposure of Kodak Gold print film will cost nd $9, and a roll of slide film costs about le that, so it's best to bring an adequate supply along with you. Blank video- for camcorders cost around $6.

you want to develop your print film in Bermuda, there are shops in the of Hamilton that have same-day pro- ng, but expect to pay upward of $25 to op and print a roll of 36 exposures. rwise, consider bringing along process- ailers to send film to a lab back home ave your photos waiting for you when eturn from your vacation.

en taking pictures, keep in mind that and water are intense reflectors, and in light they'll often leave foreground ts shadowy. You can try compensating justing your f-stop or attaching a po- g filter, or both, but the most effective ique is to take photos in the gentler of early morning and late afternoon. be careful not to leave your camera in sunlight any longer than necessary.

E

uda is in the Atlantic standard time which is four hours behind Greenwich time and one hour ahead of eastern rd time.

en it's noon in Bermuda, it is 11 am in York and Toronto, 10 am in Chicago, n Los Angeles and Vancouver, 2 am ney, midnight in Hong Kong and 4 pm don.

light saving time is in effect in Ber- from the first Sunday in April to the nday in October.

TRICITY

c current operates on 110V and 60 and a flat, two-pronged plug is used – ne as in the USA. Some hotels have rs for electric shavers.

HTS & MEASURES

gh a conversion to metric has been aken in such areas as the posting of imits, Bermuda still uses the imperial of measurement for many applica- tions. Newspapers print temperatures in degrees Fahrenheit, and most weights are measured in ounces and pounds.

For those unaccustomed to either system, there's a conversion table on the inside back cover of this book.

LAUNDRY

Most hotels offer send-out laundry services, but these tend to be quite expensive. You'll save money by using coin-operated laundries, which can be found in most parishes. Some guesthouses and apartment complexes also have a laundry room with a coin-operated machine for guest use.

TOILETS

Bermuda has standard western-style toilets. Public toilets are easy to find in major tourist areas, such as central St George and Hamilton, and at the more frequented beaches.

HEALTH

Bermuda is a healthy place to live and visit, and travelers don't need to take any unusual health precautions.

Medical Kit Check List

A small, basic medical kit is a good thing to carry. Consider including the following items.

- ❑ **Aspirin or acetaminophen** – for pain or fever
- ❑ **Antihistamine** – for allergies; to ease the itch from insect bites or stings; and to prevent motion sickness
- ❑ **Cold tablets, throat lozenges and nasal decongestant**
- ❑ **Antiseptic** – for cuts and grazes
- ❑ **Calamine lotion** – to ease irritation from sunburn and insect stings
- ❑ **Bandages and Band-Aids** – for minor injuries
- ❑ **Scissors, tweezers and a thermometer** – note that mercury thermometers are prohibited by airlines
- ❑ **Sunblock and insect repellent**

If you're visiting in the summer season and are new to the heat and humidity, you may find yourself easily fatigued and more susceptible to minor ailments. Acclimatize yourself by slowing down your pace and drinking plenty of liquids.

Predeparture Planning

Immunizations are not required to enter Bermuda.

If you need a particular medication, take an adequate supply, as foreign prescriptions cannot be filled in Bermuda. If you do run out of medication or forget to bring it, a pharmacist can refer you to a local doctor, who can write you up a new prescription. Getting replacements will be easier if you have brought a copy of the prescription itself, or part of the packaging showing both the generic and the brand name.

For all controlled drugs you're bringing into Bermuda, it's a good idea to have a legible prescription to show that you legally use the medication. Always keep the medication in its original container.

You'll want to make sure you have adequate health insurance. If your home policy doesn't cover you for overseas travel, see Travel Insurance under Visas & Documents, earlier in this chapter.

Basic Rules

Food Stomach upsets are a possibility anywhere you travel, but in Bermuda these are likely to be relatively minor.

As a general rule both at home and abroad, take care with fish and shellfish (for instance, mussels that haven't been cooked enough for their shells to open properly can be dangerous) and avoid undercooked meat.

Water Although several of Bermuda's larger resort hotels have their own desalination plants, the rest of Bermuda depends upon rain for its water supply. Because the rain is caught on rooftops and directed into individual storage tanks, the bacteria count in the water can vary. If you're staying at a guesthouse or smaller hotel, it's best to inquire with the manager about the water's suitability for drinking.

If in doubt, you can always treat the first. The simplest way of purifying wa to boil it vigorously.

Simple filtering does not remove al gerous organisms, so if you canno water, it can be treated chemically. Ch tablets kill many but not all pathc Iodine is more effective in purifying and is available in tablet form, but follc directions carefully and remember th much iodine can be harmful.

Bottled water is available in Ber grocery stores.

Medical Problems & Treatme

Island pharmacies are good places to you have a minor medical problem ar explain to the pharmacist what it is. the pharmacist or the front-desk pers at your hotel can refer you to a doc necessary.

For major problems, Bermuda's 3 King Edward VII Memorial Hospita Point Finger Rd in Paget. For medical gencies, dial ☎ 911 to get an ambulan nonemergency medical services, call th pital at ☎ 236-2345.

Environmental Hazards

Sunburn Anywhere on water and sar can get sunburned with surprising even if the sky is cloudy. Use a sunblo take extra care to cover areas that dor mally see sun – your feet, for exampl screen with an SPF (sun protection of at least 10 to 15 is recommended if not already tanned. A hat provides protection, and it may be a good idea zinc cream or some other barrier cre your nose and lips.

If you're going into the water, use screen that's water-resistant. Snorkele even want to wear a T-shirt if they pla out in the water a long time. They'll tecting not only against sunburn, but potential skin cancer and prematur of the skin.

Keep in mind the most severe between 10 am and 2 pm, and, if the precautions fail, calamine lotion is g soothing mild sunburn.

ep in mind that too much sunlight, ıer it's direct or reflected (glare), can ge your eyes. Since Bermuda is surled by water, good sunglasses are imnt. Make sure they're treated to absorb iolet (UV) radiation; if not, they'll do harm than good as they dilate your and make it easier for ultraviolet light nage the retina.

ly Heat Prickly heat is an itchy rash d by excessive perspiration trapped the skin. It usually strikes people who ust arrived in a hot climate and whose have not yet opened sufficiently to with greater sweating. Keeping cool, ng frequently or resorting to airioning may help until you acclimatize.

Exhaustion Dehydration and salt decy can cause heat exhaustion. Take o acclimatize to high temperatures, sufficient liquids and do not do anyoo physically demanding.

deficiency is characterized by fatigue, gy, headaches, giddiness and muscle s; salt tablets may help, but adding alt to your food is better.

Stroke This serious, sometimes fatal, ion can occur if the body's heatting mechanism breaks down and body rature rises to dangerous levels. Long, uous periods of exposure to high temres and insufficient fluids can leave you able to heat stroke. Avoid strenuous in open sun when you first arrive.

symptoms of heat stroke are feeling not sweating very much or at all and body temperature (39° to 41°C or 106°F). Where sweating has ceased, n becomes flushed and red. Severe, ing headaches and lack of coordinan also occur, and the sufferer may be ed or aggressive. Eventually the victim come delirious or convulse. Hospitalis essential, but in the interim get out of the sun, remove their clothing, hem with a wet sheet or towel and ally fan them. Give fluids if they are us.

Motion Sickness Eating lightly before and during a trip will reduce the chances of motion sickness. If you are prone to motion sickness, try to find a place that minimizes movement – near the wing on aircraft or close to midships on boats. Fresh air and a steady reference point like the horizon usually help; reading and cigarette smoke don't. Commercial motion-sickness preparations, which can cause drowsiness, have to be taken before the trip commences. Ginger (available in capsule form) and peppermint (including mint-flavored candy) are natural preventatives.

Jet Lag Jet lag is experienced when a person travels by air across more than three time zones (each time zone usually represents a one-hour time difference). Jet lag occurs because many of the functions of the human body (such as temperature, pulse rate and emptying of the bladder and bowels) are regulated by internal 24-hour cycles called circadian rhythms. When we travel long distances rapidly, our bodies take time to adjust to the 'new time' of our destination, and we may experience fatigue, disorientation, insomnia, anxiety, impaired concentration and loss of appetite. These effects will usually be gone within three days of arrival, but to minimize the impact of jet lag, do the following:

- Rest for a couple of days prior to departure; try to avoid late nights and last-minute dashes for traveler's checks etc.
- Try to select flight schedules that minimize sleep deprivation; arriving late in the day means you can go to sleep soon after you arrive. For very long flights, try to organize a stopover.
- Avoid excessive eating (which bloats the stomach) and alcohol (which causes dehydration) during the flight. Instead, drink plenty of noncarbonated, nonalcoholic drinks such as fruit juice or water.
- Avoid smoking.
- Make yourself comfortable by wearing loose-fitting clothes and perhaps bringing an eye mask and ear plugs to help you sleep.
- Try to sleep at the appropriate time for the time zone to which you're traveling.

Infectious Diseases

Diarrhea Simple things such as a change of water, food or climate can all cause a mild bout of diarrhea, but a few rushed toilet trips with no other symptoms are not indicative of a major problem.

Dehydration is the main danger with any diarrhea, particularly in children or the elderly, because it can occur quickly. Under all circumstances, fluid replenishment is the most important thing. Weak black tea with a little sugar, soda water or soft drinks allowed to go flat and diluted 50% with clean water are all good.

With severe diarrhea, you may need a rehydrating solution to replace minerals and salts. Seek medical advice. Stick to a bland diet as you recover.

Fungal Infections A hot, humid climate can promote a prolific growth of skin fungi and bacteria. Hot-weather fungal infections are most likely to occur between the toes or fingers, or in the groin.

Keeping your skin dry and cool and allowing air to circulate are both essential. Choose loose cotton clothing rather than synthetics, and sandals rather than shoes. If you do get an infection, wash the infected area daily with a disinfectant or medicated soap. Rinse and dry well, and then apply an antifungal powder.

HIV & AIDS Infection with the human immunodeficiency virus (HIV) may lead to acquired immune deficiency syndrome (AIDS), which is a fatal disease. Any exposure to blood, blood products or body fluids may put the individual at risk. The disease is often transmitted through sexual contact or dirty needles – vaccinations, acupuncture, tattooing and body piercing can be potentially as dangerous as intravenous drug use. In 1998, Bermuda had 17 cases of AIDS reported.

Familiar brands of condoms, such as Ramses, can be purchased in pharmacies for around $15 a dozen.

If you have any questions regarding AIDS while in Bermuda, call the AIDS/HIV Help Line at ☎ 295-0002.

Cuts, Bites & Stings

Cuts and skin punctures can get eas fected in Bermuda's humid climate an infections can be persistent. Wash a well and treat them with an antisepti as povidone-iodine. Where possible, bandages, which can keep wounds we

Coral cuts are even more suscepti infection because tiny pieces of coral c embedded in the skin. These cuts are r ously slow to heal, as the coral rele weak venom into the wound.

Unless you're allergic to them, bee are usually painful rather than dang calamine lotion will give relief, and ice will reduce the pain and swelling.

If you are stung by a jellyfish or tuguese man-of-war, quickly remo tentacles and apply vinegar or a me derizer containing papain (derived papaya), both of which act to neutral toxins – in a pinch, you could use u well. For serious reactions, including pains or difficulty in breathing, seek diate medical attention.

Bermuda's Dept of Agriculture there have been no cases of rabies fo than 40 years.

Women's Health

Some women experience irregular when traveling, due to the upset in r Don't forget to take time zones into a if you're on the pill.

Poor diet, lowered resistance due use of antibiotics for stomach ups even the use of contraceptive pills c to vaginal infections when traveling climates. Wearing skirts or loose trousers and cotton underwear will prevent infections.

WOMEN TRAVELERS

Women travelers are no more likel counter problems in Bermuda than t elsewhere, but the usual common-se cautions certainly apply when it c potentially dangerous situations lik ing alone at night, accepting ride strangers etc. Also, keep in mind that clothing is the norm only on the b uda, and it could elicit unwanted attn anywhere else.

& LESBIAN TRAVELERS

ugh Bermuda is certainly not a mecca y travelers, a century-old criminal code outlawed homosexual behavior was superseded by a gay rights amendin 1994, and homosexuality in Beris no longer against the law. Still, displays of affection – which are not on among Bermudians regardless of orientation – may well draw und attention; discretion is advised.

muda has no exclusively gay bars, me bars are gay-friendly, including ie's in the Town of St George and in the City of Hamilton.

BLED TRAVELERS

ugh Bermuda has slowly been improvcilities for disabled travelers, those pecial needs should plan ahead. A vay to start is to contact the tourism ment and request a copy of the are titled *Facilities for the Physically nged.*

wheelchair users, Bermuda's larger hotels generally have the greatest aclity with elevators, wider doorways e like, and some smaller places also heelchair-accessible guestrooms and on areas. Visitors with special needs make their requirements known at e of booking.

Bermuda Red Cross (☎ 236-2345), on d floor of the King Edward VII rial Hospital, rents walkers, wheeland crutches.

Bermuda Physically Handicapped ation (☎ 292-5035), PO Box HM 08, on HM AX, can assist disabled visihas a volunteer-operated bus with a lic lift that can be used by manual hairs; the bus is available on a firstrst-served basis.

elchair access on public transport is mited – the public buses do not have lic lifts and the ferry service has only accessibility. However, the Hamilton rminal is wheelchair accessible, so a ferry could be boarded there and taken simply as a cruise. The Hamilton-Paget ferry, for example, would make for a scenic 30-minute roundtrip tour. Another possibility is to take the ferry from Hamilton to the Royal Naval Dockyard, where the terminal, restaurants, museum, shopping center and restrooms are all wheelchair accessible.

Before the trip, physically challenged travelers might want to get in touch with national support organizations in their home country. These groups commonly have general information and tips on travel and are able to supply a list of travel agents specializing in tours for the disabled.

In the USA, the Society for the Advancement of Travel for the Handicapped (SATH; ☎ 212-447-7284), 347 Fifth Ave, Suite 610, New York, NY 10016, publishes a quarterly magazine for $13 a year and has various information sheets on travel for the disabled.

In the UK, the Royal Association for Disability & Rehabilitation (RADAR) publishes a useful guide entitled *Holidays and Travel Abroad: A Guide for Disabled People.* The book is available by post (£5) from RADAR (☎ 020-7250-3222), 12 City Forum, 250 City Rd, London EC1V 8AF.

SENIOR TRAVELERS

Bermuda is a popular destination any time of the year for senior travelers.

In addition to the usual off-season deals that are open to everyone, the Bermuda Dept of Tourism tries to attract senior visitors in February by declaring it 'Golden Rendezvous Month' and offering special events geared to travelers over 50. There's something happening for seniors every weekday in February, including bridge games, ballroom dancing, island bus tours and lectures on such topics as forts, local history, culture and flora and fauna.

Information on Elderhostel study vacations is under Organized Tours in the Getting There & Away chapter.

TRAVEL WITH CHILDREN

Although Bermudians are family oriented, Bermuda can pose some challenges to travelers with children. For instance, families who are accustomed to renting a car and piling all the kids inside will be dismayed to learn Bermuda has no car rentals. Large resort hotels don't place restrictions on children, but many other hotels and guesthouses tend to be formal and gear their activities solely to adults; a few don't accept children at all.

Still, families with children can find lots to do in Bermuda. In addition to beaches and swimming pools, there are snorkeling tours, miniature golf, a wonderful aquarium and zoo, and plenty of cool forts to explore.

Travelers with babies will readily find baby food, formula and disposable diapers at local supermarkets, although prices will be higher than at home. Some hotels can provide cribs and high chairs; if not, they can be rented from the Bermuda Red Cross (☎ 236-2345), at the King Edward VII Memorial Hospital in Paget.

For those vacationing with children, Lonely Planet's *Travel with Children*, by Maureen Wheeler, has lots of valuable tips and interesting anecdotal stories.

USEFUL ORGANIZATIONS

The Bermuda Audubon Society (☎ 297-2623), PO Box HM 1328, Hamilton HM FX, puts out a quarterly newsletter that lists upcoming events such as birdwatching field trips and lectures on local environmental projects. The membership fee is $15.

The Bermuda National Trust (☎ 236-6483), PO Box HM 61, Hamilton HM AX, is the island's leading preservation organization. For a $15 annual membership fee ($30 per family), you can receive the Trust newsletter and be entitled to free admission to Trust properties in Bermuda and in other Commonwealth countries, from Australia to Zimbabwe.

The Bermuda Zoological Society (☎ 293-2727), PO Box FL 145, Flatts FL BX, is an organization that supports the Bermuda Aquarium, Museum & Zoo. The $50 annual dues not only help with the organization's various conservation efforts, but entitle members and their family to free entrance to the Bermuda Aquarium, Museum & Zoo and a bimonthly newsletter.

For information on social and bus clubs, such as the Kiwanis Club, Rotary and Lions Club, see the yellow pages (Bermuda phone book.

DANGERS & ANNOYANCES

Theft

Although Bermuda is relatively safe, crime and drug abuse problems just lik other place. Violent crime has been c increase in recent years, and tourists a casionally targeted for muggings. Tra should use the standard precautions would use anywhere when walking al night, especially in areas that are no lit. Women carrying handbags should them close to their bodies to prevent snatchings.

Still, the most common problem en tered by visitors is moped theft, whic epidemic proportions in Bermuda. great of a problem that it's virtually i sible to get theft insurance on m anymore. Many of the bikes end up in shops' where they are stripped for pa though some just end up being taken joyride before being dumped over a you rent a moped, you can cut down odds of having it stolen by locking it time you stop and by parking in w public places.

Flora & Fauna

There are no snakes or dangerou animals in Bermuda to worry about.

Hikers should be aware that poiso abundant on some interior trails and reserves, so you may want to wear soc long pants as a precaution. In additi pencil or milk-bush tree *(Euphorbi calli)*, found in some coastal areas s Great Head Park in St David's (see David's Island section in the St G Parish chapter), has a poisonous milk and should not be touched.

Ocean Dangers

Drowning is a potential cause of acc death for visitors. If you're not famili water conditions, ask someone. It's b to swim alone in any unfamiliar place

Currents Also called riptides, rip cur- are fast-flowing currents of water n the ocean, moving from shallow hore areas out to sea. They are most ıon in conditions of high surf, forming water from incoming waves builds up the shore. Essentially the waves are ıg in faster than they can flow back out. e water then runs along the shoreline it finds an escape route out to sea, y through a channel or out along a Swimmers caught up in the current e ripped out to deeper water.

hough rip currents can be powerful, ısually dissipate 50 to 100 yards off- Anyone caught in one should either h the flow until it loses power or swim el to shore to slip out of it. Trying to against a rip current can exhaust the est of swimmers.

rtows These are common along y sloped beaches when large waves ash directly into incoming surf. The ng water picks up speed as it flows the slopes. When it hits an incoming t pulls under the wave, creating an un- . Swimmers caught up in an undertow pulled beneath the surface. The most ant thing is not to panic. Go with the t until you get beyond the wave.

Most coral cuts occur when swimmers shed onto the coral by rough waves rges. It's a good idea to wear diving when snorkeling over shallow reefs. walking on coral, which can not only ır feet, but also is very damaging to al. For the treatment of coral cuts, see Bites & Stings in the Health section in this chapter.

sh Take a peek into the water before nge in to make sure it's not jellyfish y. These gelatinous creatures, with bodies and stinging tentacles, are nes found in Bermuda. The sting of a varies from mild to severe, depend- he variety. Unless you have an aller- tion to their venom, the stings are ly not dangerous.

The Portuguese man-of-war is by far the worst type to encounter. Not technically a jellyfish, the man-of-war is a colonial hydrozoan, or a colony of coelenterates, rather than a solitary coelenterate like the true jellyfish. Its body consists of a translucent, bluish, bladder-like float, which generally grows to be about 5 inches long. In the waters off Bermuda, the Portuguese man-of-war is most prevalent from March through July.

A man-of-war sting is very painful, similar to a bad bee sting except that you're likely to get stung more than once from clusters of long tentacles containing hundreds of stinging cells. These trailing tentacles can reach up to 50 feet in length. Even touching a Portuguese man-of-war a few hours after

Beware the Portuguese man-of-war, whose trailing tentacles disguise painful stinging cells.

it's washed up on shore can result in burning stings.

For treatment of jellyfish and Portuguese man-of-war stings, see Cuts, Bites & Stings in the Health section, earlier in this chapter.

Eels Moray eels are frequently spotted by snorkelers around reefs and coral heads. They're constantly opening and closing their mouths to pump water across their gills, which makes them look far more menacing than they actually are.

Eels don't attack, but they will protect themselves if they feel cornered by fingers jabbing into the reef holes or crevices they occupy. Eels have sharp teeth and strong jaws and may clamp down if someone sticks a hand in their front door.

Sharks These are sometimes found in Bermudian waters – one of the more common varieties is the cub shark, which grows up to 12 feet in length.

Sharks are curious and will sometimes investigate divers, although they generally just check things out and continue on their way. If they start to hang around, however, it's probably time for you to go.

The best thing to do if you come face to face with a shark is to move away casually, making as little disturbance as possible. Do not panic, as sharks are attracted by things that thrash around in the water.

Some aquatic officials suggest thumping an attacking shark on the nose or sticking your fingers into its eyes, which may confuse it long enough to give you time to escape. Indeed, it's not uncommon for divers who dive in shark-infested waters to carry a billy club or bang stick.

Sharks are attracted by blood. Attacks on humans are sometimes related to spear fishing; when a shark goes after a diver's bloody catch, the diver sometimes gets in the way. Sharks are also attracted by shiny things and by anything bright red or yellow, which might influence your choice of swimsuit color.

Although unpleasant encounters with sharks are extremely unlikely, it's helpful to have a healthy respect for them.

EMERGENCIES

For emergencies involving the police, ambulance or marine rescue, dial ☎ 911

Victims of physical abuse can call the P
ical Abuse Centre hotline (☎ 297-287
the Women's Resource Centre (☎ 295-7

Lifeline, a 24-hour counseling servic
those who need emotional support, ca
reached at ☎ 236-0224 from 9 am to
and at ☎ 236-3770 from 5 pm to 9 am.

LEGAL MATTERS

For the most part, the police in Ber
tend to be lenient with tourists and few
tors are likely to have run-ins with th
For minor traffic violations, such as f
ting to put on your helmet while drivin
could be stopped by a police officer,
long as your response is polite, a
lecture will likely be the end of it.

On the other hand, any infracti
Bermuda's strict drug laws will almos
tainly land violators in court, and perh
jail as well. The importation or possess
unlawful drugs, including marijuan
other 'soft' drugs, is subject to a fine of
$10,000 or five years in prison or both

Customs officers sometimes co
body searches and students on spring
are given particular scrutiny. Those on
ships are not exempt – police have
known to search cruise ship cabins a
whiff of cannabis has wafted through t
First-time foreign offenders found wit
small amounts of marijuana are com
fined, and possession of larger amou
marijuana or any hard drugs usually
in a prison sentence.

When a visitor is arrested, the poli
call their consulate, which can u
provide advice on securing a lawye
Legal Aid Society (☎ 297-7617) ca
help visitors obtain the services of a l

BUSINESS HOURS

Shops are generally open 9 am to
Monday to Saturday, though there
ceptions – for example, grocery store
longer hours and Sunday openings, a
tourist-geared shops at the Royal
Dockyard are open every day.

›tting Married in Bermuda

ny visitors come to Bermuda not only for their honeymoons but to take their wedding vows as l. Although getting married in Bermuda requires some advance planning, there are both public ces and private wedding consultants who can help with the arrangements.

For those who want to take the public route, both the required paperwork and the ceremony can handled by the Register General's office in the City of Hamilton. For a fee of $176, this govern-nt agency will put the mandatory 'Notice of Intended Marriage' in local newspapers. Provided formal objection is raised to your marriage intention, the marriage certificate can be issued after vo-week waiting period. The registry maintains its own cozy little 'Marriage Room' where, for an itional fee of $167, a civil marriage ceremony can be performed.

Should you prefer something more tailored, there are a few wedding consultants who can nge anything from a traditional church wedding to a seaside ceremony. Of course they can arrange all of the incidentals as well, from a cake and flowers to bagpipe music and a horse carriage.

or full details on arranging a wedding in Bermuda, contact the nearest Bermuda Dept of rism office (see Tourist Offices earlier in this chapter) and request their 'Wedding & Honeymoon' hure. It includes all the nitty-gritty details and contact addresses you'll need.

vernment offices are usually open 8:30 am to 5 pm weekdays, and busi-ffices are typically open 9 am to 5 pm lays.

public holidays, all government of-nost business offices and some shops staurants close, and buses and ferries a reduced schedule.

.IC HOLIDAYS & IAL EVENTS

Holidays

hat when a public holiday falls on a ay or Sunday, it is often observed on llowing Monday. The following are da's public holidays:

ar's Day January 1
riday Friday before Easter
a Day May 24
Birthday June – 3rd Monday
tch the day before Somers Day
Day August – 1st Friday
Day September – 1st Monday
brance Day November 11
as Day December 25
Day December 26

Special Events

Bermuda offers visitors a wide variety of cultural and sporting events throughout the year. These vary with the season. For example, yachting events take place early in the summer before the hurricane season gets underway and golf tournaments are heaviest in the spring when the weather is cooler.

For some events, dates can vary a bit each year and the venues are not always the same; check with the tourist department, which maintains seasonally adjusted schedules, for the latest information.

In addition to the following events, see the boxed text on Bermuda's November-to-March activities, in the City of Hamilton chapter.

January

New Year's Day features a variety of sporting events as well as performances by costumed troupes of Gombey dancers at various locations.

The ***Bermuda International Race Weekend***, held on the second weekend in January in the City of Hamilton, includes a marathon, half marathon, 10km race, a 10km fitness walk and the Bank of Butterfield Mile.

The ***Bermuda Festival***, a seven-week festival of the performing arts, takes place from early

Spring Break

The Bermuda Dept of Tourism sponsors a spring break program throughout the month of March. Although overseas college students have been encouraged to take their spring break in Bermuda for decades, in recent years the island has made a concerted effort to keep away from a free-for-all beach-party atmosphere and instead recruits college and university sports teams – both athletes and coaches.

Consequently, the current Spring Break Sports Programme focuses on sporting events between the various visiting university teams. The tourism department, which coordinates the events, makes playing fields available and sponsors group activities such as beach barbecues and boat cruises. Sporting events include lacrosse, field hockey, soccer, rugby, track and field, tennis and golf. Although many of the activities are geared specifically to teams, individuals can participate in others.

For more information, contact the Bermuda Dept of Tourism and ask for the *Spring Break Sports* brochure.

January to late February at various locations. International artists present dance, drama and musical performances.

The ***Bermuda Dressage Group Show***, a two-day horse show, is held in mid-January at the National Equestrian Centre in Devonshire.

February

Golden Rendezvous Month, held weekdays throughout the month of February, features special activities, such as ballroom dancing and cultural lectures, geared specifically to visitors over age 50.

The ***Bermuda Festival***, which begins in January and includes various dance, drama and musical performances, continues through late February.

The weeklong ***Seniors Golf Tournament***, open to golfers 50 years and older, is held during the first week in February, and the ***Couples Golf Tournament*** is held the following week; both take place at the Port Royal Golf Course in Southampton Parish.

The annual ***Bermuda Rendezvous Bowling nament***, open to all ABC/WIBC-sanct bowlers, is held for four days in mid-Febru the Warwick Lanes in Warwick.

The weeklong ***Lobster Pot Invitational Amateur Golf Tournament***, at Port Roya Course, is held in late February.

March

Bermuda Spring Break is geared to visiting students, with sports programs and beach ties offered throughout the month.

The weeklong ***Ladies Pro-Am Golf Classi*** teams consisting of one professional and amateur women, is held in early March Port Royal Golf Course in Southampton

The ***Bermuda All Breed Championshi Shows*** are held over a week in early March Bermuda Botanical Gardens.

The ***Bermuda Men's Amateur Champion*** five-day singles match for golfers, is held March at the Mid Ocean Club.

The ***Bermuda Ladies Amateur Champion*** singles match golf event, is held for four mid-March at the Mid Ocean Club.

The ***Bermuda Cat Fanciers Association C onship Cat Show*** is held in mid-March main cruise ship passenger terminal on F in the City of Hamilton.

Bermuda Kite Festival, on Good Friday at shoe Bay, is an afternoon of kite flying, ch games and Gombey dancing.

Palm Sunday Walk is a guided annual walk by the Bermuda National Trust on Palm the location changes each year.

April

The ***Peppercorn Ceremony***, held in the To George in mid-April, reenacts the cerer which the Masonic Lodge pays an annua one peppercorn for use of the Old State

The ***FEI Show Jumping Challenge***, wh tures equestrian jumping events, is held the month at the National Equestrian C Devonshire.

The ***Agricultural Exhibition***, one of th events in Bermuda, is a three-day ex produce, flowers and livestock, along wit trian shows and other activities, held April at the Bermuda Botanical Garden

The ***XL Bermuda Open Tennis Champic*** held in mid-April at the Coral Beach Club. This USTA-sanctioned event fea ternational professional players.

·arden Club of Bermuda hosts ***Open Houses Gardens*** at distinctive island homes every ·nesday afternoon from mid-April to the end ·ay.

g ***International Race Week***, held near the of the month, yachters from Bermuda, the and North America compete in various boat ·gories.

·arden Club of Bermuda hosts ***Open Houses Garden Tours*** at distinctive island homes on ·nesday afternoons in May.

·ermuda Senior Amateur Championships, ·en age 55 and older and women age 50 and ·, is a 54-hole stroke play golf event held for days in mid-May at the Riddells Bay Golf ·untry Club.

·ansAt Daytona-Bermuda Race is a yacht held in May on odd-numbered years from ·e de Leon, Florida, to Bermuda.

Bermuda Day, a public holiday on May 24, began as a celebration of Queen Victoria's birthday, but now kicks off the summer season. It features a half-marathon that begins in Somerset, a colorful afternoon parade in the City of Hamilton and fitted dinghy races in St George's Harbour.

Beating Retreat Ceremonies, historic military reenactments performed by the Bermuda Regiment Band, take place at various times of the month in St George's, Hamilton and the Royal Naval Dockyard.

June

The ***Bermuda Amateur Stroke Play Championships*** are held for four days in mid-June at the Port Royal Golf Course. Men play 72 holes, women 54 holes, in separate events.

The Bermuda Philharmonic Society performs the ***President's Choice Open-Air Pops Concert*** in early June at King's Square in St George and at the Royal Naval Dockyard.

·wport-Bermuda Race

·Newport-Bermuda Race, the premier sailing event between the US East Coast and Bermuda, ·n in 1906, and, except for a few wartime pauses, has been running biennially ever since. This ·ric race, held in late June on even-numbered years, attracts about 150 sailboats, ranging from ·er-shaped ketches that are nearly as old as the race itself to state-of-the-art Maxis, the ·st and fastest racing boats in the world.

·e tricky and sometimes turbulent seas along the southeasterly route from Rhode ·l to Bermuda make the crossing particularly challenging. Sailors invariably have to ·nd with the Gulf Stream, the powerful northeasterly current that flows between ·S mainland and Bermuda. This warm ocean 'stream' not only generates unusual patterns, but can also bring about water temperature changes of nearly 30°F.

·e seas can become even more turbulent if there's adverse weather, but the ·n's worst storms are generally not encountered since this race, like all US-·uda races, is scheduled early in summer to avoid the peak hurricane ·n. Still, there are enough hazards that all of the crews must attend ·al safety seminars and the boats must pass strict Level 1 standards · the Offshore Racing Commission.

·ing a speed race, it's not surprising that the hottest technology of ·ay often captures the top honors at the finish line. In 1982, the launched Maxi *Nirvana* became the first boat to break the ·ot average speed, making the 630-mile crossing in just 63 hours. In 1996, a fiery new 78-foot Frers-design the ILC Maxi *Boomerang*, crossed the finish off St ·s Lighthouse in 57 hours and 31 minutes, slicing more ·ive hours off the former record!

The ***Queen's Birthday***, a public holiday on the third Monday in June, features a military parade led by the Bermuda Regiment that marches down Hamilton's Front St.

The ***Newport-Bermuda Race***, held in late June during even-numbered years, is one of the world's premier ocean races, running from Newport, Rhode Island, to Bermuda. The Royal Bermuda Yacht Club coordinates events at the Bermuda end.

Bermuda 1-2 Single-Handed Race, held in June in odd-numbered years, is a single-handed yacht race heading from Newport, Rhode Island, to Bermuda, and returning double handed to Newport.

The ***Bermuda Cruising Rally*** is a yacht race in mid-June from Norfolk, Virginia, to Bermuda. The host at the Bermuda end is the St George Dinghy & Sports Club.

The ***Bermuda Ocean Race***, held in June in even-numbered years, is another yacht race, this one from Annapolis, Maryland, to Bermuda.

The ***Marion-Bermuda Cruising Yacht Race***, held in mid-June in odd-numbered years, is an ocean race from Marion, Massachusetts, to Bermuda. The Royal Hamilton Amateur Dinghy Club is the host at the Bermuda end.

Beating Retreat Ceremonies; see the event description under May.

July

The ***Bermuda Angler's Club International Light Tackle Tournament*** is held mid-month.

Beating Retreat Ceremonies; see the event description under May.

August

The ***Cup Match Cricket Festival***, a two-day match between West End and East End cricket teams, is held on the first Thursday and Friday in August. Both days are public holidays, and numerous other activities occur on this long weekend.

SOCA is an open-air Carribbean music festival that is held late in August and takes place in St George's.

September

Labour Day, a public holiday on the first Monday of September, features music, Gombey dancers, speeches by union leaders and politicians and a small parade from Union Square in the City of Hamilton.

The ***Bermuda Jazz Festival***, a two-day event held on a weekend in mid-September, features top international jazz musicians at various venues.

The ***Bermuda Triathlon***, a swimming, bic and running competition, takes place Albouy's Point in the City of Hamilton September or early October.

Beating Retreat Ceremonies; see the event d tion under May.

October

The ***Bermuda Horse & Pony Associatio Show*** features various equestrian events Bermuda Botanical Gardens in early Oct

The ***Bermuda Open***, a golf tournament fo held for four days in mid-October at th Royal Golf Course, is open to profession amateurs with a handicap limit of 6.

At the ***King Edward VII Gold Cup Intern Match Racing Championship***, held October, Bermudians compete for prize with international boaters, including Ar Cup Match contenders.

Beating Retreat Ceremonies; see the ev scription under May.

November

The ceremonial ***Convening of Parliamer*** place at Sessions House in the City of H near the start of the month.

The ***Bermuda Four Ball Stroke Play A Championships***, a 72-hole golf event f and a separate 54-hole event for women for four days in early November at t Royal Golf Course.

Remembrance Day, a public holiday on No 11, features a military parade along Fro the City of Hamilton and the laying of wr the Cenotaph.

At the ***World Rugby Classic*** in mid-Nove ternational and local teams compete matches at the National Stadium in Dev

The ***Bermuda All Breed Championsh Shows & Obedience Trials*** take place November at the Bermuda Botanical G

The ***Bermuda Lawn Tennis Club Invi*** hosts international and local players weeks of singles and doubles matches in ber at the Coral Beach Tennis Club.

The ***Belmont Invitational Tournamen*** tournament for men, is held for four da November or early December at the Golf Club.

December

The ***Bermuda Goodwill Tournament***, a golf event for men, is held for four day December at four different golf courses

ıre various ***Santa Claus parades*** with floats narching bands in the days leading up to tmas in both the City of Hamilton and the of St George.

ing Day, a public holiday on December 26, ful Gombey dancers take to the streets all d Bermuda.

ar's Eve celebrations take place at King's e in the Town of St George with music, stalls and midnight fireworks.

RSES

ermuda Biological Station for Re- (BBSR) located in St George's Par- ers intensive three- and four-week r courses in marine zoology, ecology ceanography that explore topics g from shellfish aquaculture to the in- on between human health and the The staff includes BBSR researchers iting professors from prestigious US anadian institutes such as Harvard sity, the Smithsonian Institution and yal Ontario Museum. The courses are toward both graduate students and evel undergraduates.

on and accommodations for the pro- cost around $2500, but scholarships ilable to assist students accepted into gram. As class space is limited and ion competitive, it's best to apply as dvance as possible.

more information on these summer ns, as well as details on volunteer ns and graduate internships, contact rmuda Biological Station for Re- (☎ 297-1880, fax 297-8143), 17 Bio- Lane, St George's GE 01. You can tain an application on the Internet at sr.edu.

K

nterested in entering Bermuda for pose of employment need to obtain a rmit in advance from Bermuda's im- on authorities. Because employers on nd are required to give priority to sidents, it can be difficult for foreign- et a job, unless they have a special- ll for which there is not a suitable ndidate.

ACCOMMODATIONS

Bermuda has no truly cheap accommodations – no youth hostels, no YMCAs, no family campgrounds and no economy-chain motels.

As a general rule, the most economical options are tourist apartments, which come completely furnished, as they not only provide you with a place to stay but also have cooking facilities. Considering that the average hotel charges a good $10 per person for breakfast, being able to prepare your own coffee and toast can represent a tidy savings! Rates in such places begin around $100 a double.

Small guesthouses, which often include breakfast in their rates, also represent one of the more affordable options. These range from about $75 to $150, depending on the place and the season.

The term 'cottage colony' is generally used in Bermuda with more upmarket places that offer units in individual cottages, or in small clusters of buildings each of which contain a few units. The 'cottages' often have at least limited cooking facilities and generally have a more genteel setting with landscaped grounds, afternoon teas and the like; these typically cost a lofty $250 to $500 a double.

Small hotels are by and large just that: smaller places that usually have a restaurant, lounge and swimming pool but don't necessarily offer the array of services found at the larger resort hotels. These range from unpretentious family-oriented places to some of the island's more prestigious and intimate spots, and accordingly rates vary widely.

Bermuda has five resort hotels: the Elbow Beach Hotel, the Grotto Bay Beach Hotel, the Hamilton Princess Hotel, the Sonesta Beach Hotel and the Southampton Princess. They all have the usual resort facilities, including swimming pools, room service and restaurants. All the resort hotels are either on the beach or provide a guest shuttle to a nearby sandy strand. Depending on which resort hotel you select, the rates can vary from moderate to expensive, though if you keep an eye out for special promotions or

Meal Plans

Many Bermuda accommodations offer meal-plan packages. At some places, a specific plan is mandatory, and at others you can select from a variety of plans. The following codes are used consistently in hotel literature throughout Bermuda to represent the various options:

EP (European Plan)	Room only
CP (Continental Plan)	Room and a light breakfast
BP (Breakfast Plan)	Room and a full breakfast
AP (American Plan)	Room and all three meals
MAP (Modified American Plan)	Room with breakfast and dinner

book a package deal you can sometimes find a bargain at any one of them. For instance, in winter, the Sonesta Beach Hotel charges $130 for doubles, and the Hamilton Princess Hotel drops to $119; these rates are roughly half of their summer prices.

On top of the rates given throughout this book, all places to stay, except those with less than three guestrooms, add on a 7.25% hotel occupancy tax and almost all tack on a 10% service charge.

Long-Term Rentals

For long-term rentals a good place to look is in the classified ads section of the *Royal Gazette*. Generally, a small furnished studio costs around $1000 a month, and one-bedroom condos and apartments begin at around $1500.

If you're in Bermuda in the winter, and staying for a month or more, you can usually negotiate a reasonable monthly rate with one of the island's small hotels or apartment complexes. The best thing to do is call around and compare; a few good places to begin with are Sky Top Cottages and Salt Kettle House in Paget, and Astwood and the Surf Side Beach Club in Warw

Reservations

Many of Bermuda's small properties c easily booked through a single reserv service. If you want to inquire about s properties at once, any one of the foll room-booking services can help you:

Bermuda
Bermuda Reservation Services
(☎ 236-1633, fax 236-1662, email reservations@bspl.bm)

Canada
Bermuda Central Reservations
(☎ 416-932-8308, 800-563-9799, fax 416-485-8256, email assoc@thermrgroup.ca)

Germany
Eurep 92
(☎ 49 0 617 1910 584, fax 49 0 69 701 007, email eurep@t-online.de)

Sweden
Colibri Marketing
(☎ 46-08-32-07-00,fax 46-08-30-20-90, email tours@holiday.se)

UK
Morris-Kevan International
(☎ 0181-350-1000, fax 0181-350-1011, email mki@ttg.co.uk)

USA
Bermuda Reservation Services
(☎ 508-822-8652, 800-637-4116, fax 508-822-8649, email reservations@bspl.bm)

Camping

Although you may see Bermudians up tents, foreign visitors are not allo camp in Bermuda.

The only exception is for org groups, who may apply for permits t at group sites run by the governme handful of nearshore islands. The book each campsite is a flat $450 for a day weekend or $1030 per week. You to add on a boat fee of $85 per trip which is affordable if you're traveli 70 people, which is the full continge the larger sites can hold, but a bit st smaller groups.

Information on group camping i able from the Ministry of Youth, Sp

ation, Dept of Camping (☎ 297-7619, 5-6788), 79 Court St, Hamilton HM 12.

D

like everything else in Bermuda, tends expensive. On the plus side, Bermuda a good variety of dining options, from treet delis in the capital to superb fine- seaside restaurants.

aurants

ugh the upscale restaurants commonly on French-inspired cuisine, moder- priced eateries cover a wide ethnic from English pub fare to Chinese, ndian and Italian cuisine. Considering da's seclusion, most of the food is sur- ly authentic, and the island certainly shortage of recommendable dinner Lower-priced choices include pizze- ndwich shops, cafes and a few fast- utlets.

art casual' wear will get you a table at estaurants, but there are still a number -end restaurants that require jacket , so it's always wise to inquire about odes when making your reservation ner.

udian Cuisine

rmudian dish most often tried by vis- s Bermuda fish chowder, a tasty h-brown chowder commonly made ckfish or snapper and flavored with lack rum and sherry peppers sauce. ter is a traditional Bermudian condi- nade from sherry, peppers and spices. fish cakes became a staple in Ber- ong ago, and they're still cooked on days of the year, particularly Good Popular everyday foods are johnny- vhich are cornmeal griddle cakes, and d rice. Fresh fish plays a role in local well. Fish sandwiches, made of a filet a crisp batter, are as popular here as rgers are elsewhere.

most traditional meal is the Sunday breakfast, a huge affair to linger hich consists of codfish, eggs, boiled otatoes, bananas and avocado, with a f onions and tomatoes. Although it's most commonly served up in homes, there are a handful of restaurants on the island that offer this meal as well.

A common Christmas tradition in Bermuda is cassava pie, made with a cake-like batter that contains the grated root of the cassava plant, stuffed with a meat filling and baked. The cassava bears special significance to Bermudians, as it's credited with having helped the early settlers get through periods of famine.

DRINKS

Nonalcoholic Drinks

Bottled water, both generic spring water and the fancy carbonated variety, is readily available at grocery stores throughout the island, as are fruit juices and soft drinks.

As might be expected with their English heritage, many Bermudians fancy a cup of tea, especially as a mid-afternoon break served with finger sandwiches and pastries. If you're a coffee drinker, fret not, as coffee is readily available as well.

Because this is such a small island, it may come as a surprise that Bermuda has dairy cows and produces much of its own milk.

Alcoholic Drinks

The legal age for consuming alcoholic beverages in Bermuda is 18.

Bermuda Triangle Brewing, a microbrewery in Southampton Parish, boasts fresh, locally made brew. Among its regular offerings

Bermuda Rum Swizzle

Although every Bermudian bartender has his or her own twist, the basic rum swizzle starts out like this: mix 4oz of dark rum with 3oz of pineapple juice, 3oz of orange juice, 1oz of grenadine or other sugar syrup, the juice from one fresh lemon and a couple of dashes of Angostura bitters. Add it all to a container with crushed ice, shake it until there's a head, pour into a pair of tall glasses and garnish them with slivers of orange. If you prefer, you can substitute a lime for the lemon.

are Wilde Hogge, a German-style amber ale with a full, malty flavor, and Full Moon Pale Ale, a more traditional English bitter with lots of hops. For those more accustomed to drinking lagers, there's Spinnaker Kölsch, a pale pilsner with a golden hue that resembles conventional North American beers. Bermuda Triangle brews can be found on tap at pubs and restaurants around the island – or you can tour the brewery and sample it straight from the tank (see the Southampton Parish chapter for details).

Gosling Brothers, one of Bermuda's oldest companies, has been blending and bottling spirits on the island since the 1860s. Their cornerstone product is Gosling's Black Seal Rum, a dark rum that, until WWI, was sold from the barrel using recycled wine and champagne bottles, the cork sealed with black sealing wax – hence the name. If you pick up a bottle of Black Seal, take note that these days it comes in standard 80 proof as well as a fire-breathing 151 proof.

The dark 'n' stormy, sometimes dubbed Bermuda's national drink, is a two-to-one mix of carbonated ginger beer with Black Seal Rum; it can be purchased premixed in cans at most island liquor stores. Black Seal Rum is also the main ingredient in Bermuda's famous rum swizzle, which is far and away the most popular drink among island visitors.

Gosling produces three liqueurs as well: Bermuda Gold, Bermuda Banana Liqueur and Bermuda Coconut Rum. The one that gets the most attention is Bermuda Gold, which is made from loquats and comparable to an apricot brandy. It's commonly served straight on ice, with a twist of lemon (called a shipwreck) or with orange juice (a royal blossom).

ENTERTAINMENT

Bermuda has a number of venues with live music ranging from ballroom dancing to rock and reggae. The main music scene is in the City of Hamilton, though many of the larger hotels also have entertainment. For specifics, see the Entertainment sections in the individual chapters.

Plays and drama performances ar periodically in the City of Hamilton at the City Hall Theatre, inside City Hall, Daylesford Theatre, 11 Washington posite Victoria Park.

There are movie theaters in the C Hamilton, the Royal Naval Dockyar the Town of St George, all showing fi movies. Matinee showings generally c evening shows $7.

For the latest in what's happening, the entertainment sections of the *Be Sun* or the *Royal Gazette*, both of have comprehensive listings.

A couple of major entertainment occur annually. The biggest is the week Bermuda Festival, held from January to late February with dance, and musical performances by intern artists. In recent years, there have be pearances by the English Chamber C tra, soloists from the Bolshoi American trumpeter Wynton Marsa Cuban jazz pianist Chucho Valdés. Tic individual events cost $30. You can schedule and ticket information fr Bermuda Festival Box Office (☎ 29 email bdafest@ibl.bm) or from any of the Bermuda Dept of Tourism. I information can also be found on www.bermudafestival.com.

Also noteworthy is the two-day Be Jazz Festival, held on a weekend i September, which in recent years h tured the likes of George Bens Jarreau and Patti Austin. Tickets c per day. For ticket and schedule in tion, contact the tourist office or go o www.bermudajazz.com.

SPECTATOR SPORTS

The primary spectator sport pla Bermuda between April and Septe cricket, with scheduled matches takin at cricket fields around the islanc Sunday. Just turn to the sports sectior local paper for details and schedules.

Football (soccer) and rugby are th popular spectator sports from Septe April. Local competitions take place

‹ket Action

game of cricket was introduced to Bermuda in the early 19th century by British soldiers sta- ›d on the island. Although the first games were played between competing military teams, by) the game had caught fire with locals as well.

he first international play took place in 1891 when a Philadelphia team was invited to the island match. A decade later Bermuda's first touring team, the Hamilton Cricket Club, made its inau- l road trip, sailing to the USA to play in Philadelphia and New York. The travel restrictions and omic strains of the Great Depression and WWII put a damper on international events, and it 't until 1960 that the Bermuda team toured England for the first time. A few years later it me an associate member of the International Cricket Council (ICC) and in its most successful on, 1982, it advanced to the ICC finals without losing a match.

ill, most of Bermuda's cricket action occurs right on the island. Cricket is *the* summer spectator , attracting crowds of islanders at a variety of cricket fields. The two leading clubs, St George's Somerset, provide a long-standing east-west rivalry on the island that for Bermudians holds the thrill as interregional play in larger countries. And Bermuda's annual Cup Match Cricket Fes- is such a significant event that it's set aside as a public holiday.

and every Sunday, and the biggest for both sports are held at the Na- Stadium in Devonshire.

d hockey and sailing are two other r spectator sports.

PING

gh luxury items in Bermuda are not vily taxed as many everyday items, da is not a duty-free port, and many that you buy here may prove to be no r than they would be at home.

ch of what attracts shoppers to da is the variety of high-quality items, ng many top-name English and Euro- mports. Generally the best selections ices are found on items imported ie British Isles. These include English china, cashmere sweaters, Scottish and Irish wools and linens.

er imports commonly available in dian shops include designer Italian and silk, Swiss watches, German sil- e and French fashions. Some of the xtensively carried items are well- brands of crystal, including Baccarat aterford, and chinaware, including es, Lladro, Noritake, Royal Copenhagen, Spode and Wedgwood, as well as Goebel and Hummel figurines.

The main department stores in the City of Hamilton – Trimingham's, Smith's and AS Cooper & Sons – have the greater selection. Those stores also have branches in the Town of St George and outlets at some of the resort hotels.

Bermuda-Made Items

There are numerous Bermuda-made items that can make good souvenirs.

You can find glasswork and pottery with Bermuda themes. The Bermuda Glassblowing Studio in Bailey's Bay and Dockyard Glassworks at the Royal Naval Dockyard both create a wide variety of handblown glass, ranging from miniatures of tree frogs to expensive serving bowls and vases. Bermuda Clayworks at the Royal Naval Dockyard makes mugs, dinnerware, vases and various other pottery items with island influences.

The Bermuda Perfumery in Bailey's Bay makes perfume, eau de toilette, aftershave colognes and soaps from locally grown passion flowers, frangipani blossoms, Easter lilies, oleanders and jasmine flowers.

Duty-Free Allowances

US citizens who have been out of the USA for more than 48 hours may bring back $400 worth of goods duty-free, as long as this allowance has not been used within the past 30 days. Within their duty-free allowance each adult can include 1L of spirits and 200 cigarettes.

Canadian citizens can bring back $200 worth of goods duty-free provided they've been out of Canada for over 48 hours, and $500 worth for trips of more than seven days. Within their duty-free allowance each adult can bring in 40oz of spirits and 200 cigarettes.

UK citizens may bring back £136 worth of goods duty-free. Within their duty-free allowance each adult can bring in 1L of spirits, 2L of wine and 200 cigarettes.

For duty-free allowances for other countries, check with customs authorities before you leave home. Keep in mind that duty-free allowances can be altered without notice and that restrictions, such as those placed on the frequency the allowance can be claimed, may apply.

There are other island-made fragrances for men. Bermuda's Royall Fragrances makes four varieties of men's colognes: Royall Bay Rhum, Royall Lyme, Royall Spyce and Royall Muske.

Jewelers on the island make earrings, charms and pendants utilizing island motifs, such as tree frogs, Bermuda onions, longtail tropic birds, hog pennies – even mopeds. Any of the jewelry shops in Hamilton or St George should have a good variety of locally made items – there's also an extensive collection of jewelry at the Bermuda Craft Market in the Royal Naval Dockyard.

Bermuda designs show up on numerous other items, including silk-screened T-shirts, tea towels, refrigerator magnets, note cards and the like, any of which can make an inexpensive memento of a trip to Bermuda. Or bring home local flavor with Outerbr spicy sherry peppers sauce, local Ber honey or island-made liqueurs and readily found in shops around the is including many grocery stores.

Stamp collectors can buy comme tive stamps from the General Post Of the City of Hamilton. Overseas, they c ordered from Interpost, PO Box Malverne, NY 11565, USA, or from C Agents Stamp Bureau Ltd, 2 Carsh Rd, Sutton, Surrey SM1 4RN, UK.

Art Galleries

Bermuda inspires many artists. If you terested in picking up a watercolor, oil ing or charcoal drawing of island s some of the finer galleries are as follo

Bermuda Society of Arts (☎ 292-3824) City Hall, City of Hamilton

Heritage House (☎ 295-2615) 2 Front St, City of Hamilton

Masterworks Foundation (☎ 295-5580) Ber House Lane, 97 Front St, City of Hamilto

The Windjammer Gallery (☎ 292-7861) 87 Reid St, City of Hamilton

Carole Holding galleries (☎ 296-3431) 81 Front St in the City of Hamilton; (☎ 2 1833) on King's Square in St George; and (☎ 234-3800) at the Clocktower Mall in t Royal Naval Dockyard

Bridge House Gallery (☎ 297-8211) 1 Bridge St, St George

Bermuda Arts Centre (☎ 234-2809) Royal Naval Dockyard

Michael Swan Gallery (☎ 234-3128) Clock Mall, Royal Naval Dockyard

Terrace Gallery (☎ 234-0701) 5 Dockyard Terrace, Royal Naval Dockyard

Liquor

If you're leaving Bermuda by ship an to purchase duty-free liquor, you can despite the fact that there are no sh the dock. Bermuda's leading liquor such as Gosling's and Frith's, offer an sive selection of duty-free liquors to ship passengers heading off the isl long as arrangements are made in a

‹ way it works is that you stop by one of ›hops and pay the duty-free rate for the . You can not walk out with the bottles; d, the shop will deliver the liquor to the ship prior to departure time. There's ra charge for the delivery.

s system offers a hefty savings over ırd island prices. A liter of Gosling's Seal Rum, for example, costs about $11 ree, versus about $20 in local shops.

Orders can generally be placed anytime before 9:30 am on the day of your departure (2:30 pm the day before for Sunday and holiday departures).

Gosling's has a shop at the corner of Queen and Front Sts in the City of Hamilton and another at York and Queen Sts in St George. Frith's has shops at 57 Front St in the City of Hamilton and at the Sonesta Beach Hotel in Southampton Parish.

Getting There & Away

AIR

There are regularly scheduled direct flights to Bermuda from the USA, Canada and the UK. Travelers who arrive from other places need to connect through one of these three countries.

Airports & Airlines

Bermuda International Airport, on the eastern side of the island, is Bermuda's only airport. This small but modern facility has a couple of gift shops selling Bermuda T-shirts, books and other simple souvenirs; a duty-free shop with perfumes, cigarettes and alcohol; a bar and lounge; and a couple of food kiosks selling ice cream, pastries, coffee and sandwiches. If you have any banking needs, there's a Bank of Bermuda downstairs in the lobby that's open 10 am to 3 pm weekdays.

> **Warning**
>
> The information in this chapter is particularly vulnerable to change: prices for international travel are volatile, routes are introduced and canceled, schedules change, special deals come and go, and rules and visa requirements are amended.
>
> Airlines and governments seem to take a perverse pleasure in making price structures and regulations as complicated as possible. You should check directly with the airline, cruise operator or travel agent to make sure you understand how a fare works and what sort of restrictions your ticket will have. In addition, the travel industry is highly competitive and there are many lurks and perks.
>
> The upshot of this is that you should get opinions, quotes and advice from as many airlines and travel agents as possible before you part with your hard-earned cash. The details given in this chapter should be regarded as pointers and are not a substitute for your own careful, up-to-date research.

Air Canada, American Airlines, B Airways, Continental, Delta and US Ai have permanent, year-round counters.

Bermuda's arrival and departure fo ties and customs are generally efficie straightforward. One unusual quirk is you're flying to the USA from Ber you'll actually go through US customs Bermuda airport before your departu

Taxis meet all arriving flights. Taxi from the airport are about $10 to the of St George, $22 to the City of Hamil Elbow Beach and $30 to the Southa Princess or the Sonesta Beach Hotel.

There is also a stop in front of the a terminal for the public bus that ru tween the City of Hamilton and the T St George. Taking the bus is only prac you're traveling very light, however, bus rules require that your luggage your lap.

Buying Tickets

A number of airlines fly to Bermuda variety of fares are available. Rathe just walking into the nearest travel ag airline office, it pays to do a bit of re and shop around first. You might w start by perusing the travel sections o azines and large newspapers, such *New York Times* and the *Boston G* the USA and *Time Out* and *TNT* in th

Airfares are constantly in flux. Far with the season you travel, the day week you fly, your length of stay and th ibility the ticket provides for flight c and refunds. Still, nothing determine more than business, and when thin slow, regardless of the season, airline cally drop fares to fill the empty seats

Each airline has its own requireme restrictions, which also seem to con change. For the latest deals, browse I travel services such as www.traveloc and www.expedia.com, visit a know able travel agent or simply start call different airlines to compare fares.

en you call, it's important to ask for west fare, as that's not always the first ne airlines will quote. Each flight has limited number of seats available at eapest fare. When you make reserva- the agents will generally tell you the re that's still available on the date you hem, which may or may not be the est fare that the airline currently of- you make reservations far enough in ce and are a little flexible with travel you'll usually do better.

elers with Special Needs

have special needs of any sort – restrictions, dependence on a wheel- responsibility for a baby, a medical ion that warrants special considera- let the airline know as soon as possi- that staff can make arrangements ingly. Remind the airline when you rm your booking and again when you in at the airport. It may also be worth ng several airlines before you make ooking to find out how each of them ndle your particular needs.

st international airports will provide orted cart or wheelchair from the in desk to the plane, where needed, ere should be ramps, lifts and accessi- lets at your departure point. Aircraft , on the other hand, are likely to t a problem for some disabled pas- s; travelers should discuss this with line at an early stage and, if necessary, eir doctor. At the Bermuda end, there jetways, so wheelchair users are off the aircraft using a specialized chair.'

ines usually allow babies up to two f age to fly for 10% of the adult fare, gh a few may allow them to travel free ge. 'Skycots,' baby food and diapers be provided by the airline if re- d in advance. Children between two can usually occupy a seat for half to rds of the full fare.

rture Tax

da no longer collects departure taxes airport. Instead, the tax now gets lumped into the ever-growing tally of 'invisible' fees, such as airport landing fees and fuel surcharges, that are added on to your air ticket when you purchase it. Currently that tax is $20, but there's discussion of raising it.

Children under age two are exempt from the departure tax.

The USA

Most of Bermuda's air traffic arrives from the US East Coast. Although all the US airlines serving Bermuda operate year-round, the service is heavier in summer. From April through October, for instance, American Airlines adds a direct Boston to Bermuda service, as well as a second daily flight for New York.

Usually the best bargains are found in winter, but fare discounts can crop up at any time of the year. If you have a little flexibility and begin your planning well in advance of your trip, you'll increase the odds of finding a good deal.

On average, roundtrip excursion tickets begin at around $300 in winter and $450 at other times, though flights during the busiest summer periods, such as holiday weekends, can cost upwards of $600. Excursion fares typically require a 14-day advance purchase and allow a 30-day maximum stay.

The following airlines serve Bermuda from the USA:

American Airlines (☎ 800-433-7300) has daily nonstop flights from New York's JFK airport year-round and from Boston in summer.

Continental Airlines (☎ 800-231-0856) has daily nonstop flights from Newark Airport.

Delta Air Lines (☎ 800-221-1212) has daily nonstop flights from Boston and Atlanta.

US Airways (☎ 800-622-1015) has daily nonstop flights from Baltimore and Philadelphia.

Canada

Air Canada (☎ 800-776-3000) flies nonstop daily from Toronto and has a Saturday-only flight from Halifax. The cheapest excursion fare, with a seven-day advance purchase and a 21-day maximum stay, is typically around C$450 in the off season and C$600 in the summer.

Air Travel Glossary

Baggage Allowance For international travelers, it's usually one 20kg item to go in the hold, one item of hand luggage.

Cancellation Penalties If you have to cancel or change a discounted ticket, heavy penaltie often involved; insurance can sometimes be taken out against these penalties. Some airlines im penalties on regular tickets as well, particularly against 'no-show' passengers.

Check-In Airlines ask you to check in a certain time ahead of the flight departure (usually o two hours). If you fail to check in on time and the flight is overbooked, the airline can cancel booking and give your seat to somebody else.

Electronic Ticket If you're flying from the US mainland to Bermuda, it's possible to book flight with an electronic ticket (also called E-ticket or ticketless travel). Essentially you get a re but not an actual ticket, from your airline or travel agent; you then show identification at the counter to get your boarding pass. One big advantage is the impossibility of losing your ticke

Excursion Fare A discounted roundtrip ticket, generally marketed to leisure travelers, advance-purchase requirements and length of stay restrictions.

Full Fares Airlines traditionally offer 1st-class (coded F), business-class (coded J) and econ class (coded Y) tickets. These days, so many promotional and discounted fares are available tha passengers pay full economy fare.

Lost Tickets If you lose your airline ticket, an airline will usually treat it like a traveler's check after inquiries, issue you another one, though a fee may be involved. Legally, however, an air entitled to treat the ticket like cash; if you lose it, it's gone forever. Take good care of your ti

Onward Tickets An entry requirement for many countries is a ticket out of the country. If y unsure of your next move, the easiest solution is to buy the cheapest onward ticket to a neighb country or a ticket from a reliable airline that can later be refunded if you do not use it.

Open-Jaw Tickets These are roundtrip tickets that permit you to fly into one place but r from another. If available, these tickets can save you backtracking to your arrival point.

Overbooking Because almost every flight has some passengers who fail to show up, airlines book more passengers than they have seats. Usually excess passengers make up for the no-sh but occasionally somebody gets bumped. Guess who it is most likely to be? The passengers check in late.

Promotional Fares These officially discounted fares are available from travel agents or d from the airline.

Reconfirmation Some airlines require you to reconfirm your flight at least 72 hours prior t parture; otherwise your name may be deleted from the passenger list. Call to find out if your requires reconfirmation.

Restrictions Discounted tickets often have various restrictions, such as advance pay minimum and maximum periods you must be away, and penalties for changing the tickets.

Round-the-World Tickets RTW tickets give you a limited period (usually a year) in which cumnavigate the globe. You can go anywhere the carrying airlines go, as long as you don't track. The number of stopovers or total number of separate flights is decided before you set of these tickets usually cost more than a basic roundtrip flight.

Travel Periods Ticket prices vary with the time of year. There is a low (off-peak) season and (peak) season, and often a low-shoulder season and a high-shoulder season as well. Usually th depends on your outward flight – if you depart in the high season and return in the low seaso pay the high-season fare.

GLENDA BENDURE

s show old-fashioned facades on City of Hamilton's busy Front St.

NED FRIARY

e Park, City of Hamilton

NED FRIARY

Desmond Fountain sculpture, City of Hamilton

NED FRIARY

Sessions House, City of Hamilton

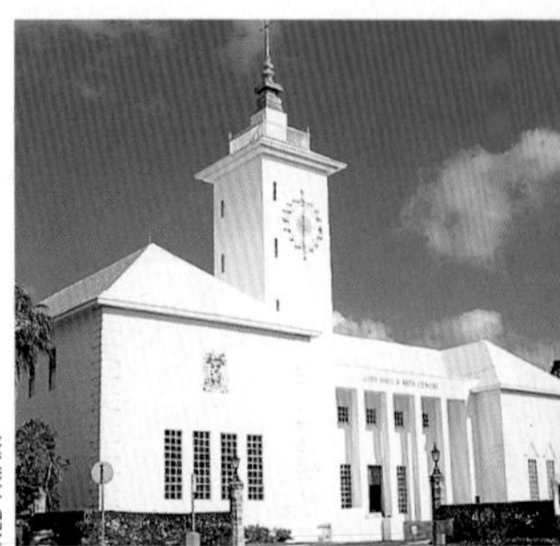
NED FRIARY

Eyebrows raised on City Hall, City of Ha

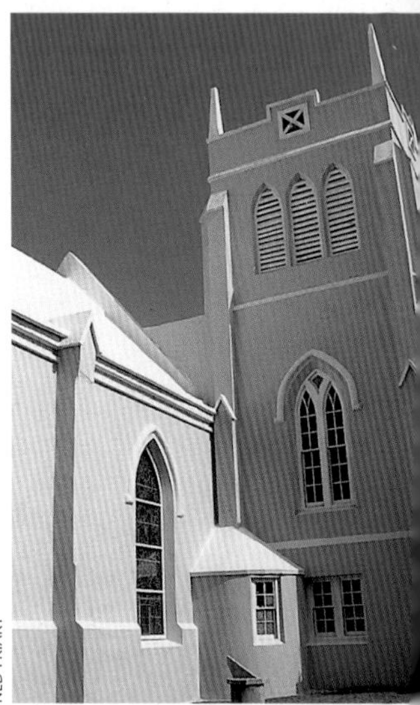
NED FRIARY

St Andrew's Church, City of Hamilton

NED FRIARY

Facade on Front St, City of Hamilton

JK

Airways (☎ 800-247-9297) flies from n (Gatwick) to Bermuda on Tuesday, lay and Saturday. The roundtrip ex- fare, with a three-day advance pur- nd a maximum stay of three months, to £600 depending upon the day of ek and the season of travel.

SE SHIP

90,000 cruise ship passengers sail to da each year. All arrive between nd October, as cruise ships suspend perations to Bermuda during the season.

typical cruise ship holiday is the ulti- ackage tour. Other than the effort in- in selecting a cruise, such a trip s minimal planning – just pay and – and for many people that is a large the appeal. Keep in mind that much time will be spent at sea, so you'll tably less time on the island than e with a vacation of comparable who takes a flight.

use cruises cover rooms, meals, en- nent and transportation in one all- e price, they can be a relatively good Although cruises cost more than d independent travel, they do not ily cost more than a conventional tour that covers airfare and ex- t a resort hotel.

travel agents have cruise ship es, complete with pictures of the d cabins, available for the taking. es also can be obtained by contact- ruise lines directly.

llowing cruise lines all offer week- ndtrip cruises to Bermuda through- ruise ship season.

Lines

Cruises (☎ 800-235-3274) sails the o Bermuda, departing from New ry Saturday between late April and ber. It docks in Bermuda at both of Hamilton and the Town of St The ship has a crew of 670 and 374 passengers. It weighs 47,255 2 feet long and has a cruising speed of 21.4 knots. Celebrity Cruises has its website at www.celebrity-cruises.com.

The Princess Cruise Line (☎ 800-774-6237) sails the *Pacific Princess* to Bermuda, departing from New York every Sunday between early May and late October. On each cruise, the ship docks at all three island ports – the Town of St George, the City of Hamilton and the Royal Naval Dockyard. The ship weighs 20,000 tons, is 553 feet long, has a cruising speed of 20 knots and carries 640 passengers. The Princess Cruise Line has its website at www.princess.com.

The Norwegian Cruise Line (☎ 800-327-7030) sails the ship *Norwegian Majesty* to Bermuda, departing from Boston every Sunday between late April and mid-October. It docks at the Town of St George. The ship weighs 38,000 tons, is 680 feet long, has a cruising speed of 20 knots and carries 1460 passengers and a crew of 550. The Norwegian Cruise Line has its website at www.ncl.com.

The Royal Caribbean Cruise Line (☎ 800-327-6700) sails the ship *Nordic Express* to Bermuda, departing from New York on Sundays from late May to mid-October. It docks at both the Town of St George and the City of Hamilton. In addition, in late April and late October the *Nordic Express* makes nine-day cruises between New York and San Juan, Puerto Rico, with a stop in Bermuda. The ship weighs 48,563 tons, is 692 feet long, has a cruising speed of 19.5 knots and carries 2020 passengers and a crew of 685. The Royal Caribbean Cruise Lines has its website at www.royalcaribbean.com.

US Customs in Bermuda

Because of a special arrangement in which US customs and immigration officers are stationed at the Bermuda International Airport, US citizens who depart from Bermuda by air clear customs and immigration in Bermuda, rather than in the USA. Their flight home is then treated as a domestic flight with no re-entry formalities upon arriving in the USA.

Costs

Cruise lines do not divide passengers into class categories, but rather provide the same meals and amenities for all passengers on each ship.

Cruises are offered at a range of rates, however, depending mainly on the size, type and location of the cabin. Bottom-end cabins might well be small and poorly located; top-end cabins are often spacious, luxurious suites. Price also depends on the dates of the cruise, the number of people in each cabin, transportation options between your home and the departure point and the cruise line you choose. In addition, discounts off the brochure rates are commonplace.

Standard rates, which for most cruises to Bermuda start between $900 and $1500, are quoted per person, based on double occupancy. Third and fourth persons (children or adults) in the same cabin are often given a heavily discounted rate.

Provisions vary for single travelers who occupy a double cabin, but the single cost is commonly about 150% of the standard rate. Some cruise lines also have a singles share program, in which they attempt to match up compatible (same-sex) cabin mates to share the double cabins.

Meals, which are typically elaborate affairs, are included in the cruise price. Alcoholic drinks usually are not included and generally are comparable in price to those in bars back home.

Entertainment shows and most onboard activities are included in the cruise price, but personal services such as hairstyling and laundry usually cost extra, as do most shoreside activities such as diving or windsurfing.

Cruise lines generally suggest that each passenger tip, per day, $3.50 to the cabin steward, $3.50 to the dining room waiter and $2 each to the maitre d' and the person who buses the tables, given in a lump sum on the last night of the cruise. For cocktail servers, a 15% tip is sometimes included in the drink price; if not, it is generally given on the spot.

Bermuda makes up for what it doesn't collect in hotel taxes by levying steep port charges. On most cruises, expect to pay between $125 to $180 in governmen and fees; these are generally paid wh buy your ticket.

Before paying for your cruise, be check the fine print about deposits, ca tion and refund policies, and travel ins

Discounts & Promotions When al and done, very few cruises are sold standard brochure rates.

Many cruise lines offer discounts f reservations and also give last-min counts. In years past, the cheapest rat those obtained at the last minute – tially standby rates for whatever cab not been booked – but the cruise lin been largely successful in reversi trend. These days, the general rule is earlier the booking is, the greater count – and, of course, the better th selection. Still, cruise lines want to so if there are seats leftover at the en will be discounts available.

And then there are the occasio motions: some cruise lines offer a 5 count for the second person on de sailings; others may offer free ca grades if certain qualifications are two-for-one specials in selected r offer discounts to senior citizens, etc

Choosing a Cruise

In addition to finding a cruise that budget, the following are some oth to consider.

Departure Point Most cruises lea New York or Boston. However, t occasional variations, including cruises from Puerto Rico to New Bermuda. The cost and ease of getti departure point should be taken i sideration when choosing a cruise.

Ship Facilities The convention ship is indeed a floating resort. Tho to Bermuda hold between 640 and sengers and have swimming pools, tertainment, casinos, multiple re and lounges.

›s generally can accommodate special vith advance notice, but verify this you book. Some ships are wheelchair ble, although passengers should care-eck details such as the measurement room clearance for wheelchairs to ure they are adequate for individual

Outside cabins are best, as their view them the least claustrophobic. Higher re also preferable, as are, of course, gest and fanciest cabins. Prices will ond accordingly. Although cruise ave stabilizers to prevent roll, if prone to motion sickness, you might get a cabin in the center of the ship, s more stable and rocks less in bad r.

nside cabins (with no portholes) on est decks are the least desirable, but st. Bottom-end cabins sometimes nk-style beds and minuscule bath- and they can be uncomfortably d. Avoid the cabins nearest the oom, as they may be noisy.

ion All cruise ships that arrive in ts are subject to unannounced US n inspections. The inspectors rate four categories: potable water sup- l preparation and holding; potential nation of food; and general cleanli- rage and repair.

mmary sheet that lists ships, the te of inspection and their ratings is d weekly and may be obtained free ng to: Chief, Vessel Sanitation Pro- ational Center for Environmental 1015 N American Way, Room 107, 'L 33132, USA.

g a Cruise

travel agent should be able to comparisons on cruise lines, facili- s and discounts. Be aware that the has also attracted the occasional ht company that advertises heavily, es the money and runs – be sure aling with a reputable agent.

Those travel agents most knowledgeable about cruises are apt to belong to Cruise Lines International Association (CLIA), an organization of cruise lines that works in affiliation with about 20,000 North American travel agencies. CLIA's website is at found www.cruising.org.

YACHT

Most yachters who sail to Bermuda depart from the US East Coast. Bermuda is approximately 640 nautical miles southeast from Virginia, 670 nautical miles from New York City and 690 nautical miles from Boston. Of course, sailing time will vary with the weather and the boat, but the typical voyage time between Bermuda and the US East Coast is five to six days.

Approach

Bermuda's two main water entrances are at the Town Cut channel and The Narrows channel, both at the eastern side of the island. Because of the vast reefs that lie as much as 10 miles offshore, the approach must be made cautiously, using updated charts. Bermuda has two lighthouses and numerous beacons, buoys and shore lights to aid navigation.

Bermuda Harbour Radio (call letters ZBM) broadcasts weather forecasts and navigational warnings. All vessels approaching Bermuda are required to contact Bermuda Harbour Radio at 2182 KHz or VHF Channel 16 for entry and berthing instructions. A call should be attempted at approximately 30 miles from the island, giving the estimated time of arrival and a description of the vessel.

Arrival & Departure

All visiting yachts are required to obtain customs, immigration and health clearance in the Port of St George before proceeding elsewhere in Bermuda. The clearance facility is at the east side of Ordnance Island and can be reached at VHF Channel 16. Instructions on departure formalities should be obtained here as well; there are no departure taxes for yachters.

Anchorages & Facilities

St George's Harbour offers anchorage for yachts at Somers Wharf, Hunters Wharf and on the north side of Ordnance Island free of charge on a first-come, first-served basis.

Anchorage is available on a fee basis at the Dockyard Marina (☎ 234-0300), a full-service marina located at the Royal Naval Dockyard. For information on how to berth in Hamilton Harbour, contact the Royal Hamilton Amateur Dinghy Club (☎ 236-2250). Bermuda Harbour Radio can also provide information on anchorage options around the island.

Because there are several yacht races between Bermuda and the US East Coast in June, yachters who are not racing may find that to be a difficult time to secure a berth.

Bermuda has boat repair yards as well as shops selling marine accessories. If you're in need of service or repairs, the clearance authorities in St George can refer you to the appropriate facilities.

Books & Charts

The Bermuda Dept of Tourism offers a a 20-page pamphlet called *Yachts (Private) Sailing to Bermuda* for anyone considering sailing to Bermuda. It includes detailed information on everything from beacon locations and customs clearance to marina facilities and where to go to pick up ice.

In addition, two recommended books are *The Yachting Guide to Bermuda*, edited by the Bermuda Maritime Museum, and *Reed's Caribbean Almanac*.

Detailed charts are essential for sailing into Bermudian waters. In Bermuda, yachting books and charts are available at PW's Marine Centre (☎ 295-3232), at Waterloo, Pitts Bay Rd, City of Hamilton.

In the USA, books and charts can be ordered from the following companies:

Armchair Sailor Worldwide Navigation (☎ 401-847-4252, 800-292-4278) 543 Thames St, Newport, RI 02840

Landfall Navigation (☎ 203-661-3176, email info@landfallnav.com) 354 W Putnam Ave, Greenwich, CT 06830

New York Nautical Instrument & Service 962-4522, email info@newyorknautical.c W Broadway, New York, NY 10013

Blue Water Books & Charts (☎ 800-94 email help@bluewaterweb.com) 1481 SE Fort Lauderdale, FL 33316

ORGANIZED TOURS

Package Tours

Conventional package tours to Be that include airfare and accommo are available from the USA, Canada UK. Most tours range from three ni one week in duration, though they of be tailored for longer stays.

As tour consolidators get steep counted rates on both airfare and h package tour typically works ou cheaply than if you were to book th hotel and flight separately. Particular are going to Bermuda for a short vacation, package tours can be econ at times the cheapest three-day tour little more than what the airfare would cost if booked independently.

From the USA, where most fl Bermuda originate, package tours a competitive. Three-day tours that inc commodations in a guesthouse c hotel and airfare from the US Ea commonly begin as low as $400 per based on double occupancy. The a in the travel sections of big-city newspapers, such as the *New York* the *Boston Globe*, are a good sour formation. Package tours in gener sent a substantial part of the boo most travel agents, and they can us you high with Bermuda tour broch

Specialized Tours

Elderhostel (☎ 617-426-8056), 75 Fe Boston, MA 02110, is a nonprofit tion offering educational programs age 55 and older. The organizatio has its origins in the youth hostels c and the folk schools of Scandinavi ally focuses on the environment an history. The Bermuda program is in conjunction with the Bermuda B

ı for Research (BBSR) in St George's
and includes marine ecology courses
BBSR, as well as history and culture
s. One-week and 10-day programs run
hout the year and start at about $800,
ng meals, classes, field trips and ac-
ɔdations. Airfare to and from Beris not included. See the Elderhostel
at www.elderhostel.org.

ƆI Travel Network International
-729-7234, email ptn@padi.com), at 30151 Tomas St, Rancho Santa Margarita, CA 92688-2125, can arrange customized dive tours to Bermuda, packaging together accommodations and diving outings. Rates vary depending upon the length of stay and the type of accommodations you select, but typically work out to be a better deal than arranging a hotel and dives on your own and paying for them separately. Check out the PADI website at www.padi.com. for more information.

Getting Around

You cannot rent cars in Bermuda. Visitors can ride public buses and ferries, use taxis, rent a moped, motor scooter or bicycle – or even hire a horse and carriage.

BUS

Bermuda has a good islandwide public bus system that you can use to reach most sights and beaches. The buses are reliable and generally run on time. Pick up a free copy of the bus and ferry schedule at one of the Visitors Service Bureaus or at the bus terminal on Washington St in the City of Hamilton.

Buses are quite busy between 3:30 and 5:30 pm on weekdays, when schoolchildren and office workers make the commute home, but at most other times, getting a seat isn't a challenge. Frequencies vary with the route and time of travel, but during the day the busier routes generally have a bus operating every 15 to 30 minutes. Sundays and holidays have substantially reduced schedules.

Schedules vary by route, but most buses begin service somewhere between 6:30 and 7:30 am. Service on some minor routes ends around 6 pm. On the two most significant routes – Hamilton to St George and Hamilton to the Royal Naval Dockyard – service continues until around 11 pm, with the schedule thinning out as the evening goes on.

Of the dozen bus routes, all, with the exception of the St George-St David's route, leave from the Hamilton bus terminal. Consequently, if you use buses often, you'll find yourself transferring there frequently.

Bus stops are marked with striped pink-and-blue posts. The posts are color coded to indicate whether buses serving that stop are inbound or outbound; the top stripe is pink for buses heading into Hamilton, blue for those heading away from Hamilton.

Fares & Passes

To ride the bus, you must have the exact fare *in coins* or have a token, ticket or transportation pass. Paper money is not accepted and change is not given.

Bermuda is divided into 14 differe zones. Fares are based either on three (meaning the trip covers one to three or 14 zones (for a journey covering 14 zones).

Beginning from the City of Hami is a three-zone fare to: the Bermuda ium, Museum & Zoo (bus Nos 10 or Bermuda Botanical Gardens (bus N or 7); Elbow Beach or Horseshoe B No 7); or Spittal Pond (bus No 1) Hamilton, it's a 14-zone fare to the Naval Dockyard (bus Nos 7 or 8). It' 14-zone fare to the airport, Bailey's St George's – all of which can be rea bus Nos 1, 3, 10 or 11.

The regular adult fare is $2.50 in $2.25 in tokens for up to three zones in coins or $3.75 in tokens for mo three zones. Children ages five to ride for $1 in coins for any number and those under age five ride for fre

Bus transfers are free as long as made with the next scheduled con bus. If you need a transfer, request the driver when you get on the first

Tickets offer a handsome discou pared to the cash fare. The cost for $15 for 15 tickets that are each vali to three zones, and $24 for 15 tick for all zones. The cost for children 15 tickets valid for all zones.

Transportation passes can be you're doing a lot of exploring, as th unlimited use of both buses and Passes valid for a single day cost $ valid for three consecutive days and those valid for seven consecu cost $34. In addition, there's a mon for $40 that is valid for the calend in which it is purchased.

Ticket books, tokens and trans passes can be purchased at the bus information booth in Hamilton fro to 5:30 pm weekdays, 8:15 am to Saturday and 8:15 am to 4:45 pm and holidays.

ket books and transportation passes so sold at most sub-post offices, but the main post office in Hamilton. The r-duration transportation passes are some hotels and guesthouses, as well ourist offices.

ou have any inquiries regarding public rvice, contact the Public Transporta- oard (☎ 292-3851) between 8:45 am om weekdays.

ous Service

ition to the islandwide public bus , a private minibus service operates in rge's Parish. The St George's Mini- rvice (☎ 297-8199) runs from around 8 pm (to 11 pm in summer) Monday rday and 9 am to 6 pm Sunday. The $2 around the Town of St George or obacco Bay, $2.75 to the Bermuda Bi- l Station and $5 to St David's.

minibus office is at the north side of rge Town Hall. The buses, which are th a yellow minibus sign on top, gen- ull into King's Square every 20 min- so. You can sometimes wave them s they come into the square; other- alk behind town hall to see if a bus is there. You can also call to arrange to ed up anywhere in the greater St area. As might be expected, the es are busiest on cruise ship days.

nformation on minibus tours of St 's, see Organized Tours later in this

D & MOTOR SCOOTER

, which are known as 'cycles' in a, are the main mode of transport ing the island independently. They a fun way of getting around, but a's narrow winding roads present es for drivers who aren't used to nditions – or who don't have moped ice.

t, enough visitors spill their cycles term 'road rash' is part of the island lar. If you're not used to riding, ure you're comfortable with the efore taking to the road. All moped ops are required to have an instruc- tor show you how to use the cycle and to provide you with an opportunity to practice. If you're not satisfied with your ability to handle the moped after your instruction, feel free to cancel the contract.

Automobile Ban

Bermudians managed to do without automobiles for some four decades after most of the rest of the Western world had become accustomed to driving around in 'horseless carriages.'

In 1906, Bermudians passed a law forbidding automobiles on the island after somebody imported a car with no mufflers and created a ruckus by spooking the horses.

It wasn't until WWII, when the US military insisted on importing motor vehicles for its own use, that Bermudians began to take to the idea of motorized transportation. In 1946, private ownership of automobiles was legalized.

There's still a strict regulation that limits the number of cars to one per household; today there are about 22,000 private cars in Bermuda and an additional 24,000 mopeds, motor scooters and motorcycles.

Road Rules

In Bermuda, as in Britain, driving is on the left. The maximum speed limit throughout Bermuda is 35km (20 miles) per hour, except in a few municipal areas such as central St George, where it drops to 25km per hour.

Bermuda has a handful of roundabouts (also known as rotaries or traffic circles) – you must give way to traffic already on the roundabout, but once you enter you have the right-of-way.

To drive a moped, you must be at least 16 years old, but if the engine is 50cc or less – as most of them are – you don't need a driver's license.

Helmets are provided by the cycle livery you rent from, and most mopeds come equipped with locks and carrying baskets. Bringing a short bungee cord from home will prove convenient for securing small packages in the basket.

Helmets are required of both drivers and passengers. Be cautious if you stop to do a lot of sightseeing, as it's easy to place the helmet in the moped's carrying basket and then forget to put it back on when you resume traveling – a situation that can draw a stern lecture from a police officer…or even from a passing citizen!

Police are not eager to ticket tourists and will generally issue warnings for traffic violations as long as the violator is apologetic.

Parking

Cycle parking is clearly marked and easy to find in the City of Hamilton and other built-up areas, and there are no parking fees. Parking a moped or motor scooter in car bays is forbidden, and can result in a $50 parking ticket.

Rental

Moped rates are competitive, and the per-day cost gets cheaper the longer you keep the cycle. You may find that you'll do just as well renting from the shop associated with your hotel or guesthouse, but if you want to seek out the best price, many cycle liveries will either pick you up and take you to their office or deliver the cycle to you.

When comparing rates, take note of the add-ons that pad up the bill. A mandatory 'repair waiver insurance' of about $18 is the most common one; this is a one-time fee that covers the entire rental period, whether it's one day or one week. The repair waiver insurance covers damages to the cycle, but with some companies there's a deductible, in which case you still could be held responsible for hundreds of dollars in damages. Be sure you understand the policy in advance.

Whichever cycle livery you rent from, and regardless of the insurance offered, you'll likely have either a large deductible for theft or find that it will not be covered at all. Because of a rash of stolen cycles (one out of every 10 motorbikes is stolen each year), mopeds have become virtually impossible to insure against theft. Incidentally, it's not just a problem for rentals – most islander had theft coverage dropped from the insurance policies. Inquire carefully the theft policy before renting; some c nies might limit your liability if yo prove you locked the cycle (ie, you ha key), but others will hold you respo under any circumstances.

Rates for a one-person moped a $30 to $40 for a one-day rental, $50 for two days, $60 to $80 for three da $110 to $140 for a week – plus the or repair waiver charge. For about $10 day you can rent a larger cycle, com referred to as a scooter, that's capa carrying a passenger. Carrying a pas isn't recommended, however, unless an experienced motorbike driver.

The mopeds come with a full tank and most have a small reserve tank need to refill on the road, there are tions throughout the island from St to Somerset.

Moped rental is available from lowing companies:

Dowling's Cycles (☎ 297-1614) is at 26 Y St George.

Elbow Beach Cycle (☎ 236-9237) is at th Beach Hotel in Paget.

Eve's Cycles (☎ 236-6247) has branche Middle Rd in Paget and 1 Water St (☎ 2 in St George.

Grotto Bay Beach Cycles (☎ 293-2378) Blue Hole Hill, near the Grotto Bay Bea in Hamilton Parish.

Oleander Cycles, a large reputable opera its main office (☎ 236-5235) on Valle Paget, has branches on Gorham Rd (☎ 2 in the City of Hamilton; at the Roy Dockyard (☎ 234-2764); and on Mi (☎ 234-0629), just north of the Port R Course in Southampton.

Rockford Cycle Livery (☎ 292-1534), on in Pembroke, boasts low rates.

Smatt's Cycle Livery (☎ 295-1180), 74 Rd, is next to the Hamilton Princess Pembroke.

Wheels Cycles is at 117 Front St (☎ 29 the City of Hamilton; at the Sout Princess hotel (☎ 238-3336), Southam

Iorth Shore Rd (☎ 293-1280) in Flatts ge. At the time of research, Wheels Cycles one of the more comprehensive repair er insurance policies.

CLE

ugh not nearly as popular as mopeds, es present another option for getting l. However, Bermuda's roads are nar-urving and often hilly, so people plan-on bicycling need to be cautious of and expect to work up a sweat. Using ilway Trail, when it's going your way, od way to avoid traffic.

ew of the moped rental shops, includ-e's Cycles and Wheels Cycles, rent bi-(generally known as pedal cycles, to ntiate them from mopeds) for $20 to the first day and lesser amounts for nal days, working out to about $75 for ly rental. Rental bicycles vary; some d bikes, but most tend to be moun-es.

ks are generally provided with bicycle Helmets are not compulsory on pe-les; some rental shops provide them e bicycles, and others do not.

HIKING

king is not illegal in Bermuda, but ely done. As one police officer re-l: 'I don't know if people would know ou're doing. They might stick their back up at you, thinking you're just a good time.'

of course, as with everywhere else in ld, hitchhiking is never entirely safe nely Planet does not recommend it. rs who make the decision to hitch-uld understand that they are taking tially serious risk. People who do to hitch will be safer if they travel in d let someone know where they are g to go.

Y

ferries, which operate daily in the ound and Hamilton Harbour, offer a lternative to the bus. As the dis-cross water are often shorter than comparable land routes, the ferries can also be quicker. The shortest ferry from the City of Hamilton to the Royal Naval Dockyard, for example, takes just 30 minutes, and the bus ride takes a full hour.

There are three different ferry routes connecting Hamilton with Paget, Warwick and the Somerset/Dockyard area. Each route leaves from the Hamilton Ferry Terminal, which is conveniently located on Front St at the end of Queen St, adjacent to the tourist office.

All fares are collected at the Hamilton terminal for both departing and arriving passengers. If you happen to be taking a ferry on intermediate stops – from the Dockyard to Somerset, for instance – there are no provisions for paying, so it's a free ride.

For details on transportation passes and tokens, which are valid on both public buses and ferries, see Fares & Passes in the earlier Bus section. If you have questions regarding ferries, contact the Hamilton Ferry Terminal (☎ 295-4506).

Paget & Warwick Routes

The Paget ferry connects the City of Hamilton with the north side of Paget Parish, making a 20-minute roundtrip loop from Hamilton that stops at Lower Ferry, Hodson's Ferry and Salt Kettle Wharf along the way. An exception is in the evening, when some sailings skip the Lower Ferry and Hodson's Ferry stops.

The Warwick ferry makes a 30-minute loop, connecting Hamilton with Darrell's Wharf, near the intersection of Harbour Rd and Cobbs Hill Rd; Belmont Wharf, near the Belmont Golf Club; and Hinson's Island.

Note that the order of the stops on both the Paget and the Warwick routes varies throughout the day, because some sailings make clockwise loops, and other sailings are counterclockwise.

The cost on either route is $2.25 one way. The boats, which operate from 7:15 am to 11 pm, leave Hamilton about once every 30 minutes. On Saturday, the first ferry leaves Hamilton at 8:45 am. On Sunday and holidays, the Warwick and Paget routes are merged

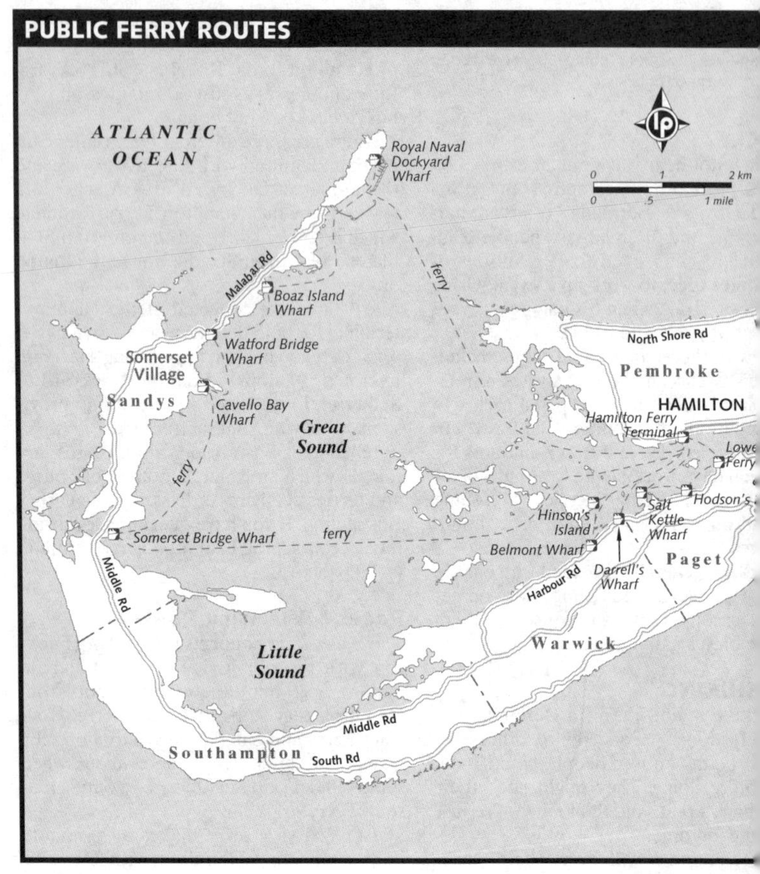

and served by a single ferry that operates every 40 minutes from 10:10 am to 7 pm.

Somerset/Dockyard Route

The Somerset/Dockyard route provides service between the City of Hamilton and the West End, with stops at the Royal Naval Dockyard, Boaz Island, Watford Bridge, Cavello Bay and Somerset Bridge. The order of stops varies with the sailing – so it can take as little as 30 minutes to get to the Dockyard from Hamilton or as long as 1¼ hours, depending on the route of the boat you catch. The whole loop rout about one hour and 45 minutes.

The one-way fare is $3.75. The So Dockyard boat is the only ferry tha you, for an additional $3.75, to moped, which gives you the option o one way and driving back.

On weekdays, the boats leave H at 6:25, 7:30, 9, 10 and 11 am; at noon 1, 2, 3, 4 and 5:20 pm. Saturday dep are the same, except that the first b 9 am. On Sunday and public holid boats depart from Hamilton at 9 an

: 1, 3 and 5 pm. Every day of the week, he 9 am and 1 pm boats make a direct nute sailing to the Dockyard.

are readily available from the airport ht times, and most larger hotels have at the waiting. In addition, there are ands in heavily touristed areas, such as St in Hamilton and King's Square in orge.

taxis are equipped with meters. The rd rate, for up to four passengers, is or the first mile plus $1.68 for each adl mile. If there are five or six passene rate is $6 for the first mile plus $2.10 ch additional mile. A 25% surcharge s between midnight and 6 am and all Sundays and public holidays.

ou need to call for a taxi, Radio Cabs -4141) has numerous vehicles and 24-ervice. Other taxi companies include axi Co-op Transportation (☎ 292-4476) ermuda Taxi Operators Company -4175).

SE & CARRIAGE

gh it's more of a romantic ride than a al means of transportation, horse-and-e rides are available in the City of on from along Front St. They usually seaside route west along Pitts Bay Rd e a circular route north on Bermudi-, west on Richmond Rd and back to t via Serpentine and Par-la-Ville Rds.

The cost per carriage, for one to four passengers, is $20 for the first 30 minutes (the minimum charge) and $20 for each additional 30-minute increment. If the carriage is drawn by two horses, as some of them are, they are allowed to carry more than four passengers, in which case the cost for the fifth and additional passengers is $5 per person per 30 minutes.

ORGANIZED TOURS

If you want to piece together your own private sightseeing tour, taxis can double as tour operators, catering a tour to your interests. The drivers are generally knowledgeable and their commentary can add plenty of local color as you explore. The cost is $30 per hour for one to four passengers, $42 per hour for five or six passengers.

In addition, the St George's Mini-Bus Service offers one-hour tours of the Town of St George, mainly on weekdays during the cruise ship season. At the height of summer there are commonly two tours in the morning and two in the afternoon. The cost is $18 per person. Inquiries can be made at the minibus office at the north side of St George Town Hall or by calling ☎ 297-8492 or 297-8199.

Public ferry rides can double as inexpensive harbor cruises; see the Ferry section earlier in this chapter. For information on sightseeing cruises, snorkeling cruises and organized walks, see the Outdoor Activities chapter.

Outdoor Activities

HIKING

Bermuda's numerous parks and nature reserves provide opportunities for short hikes. Some of the best walking destinations are the areas with the greatest acreage, such as Spittal Pond Nature Reserve in Smith's Parish and South Shore Park in Warwick and Southampton Parishes.

Railway Trail

The longest walking trails on the island aren't found in parks and nature reserves, but are along the now covered-over tracks that once carried Bermuda's narrow-gauge railway. The railway, which began operations in 1931, never gained in popularity, and the last train was taken off the tracks in 1947. The government, which had acquired the railway in its final days, sold the engines and cars to British Guiana and shipped them off to Georgetown in 1948. After that, most of the track was simply forgotten, though a few sections were lost to modernization – most notably a 3-mile stretch around the City of Hamilton that was widened into roadway.

In 1984, the government set aside the remaining sections of the old railway route for foot and bridle paths. In all, these encompass some 21 miles of trail, from Somerset Village at the West End of Bermuda to St George's at the East End.

The Railway Trail is not a single continuous route; there is a significant break between the Paget and Devonshire Parishes, as well as many shorter breaks here and there where hikers have to briefly walk along a vehicle road until the Railway Trail starts up again. Some sections are open only to hikers, bicyclists and horseback riders, but other parts are open to motorbikes and limited local car traffic.

The government publishes a nifty pocket-size booklet, *The Bermuda Railway Trail Walking Guide*, which details all seven sections of the trail, complete with a map and tidbits about the nature and history of sights you'll encounter along each section. Th
booklet can be picked up at tourist off
Bermuda after you arrive.

Organized Walks

The Walking Club of Bermuda meets a
every Sunday, rain or shine, for walk
to 7 miles. Visitors are welcome to p
pate and are not charged a fee. The lo
changes each week; look for the sche
either the current *This Week in Be*
tourist magazine, the *Royal Gazette*
Bermuda Sun.

Tim Rogers of Bermuda Lectur
Tours (☎ 234-4082) is a former high
teacher who leads informative walkin
at various locations around the island
include Devonshire on Tuesday mo
either the Ferry Point area in St G
Parish or Gibbs Hill and Church
Southampton on Thursday mornin
the Blue Hole Park area in Hamilton
on Friday mornings. The tours, which
a discussion of ecology and history, ge
begin around 10 am, last 1½ hours an
about 2 miles. The cost is $10 for ad
for children under 12. Private tours c
be arranged with Tim Rogers.

BIRDWATCHING

With only 22 species of resident bir
ing in Bermuda, it's not surprising t
peak birdwatching seasons are dur
spring and fall migrations. During
periods birdwatching can be excelle
more than 200 species of migratory b
iting the island, from warblers and t
to shorebirds and seabirds.

One of the finest all-around birdw
sites is Spittal Pond, Bermuda's
nature reserve. For sighting land bird
accessible areas include the Heydo
Estate in Sandys Parish, the Berm
tanical Gardens in Paget Parish and
boretum in Devonshire Parish. Goo
for spotting shorebirds and wadir
include Warwick Pond in Warwick

omerset Long Bay Nature Reserve in s Parish.

ood companion for birdwatchers is *A to the Birds of Bermuda*, by Eric which describes virtually every spe- f bird that has been spotted on the and gives detailed information on birding areas. Also recommended is *ecklist and Guide to the Birds of da*, by David B Wingate, which has species descriptions as well as charts seasonal distribution and abundance s.

more information on birdlife in Ber- see Birds under Flora & Fauna in the bout Bermuda chapter.

IING

ailway Trail (see the Hiking section, in this chapter) makes a good, traffic- ute for joggers. Use caution when run- other areas, as many Bermuda roads row, with heavy traffic, no sidewalks occasional blind curve.

IS

da has more than 80 tennis courts, them open to the general public. If n to play much tennis, you might want g your own equipment; however, aces that offer tennis courts also rent s and sell tennis balls. On all courts in la, proper tennis attire is preferred shoes and whites), and on some it is ory.

Government Tennis Stadium (☎ 292- t Bernard Park on Marsh Folly Rd in ke, at the north side of the City of on, has three clay and five plexicush- rts. The court cost is $8 per hour for $4 for children. Racquet rental runs our, a ball machine can be rented for hour, and lessons that cost $45 an n be scheduled. At night, there's an al $8 fee to light the courts.

following places also have tennis pen to the public. Fees are charged -hour, per-court basis.

ay Beach Hotel (☎ 293-8333), Hamilton four plexipave courts; $12 for visitors, $10 for hotel guests; night lighting $15; pro shop; lessons available

Hamiltonian Hotel & Island Club (☎ 295-5608), Pembroke; three asphalt courts; $10 for visitors, free for hotel guests; night lighting $5; lessons and ball machine available

Horizons & Cottages (☎ 236-0048), Paget; one plexipave and two grasstex courts; $10 for visitors, $4 for hotel guests

Kindley Community Tennis Courts (☎ 293-5791), St David's; four asphalt courts; $4 for adults, $2 for children

Newstead Hotel (☎ 236-6060), Paget; two clay courts; $14 for visitors, $3.50 for hotel guests

Pomander Gate Tennis Club (☎ 236-5400), Paget; four hard courts; $10 for visitors

Port Royal Tennis Club (☎ 234-0974), Southampton; four plexipave courts; $10 for visitors; night lighting $4; lessons and ball machine available

Sonesta Beach Hotel (☎ 238-8122), Southampton; six plexipave courts; $10 for visitors, free for hotel guests; night lighting $2; lessons and ball machine available

Southampton Princess, Whaler Inn Tennis Club (☎ 239-6950), Southampton; 11 plexipave courts; $12 for visitors, $10 for hotel guests; night lighting $4; lessons and ball machine available

Stonington Beach Hotel (☎ 236-5416), Paget; two plexipave courts; $10 for visitors, free for hotel guests; lessons available

Willowbank (☎ 234-1616), Sandys; two plexipave courts; $6 for visitors, free for hotel guests; lessons available

The following hotels have tennis courts that are available for their guests, but not open to the general public: Ariel Sands Beach Club

Tennis, Anyone?

The game of tennis, which originated in England in 1872, was played for the first time in the Western Hemisphere in 1873 at the Bermuda home of Sir Brownlow Gray, the island's chief justice.

Mary Outerbridge, a guest at the Gray home, was so enthralled by the game that she carried a pair of racquets with her on a trip from Bermuda to New York. She is credited with introducing tennis to the USA, in 1874.

in Devonshire, Cambridge Beaches in Sandys, Elbow Beach Hotel in Paget, Pink Beach Club in Smith's, Pompano Beach Club in Southampton and The Reefs in Southampton.

The tennis courts at the private Coral Beach & Tennis Club (☎ 236-2233), in Paget, considered the island's top tennis club, and at the exclusive Mid Ocean Club (☎ 293-0330), in Tucker's Town, are open only to members or by introduction from a member.

Schedules and information on tennis tournaments are available from the Bermuda Lawn Tennis Association (☎ 296-0834), PO Box HM 341, Hamilton HM BX.

SQUASH

At the Bermuda Squash Racquets Club (☎ 292-6881), on Middle Rd in Devonshire, are four international-size courts available on a reservation basis. The cost is $10 per person plus a court fee of $5 for 40 minutes in the afternoon, $7 in the evening. Balls and racquets can be rented.

The Coral Beach & Tennis Club (☎ 236-2233), a private club on South Rd in Paget, has two international-size squash courts, but they're generally only available by introduction from a club member.

GOLF

Bermuda has eight golf courses, six open to the public and two that require introduction by members.

All courses require 'proper golf attire,' which means shirts must have collars and shorts must be Bermuda-shorts length (to the knees); jeans, cutoff pants and sleeveless shirts are not allowed.

Reservations for tee times at the Ocean View, Port Royal and St George's golf courses, which are Bermuda's only three government-run courses, can be arranged through an automated reservation system by calling ☎ 234-4653. Tee times for the other courses are made directly.

Lessons are available at all courses for $35 to $50 per half-hour. Golf shoes can be rented at some courses for $8 to $10. Prices given for club rentals are for full sets; left-handed and right-handed sets for both men and women should be available at course. You might want to bring a supply of golf balls, but if you run shor can be purchased at the courses for a $40 to $60 a dozen.

The use of gas carts is mandatc weekends and holidays at the Ocean Port Royal and St George's golf cours at all times at the Belmont and Castl bour courses.

The following courses are open general public:

Belmont Golf Club (☎ 236-6400), Warv holes, par 70, 5769 yards; $86 on weekdays weekends, gas carts included; club rental

Castle Harbour Golf Club (☎ 298-6959), Town, St George's Parish; 18 holes, par yards; regular rate $130, but half-price rates apply after 4:30 pm; gas carts $ rentals $30

Ocean View Golf Course (☎ 295-9093), shire; nine holes, par 35, 2940 yards; $25 holes or $33 for 18 holes (sunset rate of 4 pm); pull carts $6 for nine or 18 holes, $18 per nine holes; club rentals $20

Port Royal Golf Course (☎ 234-0974), So ton; 18 holes, par 71, 6561 yards; $72 o days, $82 on weekends and on holida cheaper sunset rates; pull carts $9, gas per nine holes; club rentals $25

Southampton Princess Golf Club (☎ 2 Southampton; 18 holes, par 54, 2684 yar guests $38, others $43; sunset and mu rates available; gas carts $36 for hotel gu for others, pull carts cost $7.50 and are only with sunset rates; club rentals $20

St George's Golf Club (☎ 297-8353), St 18 holes, par 62, 4043 yards; $44, dis sunset rates available after 3 pm; pull car carts $36; club rentals $20

The following golf courses require in tion by a member:

Mid Ocean Club (☎ 293-0330), Tucker's George's; 18 holes, par 71, 6512 yards $70 if playing with a member; caddies at $25 per bag; club rentals $20

Riddells Bay Golf & Country Club (☎ 2 Warwick; 18 holes, par 70, 5713 yard weekdays, $90 on weekends and holi discounts if playing with a member; pu gas carts $40; club rentals $25

rmuda International Race Weekend

big running event of the year is the Bermuda International Race Weekend, held annually on the nd weekend of January. It centers around Sunday's running of two races: the Bank of Butter- International Marathon Bermuda, a 13-mile loop route, run twice, that begins on Front St in ilton; and the Bank of Butterfield International Half-Marathon Bermuda, held concurrently but ring only one loop of the course. Record holders for the full 26-mile marathon are Andy Holden eat Britain (2:15.20; in 1980) and Yelena Plastinina of the Ukraine (2:40.50; in 1998).

ctivities begin Friday evening on Front St in Hamilton with the Bank of Butterfield Mile, a series ile-long invitational races by elite runners, children and local celebrities. The evening is capped ith music by the Bermuda Regiment Band.

turday's event is the Bank of Butterfield International 10K & Charity Walk, a 10km race and ncurrent noncompetitive walk along the north shore starting at the National Sports Centre in nshire.

try fees are $25 for the marathon, a bit less for the other events. Total prize money for the thon is $25,000, plus a potential $30,000 combined bonus for new marathon records in both en's and women's events.

formation and an entry form can be obtained from the Bermuda Dept of Tourism (see Tourist es in the Facts for the Visitor chapter) or the Bermuda Marathon Committee, PO Box DV 397, nshire DV BX. Special hotel and air packages are offered by Marathon Tours (☎ 617-242- , 800-444-4097), 108 Main St, Boston, MA 02129, which co-sponsors the event with the of Butterfield and the Bermuda Dept of Tourism.

g Range & Miniature Golf

rmuda Golf Academy (☎ 238-8800), ustrial Park Rd in Southampton, has 320-yard driving range and miniature ilities. You can run through a bucket lls for $5 or play a round of mini golf

aments

la's golf tournaments, which are gen- eld from September to June, are both islanders and visiting golfers. nents are listed under Public Holi- Special Events in the Facts for the chapter.

information on tournaments can be d by contacting the Bermuda Golf tion (☎ 238-1367, fax 238-0983), PO 1 433, Hamilton HM BX.

EBACK RIDING

ds Riding Centre (☎ 238-8212), on Rd in Warwick, offers one-hour ides along south shore beach trails daily at 7, 10 and 11:30 am and 3 pm. In addition, from May to September evening rides are available at 4 and 6 pm on weekdays. The cost is $50 for the day rides, $37.50 for the evening rides. All rides are at a walking pace. All experience levels are accepted, including those who have never ridden before, though riders must be at least 10 years old. Reservations are required.

For information and schedules on horse shows, contact the Bermuda Equestrian Federation, PO Box DV 583, Devonshire DV BX.

BEACHES & SWIMMING

There are pleasant beaches all around Bermuda, but one singularly outstanding area is South Shore Park, a 1½-mile-long coastal park that encompasses many of the island's finest beaches. Its eastern boundary begins in Warwick Parish with the expansive Warwick Long Bay, a half-mile-long unbroken stretch of pink sand, and the western boundary runs just beyond picturesque

Who's in the Water?

Islanders say that in the off-season it's easy to tell the nationality of the people splashing in the waves. Most Bermudians don't swim after September, they say; Americans won't swim much after November; but British visitors will swim year-round.

As a general rule, Bermudians take their first swim of the year on Bermuda Day, May 24, though the more timid wait until the Queen's Birthday, in mid-June.

Horseshoe Bay in Southampton Parish. In between are nearly a dozen coves and bays of various sizes that offer protected swimming and a bit of seclusion. Coastal trails link the beaches and make exploring fun and easy. No matter where you're staying in Bermuda, be sure to include an outing here in your plans.

Other notable beaches include Elbow Beach (Paget Parish), a mile-long strand that's a favorite with beachgoers from the City of Hamilton; John Smith's Bay (Smith's Parish), which often has calm waters when westerly winds kick up the surf elsewhere around the island; and Shelly Bay Beach (Hamilton Parish), which is a favorite with families because of its shallow waters and playground facilities.

In the tourist season, lifeguards are stationed at Horseshoe Bay in Southampton Parish and John Smith's Bay in Smith's Parish.

No beaches in Bermuda allow nude or seminude sunbathing. Note that the stinging Portuguese man-of-war is sometimes found in Bermuda's waters from March to July (see Dangers & Annoyances in the Facts for the Visitor chapter).

DIVING

Despite the fact that Bermuda's coral reefs are the northernmost in the Atlantic, diving in Bermuda is quite similar to diving in Florida or the Bahamas.

The combination of shallow wate the warm ocean currents has perr Bermuda's reefs to thrive even thoug are separated by hundreds of miles c ocean water from other coral reefs. waters surrounding Bermuda harbor 24 species of hard coral, including coral and tree coral, and another two species of soft coral, including sea fa sea whips.

Many of the species of tropical fis are common to Caribbean waters ca be found feeding on the corals in Ber Some of the more colorful fish inclu clown wrasse, queen angelfish, rainbo rotfish, rock beauty, spotted puffe chromis, foureye butterflyfish, blue triggerfish, orange spotted filefish, squirrelfish and large green moray ee

Bermudian waters also hold brittl sea horses, sea spiders, sea hares, sea c bers, sea anemones, sea urchins, conchs, slipper lobsters and spiny lob

Although dive shops operate year- the most popular season and the w conditions are from May to Octobe the water temperatures range from 86°F. From November to April, wat peratures range from 65° to 71°F a wet suits are de rigueur. Although th is chilly, one plus of winter diving is visibility is excellent, ranging from 200 feet, whereas in the warmer s waters it's generally 75 to 100 feet.

Most dive operations take a b winter (generally two to four weeks uary or February), when thi slower. As these brea by operation and a good idea t reservations advance i plan di v

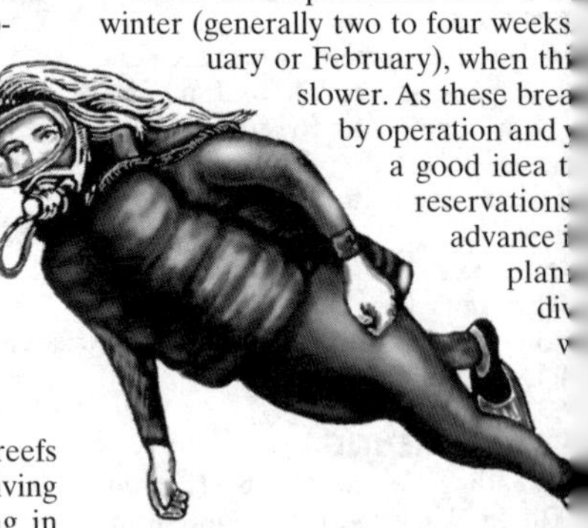

ng Edward VII Memorial Hospital in has a recompression chamber for div-no get the bends (☎ 236-2345).

ck Dives

s of shipwrecks still lie scattered along uda's treacherous reefs. Because the are relatively shallow, there are many dives suitable for both novice and nediate-level divers, in which the ship ved from the exterior without pene- the wreck itself. Since most wrecks n the reef, a wreck dive in Bermuda only doubles as a reef dive. Keep in that you should never dive inside a eck unless you have specialized train-ave the proper equipment, and are the supervision of a qualified wreck tiquity diving expert.

Constellation, a four-masted schooner ovided the inspiration for the *Goliath* r Benchley's novel *The Deep*, is a fa-among wreck divers. The ship, which is idely scattered along the ocean floor at h of only 30 feet, was en route from ork to Venezuela when it diverted to da for mechanical repairs in July 1942. approach to the island, just 7 miles est of the Royal Naval Dockyard, a carried the 192-foot schooner into ef, where – laden with a cargo of – it sank into a watery grave.

in shallow water, less than 20 yards ne *Constellation*, is the wreck of the also referred to in Bermuda as the *na*, one of its aliases. The 236-foot steamer was built in England for use ockade-runner during the US Civil aunched in 1863, it made it only as far nuda, where it sank on the reef during len voyage to the Confederate South. sections of the ship, including the wheels, remain intact and are readily even from a glass-bottom boat.

Cristobal Colon, a 500-foot Spanish at went aground in 1936, is the largest r to wreck in Bermudian waters. The hich lies 8 miles north of the island, veling with only its crew, who, due to break of civil war in Spain, were to return to their home port. Because the cruise ship grounded on the reef, rather than sinking, it was an easy target for pilferers. Although the authorities salvaged items during the day, scores of other islanders came aboard after nightfall and made off with everything from chandeliers and silverware to plumbing fixtures.

In 1937, the 250-foot Norwegian cargo ship *Aristo* sighted the still-intact *Cristobal Colon* in a position that made it appear to be sailing straight up through the reef, and the captain set his course to follow. By the time he recognized his error, the *Aristo* had a lethal gash in its hull.

During WWII, the US military decided to use the *Cristobal Colon* as a target ship, literally blowing the ship in two, with one half settling on either side of the reef. The *Aristo*, on the other hand, stands intact, its forward deck still holding a fire truck and other cargo that it was carrying to Bermuda. Both boats sit in about 50 feet of water.

In the same general area is the *Taunton*, a 228-foot freighter that sank, weighed down with a load of American coal, as it arrived in Bermuda in 1920. This is a good wreck dive for novices, as it's just 20 feet beneath the surface.

One of the newest and most intact of the shipwrecks is the *Hermes*, a 165-foot freighter that was built during WWII. In the early 1980s, after the *Hermes* was abandoned in Bermuda, the government decided to scuttle the boat and turn it into a dive site. First they stripped the hatches and other potential hazards so that it could be used safely for penetration dives, and then they towed it out to sea. The boat sits upright in 75 feet of water about a mile south of Warwick Long Bay and Bermuda's south shore.

Dive Operations

There are five dive operations in Bermuda. In addition to dives for certified divers, all offer a half-day introductory course for people who want to experience diving for the first time; the course includes a condensed basic scuba lesson and a supervised shallow dive.

If you're interested in a full certification course, programs are offered by all of

Bermuda's dive operators. Two of the companies, Fantasea Diving and Nautilus Diving, have a PADI five-star rating; Nautilus also has a PADI five-star Instructor Development Center. Although PADI programs are the most common, NAUI and SSI certification are also available.

Prices are competitive, but you should inquire as to what gear is included in the dive price, as it can vary depending upon the dive program and operation. If you need gear, expect to pay an extra $8 to $10 each for rental of a regulator and gauge, a BCD, a wet suit, or a set including mask, fins and snorkel.

Underwater cameras can be rented from most dive shops, but if you're planning on this, you should call in advance to get information on what equipment is available. Night dives, suitable for experienced divers only, can be arranged for around $60 from Blue Water Divers, Fantasea Diving, Scuba Look and South Side Scuba Watersports.

Fantasea Diving (☎ 236-6339, fax 236-8926, email info@fantasea.bm), Darrell's Wharf, Harbour Rd, Paget PG 01, offers a $95 'Discover Scuba' course for beginners, which includes an hour-long introductory lesson at either a hotel pool or the beach and a supervised shallow wreck dive. The price includes all equipment – just bring a bathing suit. For experienced divers, Fantasea offers a one-tank wreck and reef dive for $50 and a two-tank dive for $70.

Blue Water Divers (☎ 234-1034, fax 234-3561, email bwdivers@ibl.bm), at Robinson's Marina, PO Box SN 165, Southampton SN BX, offers a $95 introductory scuba course similar to Fantasea's, as well as an $80 follow-up beginner's dive. One-tank dives, in depths that vary from 30 to 80 feet depending upo diver's experience, cost $50, and two dives cost $70.

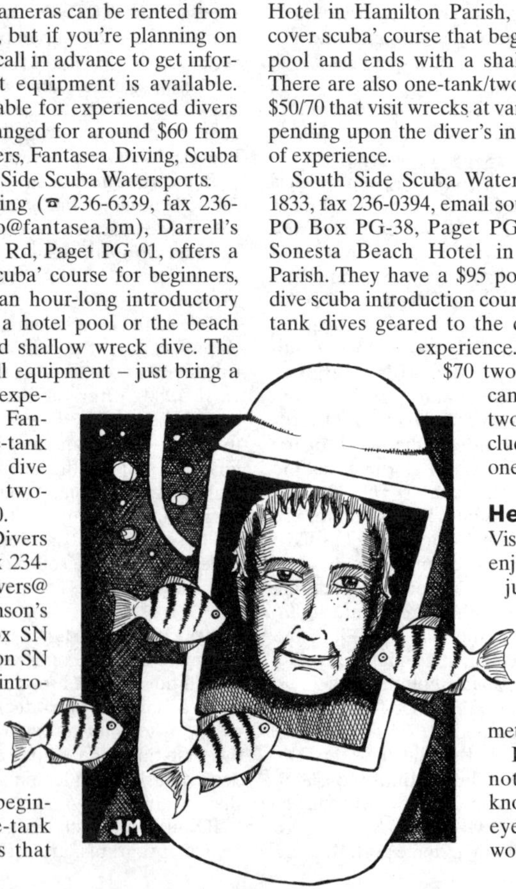

Nautilus Diving (☎ 238-2332, fax 5180, email nautilus@ibl.bm), PO Bo 237, Hamilton HM AX, has locations a the Southampton Princess hote Southampton Parish and the Ham Princess Hotel in Pembroke Parish. Na offers a $99 scuba introduction cours includes a lesson in the pool followe shallow reef dive, as well as standar tank/two-tank dives for $50/75.

Scuba Look (☎ 293-7319, 295-2421, scubaluk@ibl.bm), at the Grotto Bay Hotel in Hamilton Parish, has a $9 cover scuba' course that begins in the pool and ends with a shallow reef There are also one-tank/two-tank div $50/70 that visit wrecks at various dep pending upon the diver's interest an of experience.

South Side Scuba Watersports (☎ 1833, fax 236-0394, email southsid@ib PO Box PG-38, Paget PG BX, is Sonesta Beach Hotel in Southa Parish. They have a $95 pool-and-sh dive scuba introduction course and $5 tank dives geared to the diver's le experience. There's $70 two-tank di can either t two wrecks clude one re one wreck.

Helmet D

Visitors who enjoy a cha jump bel surface water master ing sk check c met diving.

In fact, not even h know how t eyeglasses worn, and c

nsiderations for Responsible Diving

sites tend to be located where the reefs and walls display the most beautiful corals and ıges. It only takes a moment – an inadvertently placed hand or knee, or a careless brush or kick a fin – to destroy this fragile, living part of our delicate ecosystem. By following certain basic elines while diving, you can help preserve the ecology and beauty of the reefs:

Never drop boat anchors onto a coral reef, and take care not to ground boats on coral. Encourage dive operators and regulatory bodies in their efforts to establish permanent moorings at appropriate dive sites.

Practice and maintain proper buoyancy control, and avoid over-weighting. Be aware that buoyancy can change over the period of an extended trip. Initially you may breathe harder and need more weighting; a few days later you may breathe more easily and need less weight. Tip: Use your weight belt and tank position to maintain a horizontal position – raise them to elevate your feet, lower them to elevate your upper body. Also be careful about buoyancy loss: as you go deeper, your wetsuit compresses, as does the air in your BC.

Avoid touching living marine organisms with your body and equipment. Polyps can be damaged by even the gentlest contact. Never stand on or touch living coral. The use of gloves s no longer recommended: gloves make it too easy to hold on to the reef. The abrasion caused by gloves may be even more damaging to the reef than your hands are. If you must hold on to the reef, touch only exposed rock or dead coral.

Take great care in underwater caves. Spend as little time within them as possible, as your air bubbles can damage fragile organisms. Divers should take turns inspecting the interiors of small caves or under ledges to lessen the chances of damaging contact.

Be conscious of your fins. Even without contact, the surge from heavy fin strokes near the reef can do damage. Avoid full-leg kicks when diving close to the bottom and when leaving a photo scene. When you inadvertently kick something, stop kicking! It seems obvious, but some divers either panic or are totally oblivious when they bump something. When treading water in shallow reef areas, take care not to kick up clouds of sand. Settling sand can smother the delicate reef organisms.

ecure gauges, computer consoles and the octopus regulator so they're not dangling – they are ke miniature wrecking balls to a reef.

When swimming in strong currents, be extra careful about leg kicks and handholds.

Photographers should take extra precautions, as cameras and equipment affect buoyancy. Changing f-stops, framing a subject and maintaining position for a photo often conspire to prohibit the ideal 'no-touch' approach on a reef. When you must use 'holdfasts,' choose them intelligently (ie, use one finger only for leverage off an area of dead coral).

esist the temptation to collect or buy coral or shells. Aside from the ecological damage, taking ome marine souvenirs depletes the beauty of a site and spoils other divers' enjoyment.

nsure that you take home all your trash and any litter you may find as well. Plastics in particlar pose a serious threat to marine life.

esist the temptation to feed fish. You may disturb their normal eating habits, encourage agressive behavior or feed them food that is detrimental to their health.

Minimize your disturbance of marine animals. Don't ride on the backs of turtles or manta rays, s this can cause them great anxiety.

as young as five years can participate. All you bring is a bathing suit and towel.

Participants don a headpiece, called a helmet, that has a clear face plate and works on a similar premise to a glass held upside-down in water. The helmet rests atop one's shoulders and is connected to a hose that pumps in fresh air from the boat above. The 'dive,' which lasts about 30 minutes, occurs at the sandy edge of the reef in about 10 feet of water, allowing fish and coral to be viewed up close.

Around 30 people can go out with the boat, but generally only six people go underwater at any one time. The entire outing lasts about 3½ hours. There's a shower on the boat, and wet suits are provided when the water temperature drops below 80°F.

Two companies in Bermuda offer helmet diving daily from April to November. At the height of the season, the operations have both morning and afternoon outings.

Greg Hartley's Under Sea Adventure (☎ 234-2861, email hartley@ibl.bm) departs from the Watford Bridge dock in Sandys Parish and has the advantage of going a bit farther offshore, where the water tends to be clearer. Bermuda Bell Diving (☎ 292-4434, email heldive@ibl.bm) departs from Flatts Inlet in Smith's Parish. Both charge $48 for adults, $36 for children.

SNORKELING

Snorkeling, like swimming and diving, is far more popular in the summer months, when the waters are at their warmest.

Two of the best places for snorkeling right from the beach are Church Bay, in Southampton Parish on the south shore, and Tobacco Bay, north of the Town of St George. There are also a number of other beaches where you'll find coastal outcrops that harbor colorful fish – essentially any rocky shoreline in calm waters is a potential snorkeling site.

Some of the best and most pristine snorkeling spots are too far offshore to be reached without a boat. One advantage of joining snorkeling cruises is that they often include a visit to a shipwreck – an easy task, since most wrecks tend to be found along coral reefs.

Equipment Rentals

You can save money by bringing you snorkeling equipment, but snorkel (mask, snorkel and fins) can be rent several locations around Bermuda. places give discounts for rentals lasting er than one day. If you don't use a credi a deposit of about $30 is usually requi

Adventure Enterprises (☎ 297-1459), at the erance in the Town of St George, rents s sets for $5 an hour, $20 a day.

Blue Hole Water Sports (☎ 293-2915), at Bay Beach Hotel in Hamilton Parish snorkel sets for $6 an hour, $18 a day.

Blue Water Divers (☎ 234-1034), at Rob Marina in Sandys, rents snorkel sets for $2

Fantasea Diving (☎ 236-6339), at Darrell's in Warwick, rents snorkel sets for $20 a d

Horseshoe Bay Beach House (☎ 238-2 Horseshoe Bay in Southampton Paris snorkel sets for $15 a day.

Mangrove Marina Ltd (☎ 234-0914), at S Bridge in Sandys, rents snorkel sets fo hour, $10 a day.

Nautilus Diving, at both the Southampton (☎ 238-2332) in Southampton, and the H Princess Hotel (☎ 295-9485) in Pembrok snorkel sets for $8 an hour, $24 a day. T provide masks with prescription lenses.

South Side Scuba Watersports (☎ 238-183 Sonesta Beach Hotel in Southampto snorkel sets for $6 an hour, $18 a day.

Tobacco Bay Beach House (☎ 297-2 Tobacco Bay in St George's, rents sno for $20 a day.

Windjammer Watersports (☎ 234-0250) Royal Naval Dockyard, rents snorkel set a day.

Snorkeling Cruises

Dive companies (see Diving) take s ers out on their boats to snorkel ab reefs while the divers are bene surface. The cost ranges from $35 snorkeling gear included.

However, most snorkelers are be going on a cruise designed specific snorkelers. As a rule, these sn designated tours take you to shallo where you can better view the fish f surface, rather than peering down at t

gh 20 to 40 feet of water, which com-
/ happens when you go out with divers.
st of the snorkeling cruises are combi-
n sightseeing tours; some use glass-
m boats. All include complimentary
snorkeling equipment and a bit of in-
ion for first-time snorkelers. A few
complimentary drinks; others have a
ar.

main season is from May to October. tours begin as early as April and con- nto November, but they only operate have enough customers to make it while – so the farther from summer, wer the outings offered. It's best to reservations a day or so in advance – n secure your place during busy times operators know they have customers slow periods.

ises generally last 3½ to four hours. er, if you're going along primarily for orkeling, it's a good idea to inquire he length of time that will be spent in ter, as it can vary significantly among mpanies.

ause boats depart from different piers the island, it's usually possible to one close to where you're staying.

dren's prices are usually half the re.

a Longtail Party Boat (☎ 292-0282), which s near the ferry terminal in the City of ton, uses a 65-foot motor catamaran and 35.

a Water Tours (☎ 236-1500), which departs e ferry terminal in the City of Hamilton, 50-foot glass-bottom boat. The cost is $45.

d's Snorkelling & Glass Bottom Boat s (☎ 236-9894) departs near the ferry ter- n the City of Hamilton on a 54-foot mo- that has an easy-access platform. This cally oriented operation typically goes to ne reef site not far from the *Constellation* eck. The cost is $45.

mes Cruises (☎ 296-5801) departs from 's Point in the City of Hamilton and also p passengers at Darrell's Wharf in War- has both 48-foot and 57-foot boats and $45.

Snorkelling (☎ 234-0700) departs from on's Marina at the Somerset Bridge in Sandys. Conducted by Joffre Pitman aboard his 44-foot glass-bottom motorboat, this tour includes plenty of colorful commentary and takes you farther out than most of the competition, to a splendid section of reef. The cost is $45.

Salt Kettle Boat Rentals (☎ 236-4863) departs from Salt Kettle in Paget aboard a 35-foot motorboat. It charges $45 but only goes out with a minimum of 12 passengers.

Snorkel Look (☎ 293-7319) departs from the dock at Grotto Bay Beach Hotel in Hamilton Parish aboard a 34-foot catamaran and charges $35.

Sun Deck Too Cruise (☎ 293-2640) departs from St George's aboard a 60-foot glass-bottom catamaran and charges $40.

Snorkel Park

The Bermuda Snorkel Park (☎ 234-1006), at the northwest side of the Royal Naval Dockyard, has a shallow lagoon and a nearshore reef that offers easy beach-access snorkeling.

The park's waters contain a handful of colonial-era cannons and a few dozen varieties of tropical fish, including colorful butterflyfish, turquoise wrasses and large coral-chopping parrotfish.

For $2 visitors can go in and use the beach or for $17.50 rent a snorkel, mask, fins and buoyancy vest for the day. If you want to spend only a short time in the water, you can also rent the gear for just one hour at $10. There are showers and changing rooms on site.

The snorkel park is open 9:30 am to 6 pm daily during the months of May through October.

WINDSURFING

Windsurfing has not taken off in a big way in Bermuda, but it does have its enthusiasts. Conditions tend to be best in the winter. The Great Sound sees the most windsurfing action, but the best locations change with the wind. When winds come from the south, the south shore can have decent waves for wave sailing.

Pompano Beach Club (☎ 234-0222), in Southampton, rents beginner and intermediate boards. The cost is $20 an hour or $45 for four hours.

Blue Hole Water Sports (☎ 293-2915), at the Grotto Bay Beach Hotel, rents windsurfing equipment at $25 for the first hour, $10 for each additional hour.

Windjammer Watersports (☎ 234-2050), at the Royal Naval Dockyard, rents windsurfing equipment at $35 for the first hour, $10 each additional hour.

FISHING

Ocean fishing is possible at any time of the year, but the best conditions are generally from May through November.

Game fish in Bermuda's waters include Atlantic blue marlin, white marlin, blackfin tuna, yellowfin tuna, skipjack tuna, dolphinfish (not the marine mammal), wahoo, great barracuda, greater amberjack, almaco jack, gray snapper, yellowtail snapper, Bermuda chub, bonefish, pompano and rainbow runner.

In the interest of Bermuda's conservation efforts, sport fishers are encouraged to tag and release game fish, particularly marlin and other billfish, unless they're being taken for food. Marlin, incidentally, are most prevalent from June through August. Of the approximately 200 billfish caught annually aboard charter boats off Bermuda, nearly 95% are currently being released.

Shore Fishing

Those who want to try their luck at fishing from shore can rent rods, reels and tackle for $15 a day from Windjammer Watersports (☎ 234-0250) at the Royal Naval Dockyard. Mangrove Marina (☎ 234-0914), at Robinson's Sports Centre, Somerset Bridge, Sandys, also rents equipment for $15 a day, but only for those who also rent a boat. Both places sell bait.

No licenses or fees are required to fish from shore; catches can typically include gray snapper, great barracuda, bonefish and pompano.

Deep-Sea Fishing

Boat charters are available for deep-sea fishing by either the half day or full day.

Rates vary according to the size of the boat, trip location, number of people on board etc. To charter the whole boat, expect to pay about $650 for a half day, $900 for a

Marine Life Protections

The following marine life is protecte Bermuda and may not be killed or other taken: sea turtles, all types of corals (inc ing sea fans), conchs, scallops, helmet sh bonnet shells, netted olive shells, Berm cone shells, Atlantic pearl oysters, c clams and West Indian top shells. Lob may only be taken by licensed residents only from September through March.

Spear guns are banned. Spear fishi not allowed within 1 mile of shore, an more than two fish of a single species ma speared within a 24-hour period.

full day. Individuals who join up group typically pay $85 to $110 for day, $115 to $150 for a full day. Prices i all fishing equipment; lunch and bev are not included.

Charter boats can be booked thro following offices:

Bermuda Sports Fishing Association (☎ 295-2370), Creek View House, 8 Tulo Lane, Pembroke HM 02

St George Game Fishing & Cruising Association (☎ 297-8093), PO Box GE 10 St George's GE BX

WATERSKIING

The following two companies offer skiing for all levels, from beginner vanced, and can provide instruc necessary. Rates are $40 for a quart $70 for a half hour and $120 for an h

The Bermuda Waterski Centre 3354), at Robinson's Marina, at S Bridge in Sandys, is open daily fr through September. They offer slal skis, tubes, knee boards and wake b

Blue Hole Water Sports (☎ 293-2 cated at the Grotto Bay Beach H Hamilton Parish, operates daily fr to October, weather permitting. Th slalom, knee boards, tubes, trick sk boards and children's skis.

KING

ent years, kayaking has gained in pop-
' in Bermuda. You can paddle along
ful mangrove-lined shoreline, visit
ore islands or make your own snor-
outing.

following places rent kayaks:

ole Water Sports (☎ 293-2915), at Grotto
Beach Hotel in Hamilton Parish, rents one-
n kayaks for $15 for one hour, $40 for four
, $60 for eight hours. Two-person kayaks
20/50/70 for one/four/eight hours.

ater Watersports (☎ 232-2909, ext 8919), at
bow Beach Hotel, rents one-person kayaks
7 an hour and $48 for four hours; two-
n kayaks cost $22/53 for one/four hours.

cean Watersports (☎ 235-3696), at Black-
s Hideout at Achilles Bay in St George's,
wo-person kayaks for $25 an hour, $65 for
ours.

ve Marina (☎ 234-0914), at Robinson's
a in Sandys, rents one-person kayaks for
one hour, $40 for four hours, $60 for eight
Two-person kayaks or canoes cost
70 for one/four/eight hours.

o Beach Club (☎ 234-0222), in Southamp-
nts one-person kayaks for $15 an hour,
four hours.

ide Scuba Water Sports (☎ 238-1833), at
a Beach Hotel in Southampton Parish,
ne-person kayaks for $20 an hour and
rson kayaks for $30 an hour.

nmer Watersports (☎ 234-2050), at the
Naval Dockyard, rents one-person kayaks
)/50/75 for one/four/eight hours, two-
kayaks for $25/55/80.

r option, besides renting a kayak on
vn, is to join one of the organized
g tours offered by the following
ies:

er Watersports (☎ 232-2909, ext 8919), at
Beach Hotel, offers 1½-hour kayak tours
he reef for snorkeling. The cost is $45.

Cruises (☎ 236-1300), at Darrell's Wharf
t, offers tours that take in interesting
e scenery and beaches; tours last two to
ours and cost $35 to $45.

fari (☎ 297-4223), at Ordnance Island in
n of St George, kayaks around unspoiled
in a tour that lasts about 1½ hours and
).

SAILING

If you know how to handle a small sailboat and want to head off on your own, there are several options.

Windjammer Watersports (☎ 234-0250), at the Royal Naval Dockyard, rents Sunfish sailboats that can hold two people for $30/55 for one/four hours and 17-foot Daysailers that have a capacity of up to four people for $45/90.

Blue Water Watersports (☎ 232-2909 ext 8919), at the Elbow Beach Hotel, and Blue Hole Water Sports (☎ 293-2915), at the Grotto Bay Beach Hotel, both rent two-person Sunfish sailboats at rates comparable to Windjammer Watersports.

In addition, Rance's Boatyard (☎ 292-1843), at Crow Lane in Paget, has a 16-foot Cape Cod Gemini with a capacity of up to six people that rents for $75 for four hours, $110 for eight hours.

SIGHTSEEING CRUISES

A number of companies offer sightseeing boat cruises that take in coastal scenery. Some operate in glass-bottom boats that allow you to view coral, fish and shipwrecks. In addition to the following cruises, see the earlier Snorkeling Cruises section.

Argo Adventures (☎ 297-1459), which departs from Ordnance Island in the Town of St George, has a 25-foot motorboat and a 36-foot trimaran and offers cruises to nature reserves, beaches and reefs for $40.

Bermuda Island Cruises (☎ 292-8652), which departs from the ferry terminal in the City of Hamilton, uses a 68-foot motor yacht with a glass bottom and charges $30 for a two-hour tour.

Bermuda Water Tours (☎ 236-1500), which departs near the ferry terminal in the City of Hamilton, offers a glass-bottom boat cruise that lasts two hours and costs $30.

Coral Sea Cruises (☎ 297-4223) operates a 60-foot glass-bottom boat from Ordnance Island in the Town of St George on a one-hour cruise to a coral reef for $20.

Fantasea Cruises (☎ 236-1300), at Darrell's Wharf in Paget, has a 55-foot catamaran and offers a variety of sailing options, including dinner and sunset cruises, with prices from $40.

Charter Cruises

If you're traveling with a group and want to draw up your own itinerary, it's possible to charter a skippered yacht for day cruises. The tourist office maintains an updated list of about a dozen boats that are available for chartering.

Prices vary depending upon the boat. Near the low end is Starlight Sailing Cruises (☎ 292-1834), which has the 31-foot sloop *Starlight* and charges $200 for up people on a three-hour sail, $400 for hour sail. At the high end is Salt Kettle Rentals (☎ 236-4863), which has the 5 sloop *Bright Star* and charges $500 for eight people for a three-hour sail or $8 a six-hour sail. These two companies, a as most of the other charter yacht include swimming and snorkeling st part of the cruise.

ty of Hamilton

ity of Hamilton is the hub of Bermuda, g as both its capital and commercial . Although it's not a large city, it has a sing amount of hustle and bustle – at n comparison to the rest of the island. milton has the main government of- a handful of interesting sightseeing and the island's largest collection of In addition, Hamilton rates as the ining locale in Bermuda, in terms of election and price.

nilton's pulse is Front St, a harbor- road lined with Victorian buildings in pastels of lemon, lime, apricot and sky Many of them have overhanging ve- , where you can linger over lunch and the boats ferry across the harbor.

nilton serves as a central terminus and r point for island buses, so you can to visit the city frequently if you use blic bus system. Note that Hamilton is nly called 'town' by Bermudians, so to town' means, without a doubt, o Hamilton.

City of Hamilton is in Pembroke sights and accommodations outside y boundaries are described in the oke Parish chapter.

ry

y is named for Sir Henry Hamilton, rmuda governor (1788-94) who en- ed the building of a town in the part of Bermuda in order to have a ent convenient to all islanders. The wn adopted the motto *Hamilton Collegit*, meaning 'Hamilton has t together the scattered,' which can found on the town's coat of arms.

'90, the grand design of Hamilton was , with 50-foot-wide streets in a neat ttern that covered an area of about es and spread north half a dozen from a new commercial harbor. By e town had taken shape and the first al elections were held in the new ll.

Highlights

- Linger over a drink at one of the veranda restaurants overlooking Front St
- Delve into the past at the Bermuda Historical Society Museum
- Walk up to Fort Hamilton for a fine hilltop view of the city

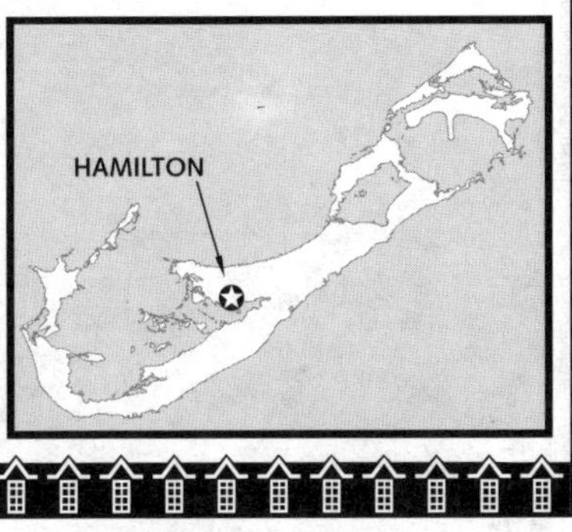

Hamilton prospered and grew so quickly that in just two decades it had become the biggest town in Bermuda. In 1815, the capital was relocated from St George to Hamilton. In 1897, Hamilton's status was changed from that of a town to a city.

Although little more than 1000 people live in the narrow boundaries of the city itself, nearly a quarter of the island's population lives within a 2-mile radius of the city.

Information

Tourist Offices The Visitors Service Bureau (☎ 295-1480), at 8 Front St, next to the ferry terminal, is open 9 am to 5 pm Monday to Saturday. The hours are currently the same year-round, but in the past the office has closed at 2 pm in winter, so if you're planning on dropping by in the off-season, it's probably a good idea to get there early. This is a good place to pick up islandwide tourist brochures and maps, as well as get specific

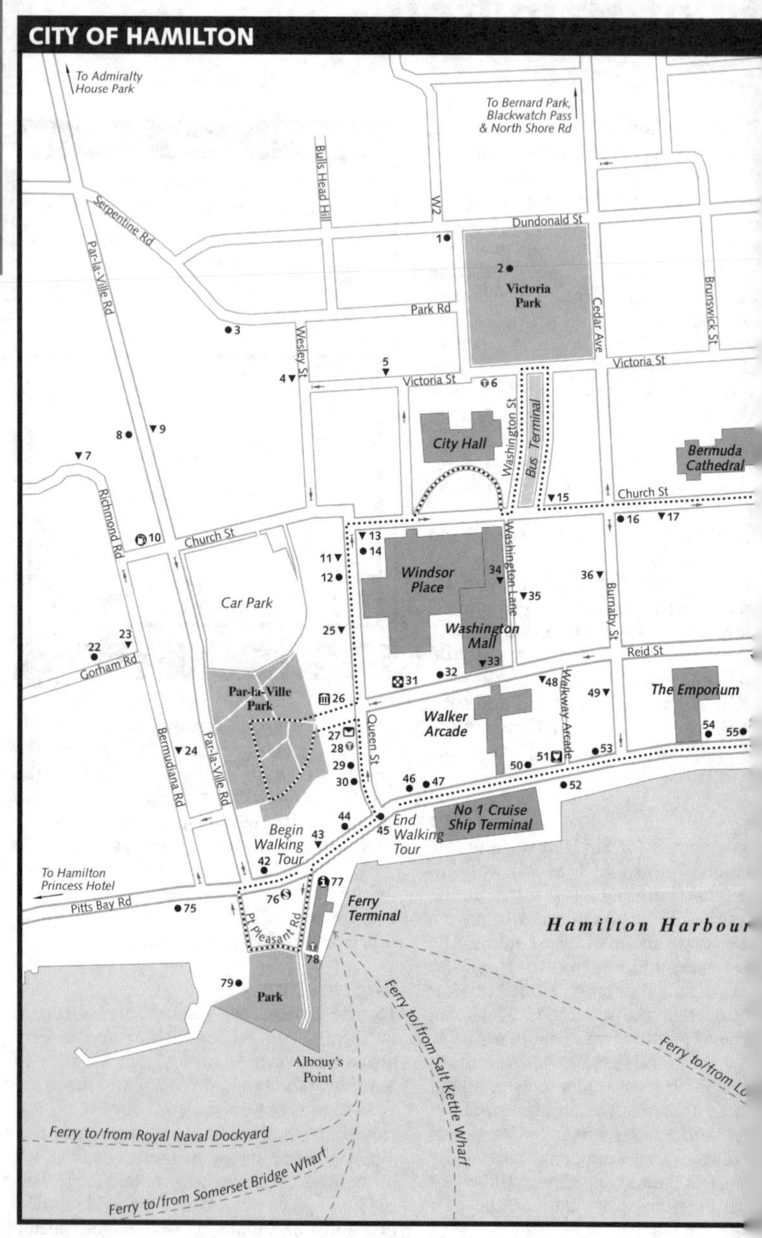
CITY OF HAMILTON
To Admiralty House Park
To Bernard Park, Blackwatch Pass & North Shore Rd
Bulls Head Hill
W2
Serpentine Rd
Dundonald St
Par-la-Ville Rd
Victoria Park
Park Rd
Cedar Ave
Brunswick St
Wesley St
Victoria St
City Hall
Washington St
Bus Terminal
Bermuda Cathedral
Richmond Rd
Church St
Windsor Place
Washington Lane
Washington Mall
Burnaby St
Car Park
Gorham Rd
Reid St
Par-la-Ville Park
Walker Arcade
Walkway Arcade
The Emporium
Bermudiana Rd
Queen St
No 1 Cruise Ship Terminal
Begin Walking Tour
End Walking Tour
To Hamilton Princess Hotel
Pitts Bay Rd
Pt Pleasant Rd
Ferry Terminal
Hamilton Harbour
Park
Albouy's Point
Ferry to/from Salt Kettle Wharf
Ferry to/from Royal Naval Dockyard
Ferry to/from Somerset Bridge Wharf

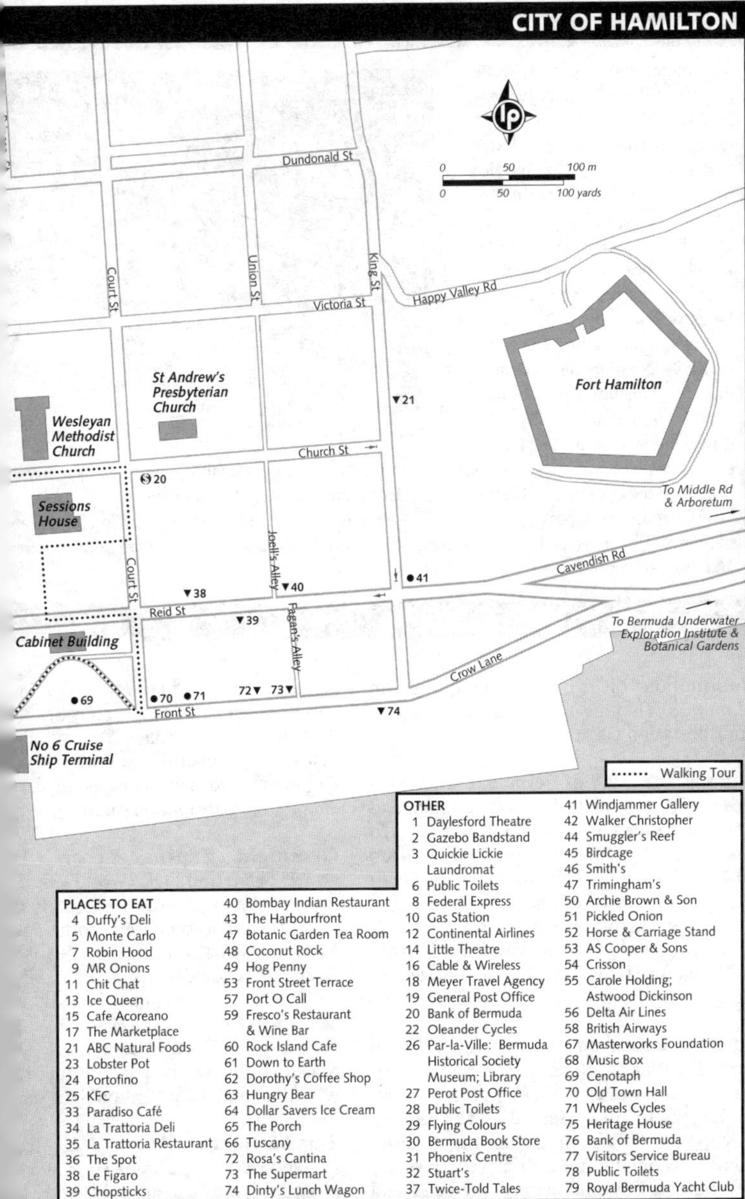
CITY OF HAMILTON
0 50 100 m
0 50 100 yards
Dundonald St
Court St
Union St
King St
Victoria St
Happy Valley Rd
St Andrew's Presbyterian Church
Fort Hamilton
Wesleyan Methodist Church
Church St
20
21
Sessions House
To Middle Rd & Arboretum
Joell's Alley
40
41
Cavendish Rd
38
Reid St
39
Fagan's Alley
To Bermuda Underwater Exploration Institute & Botanical Gardens
Cabinet Building
Crow Lane
69
70
71
72
73
Front St
74
No 6 Cruise Ship Terminal
Walking Tour
PLACES TO EAT
4 Duffy's Deli
5 Monte Carlo
7 Robin Hood
9 MR Onions
11 Chit Chat
13 Ice Queen
15 Cafe Acoreano
17 The Marketplace
21 ABC Natural Foods
23 Lobster Pot
24 Portofino
25 KFC
33 Paradiso Café
34 La Trattoria Deli
35 La Trattoria Restaurant
36 The Spot
38 Le Figaro
39 Chopsticks
40 Bombay Indian Restaurant
43 The Harbourfront
47 Botanic Garden Tea Room
48 Coconut Rock
49 Hog Penny
53 Front Street Terrace
57 Port O Call
59 Fresco's Restaurant & Wine Bar
60 Rock Island Cafe
61 Down to Earth
62 Dorothy's Coffee Shop
63 Hungry Bear
64 Dollar Savers Ice Cream
65 The Porch
66 Tuscany
72 Rosa's Cantina
73 The Supermart
74 Dinty's Lunch Wagon
OTHER
1 Daylesford Theatre
2 Gazebo Bandstand
3 Quickie Lickie Laundromat
6 Public Toilets
8 Federal Express
10 Gas Station
12 Continental Airlines
14 Little Theatre
16 Cable & Wireless
18 Meyer Travel Agency
19 General Post Office
20 Bank of Bermuda
22 Oleander Cycles
26 Par-la-Ville: Bermuda Historical Society Museum; Library
27 Perot Post Office
28 Public Toilets
29 Flying Colours
30 Bermuda Book Store
31 Phoenix Centre
32 Stuart's
37 Twice-Told Tales
41 Windjammer Gallery
42 Walker Christopher
44 Smuggler's Reef
45 Birdcage
46 Smith's
47 Trimingham's
50 Archie Brown & Son
51 Pickled Onion
52 Horse & Carriage Stand
53 AS Cooper & Sons
54 Crisson
55 Carole Holding; Astwood Dickinson
56 Delta Air Lines
58 British Airways
67 Masterworks Foundation
68 Music Box
69 Cenotaph
70 Old Town Hall
71 Wheels Cycles
75 Heritage House
76 Bank of Bermuda
77 Visitors Service Bureau
78 Public Toilets
79 Royal Bermuda Yacht Club

Greetings from Johnny

BERMUDA DEPARTMENT OF TOURISM

You might be surprised to be greeted at the Hamilton city limits by a cheery gentleman waving with both hands, blowing kisses and shouting, 'I love you.' No, he's not running for public office, nor has he slipped off the deep end. But he may well be the friendliest person in Bermuda.

Johnny Barnes, who is sometimes referred to as 'Bermuda's goodwill ambassador,' has been faithfully greeting the Hamilton morning commuters for the past 20 years. A retired bus driver, this spry octogenarian sporting a generous silver beard and a straw hat stands at the Crow Lane roundabout, just east of the Berr Underwater Exploration Institute (BUEI), 5 to 10 am each weekday morning.

If you happen to pass by outside of these hours, you can still be greeted by Johnny Barne the form of a bronze statue, hands outstretched, on the ocean side of the road between the and the roundabout.

information on current happenings in Hamilton. They also sell phone cards and transportation passes.

Money The Bank of Bermuda, with an office on Front St near the ferry terminal and another on the corner of Court and Church Sts, is open 9:30 am to 4 pm Monday, 8:30 am to 4 pm Tuesday to Thursday and 8:30 am to 4:30 pm Friday. If you have a major credit card or a Cirrus or Plus system banking card, you can get cash withdrawals from sidewalk ATMs available at either branch 24 hours a day.

Post & Communications The General Post Office, at the corner of Church and Parliament Sts, is open 8 am to 5 pm weekdays and 8 am to noon Saturday. The branch Perot Post Office on Queen St, opposite Reid St, is open 9 am to 5 pm weekdays.

You can buy phone cards or send and receive faxes, telegrams and telexes at the Cable & Wireless office (☎ 297-7022), corner of Church and Burnaby Sts; it' 9 am to 5 pm weekdays. You can als faxes at the General Post Office. See Communications in the Facts for the chapter for information on price.

Overnight Express Federal E (☎ 295-3854) and DHL Worldwide E (☎ 295-3300) operate express delive vices. The cutoff time for sending a p for next-day delivery to the USA is 3 pm. The Federal Express office at Ville Place, 14 Par-la-Ville Rd, i 8:30 am to 6 pm weekdays and 9 am Saturday. The DHL office, at the Was Mall, 16 Church St, is open 8:30 am to weekdays and 9 am to noon Saturda

Email & Internet Access Twice-To (☎ 296-1995), a used-book store at 34 ment St, has two computers with I access at $7 an hour, but there can b

t's open 8 am to 5 pm weekdays and to 4 pm Saturday.

t Chat (☎ 292-3400), a cybercafe at 27 ı St, has a dozen computers and the connections, at 128K. The cost is $4 lf-hour. It's open 11 am to 10 pm Mon- Saturday.

MR Onions restaurant (☎ 292-5012), -la-Ville Rd, has six Internet-connected ıters set up in its lounge. The cost is r the first hour and $5 for each addi- hour. It's open noon to 1 am nightly.

Agencies There are a number of agents in the city center, including Travel Agency (☎ 295-4176) at 35 h St, opposite the General Post Office.

e Offices British Airways (☎ 293- is at 89 Front St; Delta Air Lines -1024) is nearby at 85 Front St. Air a (☎ 295-4587) and American Airlines -1420) are on the 2nd floor of Windsor on Queen St, and Continental Airlines -6329) is at 27 Queen St. All of these ket offices are open 9 am to 5 pm ays, except for American Airlines, s open 8 am to 5:15 pm weekdays and 1 pm Saturday.

tores The Bookmart, upstairs in the x Centre at 3 Reid St, is Bermuda's d biggest bookstore, with a good se- of books about Bermuda as well as tional best-sellers. The Bermuda tore, on Queen St just north of Front naller but also has an extensive col- of island books.

e-Told Tales, 34 Parliament St, sells eneral-interest books at reasonable and also has rare 1st-edition books Bermuda.

tands Newspaper Express, on the floor of the Phoenix Centre, 3 Reid a wide variety of US, Canadian and newspapers, including most of the loids.

ington Mall Magazines, in the Wash- Mall, carries the most international n of newspapers and magazines, with a far-flung range that includes Italy's *La Stampa* and the *New Zealand Herald*.

Libraries The public library (☎ 295-2905), in the Par-la-Ville building at 13 Queen St, has a good reference collection of books about Bermuda and subscribes to international newspapers, including the *Boston Globe*, the *New York Times*, the *Guardian* and Britain's *Sunday Times*. Its normal opening hours are 9 am to 6 pm weekdays and 9 am to 5 pm Saturday, but on at least a temporary basis the library has also been open most evenings until 8 pm and on Sunday afternoons as well.

Laundry Quickie Lickie Laundromat (☎ 295-6097), 74 Serpentine Rd, just north-west of the city center, has coin-operated washing machines and dryers. It's open 6 am to 10 pm Monday to Saturday and 6 am to 6 pm Sunday.

Toilets Public toilets can be found in numerous places around the city, including in back of the tourist office; just south of Perot Post Office on Queen St; and on Victoria St, around the corner from the bus terminal.

Photo Shops Bermuda Photo Craftsmen (☎ 295-2698), in the Walker Arcade, carries print and slide film, though prices are high. For example, the purchase price for a 36-exposure roll of Kodak Gold print film is $9, and the cost to develop and print 36 exposures is around $28.

Camcorder videotapes can be purchased for $6 at Stuart's (☎ 295-5496), on Reid St just west of the Washington Mall. Stuart's also carries camcorder batteries and accessories.

Emergency Hamilton's police station (☎ 295-0011) is at 42 Parliament St. Dial ☎ 911 for ambulance, police and fire emergencies. There are numerous pharmacies in Hamilton, including the Phoenix Drug Store (☎ 295-3838), in the Phoenix Centre, 3 Reid St.

Dangers & Annoyances The north side of Hamilton, called 'back of town' or 'backside' by islanders, is not well regarded for safety, particularly after dark. Back of town has higher-than-average issues with violent crime, theft and drugs. Simply put, it is best to avoid walking at all in the area north of Victoria St at night, and even during the day it's not wise to carry a purse or other obvious valuables.

Also note that the heavily walked section of Pitts Bay Rd between town and the Hamilton Princess Hotel has seen a fair share of purse snatchings. One precaution to thwart drive-by snatchers is simply to carry your bag close to your body, away from the road.

Walking Tour

Sights marked with an asterisk (*) are given more detail under separate headings at the end of this Walking Tour section.

The tourist office on Front St is a good starting point for an enjoyable half-day walking tour that takes in the main sights of central Hamilton. You can explore this part of the waterfront before beginning your walk. Behind the Bank of Bermuda you'll find the picturesque salmon-colored building that quarters the **Royal Bermuda Yacht Club**, as well as **Albouy's Point**, where there's a little grassy park with benches and water views. The Bank of Bermuda itself has the island's most notable **coin collection***.

At the intersection of Queen and Front Sts, there's a colorful box that's sometimes used by a bobby (police officer) for directing traffic. With its supporting posts and little roof, it's easy to see why it's nicknamed the **birdcage**.

If you head north on Queen St, you'll shortly come to the **Perot Post Office**, which occupies a classic Bermudian building, whitewashed with black shutters, that was erected by Postmaster William Perot on his own property in 1842. As is duly noted on the bronze plaque fronting the building, it was here, in 1848, that Perot issued the first Bermudian postage stamps. Although the main post office has long since moved to larger quarters, this historic building still functions as a neighborhood post office.

Next to the post office is **Par-la-Ville**, a graceful Georgian-style house built in 1814 by William Perot, father of the aforemen-

tioned Hamilton postmaster. This b now houses the public **library** a **Bermuda Historical Society Museum** the family gardens have been turn **Par-la-Ville Park**. This public park c pleasant respite of birdsong in the ci ter and has lawns, flowers and a va trees, including Bermuda cedar and India rubber tree, both found at the e of the grounds. The rear entrance off Ville Rd, at the southwestern end of th is spanned by Bermuda's oldest moo

The **rubber tree** *(Ficus elastica)*, shades the library, was planted by p ter Perot in 1847 using a seed se British Guiana by his son Adolphu often the case with exotics, the tree h its environment as well as it may app extensive root system not only beyond the library and post office, spread clear down to the waterfront its way through cement en route! S tree's historic significance has thus f it from the ax.

Continuing north on Queen St, be on Church St and you'll arrive at **ci**

houses two art galleries and has a
ɛr of other interesting features both
and out.

Washington St, the site of the main
rminal, you can make a detour one
north to **Victoria Park**, a quiet green
with shaded lawns, tall trees and a
ıan-style bandstand that, fittingly, was
d in 1887 in Queen Victoria's honor.

ɔu make your way back to Church St,
almost immediately come to the An-
Bermuda Cathedral, a weighty neo-
building that is one of the city's most
ant landmarks. Construction on the
ıg began in 1894, after an arsonist
down the original church, and the
t structure wasn't completed until
Built of native limestone block, the
ral has lofty arches and handsome
-glass windows. Entry to the cathe-
ree. For $3 you can climb the 157 steps
op of the church tower for a sweep-
-degree view of greater Hamilton.

ou continue on Church St, it's easy to
v the street got its name, as there's a
on every block. **Wesleyan Methodist**
is first up, followed **St Andrew's Pres-**
ı Church, a pretty pink building that
o 1846, which makes it the oldest
still standing in the city.

ding south on Court St, you'll pass
da's two 19th-century government
gs, **Sessions House*** and the **Cabinet**
g*, both of which are open to the

ıe east corner of Court and Front Sts
ld town hall, a building with one of
gest histories in Hamilton. It was
in 1794 as a warehouse for customs,
ıs a meeting place for the House of
ly from 1815 to 1822 and was con-
nto Hamilton's city hall in the late
ıtury. It is currently used as the Reg-
the Supreme Court.

ınue west on Front St to view the
h, a war remembrance monument
Bermuda limestone. The corner-
as laid in 1920 by the Prince of
The monument is a replica of the
h that stands in Whitehall, London.

As you walk west on Front St, back toward the tourist office, you'll pass Hamilton's cruise ship docks on the left and the city's most fanciful Victorian buildings on the right.

Coin Collection

A fascinating coin collection, displayed in half a dozen glass cases, can be viewed on the 2nd-floor mezzanine of the Bank of Bermuda on Front St.

Many of the coins were collected by the late E Rodovan Bell, who focused on acquiring coins that over the years would have been accepted as a currency of trade in Bermuda. These include British coins from

A Pretty Penny

William Benet Perot, Hamilton's first postmaster, was a colorful character best known in posterity for the postage stamps he created.

After the Post Office Act of 1842 established the cost of mailing a domestic letter at one penny, Perot set up two boxes in his post office, one where customers dropped the letter to be mailed and the other where they dropped a penny coin to cover the postage. Over time, Perot discovered that he was collecting more letters than pennies.

To stem his losses, in 1848 Perot decided to drop the honor system and create his own stamps. He stamped them 12 to a sheet, using a cancellation seal so that each circular imprint read 'Hamilton, Bermuda' along with the year. Perot then wrote 'one penny' where the date would normally appear and signed each 'WB Perot.'

Not only did the stamps generate enough money for Perot to keep the postal system solvent, but a century and a half later they've become prized collector's items, a single one having fetched £185,000 at a Christie's auction in London. Of the thousands of stamps Perot created, only 11 are known to still exist, and seven of these are in the royal stamp collection of Queen Elizabeth II.

1603 to the present, coins and tokens of the English-American colonies and early US coins. Many of the coins are made of gold or silver.

Of greatest interest is the complete set of 'hog money,' which was Bermuda's original currency and the first British colonial coins ever made. These were rough-stamped in Bermuda from 1614 and show a sailing ship on one side and the imprint of a hog on the other. This rare collection includes twopence, threepence, sixpence and shilling coins.

The hog, incidentally, takes its lofty status from having been a significant food source for the earliest British settlers, who shipwrecked on the island in 1609. Although hog money hasn't been minted for two centuries, it continues in a modified form, with the hog appearing on the back of present-day Bermudian pennies.

To get to the collection, take the elevator in the front lobby and push 'M' for the mezzanine. The bank hours are 9:30 am to 4 pm Monday, 8:30 am to 4 pm Tuesday to Thursday and 8:30 am to 4:30 pm Friday.

Bermuda Historical Society Museum

The Bermuda Historical Society Museum occupies the front rooms of Par-la-Ville, the Queen St building that also houses the public library.

In the lobby you'll find models of the ill-fated *Sea Venture* and the two ships that Admiral George Somers built to replace it. In the same room is Somers' sea chest, made of Italian cypress, flanked by portraits of Somers and his wife.

Other items on display from that period include the lodestone that Somers used to magnetize his compass, a 1615 'hog money' shilling and a map of Bermuda drawn in 1622. There are also portraits of the Perots, who built this house in 1814, pieces of period china painted by Josiah Wedgwood and two rooms of 18th-century furniture b
Bermuda cedar. The museum has
quirky items as well, including a Cor
ate officer's sword that was forg
London and items made by Boer pri
of war during their stay in Be
at the end of the 19th ce

One other curious i
display is a copy of a
written by George
ington in 1775 re
ing the support
people of Berm
the American st
for independence

The Bermuda H
cal Society Muse
open 9:30 am to 3:
Monday to Saturday. A
sion is free, but donatio
welcomed.

City Hall

The whitewashed city hall on Chur
handsome building of limestone blo
struction, was designed by Bermudia
tect Wilfred Onions and completed i

Exterior features include a promin
foot-high tower; a colorful insignia
city crest; and pointy 'eyebrows,' a
decorative detail crowning the wind
the building's right side. If you step
bit and stare up to the top of the
you'll be able to see a weathervane
with a bronze replica of the *Sea Vent*
boat that brought Bermuda's first
The water fountain fronting city h
tains two lifelike statues of playful c
created by renowned Bermudian s
Desmond Fountain.

Inside, the foyer walls are decorat
the portraits of the former mayors of
ton, some painted by Antoine Verp
French artist who retired to Bermud
1930s. The foyer also contains an oil p
of Queen Elizabeth; another conter
statue by Desmond Fountain; and
chandeliers made of Canadian p
though they bear an odd resembl
cement. The most attractive woodw
staircase and doors, is made of nativ

NED FRIARY

ɪ 'cake icing' roofs collect rainwater on a typical Bermudian inn.

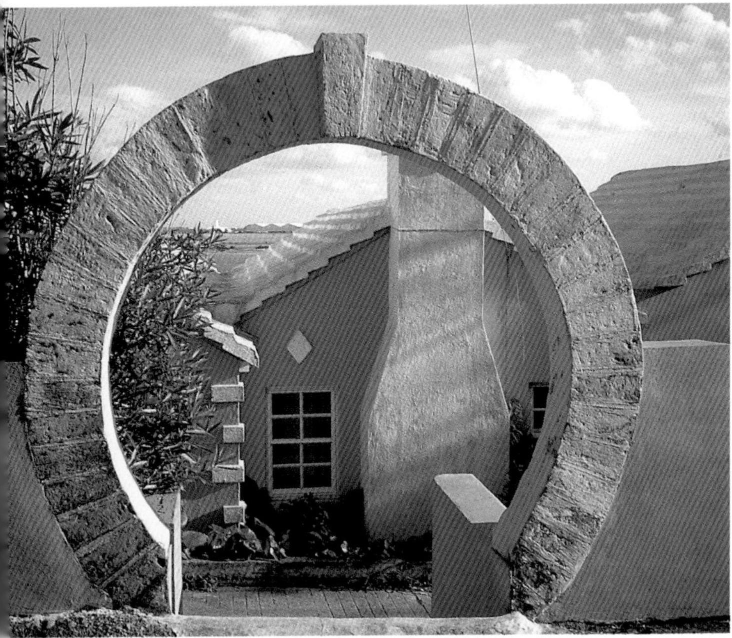

NED FRIARY

tes are said to bring good luck to those who pass through them.

NED FRIARY
The Bermuda Cathedral, City of Hamilton

NED FRIARY
Spinnaker's building, Front St, City of Har

NED FRIARY
Bermudian windows, gabled and shutter

NED FRIARY
City of Hamilton's waterfront

PIERCE & NEWMAN

g with an ocean view

LAWSON WOOD

Boating near Boaz Island

LAWSON WOOD

n the *Nola*, Western Blue Cut

NED FRIARY

Cottages look out on Little Sound.

LAWSON WOOD

Spanish Point Cave, Pembroke Parish

the left side of the foyer is a 378-seat r that is used for local plays and con- as well as for international perform- which in the past have included the h Chamber Orchestra and the Royal a Ballet.

ou're interested in postage stamps, n find one of the island's best collec- a the city office at the right side of the Known as the Benbow Collection, mps were donated by Colin Benbow, er member of Parliament and the curator of the Bermuda Historical Museum.

city hall is open 9 am to 5 pm week- ough the foyer is usually open on ds as well.

da National Gallery The national established in 1992, occupies the east he 2nd floor of city hall.

Hereward T Watlington Room con- e gallery's initial collection, some 18 an paintings spanning the 15th to nturies. These include a portrait of an patriot Thomas Paine by George and works by Thomas Gainsbor- shua Reynolds and Cornelius de Vos. allery's permanent collection also in- Vest African sculptures, ceremonial and masks, a few 18th- and 19th- Bermudian portraits, and contem- photography by islanders Richard s and deForest Trimingham.

lition, there are temporary exhibits d art that have ranged from the f 19th-century Bermudian water- sts to an international collection of orary Azorean art.

llery (☎ 295-9428) is open 10 am to nday to Saturday. Admission is $3 , free for children under 16.

a Society of Arts Gallery At side of the 2nd floor of city hall, uda Society of Arts displays and ks by resident and visiting artists. these pieces, which include both nd realistic works, depict scenes da through the media of water- stels and oils. The gallery is open 10 am to 4 pm Monday to Saturday, and admission is free.

Sessions House

Hamilton's centerpiece building, the Sessions House, dates to 1817, though it owes much of its grand appearance, including the landmark clock tower, Italianate ornamentation and terra-cotta colonnade, to additions made in 1887 marking Queen Victoria's golden jubilee.

Bermuda's parliamentary meeting house for the 40-member House of Assembly, Sessions House also serves as the chambers of the Supreme Court.

The House of Assembly meetings take place on the 2nd floor, where the speaker of the house, outfitted in typical British wig and robes and flanked by paintings of King George III and Queen Charlotte, presides over parliamentary debate.

The desk of the speaker's clerk, which stands between the speaker and the assembly, is inset with the coat of arms of the Virginia Company; whenever the House is in session, it is topped by a silver mace that symbolizes the speaker's authority. The members of the House, in typical Westminster style, are arranged in rows on either side of the chamber, with the two major parties facing each other.

House sessions, which are open to the public, are held at 10 am on Friday from late October through July. If you happen to be around at budget time (in February and March), the House often convenes on Monday and Wednesday as well as Friday.

In addition, the assembly meeting room is open year-round for public viewing from 9 am to 12:30 pm and 2 to 5 pm weekdays. Photography is only allowed when the House is not in session.

Cabinet Building

The 19th-century Cabinet Building, a stately two-story limestone structure, contains the meeting chamber of Bermuda's Senate. From 9 am to 5 pm weekdays year-round, visitors are free to climb the steps to the 2nd-floor chamber, which holds the round table where the 11 members of the Senate

NED FRIARY

The Cabinet Building, City of Hamilton

conduct business. Their sessions, which are open to the public, are held at 10 am each Wednesday from late October to July.

The Cabinet's round table, although not its chamber, has also been used for meetings between international heads of state. In 1953, the table was dismantled and removed to a private location for a conference between Sir Winston Churchill and President Dwight Eisenhower. In 1971, the table was moved, this time to Government Hou a meeting between Prime Minister E Heath and President Richard Nixon.

Fort Hamilton

This substantial hilltop fort was or series of island fortifications erected mid-19th century during a period o tensions between Great Britain and th

Fort Hamilton remains intact, i parts mounted with 10-inch rifled r loader guns that were capable of 400lb cannonball through an 11-inc iron plate – more than enough pene force to have sliced any iron-hullec that sailed the seas. But as history have it, no enemy ships ever appear

Today this carefully renovated fc much park as historic site and make joyable place to explore. The sout ramparts offer a bird's-eye view of H Harbour. You can also scurry abou fortification's dungeon-like magazin you'll find gun embrasures, shell ho nitions storage rooms and the like.

Don't miss taking a stroll thro fort's narrow moat, which has bee

'November to March' Activities

To lure more people to the island in the off-season, the Bermuda Dept of Tourism offers v special series of weekly activities from November 1 to March 31. All of the activities are fre

At 10 am on Monday, a guided walking tour of the City of Hamilton begins at the wa tourist office. At 11:15 am there's a tour of the parliamentary Sessions House and at noon t colorful skirling ceremony at historic Fort Hamilton; both are included in the walking tour o taken in separately. At 3 pm, there's a Tea & Fashion Show at the No 1 cruise ship passenge nal on Hamilton's Front St.

At 10:30 am on Tuesday in Hamilton, there's an hour-long Heritage & Cultural Trail W covers the city's history and starts at the Cabinet Building. At 3 pm, also in the City of Har performance by a troupe of costumed Gombey dancers takes place at the No 1 cruise ship ger terminal, complete with fruit punch and cookies. If you prefer to do your own dancing ballroom dancing at the Hamilton Princess Hotel from 8 to 11 pm.

On Wednesday, the Town of St George offers an hour-long walking tour from King's S 10:30 am, ending with a greeting from the mayor in town hall, and a noontime reenactme ducking-stool punishment that was once meted out to gossipers. If you miss the first walk

ne of Hamilton's more unusual gar-
andwiched between the steep walls of
t's inner and outer ramparts, this dry
is cool and shady with a luxuriant
of ferns, bamboo and other tropical
tion; some of the plants are identified
ame plaques.

somewhat inconspicuous entrances
magazine and moat are both to the
the main fort entrance, immediately
ou cross the bridge over the moat.
amilton is open 9:30 am to 5 pm daily
try is free.

u're in Bermuda during the winter
(November through March), try to
ur visit to coincide with the colorful
performance held at noon on
ys by the kilted bagpipers and drum-
the Bermuda Islands Pipe Band. If
nt to linger a little after the skirling
nance, a small volunteer-run tea
pens at that time, selling inexpensive
ea and scones.

et to the fort from the city center,
st on Church St, which terminates at
, where you'll turn left. Continue
King St for a block; at the top of
make a sharp right onto Happy
Valley Rd – the fort is about 150 yards farther east. Although it's just a 10- to 15-minute walk from town, not many visitors come up this way, making it a peaceful retreat from the city's hustle and bustle.

Places to Stay

There are no places to stay within the strict boundaries of the City of Hamilton, but there are numerous places within walking distance of town; these are detailed in the following Pembroke Parish chapter.

Places to Eat – Budget

Markets *The Supermart (125 Front St)* is a good-size grocery store near the waterfront that's open 7:30 am to 8 pm Monday to Saturday and 1 to 5 pm Sunday. The store's biggest draw, especially among lunchtime office workers, is its extensive take-out salad bar ($5.75 per pound) that has the usual greens and veggies as well as more than a dozen hot dishes including macaroni and cheese, fried chicken and spareribs.

The Marketplace, a popular grocery store on Church St near the Bermuda Cathedral, is open 7 am to 10 pm Monday to Saturday and 1 to 5 pm Sunday. This large, well-stocked

'November to March' Activities

another one at 1:30 pm. For those who want to learn about Bermudian cuisine, a cooking
stration is given from 2:30 to 4 pm at the No 1 cruise ship passenger terminal in the City of
n.

sday features Bermuda's West End, with an hour-long walking tour of Somerset departing at
from the Somerset County Squire restaurant on Mangrove Bay.

y is for nature lovers. At 10:30 am there's a tour of the Bermuda Botanical Gardens in Paget
beginning at the garden's visitor center, and at 1 pm there's a tour of Spittal Pond Nature
in Smith's Parish, beginning at the east-end parking lot.

day again features an hour-long walking tour of the Town of St George, starting at King's
at 10:30 am. As with the Tuesday tour, this includes a greeting from the mayor in town hall
noontime ducking-stool reenactment.

nain Sunday events are at the Royal Naval Dockyard, where a walking tour with a focus on
egins at the Clocktower Mall at 11:15 am; meet outdoors at the anchor fountain, between
clock towers. At 2:15 pm a more conventional walking tour of the Dockyard begins at the
to the craft market.

store has a produce section; a selection of wines, beer and spirits; a bakery with inexpensive doughnuts and muffins; a deli with salads and sandwiches; and a simple salad bar with fruit, greens and fried chicken for $5 per pound.

Down to Earth *(56 Reid St)* is Hamilton's biggest and best natural foods store. A friendly owner-run place, it carries vitamins, wholesome snacks such as trail mix and rice cakes, soy-based yogurt, rennetless cheese, organic cereals and frozen foods. There's also a juice bar that whips up a variety of tasty tropical fruit smoothies ($3) that can be spiked with add-ins such as ginseng, spirulina and bee pollen. The store is open 9 am to 5:30 pm Monday to Saturday, the juice bar 10 am to 4:30 pm.

Also centrally located but with a much more limited selection is ***The Health Store***, at the Washington Mall, which is open 9 am to 5 pm Monday to Saturday; try the healthy homemade cookies (25¢). The Seventh-Day Adventist church, on the east side of the city, operates ***ABC Natural Foods*** *(41 King St)*, which has packaged foods, bulk grains and vitamins; it's open 9 am to 5:15 pm Monday to Thursday, 9 am to 1:15 pm Friday and 10 am to 2 pm Sunday.

Cafes, Delis & Fast Food The only international fast-food chain in Bermuda is ***KFC*** *(☎ 296-4532, 23 Queen St)*, which features the colonel's standard menu; two pieces of chicken and a roll will set you back $5. It's open 11 am to 10 pm Monday to Saturday and 11 am to 9 pm Sunday.

Ice Queen *(☎ 292-6497)*, on the corner of Queen and Church Sts, is a tidy little fast-food eatery that doubles as the refreshment stand for the Little Theatre. Virtually everything is priced under $5, including beef burgers, gardenburgers, fried chicken and soft-serve ice cream. It's open 10 am to midnight daily.

Dollar Savers Ice Cream *(☎ 292-5732, 95 Front St)*, a cubbyhole shop at the side of Dollar Savers convenience store, sells island-made ice cream. For a treat, try the rum and ginger flavor, a tangy local favorite; the large cone ($2.75) is stacked high enough to satisfy any craving. Op hours are 7:30 am to 10 pm weekdays to 6 pm Saturday and 9 am to 2 pm S

Anyone in Bermuda can point y ***Dorothy's Coffee Shop*** *(☎ 292-413* Chancery Lane, for the best burgers country. It's a simple little breakfa lunch spot with stools set around shaped counter. Hamburgers cost ab cheeseburgers $3.50, and omelette toast start at $5. It's open 7:15 am t weekdays, 8 am to 2 pm Saturday.

La Trattoria Deli *(☎ 295-9499)*, a h the-wall on Washington Lane, sells ge $3 slices of pizza, as well as lasagna with meatballs and other Italian ite around $5, all for take-out only. If yo to eat light, they also make a recon able vegetarian avocado wrap for jus The food, which is prepared in the kit La Trattoria Restaurant across the arguably the best lunch deal in town 11 am to 5 pm Monday to Saturday, attracts long queues of office workers

Duffy's Deli *(☎ 295-7155, 4 Wesle* inconspicuous little basement shop west of city hall, has good take-ou wiches for around $5, including grilled-chicken and cold-cut sand They also have tabbouleh salad an inexpensive hot dishes. It's open 3 pm weekdays.

The Deli *(☎ 295-5890)*, in the Was Mall, also specializes in take-out fa pizza by the slice for $3.25 and str ward sandwiches or salads for arc It's open 8 am to 5 pm weekdays an 4 pm Saturday.

Dinty's Lunch Wagon, which east end of Front St, serves up fish cheeseburgers and chicken sandwi $4 and a few more substantial items and chips for around $10. The wag ates 11 am to 7 pm weekdays and around 3 am weekends.

Cafe Acoreano *(☎ 296-0402)*, Ch Washington Sts, is an unpretentiou across from the bus terminal. It has of tempting Portuguese pastries $1.50, quiches and sandwiches fo reasonably priced tea and coffee. T

ıbles where you can sit and eat. It's
ϛ:30 am to 4 pm Monday to Saturday.
ıgry Bear (*☎ 292-2353*), an espresso
d cafe on Chancery Lane, is an unhur-
ace to enjoy a cup of coffee. You can
agel or croissant with cream cheese or
: just $2, as well as inexpensive scones,
s, salads and sandwiches. It's open
› 4:30 pm weekdays.
k Island Cafe (*☎ 296-5241, 48 Reid*
ı casual coffee shop where you can
ı an easy chair and read the newspa-
ʼou linger over an espresso or cafe au
e cafe has reasonably priced baked
as well as creative sandwiches and
pecials, such as char-grilled veggies
ozzarella, for around $5. It's open
› 6 pm weekdays and 8 am to 6 pm
ıy.
y's Kaffee (*☎ 295-5203, 69 Front*
mple little cafe in the back of The
um, sells inexpensive breakfast fare,
hes, burgers, falafels and gyros, most
5 to $7 range. It also has pies, cakes
coffee. Kathy's is open 8 am to 5 pm
ı to Thursday, 8 am to 4 pm Friday
0 am to 4 pm Saturday.
Five (*☎ 295-4903*), upstairs at the
gton Mall, is a locally popular cafe
ncakes, fish chowder, burgers and
hes for around $5. On Saturday, you
ı traditional Bermuda codfish break-
$11.75. It's open 7 am to 3:30 pm
to Saturday.
liso Café (*☎ 295-3263, 7 Reid St*) is a
European-style cafe at the Reid St
ıe Washington Mall. Vegetarian and
ıdwiches for $5 to $6 are the main-
ıt it also serves specialty salads,
elgian waffles, tiramisu, chocolate
Danish pastries and a variety of
nd teas at reasonable prices. The
lrawback is that Paradiso is often
particularly at lunchtime, when get-
le can be a challenge. It's open 7 am
veekdays, 8 am to 5 pm Saturday.
Vashington Mall also has ***The
Garden***, a deli-style cafe with
pies and cakes, as well as scones,
; and bagels. It boasts what may be
's cheapest gourmet-blend coffee,
at $1 a cup with a free refill. From 7 to 11 am, there's a full menu of egg dishes, pancakes and breakfast sandwiches for $5 to $8. Lunch, which is also reasonably priced, is available from 11:30 am to 3:30 pm and focuses on salads, hot and cold sandwiches and pasta dishes. It's closed on Sunday.

The ***Botanic Garden Tea Room*** (*☎ 295-1183, 37 Front St*), on the 3rd floor of Trimingham's department store, is an inexpensive place offering afternoon tea and scones for $4 and basic sandwiches, quiches and salads for around $5. Despite the alluring name, the setting is in a bland corner of the store; the nod to 'garden' apparently derives from floral wallpaper and the artificial flowers that decorate the tables. It's open 9:30 am to 4:30 pm Monday to Saturday.

More atmospheric is the ***Front Street Terrace*** (*☎ 296-5265, 59 Front St*), on the 2nd floor of the AS Cooper & Sons department store, which has veranda dining overlooking Front St. At breakfast, two scrambled eggs, cheese and ham on a bagel cost $6. For lunch, there's always a soup and half-sandwich deal for $10 and a changing daily special, such as Indian curry over rice, for around $8. Various afternoon tea combinations with scones and finger sandwiches cost $6 to $9. It's open 9 am to 4 pm Monday to Saturday.

The Spot (*☎ 292-6293, 6 Burnaby St*) is Bermuda's version of a neighborhood diner, serving simple fare at reasonable prices. A hot roast-beef sandwich, a Reuben on rye or a tuna melt, served with fries, costs around $9, as does a chef's salad. At breakfast you can order French toast, waffles or omelettes for $5 to $8. It's open 6:30 am to 7 pm Monday to Saturday.

Chit Chat (*☎ 292-3400, 27 Queen St*), an Internet cafe, serves salads, sub-style sandwiches, lasagna and other simple eats for $8 to $10. It's open 11 am to at least 10 pm Monday to Saturday. For details on the Internet service, see Information, earlier in this chapter.

Places to Eat – Mid-Range

La Trattoria Restaurant (*☎ 295-9499, 22 Washington Lane*) is a large Italian restaurant that packs in a crowd each noon with its inexpensive lunch menu that includes sub sandwiches for $7; a good vegetarian pizza loaded with artichokes, mushrooms and olives for $9; and numerous other hot dishes for around $10. At dinner, pizzas begin at around $10, pastas $15 and steak and fish dishes $25. You can also order pastas and pizzas for take-out. It's open 11:30 am to 3:30 pm Monday to Saturday and 5:30 to 10:30 pm nightly.

For local character, it's hard to beat the ***Hog Penny*** *(☎ 292-2534, 5 Burnaby St)*, which has a dark, publike interior and good British, Bermudian and East Indian fare. There's an award-winning fish chowder at $5 a bowl, Caesar and spinach salads for $6 and other appetizers, such as vegetable crepes or garlic-buttered escargot, for a few dollars more. Entrees average $20 and include prime rib, lamb curry or catch of the day. There's also a simple pub-fare menu with traditional English dishes such as bangers and mash (sausages with mashed potatoes) or shepherd's pie for around $14, or a burger-and-fries plate for $10. It's open for lunch 11:30 am to 4 pm Monday to Saturday and for dinner 5:30 to 11 pm nightly. The bar stays open until 1 am.

Chopsticks *(☎ 292-0791, 88 Reid St)* serves reasonably priced Chinese and Thai fare. There's a nice, spicy hot and sour soup ($3.75) and a full dinner menu of pork, beef, poultry and vegetarian dishes for $11 to $16. In addition, from noon to 2:30 pm on weekdays, the restaurant offers a lunch special of soup, rice and an entree for $10. Dinner is from 5 to 11 pm nightly. There's also a take-out service at the side of the restaurant.

The ***Bombay Indian Restaurant*** *(☎ 292-0048, 75 Reid St, 3rd floor)* has a pleasant East Indian atmosphere. From noon to 2:30 pm on weekdays there's a recommendable all-you-can-eat lunch buffet that includes salad, basmati rice, lentils, potato curry, roti and a few meat dishes for $12 (or $10 if you select only the vegetarian dishes). At dinner, from 6 to 11 pm Monday to Saturday, main dishes such as lamb curry or tandoori chicken are priced from $15 to $20 and are served with rice and salad.

The bustling ***Rosa's Cantina*** *(☎ 295*
121 Front St) is Hamilton's Tex-Mex r
rant. At lunch, salads, sandwiches and
tos cost under $10. At dinner you c
various combination plates or s
chicken fajitas for $12 to $16. M
dishes can be ordered with different
of spiciness, from mild to hot, and th
a number of vegetarian offerings
organic black beans. The menu also in
barbecued chicken and ribs, steak
shrimp. For starters, try the cheese-
jalapeño peppers, called Iguana Egg
and wash them down with a frost
garita. Rosa's is open noon to 1 am d

Coconut Rock *(☎ 292-1043, 20 Re*
a trendy meeting place with music
and some creative sandwiches, incl
'Blues Burger' of lean ground beef
with blue cheese; a vegetarian lentil
with guacamole; and the 'C-Rock Sa
of grilled chicken breast with bac
Swiss cheese. All of these sandwic
served with fries and coleslaw and c
under $10. There are also reasonabl
salads, pastas and fish dishes. Lunch
11:30 am to 2:30 pm Monday to S
dinner from 6 to 10:30 pm nightly.

MR Onions *(☎ 292-5012, 11 Par*
Rd) is a popular restaurant with
dining and family-style fare. The $2
bird specials, available 5 to 6:15 pm
include dessert, a choice of appetiz
main dishes such as barbecue ribs,
teriyaki or pan-fried fish. Otherwise
begin at around $15 for pasta dishes
for meat and seafood. At lunch, the
cludes Greek and other specialty s
well as burgers and hot sandwiche
with fries, for around $10. Lunch
noon to 5 pm on weekdays, dinner f
10 pm nightly. The restaurant also h
and Internet-connected comput
details on the Internet service, see
tion, earlier in this chapter).

Robin Hood *(☎ 295-3314, 25 R*
Rd), at the north side of town, is a
English-style pub that makes the
best pizza. You can get a 12-inc
version that can feed two people f
17-inch one that can handle up

e for $15. A variety of toppings can be
for $1 each. Naturally there's also a
nenu of 'pub grub' items such as
rs and mash or fish and chips – mostly
around $12. It's open noon to 1 am

often jam-packed ***Portofino*** *(☎ 292-
20 Bermudiana Rd)* has good Italian
a bright upbeat setting and attentive
, though it can be rushed when it's
oups, salads and starters such as cala-
ritti in a spicy tomato sauce are all
ately priced. There are a dozen vari-
f 10-inch pizzas for around $13, nu-
s pasta dishes for around $16 and
n, fish and steak dishes for $25. It's
1:30 am to 3:45 pm weekdays and
o around midnight nightly. Portofino
s a take-out operation at the side of
taurant that offers hearty portions of
ishes for around $10.

any *(☎ 292-4507, 95 Front St)*, with its
ce on Bermuda House Lane, also
authentic Italian food but with a less
l atmosphere. You can dine inside
h frescos of Tuscany scenes or out-
n the balcony overlooking Front St.
sti, which include carpaccio, smoked
and fried calamari, cost around $10.
verage $12, lasagna, ravioli and other
shes $15 and meat or fish dishes $22.
re early dinner deals offered until
n and at lunch you can get seafood
r your choice of pasta for $11.50. It's
onday to Saturday; lunch is served
2:45 to 2:30 pm, dinner from 6 to
n.

Porch *(☎ 292-4737, 93 Front St)*, op-
he No 6 cruise ship terminal, has a
r balcony overlooking the harbor.
h you'll find pasta or Greek salads,
andwiches and veggie burgers for
$10. At dinner the menu includes the
rack of lamb, shrimp Creole and
urry chicken for $15 to $25. There's
9 early-bird dinner from 5 to 7 pm
ludes soup or salad, blackened
hi or grilled teriyaki beef and a
f ice cream or carrot cake. It's open
10 pm daily and usually has jazz or
tertainment at dinner.

Places to Eat – Top End

Le Figaro *(☎ 296-4991, 63 Reid St)* is an unpretentious place with a casual atmosphere that serves up some of the island's best French food. Traditional baked onion soup costs $5, and appetizers such as escargot Chablis or duck liver paté cost around double that. Main dishes, which are priced from $16 to $20, include the likes of pan-seared tuna in a red wine sauce, rosemary chicken with garlic potatoes and duck à l'orange. Although it's also open at lunch, the restaurant is at its best at dinner, when more attention is given to the food preparation and candlelight softens the decor. There's a good French wine selection, including more than a dozen varieties at $5 a glass. It's open noon to 2:30 pm weekdays and 6 to 9:30 pm nightly.

The Harbourfront *(☎ 295-4207, 21 Front St)*, opposite the tourist office, is a cozy bar and restaurant with a balcony offering harborview dining. Its contemporary menu includes appetizers such as beef carpaccio or grilled vegetables with goat cheese and pesto for around $12. Entrees, which cost $20 to $30, range from creative pastas to Curacao duck and rack of lamb. There's also a sushi bar with sashimi, nigiri and norimaki priced at $6 per plate. Lunch, which includes reasonably priced burgers and fish and chips, is served Monday to Saturday from 11:30 am to 5 pm, dinner from 6 to 10 pm. If you arrive before 6:30 pm, there are good-value early dinner specials that include a choice of appetizer, main course and coffee for $20 to $25.

Port O Call *(☎ 295-5373, 87 Front St)* has good seafood and an upmarket nautical decor. Chowder, lobster bisque and appetizers like escargot are $6 to $10. Innovative main courses, which include the likes of spicy yellowfin tuna on spaghetti squash, grilled Bermuda wahoo on Thai noodles and tandoori salmon with cilantro potatoes, cost $20 to $25. At lunch the menu includes sandwiches and pastas for $10 to $15. The lengthy wine list includes numerous choices available by the glass. It's open for lunch from noon to 3 pm weekdays and for dinner from 6 pm nightly.

Fresco's Restaurant & Wine Bar *(☎ 295-5058)*, Chancery Lane off Front St, is an atmospheric wine bar that offers good Mediterranean-influenced food. The extensive menu includes starters such as duck carpaccio, goat cheese terrine or snails provencale for around $10. At lunch there are sandwiches, creative salads and seafood dishes priced from $10 to $15. At dinner, vegetarian crepe and pasta dishes cost around $18, and other main dishes such as rare-seared tuna or rack of lamb average $25. Desserts include an award-winning baked chocolate mousse ($7.50) and similar indulgences. There's a good selection of international wines, as well as specialty coffees. It's open for lunch from noon to 2:30 pm weekdays and for dinner from 6:30 to 10:30 pm nightly.

Monte Carlo *(☎ 295-5433, 9 Victoria St)*, in back of city hall, is a well-regarded restaurant that blends Italian and southern French influences. Appetizers such as eggplant with mozzarella or marinated tuna average $10. Vegetarian main dishes such as crepes Florentine or angelhair pasta with black olives and sundried tomatoes cost around $15. Meat and seafood main dishes, including seafood bouillabaisse or pistachio-coated tenderloin, average $25. Meals are a la carte but do include a nice focaccia bread. It's open noon to 3 pm and 6 to 10:30 pm Monday to Saturday.

The ***Lobster Pot*** *(☎ 292-6898, 6 Bermudiana Rd)* has a good reputation for its fresh lobsters and other seafood. Appetizers such as coconut shrimp or oysters Brittany average $16. Main dishes range from shiitake grouper for $26 to a seafood lover's plate that includes clams, mussels, shrimp, crab claws and half a Maine lobster for $33. At lunch there's lighter fare, such as seared tuna on green salad, for around $15. It's open for lunch from 11:30 am to 2:30 pm weekdays and for dinner from 6 to 10 pm Monday to Saturday.

Entertainment

Oasis *(☎ 292-4978, 69 Front St)*, on the 3rd floor of The Emporium, is the city's top dance club and a popular place for singles and others under 40. The music is pu up and runs the gamut from rock and R&B and techno. There are two se open 9 pm to 3 am nightly, one with a other with a live band. The cover ch usually $10.

Flanagan's *(☎ 295-8299, 69 Front* Irish pub and sports bar in The Emp often has some sort of music, either reggae group or a pianist who plays Music typically begins at 10 pm, and no cover.

Pickled Onion *(☎ 295-2263)*, Front popular 2nd-floor pub with live ent ment from 10:30 pm to 1 am nightl cally blues or Top 40, and no cove around the corner at 5 Burnaby St ***Hog Penny*** *(☎ 292-2534)*, an atmos English pub that has good grub and entertainment – usually a guitaris 10 pm to 1 am.

Coconut Rock *(☎ 292-1043, 20 Re* combination restaurant and bar, is a gathering place that packs in a There's no dancing, but music vide continuously, except on Sunday nigh there's an open mike with poetry re singing and music. It's open 11:30 around 1 am, and there's no cover.

Robin Hood *(☎ 295-3314, 25 Ri Rd)*, at the north side of town, is a with an English flavor that carries Eu soccer games on big-screen TV. It noon to 1 am daily.

Open-air concerts ranging from g big band jazz are held one Sunday a typically the second or third Sunday to 8 pm, in the ***gazebo bandstand*** at Park; for schedule information, ask hotel or the tourist office or call ☎ 2

City Hall Theater, in Hamilton's has plays, concerts and other perfo throughout the year, including thos ternational artists during the Berm tival in January and February. Call t office *(☎ 292-2313)* for schedule ar information.

The smaller ***Daylesford Theatre*** *0848, 11 Washington St)*, opposite Park, is the home theater of the Musical and Dramatic Society, whi mances of Shakespeare, Chekhov and casional contemporary work. Prices vith the performance and seating, but generally cost around $30.

first-run Hollywood movies, there's *ittle Theater* (☎ *292-2135, 30 Queen* the city center. The cost is $7 in the g, $5 for an afternoon matinee.

ping

ton offers shoppers Bermuda's great-ection of both goods and shops.

island's largest department stores, gham's, Smith's and AS Cooper & ll have their main shops on Front St, block between Queen and Burnaby ese are good places to get an idea of on and costs, as they carry everything Waterford crystal, Wedgwood china nternational designer clothing to da shorts, Royall Bay Rhum cologne niature replicas of Bermuda cottages ongates.

nie Brown & Son, 51 Front St, has a uality selection of Scottish cashmere, kilts and Irish woolens.

more casual clothing needs, Smug-Reef, 29 Front St, has lots of interest-hirts with Bermuda slogans. Flying s, 5 Queen St, also has stylish T-shirts k tops, as well as numerous other r items with Bermuda logos.

y Jewelry stores abound and all carry ems that would make interesting sou-The Gem Cellar, in the Walker Ar-n Front St, sells affordable charms ndants with Bermuda motifs such as gs, longtail birds and hog pennies, ght on the premises. Astwood Dick-35 Front St, carries similar island-ewelry and has watches ranging from sive Seikos to pricey Omega models. 71 Front St, specializes in exclusive ch as Rolex watches, diamonds and ional designer jewelry, but also has a-themed pendants and bracelets. Christopher, 9 Front St, specializes ntique jewelry, rare gems and such s as gold doubloons recovered from entury Spanish shipwreck.

Arts & Crafts The Bermuda Society of Arts, which has a gallery and showroom on the 2nd floor of city hall, sells artwork by resident and visiting artists, most with local themes. The mediums are varied, often including watercolors, pastels, acrylics, oils and sculptures.

Another good gallery is the nonprofit Masterworks Foundation, on Bermuda House Lane between Reid and Front Sts, which sells quality Bermuda-inspired prints as well as some souvenir arts and crafts items, including Staffordshire enamel boxes hand-painted with the Bermudiana flower.

Carole Holding, which is both the name of a watercolor artist and a shop at 81 Front St, sells attractive, reasonably priced prints and notecards depicting Bermuda scenes. The shop also has a wide variety of souvenir items including antique-style maps, ceramic cottages and banana-leaf dolls.

The Windjammer Gallery, on the corner of Reid and King Sts, sells original watercolors, oils and bronzes, including those of Bermuda's best-known sculptor, Desmond Fountain. They also sell posters, prints, cards and calendars that have a Bermuda theme.

Stamps, Antiques & Collectibles Stamp collectors can buy commemorative stamps at the Bermuda Philatelic Bureau window inside the General Post Office on Parliament and Church Sts. Portobello, in The Emporium building on Front St, carries old stamps, coins and small antique items.

Pegasus Prints and Maps, 63 Pitts Bay Rd, a small shop on the west side of town, specializes in antique maps and prints.

Heritage House, in the York House building on Front St, opposite Bermudiana Rd, carries upmarket British antiques, including paperweights and china.

Music The Music Box, 58 Reid St, has a good selection of CDs and cassettes by local musicians, including steel band and other music. For something more offbeat, the Music Box also sells recordings of Bermuda's tree frogs. The store has a handy headphone setup that allows you to sample the tunes before deciding if you want to buy.

Getting There & Around

All public buses and ferries terminate in Hamilton. You can pick up a bus to anywhere on the island at the open-air bus terminal on Washington St. Ferries leave from the terminal adjacent to the tourist information office on Front St.

Moped rentals are available at Wheels Cycles (☎ 292-2245), 117 Front St, and Oleander Cycles (☎ 295-0919), on Gorha
just off Bermudiana Rd.

The cruise ship wharves are conven
located along Front St, just minutes fr
tourist office and all central city sights

For information on horse-and-ca
rides around the City of Hamilton and
on other public transportation, see th
ting Around chapter, earlier in this bo

›embroke Parish

an estimated 12,500 residents, Pem- is the most heavily populated of ıda's nine parishes. It encompasses the 's capital, the City of Hamilton, and combined with its central location – ; Pembroke the busiest and most fre- 'y visited place in Bermuda.

parish's primary sightseeing attrac- ıre in the City of Hamilton, but there ıandful of sights outside the city that explored as well.

ıbroke offers plenty of places to stay, ey're not on sandy beaches, so these modations are best suited to those alue being within easy reach of the , with its restaurants, shops and other ıiences.

information on Fort Hamilton and within the City of Hamilton, see the Hamilton chapter.

Highlights

- Enjoy a gourmet meal in a fancy setting like Ascots or as an affordable take-out at Miles Market
- Discover wonders of the marine world at the Bermuda Underwater Exploration Institute
- Visit Admiralty House Park for its wooded trails and sheltered swimming cove

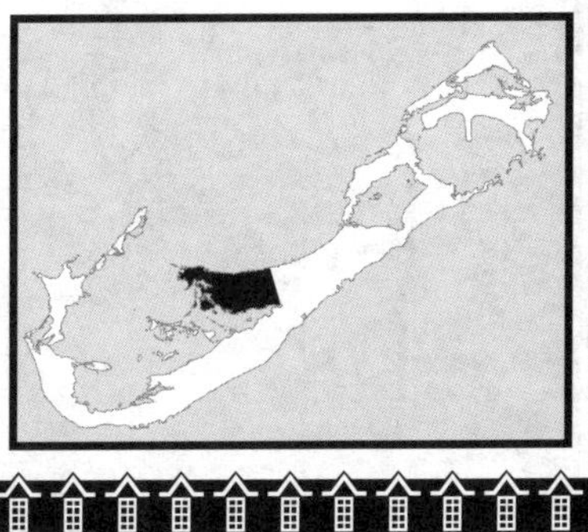

›uda Underwater ›ration Institute

ınd's newest attraction, the Bermuda water Exploration Institute (☎ 292- 40 Crow Lane, is an ambitious facility ıed to the underwater world.

exhibits in the extensive array take cational approach, with lots of de- ınformation boards and interactive s featuring state-of-the-art sound and echnology.

exhibits begin with the history of including a 19th-century hard-hat uit attached to a primitive air pump oks like something out of a Jules ıovel. There's also a full-scale model riginal bathysphere, the submersible er that William Beebe and Otis used for their record-setting (3028 ıderwater descent off Bermuda in his is followed by displays on reef and a superb collection of seashells. highlight is a simulated dive, in a ıne-shaped theater, that creates the descending to a depth of 12,000 feet, eldom-seen jellyfish and giant squid roam the ocean floors. To add a realistic element to the experience, the theater actually moves along an elevator shaft, depositing you, after the end of the seven-minute presentation, at the institute's lower level, which fittingly is dedicated to the sea floor. Here you'll find exhibits detailing everything from deep-sea creatures to Bermuda's geologic formation from an underwater volcano.

Not surprisingly, considering the abundance of ships that sank to watery graves along Bermuda's reef-entangled coast, there's a whole section dedicated to shipwrecks. This includes interesting video footage of ships in distress, followed by scenes of diving the wrecks.

One exhibit, complete with morphine-filled glass ampules, is of the *Constellation*, a four-masted schooner that went down during

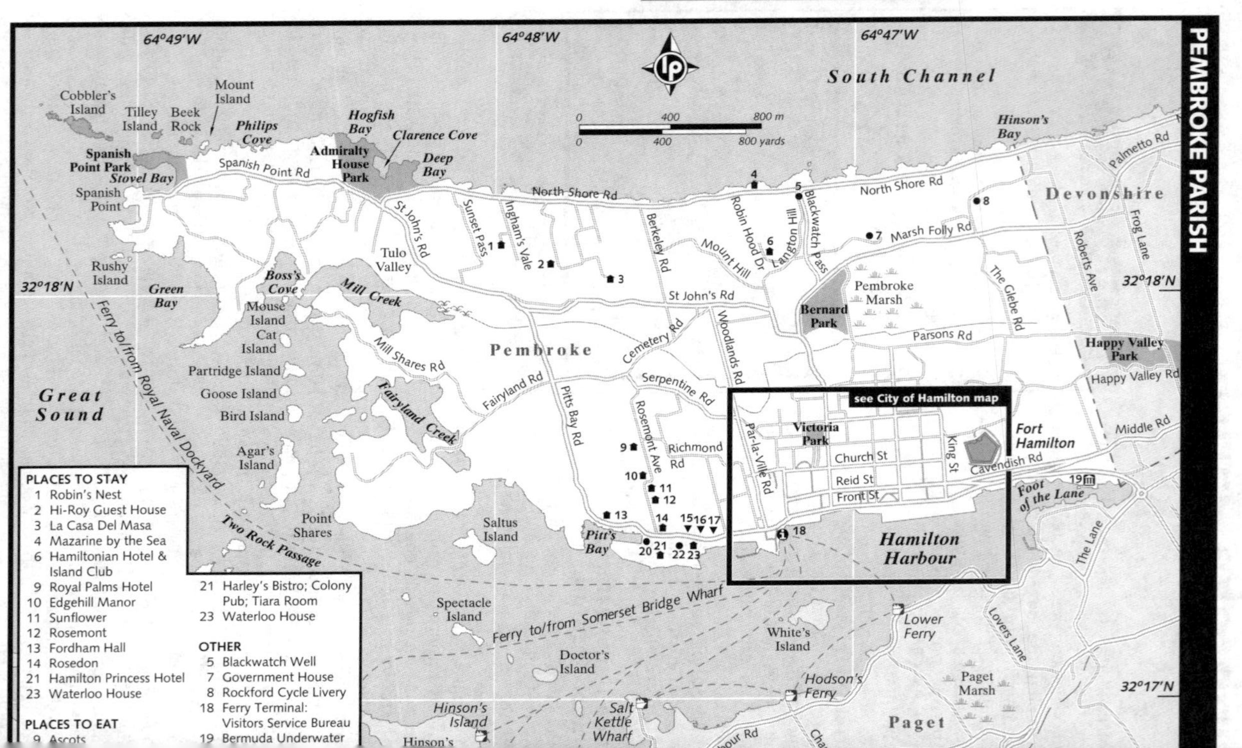
PEMBROKE PARISH
South Channel
Great Sound
Hamilton Harbour
Devonshire
Pembroke
Paget
see City of Hamilton map
64°49'W
64°48'W
64°47'W
32°18'N
32°17'N
0
400
800 m
0
400
800 yards
Cobbler's Island
Tilley Island
Beek Rock
Mount Island
Philips Cove
Spanish Point Park
Stovel Bay
Spanish Point
Spanish Point Rd
Hogfish Bay
Clarence Cove
Admiralty House Park
Deep Bay
North Shore Rd
St John's Rd
Sunset Pass
Ingham's Vale
Tulo Valley
Rushy Island
Green Bay
Boss's Cove
Mill Creek
Mouse Island
Cat Island
Partridge Island
Goose Island
Bird Island
Agar's Island
Mill Shares Rd
Fairyland Creek
Fairyland Rd
Point Shares
Two Rock Passage
Ferry to/from Royal Naval Dockyard
Berkeley Rd
Mount Hill
Robin Hood Dr
Langton Hill
Blackwatch Pass
Marsh Folly Rd
Pembroke Marsh
Bernard Park
Parsons Rd
The Glebe Rd
Hinson's Bay
Palmetto Rd
Frog Lane
Roberts Ave
Happy Valley Park
Happy Valley Rd
Middle Rd
Cemetery Rd
Woodlands Rd
Serpentine Rd
Pitts Bay Rd
Rosemont Ave
Richmond Rd
Pitt's Bay
Par-la-Ville Rd
Victoria Park
Church St
Reid St
Front St
King St
Cavendish Rd
Fort Hamilton
Foot of the Lane
The Lane
Saltus Island
Spectacle Island
Ferry to/from Somerset Bridge Wharf
Doctor's Island
White's Island
Lower Ferry
Lovers Lane
Hodson's Ferry
Paget Marsh
Hinson's Island
Salt Kettle Wharf
PLACES TO STAY
1 Robin's Nest
2 Hi-Roy Guest House
3 La Casa Del Masa
4 Mazarine by the Sea
6 Hamiltonian Hotel & Island Club
9 Royal Palms Hotel
10 Edgehill Manor
11 Sunflower
12 Rosemont
13 Fordham Hall
14 Rosedon
21 Hamilton Princess Hotel
23 Waterloo House
PLACES TO EAT
9 Ascots
21 Harley's Bistro; Colony Pub; Tiara Room
23 Waterloo House
OTHER
5 Blackwatch Well
7 Government House
8 Rockford Cycle Livery
18 Ferry Terminal: Visitors Service Bureau
19 Bermuda Underwater

I. The ship was made famous in Peter
ıley's book *The Deep*, whose plot de-
ed around recovering the wreck's
of opiates. Although the *Constellation*
e Bermuda's most famous shipwreck,
wrecks have also produced an abun-
of recovered items, ranging from
entury guns, cannons and ballast
to cutlery and gold jewelry. Amaz-
the lion's share of the items displayed
were recovered by just one islander,
Tucker, during his 40-year diving
. Tucker and Benchley are two of the
eople behind developing the non-
Bermuda Underwater Exploration
ıte.

a 10-minute walk east from the City
nilton, the institute's exhibits are open
to 5 pm daily, with the last entry
d at 4 pm. Admission costs $9.75 for
$5 for children ages seven to 17; chil-
x and under are free.

re's an on-site restaurant, La Co-
with moderately priced lunches and
ive dinners; see Places to Eat, later in
apter.

ish Point Park

3, a Spanish galleon passing Bermuda
a rock on the reef, forcing its captain,
Ramirez, to come ashore at Stovel
here the crew stayed for three weeks
ir the ship to a seaworthy condition.
rs later, when the first English settlers
shore on Bermuda, they discovered
ıts of the camp here, at the northwest
Pembroke Parish – hence the name
h Point.'

y, the north side of Stovel Bay has
ırned into the 7-acre Spanish Point
he bay is a mooring area for small
nd the park consists mainly of grassy
lotted with casuarina trees. A short,
ootpath leads from the bay to the tip
point, from where there's a clear-on
the Royal Naval Dockyard's twin
which sit 2 miles across the Great
o the northwest.

ll also see what looks like a ship-
ff the west side of the point; actually,
old drydock that sank here in 1902.

Bermuda's waters are home to sea anemones.

Windsurfers sometimes launch from the park, but the main activity is picnicking.

Admiralty House Park

Once home to the admiral who served as the regional commander-in-chief of the British naval forces, Admiralty House Park is now a 16-acre recreational area. A network of short trails leads through shaded woods filled with birdsong and along low cliffs with coastal views.

Admiralty House, built in 1812 as a naval hospital, was turned into the admiral's residence in 1816 and served that function until the late 1950s, when the navy withdrew and turned over the property to the island government. In 1974, the grounds were converted into a park. Some of the buildings that previously were used by the navy now house the offices of community groups and youth organizations, such as the Boy Scouts.

The park encompasses **Clarence Cove**, a sheltered cove with shallow waters and a tiny sandy beach, making it a popular destination for families on weekend outings. You may also see divers here, as the Bermuda Sub-Aqua Club, a private dive club, operates out of the park.

On the south side of the road, **Tulo Valley**, currently a parks department nursery, was originally the vegetable garden for Admiralty House. A tunnel, now blocked off, once connected the two areas.

Blackwatch Pass

The island's most impressive road engineering feat is the Blackwatch Pass, a tunnel-like pass cut more than 50 feet deep into the limestone cliffs separating the north shore of Pembroke from the City of Hamilton.

Along the north side of Blackwatch Pass, near the intersection with Langton Hill road, is the site of **Blackwatch Well**, which is marked by a small enclosure. The well, now capped, was dug during a severe drought in 1849 to provide the area with a more reliable source of water.

Government House

The official residence of Bermuda's governor, Government House is generally not open to the public, but it can be seen from neighboring roads. Built in 1892 atop the 112-foot Langton Hill, this stately stone house has more than 30 rooms, as well as extensive verandas and an outdoor swimming pool. It was on the 33-acre estate grounds that governor Sir Richard Sharples, along with his bodyguard and the Great Dane that Sharples was walking, were gunned down by an assassin on March 10, 1973.

For more than a century, dignitaries visiting Government House have traditionally been invited to ceremoniously plant a tree, which is then endowed with a plaque. More than 100 of these commemorative plantings dot the grounds, including a mango tree planted in 1880 by the future King George V, a princess palm planted by Ethiopian King Haile Selassie in 1963 and a queen palm planted by Queen Elizabeth in 1994.

Outdoor Activities

The Government Tennis Stadium is in Bernard Park, north of the City of Hamilton, and there are also tennis courts at the Hamiltonian Hotel & Island Club. Details on both are in the Outdoor Activities chapter, earlier in this book.

Places to Stay

West of Hamilton The western outskirts of the City of Hamilton have a waterfront dominated by the Hamilton Princess Hotel. Inland from the Princess is a quiet neighborhood of wealthy homes that includes a number of small hotels and guesthouses. Collectively, these hostelries offer a nice variety of accommodations, ranging moderate to upscale. All are within minute walk of the city center.

Fordham Hall *(☎ 295-1551, 800-53 in the USA, fax 295-3906, 53 Pitts B PO Box HM 692, Hamilton HM C* guesthouse a few minutes' walk beyo Princess. From the exterior it has the appearance of a mid-19th century house, though the interior is quite inf The guesthouse has a dozen simple some a bit worn, but all with private rooms. There's a spacious guest loung cable TV and a breakfast room with of Hamilton Harbour. The rate for singles or doubles begins at $80/ winter/summer and includes a ge continental breakfast of juice, muffins, and fresh fruit. One downside is that i stretch of busy Pitts Bay Rd that have a sidewalk, so the walk to town partly in the street.

Sunflower *(☎ 296-0523, fax 29 email sunflower@ibl.bm, 31 Rosemo Pembroke HM08)* is a cozy studio home of Tricia Thompson-Browne. Th room unit is compact but has two tw a private bath, air-conditioning, TV, a and a little table with two chairs. Ther a 'micro-kitchen,' suitable for pre simple meals, that consists of a mic toaster oven, small refrigerator a feemaker. The studio is pleasantly de and has its own private entrance. T for either singles or doubles is $10 winter/summer, and there are no ad taxes or gratuities.

Edgehill Manor *(☎ 295-7124, f 3850, email edgehill@bermuda.com, mont Ave, PO Box HM 1048, Hamil EX)* is a small guesthouse with an ag down-to-earth atmosphere and f management. The nine rooms vary, b is pleasant and sports a TV, refrigera vate bath, ceiling fan and air-condi The upstairs rooms have balconi hilltop views, and the downstairs roo patios. Some have a pair of twin b others have a king bed. Singles/doul $100/124; for an extra $10 you can b of the two rooms with kitchens. Som a sofa bed that could accommodate a (\$15 extra). A homemade continental fast is included in the rates, and there's .

emont (☎ *292-1055, 800-367-0040 in A,* ☎ *800-267-0040 in Canada, fax 295- email rosemont@ibl.bm, 41 Rosemont O Box HM 37, Hamilton HM AX)* is a tyle complex with a hilltop location. d and operated by the Cooper family, opular place with return visitors. All dio and one-bedroom units are mod- d equipped with kitchen facilities that e four-burner stoves and full-size re- tors. All units have air-conditioning, TV and phones. Studio units in the three-story building that fronts the ost \$120/156 in winter/summer; there o a few studios in gardenside cottages 16/150. For those who need more there's a new wing with one-bedroom ents for \$140/180 that have a sofa bed living room and either a king or two eds in the bedroom. The above rates up to two people; additional guests 2 to \$25 each, depending upon the and whether they are children or There's complimentary coffee and pers, free local phone calls and pro- for late check-outs. Rosemont has a at www.rosemont.bm.

al Palms Hotel (☎ *292-1854, 800-678- the USA,* ☎ *800-799-0824 in Canada, -1946, email rpalms@ibl.bm, 24 Rose- ve, PO Box HM 499, Hamilton HM* an intimate family-run hotel in a 903 home. The main house has 13 each individually decorated but all steful Victorian furnishings, private Vs, air-conditioning and coffeemak- ddition, there's a newer section, con- in the same architectural style as tury-old main house, that contains a uites and cottages with kitchen facil- ere are lots of pleasant personal throughout. Rates, which include a ntal breakfast of pastries, fruit and begin at \$127/170 in the winter/ for singles, \$143/180 for doubles. nd cottages begin at \$137/195 for and \$159/210 for doubles. The well-regarded Ascots restaurant is located on site, so lunch and dinner can also be taken at the hotel. Royal Palms has a website at www.royalpalms.bm.

Rosedon (☎ *295-1640, 800-742-5008 in the USA, fax 295-5904, email rosedon@ibl.bm, 61 Pitts Bay Rd, PO Box HM 290, Hamilton HM AX)*, directly opposite the Hamilton Princess Hotel, is a small hotel with the character of a genteel guesthouse. The main house, built in 1906, has a cozy living room with fireplace where afternoon tea is served and a couple of atmospheric 2nd-floor guestrooms with Victorian furnishings. However, most of the hotel's 43 rooms are in two modern two-story wings that flank the heated pool and gardenlike grounds behind the main house. All rooms come with private baths, TVs, phones, ceiling fans, air-conditioning, coffeemakers, refrigerators and wall safes. Standard rooms, including No 42, a nicely appointed room in the main house, cost \$134/178 for singles and \$166/200 for doubles in winter/summer, breakfast included. Rosedon also offers wedding and anniversary packages. A complimentary taxi service is provided to Elbow Beach. The hotel has a website that can be found at www.rosedonbermuda.com.

Waterloo House (☎ *295-4480, 800-468-4100 in the USA, fax 295-2585, 100 Pitts Bay Rd, Hamilton HM BX)* is a small upmarket hotel that's a member of the Relais et Chateaux chain. Located in a restored 19th-century manor house, Waterloo has a quiet harborside location just a few minutes west of central Hamilton. The inn's sitting room is furnished with antiques, as are the 32 guestrooms and suites. No two guestrooms are the same, but all are spacious and have air-conditioning and twin beds that can be made up as a king. In winter, the double rates are from \$150 to \$260; in summer, from \$195 to \$340. Single rates are \$50 to \$65 less. All rooms are essentially of the same standard, with the lower prices for city views and the highest for views of the harbor. Rates include a full breakfast. For an additional \$40 per person, a four-course dinner can be added on and taken at the restaurant here or at either of the hotel's sister properties,

Horizons and Coral Beach Club, both in Paget Parish.

Hamilton's only large hotel is the ***Hamilton Princess Hotel*** *(☎ 295-3000, 800-441-1414 in the USA and Canada, ☎ 0171-389-1126 in the UK, fax 295-8052, email reservations@cphotels.com, 76 Pitts Bay Rd, PO Box HM 837, Hamilton HM CX)*, a member of the Fairmont chain. The Princess is a five-minute walk west of the city center. As Bermuda's oldest 1st-class hotel, opened in 1884, it has hosted presidents, princes and luminary travelers such as Mark Twain; these days it's a favorite among business travelers. The hotel has just begun an extensive three-year-long renovation but will remain open during the process. The 413 rooms have the expected amenities, including air-conditioning, cable TV, room safes, phones, a king or two queen beds and either a balcony or patio. Rates without breakfast start at $119 in winter and $199 in summer for both singles and doubles. There's a heated swimming pool, a fitness center, a putting green, a pub, banquet halls and numerous shops and restaurants. The harborside locale is not well-suited for swimming, but free transportation is provided to its sister hotel, the Southampton Princess, where there's an appealing beach and other recreational offerings.

North Pembroke The following places are in residential neighborhoods north of the City of Hamilton.

Hi-Roy Guest House *(☎ 292-0808, 22 Princess Estate Rd, Pembroke HM 04)* is a friendly little place about a mile northwest of Hamilton center. 'Soul spoken here' reads a sign in the back room, above a wall of musicians' photos. Everard 'Jonesy' Jones, DJ for a local radio jazz show, runs the place. No two rooms are decorated the same – expect bright colors and a homey ambiance. Each of the six guestrooms has a private bath, air-conditioning, ceiling fan and TV. There's a large lounge, outdoor patio, refrigerator and phone that guests can use. Rates are the same year-round and include home-cooked meals: singles/doubles cost $60/120 with breakfast, or $80/160 with breakfast and dinner.

Nearby is ***La Casa Del Masa*** *(☎
8726, 800-637-4116 in the USA, fax 295-
email lac@bspl.bm, 7 Eves Hill Lan
Box HM 2494, Hamilton HM GX)*,
has three units, each with a bedroom
two double beds, a separate kitchen
vate bath, TV, phone, ceiling fan an
conditioning. There's a patio, barbecu
and pool for guest use. An apartme
one or two people costs $100 year-r
add another $10 for an upper-floor u
Casa Del Masa is atop a little hill, ma
a somewhat hefty climb for walking
but also affording a panoramic view
north shore.

In the same north shore neighborh
Robin's Nest *(☎/fax 292-4347, 80
4116 in the USA, email rob@bspl.b
Vale Close, Pembroke HM 04)*, whi
four modern rental units: a studio,
bedroom apartment and a pair o
bedroom apartments. Each has a bat
with both shower and tub, a kitchen
TV, air-conditioning, ceiling fan
phones. Year-round rates are $125 f
adults, $175 for three and $200 for fo
$10 for children ages two to 12, but
under two are free. Milt and Terri Ro
operate this quiet, somewhat seclude
and there's a pleasant swimming poo

Mazarine by the Sea *(☎ 292-169
441-7087 in the USA, fax 292-9077,
mazarinebythesea@ibl.bm, PO Bo
3153, Hamilton HM AX)* has seven ur
two-story building perched abo
water's edge on North Shore Rd. The
sandy beach, but steps in the backya
down to a good snorkeling spot and t
small pool with an ocean view. Th
have kitchens, private baths, T
phones. The cost is $125 for doubles, $
three. Mazarine by the Sea shuts do
month each year from mid-October t
mid-November.

The ***Hamiltonian Hotel & Islan***
*(☎ 295-5608, 800-203-3222 in the U
Canada, fax 295-7481, PO Box H
Hamilton HM GX)*, on a knoll abo
minute walk north of Hamilton, is
story timeshare complex. There
contemporary, one-bedroom cond

with a TV, phone, oceanview balcony, nditioning, toaster, microwave, cofker and mini-refrigerator. Those units ave not been booked by timeshare ers can be rented by the general and are a particularly good deal in . Winter/summer rates are $74/130 for s and $88/156 for doubles. There's a pool and three tennis courts, two of are lit for night play.

s to Eat

the places listed in this section are just f the City of Hamilton, with the exn of La Coquille, which is on the outskirts of the city. In addition, visan take advantage of the full array of rants in Hamilton, which is within g distance of most Pembroke accomions (see the Places to Eat section in y of Hamilton chapter).

Buttercrust Shop, on Pitts Bay Rd te Waterloo House, sells breads and ome pastries, including a tasty apple for 90¢. It also has simple take-out r sandwiches for $3 to $4. The shop is eekdays only, 8 am to 4:45 pm.

s Market *(☎ 295-1234, 90 Pitts Bay* the rear of the new multistory 'The ront' building, is hands-down the best grocery store, with an impresection of imported items and natural nging from Indian nan to organic ge chicken. There's a bakery with rain bread, croissants and tempting a deli with gourmet-quality grilled and roasted chicken; and a fresh r. It's open 7:30 am to 7 pm Monday day, 1 to 5 pm Sunday. If you opt for e-out, there are a couple of covered utside where you can sit and eat.

y's Restaurant *(☎ 295-5759, 75 Pitts* *)* is a local favorite, about midway Front St and the Hamilton Princess Breakfast includes standards such as toast or eggs, bacon and toast for 7. Lunch features sandwiches for $6 dishes like curried chicken with rice d for $12. At dinner there's a range en, meat and fish dishes for $15 to breakfast menu is available from 7:30 am to 2:30 pm daily, lunch from 11:30 am to 2:30 pm daily. Dinner is served from 5:30 to 10 pm Monday to Saturday.

Ristorante Primavera *(☎ 295-2167, 69 Pitts Bay Rd)* is an Italian restaurant with an extensive menu. Antipasto items such as carpaccio or fried calamari cost around $12. Pasta main dishes are priced from $15, chicken dishes average $20 and fish and steak dishes cost around $25. It's open for lunch from 11:45 am to 2:30 pm weekdays and for dinner from 6:30 to 10:30 pm nightly.

Ascots *(☎ 295-9644, 24 Rosemont Ave)*, in the Royal Palms Hotel, a 10-minute walk west of Hamilton center, has a Victorian setting, both indoor and al fresco dining, and excellent continental fare. The varied menu includes starters such as wahoo gravlax or tiger shrimp brochette for around $10 at lunch and $15 at dinner. Main dishes, which average $18 at lunch and $30 at dinner, include the likes of grilled lamb in tarragon sauce, yellowfin tuna with citrus salsa or pan-fried rockfish with bananas and rum. The menu has a few vegetarian offerings as well. An indulgent dessert is crepe garibaldi ($8.25), with fresh strawberries and hazelnut chocolate sauce. At lunch there's also a 'house specialities' menu that features a half-dozen choices, such as Bermuda fishcakes with chutney sauce or homemade butter-squash ravioli, served with salad, for around $13. Another good value is the three-course Sunday lunch special for $19.50, with a limited choice that typically includes roasted artichoke on greens or lobster gazpacho; leg of lamb, sirloin or chicken; crepe garibaldi and coffee. Ascots has an extensive wine list. Lunch is from noon to 2:30 pm Sunday to Friday, dinner from 6:30 to 10 pm nightly.

There are a handful of restaurants at the Hamilton Princess Hotel *(☎ 295-3000, 76 Pitts Bay Rd)*, including the trattoria-style ***Harley's Bistro***, which has pizzas and pastas for around $15 and meat or fish dishes for double that, and the ***Colony Pub***, a New York-style steakhouse restaurant featuring cuts of Angus beef from around $25. Both are open daily for lunch from noon to at least 2:30 pm and for dinner from 6:30 to 10 pm. There's also an expensive fine-dining dinner restaurant, the ***Tiara Room***, which specializes in seafood dishes with a French influence; it's open 6:30 to 9 pm daily.

Waterloo House *(☎ 295-4480, 100 Pitts Bay Rd)*, an upmarket restaurant at the Waterloo House hotel, has a formal English-style dining room with a harbor view and an international menu. Starters such as shrimp risotto or tartlet of smoked salmon cost $16, and main dishes such as grilled black grouper or lamb cutlets with Yorkshire pudding average $32. Men are required to wear jackets and ties at dinner, which is from 7:30 to 9:30 pm daily. There's a less expensive lunch menu from noon until 2:30 pm, which is served on the harborside terrace.

La Coquille *(☎ 292-6122, 40 Crow Lane)* is a new French restaurant at the Bermuda Underwater Exploration Institute. Located right on the harbor, it has a fine water view and a menu that emphasizes French Provence cuisine. Lunch, which is served daily from noon until 2 pm, features salads, baguette sandwiches and quiche lorraine for $10 to $14, as well as a few hot dishes like seafood crepes or salmon fillet for around $20. Dinner, daily from 6:30 to 10 pm, is a pricier affair with elaborate dishes like beef tenderloin topped with foie gras and wild mushrooms for around $30; appetizers such as lobster-meat ravioli cost half that.

Entertainment

The Colony Pub at the ***Hamilton Princess Hotel*** *(☎ 295-3000)* has music most nights, ranging from piano and vocals to a jaz and rhythm and blues. There's also s times a cocktail theater in the hotel's lounge, with performances ranging island-style musicals and the songs of Holiday to British farces.

For other entertainment in the are the Entertainment section in the C Hamilton chapter.

Getting There & Around

Bus No 4 runs west from the City of H ton along St John's Rd to Spanish Poin and returns to Hamilton along North Rd; the route direction is occasiona versed at rush hour. Monday to Sat the bus runs at least hourly from 8 6 pm, but on Sunday there are only dozen runs.

Bus No 11, which terminates in the of St George, connects the City of Ha with the northeast coast of Pembro Blackwatch Pass. Monday to Saturd bus runs from 6:45 am to 11:45 pm, w partures every 15 minutes at the he the day, but as infrequently as once a in early morning and during the eveni Sunday bus No 11 runs once an hou 7:45 am to 10:45 pm.

Moped rentals are available from Cycle Livery (☎ 295-1180), on Pitts next to the Hamilton Princess Hot from Rockford Cycle Livery (☎ 292 on Glebe Rd.

: George's Parish

·orge's, Bermuda's easternmost parish, site of the historic Town of St George. unspoiled town, which overlooks St ge's Harbour, was Bermuda's first l and remains its most fascinating eeing area.

 Town of St George has done an ex- nal job of preserving its historic sites, ing the instituting of a Town Heritage hat keeps modern eyesores, such as ead utility lines, to a minimum. Recog- its preservation accomplishments, 's Minister of Culture nominated the of St George to UNESCO in 1999, the ep in having it considered for selection orld Heritage Site.

ddition to the town, St George's Parish cludes the remainder of St George's which boasts forts and beaches; St s Island, with the airport and a couple oric sites; and ritzy Tucker's Town, is located – somewhat confusingly – southwest side of Castle Harbour with l connection to the rest of the parish.

 best spots for hiking are along the y Trail at the westernmost part of St 's Island and on the footpaths at Head Park in St David's. These two locales are also two of the parish's omising birdwatching venues.

 area's best swimming and snorkel- ches can be found north of the Town George and are described under St 's Island, later in this chapter.

formation on St George's Golf Club own of St George, and on snorkeling departing from St George's Harbour, Outdoor Activities chapter, near the the book.

parish population is approximately

Highlights

- Stroll the cobbled streets of the Town of St George, with its profusion of historic sights
- Visit the museum at Fort St Catherine and then take a dip at nearby Tobacco Bay
- Soak up the panoramic vista from St David's Lighthouse

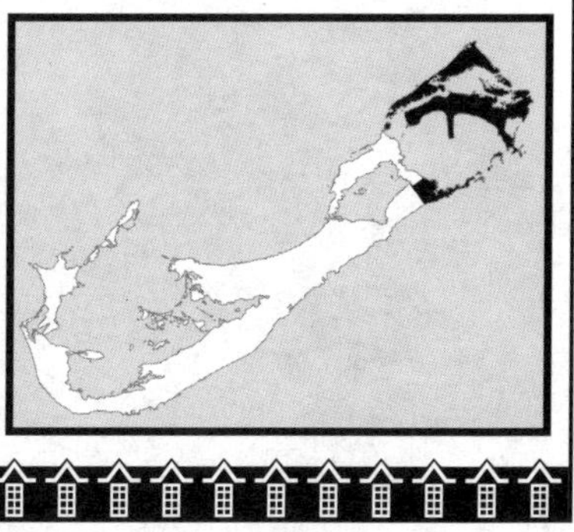

OF ST GEORGE

 its history as Bermuda's original and Britain's second-oldest settle- the New World, St George is in period charm. Many of its origi- nal twisting alleyways and colonial-era buildings remain intact. Some of these centuries-old structures have been set aside as museums, but others continue to function as public meeting places, churches and shops. Even the names of the public ways – King's Square, Old Maid's Lane and Feath- erbed Alley, to name a few – conjure up images of the past.

St George has a pleasantly slow pace that sets it aside from the bustle of Hamilton, Bermuda's present-day capital. With the ex- ception of outlying forts and beaches, all of the main sights are within easy walking dis- tance of the town center and are best ex- plored on foot.

If you enjoy shopping as much as historic sights, you'll find a run of quality shops in the center, west of King's Square. There are also a handful of waterfront restaurants that can make for atmospheric dining.

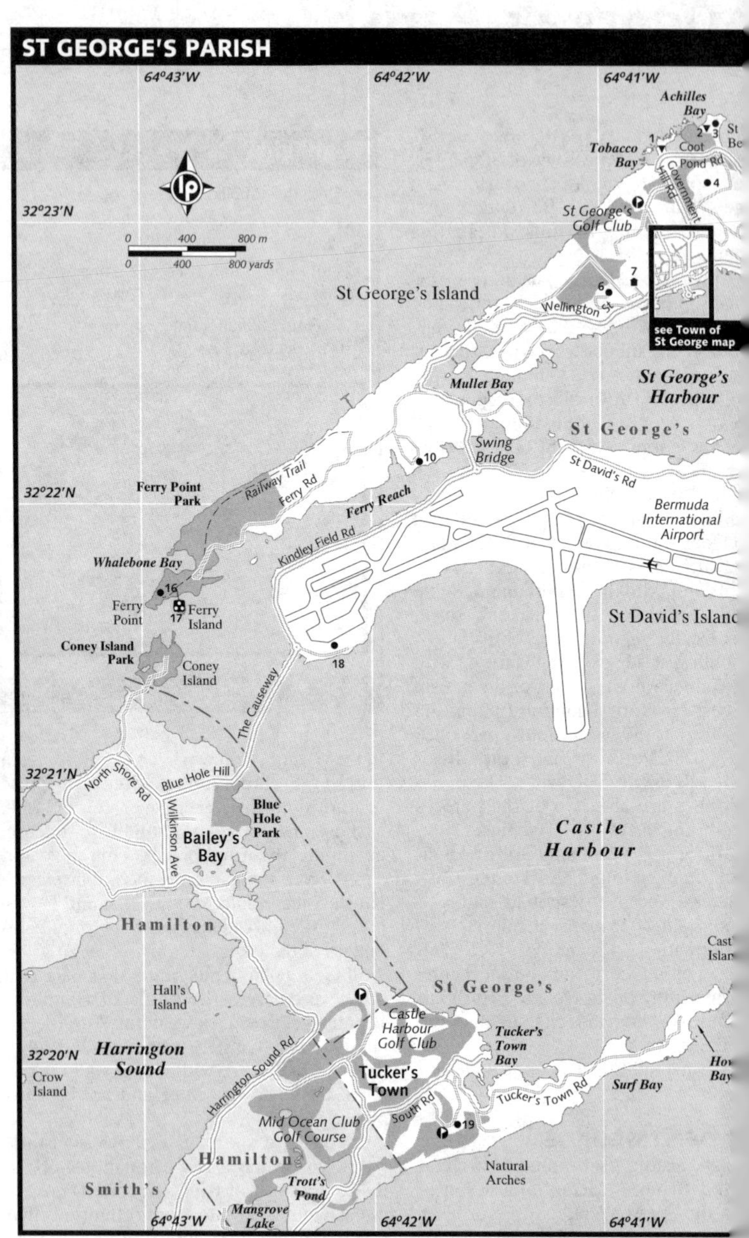
ST GEORGE'S PARISH
64°43'W
64°42'W
64°41'W
32°23'N
32°22'N
32°21'N
32°20'N
0 400 800 m
0 400 800 yards
Achilles Bay
Tobacco Bay
Coot Pond Rd
Government Hill Rd
St George's Golf Club
St George's Island
Wellington St
see Town of St George map
St George's Harbour
Mullet Bay
Swing Bridge
St George's
St David's Rd
Bermuda International Airport
Ferry Point Park
Railway Trail
Ferry Rd
Ferry Reach
Kindley Field Rd
Whalebone Bay
Ferry Point
Ferry Island
St David's Island
Coney Island Park
Coney Island
The Causeway
North Shore Rd
Blue Hole Hill
Wilkinson Ave
Bailey's Bay
Blue Hole Park
Castle Harbour
Hamilton
Hall's Island
Harrington Sound
Crow Island
Harrington Sound Rd
Castle Harbour Golf Club
Tucker's Town Bay
Tucker's Town
South Rd
Tucker's Town Rd
Surf Bay
Mid Ocean Club Golf Course
Natural Arches
Trott's Pond
Mangrove Lake
Smith's
1
2
3
4
6
7
10
16
17
18
19

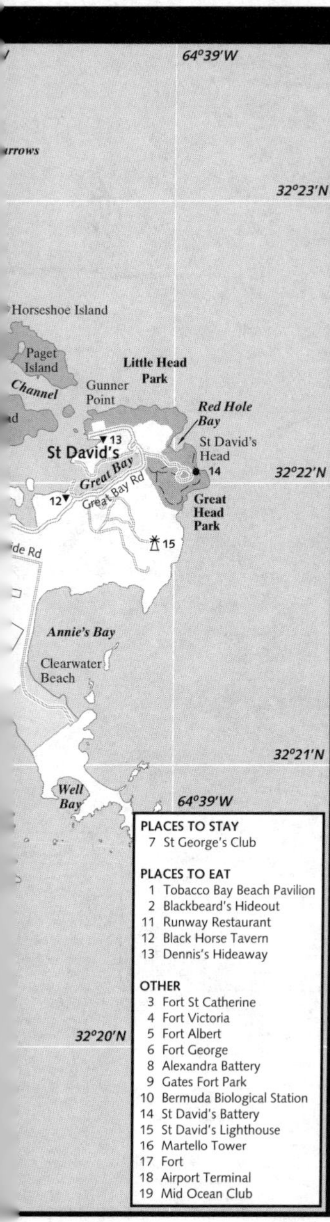

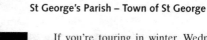

If you're touring in winter, Wednesday can be a convenient day to visit St George, as it's the one day of the week when the Old State House and the Old Rectory are open to the public. If you're visiting in the summer, keep in mind that cruise ships dock at St George during the week so it tends to be much quieter on weekends.

Information

Tourist Offices The very helpful Visitors Service Bureau (☎ 297-1642), at the south side of King's Square, offers brochures covering all of Bermuda, provides sightseeing information and sells bus tokens and passes. The office is open 9 am to 5 pm Monday to Saturday.

A branch of the Visitors Service Bureau opens in the Penno's Wharf cruise ship terminal on mornings when cruise ships arrive.

Money There are two banks on King's Square. The Bank of Butterfield is open 9 am to 3:30 pm Monday to Thursday, 9 am to 4:30 pm Friday. The Bank of Bermuda is open 9:30 am to 3 pm Monday to Thursday, 9:30 am to 4:30 pm Friday. Both banks have ATMs that are accessible 24 hours a day.

Post & Communications St George's post office (☎ 297-1610), at 11 Water St, a block west of King's Square, is open 8 am to 5 pm weekdays.

There are pay phones at King's Square, including one inside the tourist office.

Bookstores The Book Cellar (☎ 297-0448), on the corner of Water St and Barber's Alley, is a nice little bookstore with books about Bermuda, travel literature and a choice selection of British and American novels.

Robertson's Drug Store, on York St, carries foreign magazines and newspapers, as well as some Bermuda-themed books.

Laundry There's a coin laundry, Tic-O-Matic Laundromat (☎ 293-9823), on Shinbone Alley just north of York St. It's open 7 am to 9 pm Monday to Saturday and 7 am to 6 pm Sunday.

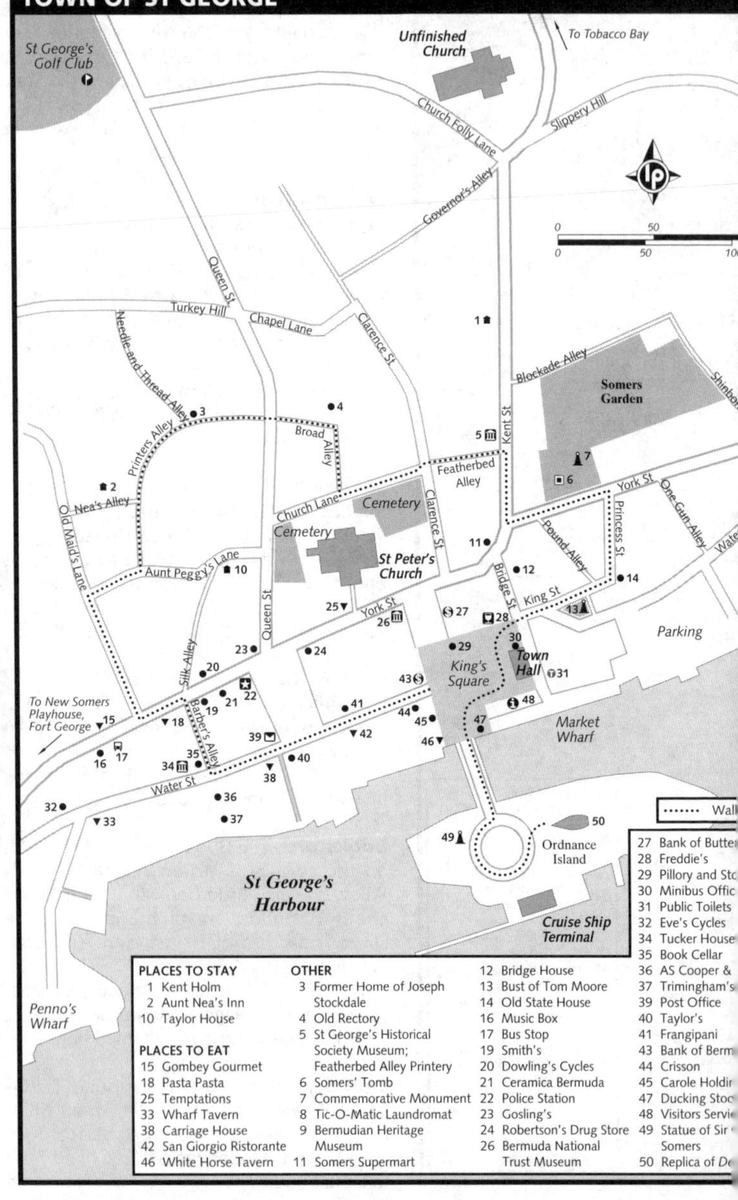
TOWN OF ST GEORGE
St George's Golf Club
Unfinished Church
To Tobacco Bay
Church Folly Lane
Slippery Hill
Governor's Alley
Queen St
Turkey Hill
Chapel Lane
Clarence St
Needle-and-Thread Alley
Printers Alley
Broad Alley
Blockade Alley
Somers Garden
Kent St
Featherbed Alley
Church Lane
Cemetery
Cemetery
St Peter's Church
Nea's Alley
Old Maid's Lane
Aunt Peggy's Lane
York St
Pound Alley
Princess St
One Gun Alley
Bridge St
King St
Parking
Silk Alley
King's Square
Town Hall
Market Wharf
Barber's Alley
Water St
To New Somers Playhouse, Fort George
Ordnance Island
St George's Harbour
Cruise Ship Terminal
Penno's Wharf
Wall
PLACES TO STAY
1 Kent Holm
2 Aunt Nea's Inn
10 Taylor House
PLACES TO EAT
15 Gombey Gourmet
18 Pasta Pasta
25 Temptations
33 Wharf Tavern
38 Carriage House
42 San Giorgio Ristorante
46 White Horse Tavern
OTHER
3 Former Home of Joseph Stockdale
4 Old Rectory
5 St George's Historical Society Museum; Featherbed Alley Printery
6 Somers' Tomb
7 Commemorative Monument
8 Tic-O-Matic Laundromat
9 Bermudian Heritage Museum
11 Somers Supermart
12 Bridge House
13 Bust of Tom Moore
14 Old State House
16 Music Box
17 Bus Stop
19 Smith's
20 Dowling's Cycles
21 Ceramica Bermuda
22 Police Station
23 Gosling's
24 Robertson's Drug Store
26 Bermuda National Trust Museum
27 Bank of Butte
28 Freddie's
29 Pillory and Sto
30 Minibus Offic
31 Public Toilets
32 Eve's Cycles
34 Tucker House
35 Book Cellar
36 AS Cooper &
37 Trimingham's
39 Post Office
40 Taylor's
41 Frangipani
43 Bank of Berm
44 Crisson
45 Carole Holdi
47 Ducking Stoc
48 Visitors Servi
49 Statue of Sir Somers
50 Replica of D

ST GEORGE'S PARISH

s Public toilets are located east of the office.

gency The police station (☎ 297-1122) eorge is in the town center at 22 York bertson's Drug Store (☎ 297-1736), on York St, is a large, well-stocked acy that's open 8 am to 7:30 pm ay to Saturday and 4 to 6 pm Sunday.

ing Tour

llowing walking tour takes in most of vn's main sights and a ramble along f its old alleys and backstreets. If you all of the museums and attractions ne way, you could easily fill a leisurely y.

ood place to begin your walking tour iny Ordnance Island, which once as a British arsenal. Today it has a hip dock and two sights commemo- arlier visitors.

he west side of Ordnance Island is a **of Sir George Somers**, Bermuda's cked founder, created by local sculp- mond Fountain. On the east side of nd is a **replica of *Deliverance***, the ship that Somers built in 1610 in continue his journey to the Virginia of Jamestown. For a $3 admission fee, n walk through the boat's holds, simple exhibits using mannequins limpse of what life was like in these d quarters.

ort bridge leads from Ordnance historic King's Square, the heart of ge. **Town Hall**, erected in 1782 and ed with the parish's colorful seal, e square's eastern flank. This attrac- ding, where the mayor and council t, retains its original period charac- walls of Bermuda cedar and por- former mayors. Visitors are free to ok inside 10 am to 4 pm Monday to .

e north side of the square are rep- he **pillory and stocks**, once used to chastise male residents who of- colonial mores with such mis- excessive drinking and disorderly .

On the south side of the square, near a couple of old cannons, is the **ducking stool**, where punishment to colonial women was meted out. The ducking stool has a seat at the end of a long seesaw-like plank that's hung over the water's edge. Women accused of gossiping or other petty offenses were forced to endure the humiliation of being dunked into the harbor. These days, costumed actors reenact the scene at noon on Wednesday and Saturday in winter, and every day except Friday and Sunday in summer.

Head east from King's Square and make a short detour north on Bridge St to **Bridge House**, a 300-year-old house maintained by the Bermuda National Trust; it was once home to island governors and now contains a gift shop and the studio of watercolorist Jill Amos Raine.

Return to King St and proceed east, where you'll come to a little green space containing the **bust of Tom Moore**, an Irish poet who sojourned in Bermuda in 1804.

The **Old State House**, at the east end of King St, dates to 1620 and is the oldest building in Bermuda. Although modest in size, the building incorporates Italianate features and has a stately appearance apropos of its former role as colonial Bermuda's parliamentary house. After the capital was moved to Hamilton in 1815, the Freemasons were granted the building as a meeting hall in exchange for the nominal rent of a single peppercorn. Prince Charles officiated at the reopening of the building in 1970 after it had gone through an extensive restoration. The ornate chamber, where island lawmakers met for nearly 200 years, can be entered 10 am to 4 pm Wednesday. Admission is free.

Go north on Princess St and then cross York St to get to **Somers Garden**, a little park with tall royal palms and a monument erected in 1909 to commemorate the 300th anniversary of the founding of Bermuda by Sir George Somers. Admiral Somers, as islanders like to note, left his heart in Bermuda – and they mean this quite literally. Somers' heart, along with his entrails, are contained in a modest tomb at the southwest corner of the park. As was customary

Joseph Hayne Rainey

Joseph Hayne Rainey (1832-1887), born into slavery in South Carolina, went on to become the first black member of the US House of Representatives.

During the Civil War, Rainey was compelled to work on a Confederate blockade-runner, but he took the opportunity to jump ship after arrival in Bermuda in 1862. In the Town of St George, Rainey set up a barbershop in the building that is now the Tucker House Museum. Today the side street adjacent to the museum, named Barber's Alley, commemorates Rainey's enterprise.

After the war ended, Rainey returned to South Carolina in 1866. For the next few years he was involved in state politics, and then in 1870 he was elected to the US House of Representatives. He served four terms before being defeated in 1878.

A vocal supporter of civil rights legislation – not only for African Americans, but all minorities – Rainey was also a member of the Committee on Indian Affairs. In 1874, during a debate over the Indian Appropriation Bill, Rainey became the first African American man to preside over a session of the House.

at the time, the rest of his body was sh back to England.

From the garden, head north along St to Featherbed Alley and the **St Ge Historical Society Museum**. This mu which is in an early 18th-century ho decorated with period furnishings, inc four-poster beds, a wood-fired oven, Bible, an 1813 rifle, a collection of old and the like. In the basement of the building, but with a separate entrance **Featherbed Alley Printery**, where sides are still imprinted occasionally a centuries-old press. Volunteers st museum and the printery and will show you around and point out int little oddities. Combined admission t sites is $4. Hours are not set in sto they're typically 10 am to 4 pm week summer, and 11 am to 3 pm on Wed and Saturday in winter.

From Featherbed Alley head w Church Lane, which passes the back **St Peter's Church**, and turn north up Alley to the **Old Rectory**, which visited on Wednesdays in winter or from the gate any day. Both the chu the Old Rectory are described below

The winding streets and alleys wes Old Rectory have picturesque hou are fun to wander. A plaque on the of Printers Alley and Needle and Alley marks the **former home of Stockdale**, who in 1783 brought t printing press to the island and foun *Bermuda Gazette* newspaper, the f ner of the current *Royal Gazette*. St incidentally, also started Bermud postal service, a horseback operati George's Parish that began in 1784.

If you continue south on Old Mai and Barber's Alley to Water St, you the Tucker House Museum on you to King's Square.

Tucker House Museum

Built in the early 18th century, the House on Water St has been w served, with rooms that maintain look. The house is named for the f Henry Tucker, the colonial treasu

ST GEORGE'S PARISH

rnor's Council president who purd it in 1775 and lived there for more hree decades. The Tuckers were one of ost prestigious families in Bermuda, any of the furnishings, silver and china re displayed here come from their

museum's collection includes numerrtraits of Tucker family members, as s many fine pieces of furniture, some l cedar and others of imported may. In the basement, there's a little logical exhibit that details the history property.

ker House Museum, which is owned n by the Bermuda National Trust, is 0 am to 4 pm Monday to Saturday. sion is $3, or for $5 you can get a comn ticket that also allows entry to the Bermuda National Trust Museum as the Verdmont Museum in Smith's

ectory

d Rectory, on Broad Alley, was built notorious pirate George Dew, who American colonies for Bermuda e converted to the good life, becomhurch warden and lawyer. Although ct date of construction is not known, se was standing by 1705. It was one first houses in Bermuda to have a of, rather than palmetto thatch. The ere made of limestone quarried from the house foundation, a technique created a cellar in the process.

Old Rectory takes its name from a ner, Alexander Richardson, a miniswas given the property in the midntury as a wedding gift from the f his Bermuda-born bride. Today it's arming little house with period fur, cedar ceilings and a solidly colonial r.

building is now owned by the a National Trust and is lived in by storian Brendan Hollis, who graopens the property free of charge rs noon to 5 pm Wednesday from er through March. At other times, view it from outside the gate only.

Bermuda National Trust Museum

This museum, on the corner of York St just north of King's Square, occupies a well-preserved colonial structure that was erected in 1700 by Bermuda governor Samuel Day. In the mid-1800s it was turned into a hotel called The Globe, and in 1863 the hotel became the base for Major Norman Walker, an agent for the Confederate government.

During the US Civil War, Bermuda was an important transshipment center for the Southern cotton headed toward England. Because of the Union blockade, swift steamships were employed as blockade-runners by the Confederacy to get the cotton as far as Bermuda, where it was then transferred to more seaworthy cargo vessels for the transatlantic passage. During this period, St George enjoyed unprecedented economic activity, its harbor bustling with North American ships and its waterfront warehouses piled high with cotton.

The upper floor of the museum focuses on the role Bermuda played during the US Civil War, mainly through interpretive signboards that cover such topics as Confederacy money as well as blockade-runners. Downstairs there's a model of the *Sea Venture*, the flagship that carried the first English settlers to St George, and a 12-minute video presentation on Bermudian history.

The museum is open 10 am to 4 pm Monday to Saturday. Admission is $4, or for just $1 more you can get a combination ticket that also allows entry to the Tucker House Museum in St George and the Verdmont Museum in Smith's Parish. Children under six are free.

Bermudian Heritage Museum

Dedicated to the history of black Bermudians, the Bermudian Heritage Museum, at the eastern intersection of York and Water Sts, is the town's newest museum. It's the culmination of efforts by the Bermuda Heritage Association, which formed in 1994 to research and preserve the history and accomplishments of black islanders.

Displays cover the impact of slavery from 1616, when the first two slaves were brought

The Tempest

When the first English castaways washed up on Bermuda's shores in July 1609, they may well set the stage for William Shakespeare's final work, *The Tempest*. Shakespeare is thought to begun work on that play in 1610, after the first reports of the *Sea Venture*'s wreck in a temp ous storm appeared in England.

It seems that Shakespeare, who knew several of the shareholders of the Virginia exped probably had a copy of the account entitled 'A Discovery of the Bermudas, otherwise called th of Devils' at his disposal when he wrote the play. Although the plot of *The Tempest* is not Bermuda, the description of the storm and shipwreck bear a close resemblance to the event rounding the ill-fated *Sea Venture*. Indeed, in Act 1, Scene II, Shakespeare appears to make a reference to the islands with a mention of the 'still-vex'd Bermoothes.'

to Bermuda to dive for pearls, up until emancipation in 1834. Also detailed are the 'friendly societies' that were organized in the years surrounding emancipation to create economic and social opportunities for black residents.

Other exhibits touch upon the barriers of segregation and the extensive contributions of black Bermudians in fields ranging from the construction trades and medicine to cricket and government service.

The Bermudian Heritage Museum is open 10 am to 4 pm Tuesday to Saturday. Admission is $3 for adults and $2 for senior citizens and children (free for children under five).

St Peter's Church

One of the oldest Anglican churches in the Western Hemisphere, the original St Peter's Church was built of wood and thatch in 1612. A more permanent structure followed a few years later, and much of the present church was built in the early 1700s.

It's a thoroughly historic building with open beams of timber, hanging chandeliers and a wall of marble memorial stones whose epitaphs honor early governors, business leaders and clergy. At the east wing you can see the oldest piece of Bermudian furniture on the island, a simple mahogany altar made under the direction of the first governor.

Other early colonial period items are in the vestibule behind the main altar, where a vault with a glass door contains a chalice that was given to the church by the Bermuda Company. The chalic graved with the company's coat of arn scene of the *Sea Venture* grounding on There's also a second 17th-century this one presented by King William I

The **churchyard**, like St Peter's itself, once had segregated areas fc and white parishioners, with the gra slaves confined to the west side of t in the walled area closest to Queen the church's east side is the grave Richard Sharples, the Bermudian g who was gunned down in March 19 incident is described under History Facts about Bermuda chapter). The nor is buried alongside his bod Captain Hugh Sayers of the Welsh who was murdered by the same assa the grounds of Government House.

The church is open daily, typically to 5 pm, and admission is free.

Unfinished Church

Although it looks like the ruins of grandiose Gothic church, the Un Church at the north end of Kent St i the hollow shell of a 'new' Anglican It was intended to replace St Peter' had fallen into disrepair by the mi Construction began on this repla church in 1874 and piecemeal work ued for two decades. Meanwhile, b en parishioners – some who supported ›w church and an increasing number avored restoring St Peter's – eventu- ought the project to a halt.

Bermuda National Trust, which now ains the church grounds, has under- restoration work to stabilize the walls. hat work is completed, the Unfinished h can only be viewed from the outside.

George

eorge is perched on a hillside about a ute walk west of the town center. ally erected in 1612 as a watchtower, of the current structure dates to the 19th century. It's a small fort with masonry walls that reach about 150 ross and a central keep now used as a ment communications facility (Ber- Harbour Radio) to coordinate ocean in Bermuda's waters.

site remains off tourist maps, as the s been in a state of disrepair and visi- ve not been particularly encouraged ore it. However, the parks depart- s in the process of bringing Fort under the national parks umbrella e hopes of restoring it and eventually g it to tours.

ne meantime, visitors can take Fort Hill Rd to the top for a view of St and St David's, as well as a peek at and one of its 25-ton, 11-inch guns (a nuzzleloader dating to 1871), which usly aimed right at the cruise ship 's a fairly steep climb and there's a log en route, so it's a site that's best ated by those with a moped.

s to Stay

olm *(☎ 297-0528, Kent St, St George's)* is a small family-run guesthouse at ne of Grace Smith. Situated on the the Unfinished Church, it's a short anywhere in the town center and 0 minutes to Tobacco Bay. There's a room for $70 that has one double single bed, a small refrigerator and ate that can be used to boil water. se who want to do more extensive , there's also a studio unit that is equipped with a full kitchen and costs $90 a day. Rates are the same year-round.

Taylor House *(☎ 297-1161, email mark@bermudagetaway.com, Aunt Peggy's Lane, St George's GE BX)* is a delightful split-level apartment in the circa 1690 home of Mark Rowe. Just minutes from the town's central sights, the place has all the comforts of a home away from home. Downstairs there's a living room with a couple of armchairs, as well as a fully equipped kitchen with a refrigerator, stove, microwave and blender. Upstairs is a roomy bedroom with a queen bed and a single bed. Both the living room and bedroom are equipped with cable TV, phones, ceiling fans and air-conditioning. The rate is $95/110 in winter/summer for stays of up to six nights and $80/95 for stays of a week or more. There's no housekeeping service, but Mark will provide guests with clean towels and sheets as needed, and no service fees or taxes are added onto the bill.

Aunt Nea's Inn *(☎ 297-1630, fax 297-1908, email auntneas@ibl.bm, PO Box GE96, St George's GE BX)*, at 1 Nea's Alley, is a pleasant upmarket bed and breakfast in a quiet residential neighborhood just a few minutes' walk from the center of town. The inn has recently been renovated and the rooms are furnished with antiques including either four-poster or sleigh beds. There are 10 rooms in all, most in the 18th-century main house, although a few are in cottages out back. All have phones, air-conditioning and private baths. Guests have access to a lounge with cable TV, a refrigerator and a microwave oven. Rates, which include breakfast, are $130 to $170 in summer and $110 to $145 in winter; the higher rates are for rooms with both a whirlpool and fireplace. Aunt Nea's maintains a website at www.auntneas.com.bm.

The ***St George's Club*** *(☎ 297-1200, fax 297-8003, email stgeorgeclub@ibl.bm, PO Box GE 92, St George's GE BX)* is a modern timeshare condominium complex with a hilltop location, about a 10-minute walk west of the town center. The 69 units are contemporary and comfortably furnished, each with a living room, complete kitchen, spacious bathroom, TV, phone and air-conditioning. Many have nice views of the town and surrounding water. A one-bedroom unit for up to four people costs $165/250 in winter/summer. A two-bedroom unit for up to six people costs $250/350. There are three pools (one heated), three tennis courts and a putting green. An affiliate of Resort Condominiums International (RCI), the units can also be booked in the USA by calling ☎ 800-338-7777 and viewed online at www.rci.com.

Places to Eat

The ***Gombey Gourmet*** *(☎ 297-8371, 13 York St)*, at the bus stop, is a pleasant little place specializing in $2 ice cream cones and inexpensive homemade baked goods. You can get a nice slab of gingerbread for just $1 and generous Cornish pasties and quiches for around $3. Although it's mostly geared for take-out, there is a cafe table. It's open 10 am to 4 pm Tuesday to Friday and 11 am to 4 pm Monday and Saturday.

Temptations *(☎ 297-1368, 31 York St)*, in the center of town near St Peter's Church, is a cross between a bakery and cafe. In addition to good, reasonably priced pies, cakes and pastries, they sell cappuccino and other drinks, and have simple meat and vegetarian sandwiches for around $4. It's closed on Sunday but is otherwise open 8 am to 6 pm (to 5 pm Saturday).

San Giorgio Ristorante *(☎ 297-1307)*, Water St, is St George's leading Italian restaurant, with a full menu of pizzas and pastas. At lunch, from 11 am to 3 pm Monday to Saturday, they serve nice fresh salads for around $6 and have a two-slice pizza deal for $5. Full pizzas range from $9 to $14, depending on the toppings, and pasta dishes start at $12. Dinner is served nightly from 6:30 to 10 pm. There's both inside dining and an open-air waterfront patio.

If you just want something quick and inexpensive, ***Pasta Pasta*** *(☎ 297-2927, 14 York St)* is a simpler eatery with both eat-in and take-out pizza and pasta options. A small one-person pizza, pasta dish or salad costs around $7. It's open 11:30 am to 10 pm Monday to Saturday and 5 to 10 pm Sunday.

For atmosphere and setting, it's h beat the ***White Horse Tavern*** *(☎ 297-* right on King's Square. This casual r rant and pub has indoor dining as wel open-air waterfront patio. You ca salads, sandwiches or burgers with fr around $10; go for an English pub lu steak and kidney pie for $14; or get sta meat and fish dishes for around $2 open 11 am (noon on Sunday) to 1 am

The ***Wharf Tavern*** *(☎ 297-1515, 14 St)* is a local pub with patio tables ri the water. It's most popular for its v burgers that range from $8 for a vege version to $12 for a beef burger toppe bacon and fried onions. There are also in the same price range and pub gru as shepherd's pie or fish and chi around $15. It's open for meals 8 10 pm Monday to Saturday, and around 1 am for drinks.

The town's favorite fine-dining r rant, the ***Carriage House*** *(☎ 297-173* cupies an 18th-century building on W and has an upmarket English ambie addition to the brick-vaulted dining r warm weather you can dine al fresco harborfront terrace. At lunch, from 1 to 4:30 pm, various sandwiches, sala quiches cost around $10, fish and about $15. At dinner, from 5:30 to 9:3 la carte meat or fish dishes begin $25, or you can order a four-course bird dinner before 6:45 pm for $20. also the place for a fancy Sunday br from noon to 2:30 pm, there's a buf includes salads, smoked salmon, shri of lamb, caviar, pastries and a glass o pagne for $28. Traditional afternoon scones, dainty sandwiches and a pot served 2:30 to 4:30 pm Monday to S for $9.50.

You can pick up groceries at ***Som permart***, on the corner of York an Sts. It's open 7 am to 8 pm Monday t day, 7 am to 6 pm Sunday.

Entertainment

In St George, the entertainment g varies with the time of year, with t y occurring during the tourist season :he cruise ships are in dock.

White Horse Tavern *(☎ 297-1838)*, Square, is one of St George's main ainment venues. During the summer typically a band playing live rock and y on Tuesday nights and reggae and n Wednesday and Thursday nights.

Wharf Tavern *(☎ 297-1515, 14 Water*) has live entertainment with a some- exible schedule. It's typically karaoke ndays, a rock band on Tuesdays and a ssion on Thursdays.

ldie's *(☎ 297-1717)*, King's Square, has ty sports bar downstairs with a big- satellite TV that tunes in to Boston- games. In summer the upstairs lounge s an entertainer singing standard pub tunes and is a popular entertainment venue for cruise ship crews.

If you want to catch a movie, there's the ***New Somers Playhouse*** *(☎ 297-2821, 37 Wellington St)*, a cinema at the west side of town.

On Tuesdays during the summer months, St George holds Heritage Nights from 7 to 9:30 pm with craft and food stalls set up in King's Square, an appearance by the town crier, a ducking-stool reenactment and Gombey dancers.

Shopping

There are lots of shopping possibilities in St George. All the main Hamilton department stores – Trimingham's, Smith's and AS Cooper & Sons – have branches at the west

BERMUDA DEPARTMENT OF TOURISM

Costumed Gombey dancers give travelers a taste of Bermuda's African heritage.

side of the town center. Trimingham's and AS Cooper & Sons are at the Somers Wharf complex on Water Street, and Smith's is just a two-minute walk to the north at the corner of York St and Barber's Alley. These stores carry a wide variety of items, including top international brands of china, crystal, designer clothing, jewelry and perfumes. They also have swimsuits, sportswear and some local items such as Bermuda shorts and Royall Bay Rhum cologne.

There are a couple of interesting clothing shops on Water St. Taylor's, 30 Water St, sells imports from Scotland, ranging from Shetland and cashmere sweaters to kilts and tartans for both men and women. Frangipani, diagonally across the street, specializes in casual women's clothing in light cottons and tropical designs.

The Bridge House Gallery, at the Bridge House on Bridge St, sells quality watercolors of island scenes by artist Jill Amos Raine, both originals and prints. It also has a selection of island-made handicrafts, such as cedar bowls and banana-leaf dolls, and sells other gift items including locally made jams and period postcards.

Another excellent place to look for attractive watercolor paintings of Bermudian themes is at Carole Holding, which is both the name of the artist and the gallery on King's Square.

Ceramica Bermuda, on York St near the police station, features a variety of ceramics. Although most are imported from Spain, there are some by Bermudian artists with local designs of tropical flowers and fish.

Crisson, a jewelers on Water St just behind the Carole Holding gallery, has a wide collection of watches ranging from elite brands like Rolex and Cartier to moderately priced items made by Seiko and Casio. It also carries expensive imported jewelry and gemstones as well as Bermudian-themed pendants and bracelets with sea turtles, seashells and similar designs. The Music Box, 8 York St, is the place to buy CDs and cassettes by various Bermudian musicians, steel bands, the Bermuda Regiment Band, and even tree frogs! For books, see the Information section, earlier in this chapter.

Gosling's, on the corner of Yor Queen Sts, sells wines and spirits, inc their namesake Gosling's Black Seal

Getting There & Around

Bus Nos 1, 3, 10 and 11 connect St C with the City of Hamilton. Service quent during the day, with at least these buses operating every 15 minute 6:45 am to 7 pm; bus No 11 provides ing service once every hour until 11: (10:45 pm on Sunday).

Bus No 6 connects St George w David's once an hour from 6:15 6:15 pm on weekdays; on weeken service starts an hour or two later but erwise the same.

In addition, if you want to catch a the beach or out to one of the parish' distant sightseeing spots, the St Ge Mini-Bus Service (☎ 297-8199) ru demand throughout the greater St C area and to St David's. The minibus c at the north side of St George Tow For more details, see Minibus Service Getting Around chapter.

Dowling's Cycles (☎ 297-1614), 2 St, rents mopeds. Eve's Cycles (☎ 236 1 Water St, also called St George's Livery, rents both mopeds and bicycl

You can pick up a taxi at King's S

ST GEORGE'S ISLAND

Fort St Catherine

At the northeastern tip of St G Island, Fort St Catherine overloc beach where Sir George Somers shipwrecked crew scurried ashore i Bermuda's first governor, a carpente name of Richard Moore, constructed itive timber fortification here a fe later. The fort has since been rebuilt times; most of the current concrete st dates to 1865.

This substantial fort has a drawb moat, ramparts, a maze of tunnels powerful 18-ton muzzleloader gu have never been fired in anger.

Fort St Catherine was set asi museum in the 1950s. Its old powde zine now contains a collection of

asion Anxiety

mile-long northeast coast of St George's d faces The Narrows, a navigable reef nel of strategic importance. Conse-tly, this stretch of coastline was heavily ied by British colonists to fend off po-al invaders.

e handful of forts that still stand today an interesting glimpse of the invasion ty that gripped islanders for more than centuries. Despite the energy exerted eir defenses, Bermuda has never been bject of a foreign attack.

actuality, only once in its entire history ermuda even had the opportunity to s guns in anger, and that was way back 14, when two small Spanish ships sur-g the new British colony decided to h a skiff near the entrance of Castle our. The skiff drew immediate fire and paniards beat a quick retreat, marking rst and last of Bermuda's military 'skir-s.' The incident did, however, serve to ot the construction of some 50 forts in ears that followed.

s, the artillery storeroom has diora-picting colonial history and other have various displays ranging from iovisual presentation on Bermuda's a wax figure of Queen Elizabeth II licas of Britain's crown jewels. The n (☎ 297-1920) is open 10 am to 1 every day except Christmas, with st entry allowed at 4 pm. Admission adults and $2 for children.

St Catherine is about a mile north of n of St George. To get there, turn Sapper Lane, north of the Unfin-hurch, and continue on Victoria Rd.

Fortifications

unds of the former Club Med hotel ted on the remains of two forts, on ide southwest of Fort St Catherine. **toria**, just south of the hotel, and **Fort** ust east of the tennis courts, both date to the 19th century and are of a similar Wellington construction. The four guns at Fort Albert were of the same class as those displayed at Fort St Catherine, and the guns at Fort Victoria weighed in at 23 tons and shot massive 540lb shells.

A mile southeast of Fort St Catherine, along the coastal Barry Rd, are two adjacent waterfront fortifications. **Alexandra Battery**, which was begun in the 1870s and extensively remodeled in the early 1900s, has a cannon with a unique cast-iron faceplate that was intended to protect the gunner from return fire. The battery overlooks the site where the marooned English colonists constructed and launched the *Deliverance* in 1610.

Gates Fort Park, at the point where Barry Rd changes to Cut Rd, holds the remains of a small battery with a couple of cannons and a lookout tower that offers a view of Town Cut, the strategic channel into St George's Harbour.

Beaches

There are a couple of small sandy beaches on the northeastern tip of the parish that are within walking distance of the Town of St George.

The main public beach, **Tobacco Bay**, can be reached by taking Government Hill Rd north to its end. Tobacco Bay is a good choice for swimming and snorkeling, as it has sheltered waters and interesting limestone rock formations that attract tropical fish. There are also restroom facilities and a concession stand that sells food and rents snorkeling gear ($20 a day for the set) from April through October. Tobacco Bay, incidentally, played a part in the American Revolution, when gunpowder stolen from St George's magazine was brought down to this bay and loaded onto small boats that then scurried it across the reef to a waiting American ship, which in turn delivered the desperately needed gunpowder to Washington's armies. (See History in the Facts about Bermuda chapter for more on this incident.)

At the west side of Fort St Catherine, **Achilles Bay** has a pleasant cove with a tiny public beach that's also good for swimming and snorkeling. The cove is backed by Blackbeard's Hideout, a bar and restaurant; see Places to Eat, later in this section.

St Catherine's Beach, at the south side of Fort St Catherine, is a longer and broader beach but with less-protected waters. St Catherine's was formerly the private beach of the now-defunct Club Med.

Railway Trail & Ferry Point Park

The easternmost section of the Railway Trail, a 2¾-mile-long stretch, begins west of the Town of St George, off Wellington Lane, and follows the northern coastline to the western tip of St George's Island at Ferry Point Park. Near the midway point, a section of the trail connects back to the main vehicle road for about half a mile to loop around oil storage facilities that are closed to the public.

Just before Ferry Point, at the south side of picturesque Whalebone Bay, you'll find the foundations of a 19th-century gunpowder magazine and the Martello tower, a circular stone gun tower that offers a go degree view. At Ferry Point itself th two other historic remains – those early 17th-century fort and concret ings that stand as the sole remnan trestle that once provided a rail Coney Island.

The nearby Ferry Island, which car cessed via a causeway, has more century fortification ruins that c explored. Ferry Island, incidentally, t name from its former duty as the te for the ferry link that once provided t connection between St George's Isla the rest of Bermuda.

When you're ready to leave, y either backtrack along the Railway simply return via Ferry Rd.

Bermuda Biological Station

Officially named the Bermuda Bic Station for Research (BBSR), this was founded in 1903 as a joint ven Harvard University, New York Un

BERMUDA DEPARTMENT OF TOURISM

Bermuda's failed railway system became the Railway Trail, a boon to hikers and biker

LAWSON WOOD

Bay, St George's Parish

NED FRIARY

d Church, Town of St George

BERMUDA DEPARTMENT OF TOURISM

se Tavern, Town of St George

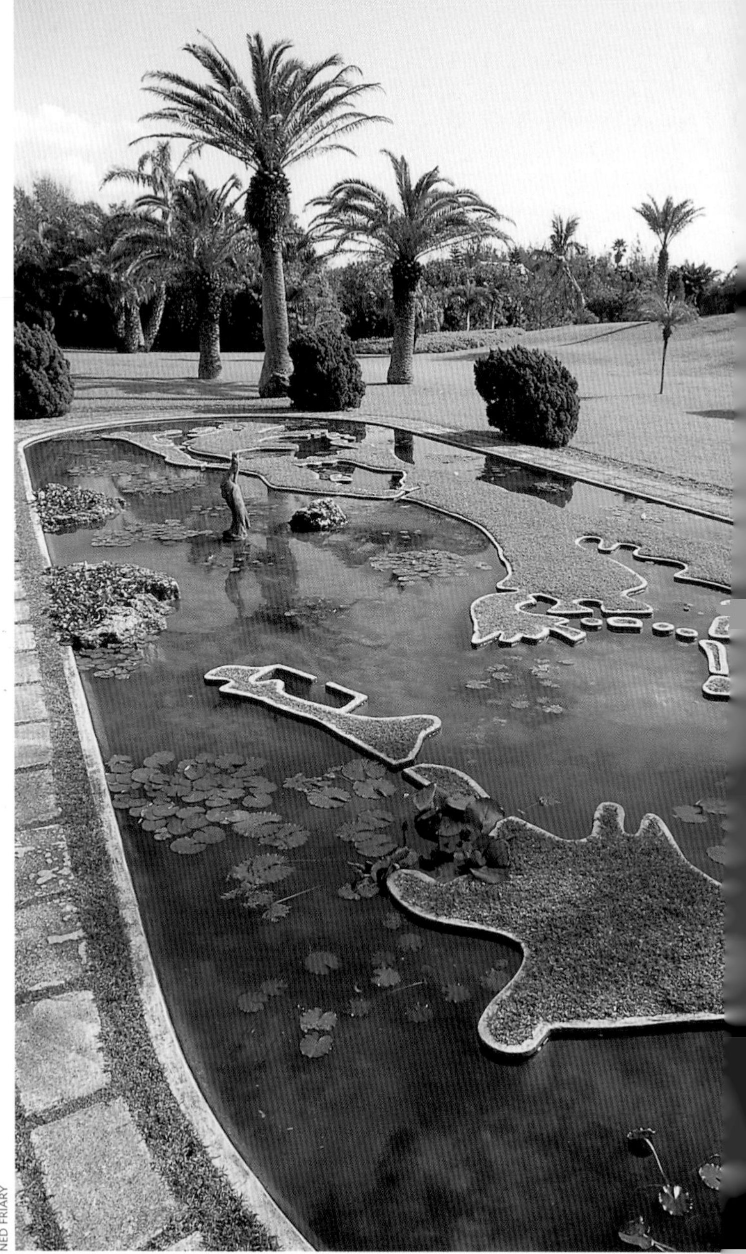
NED FRIARY

Palm Grove Garden, Devonshire Parish

ie Bermuda Natural History Society. the station provides facilities for both nt staff and visiting scientists and stu- BBSR conducts research on marine ;, ranging from coral reef ecology to .cal oceanography. Some of its work is efront environmental fields – the geoscience program, for example, ; the effects that oceans have on : in order to better understand global changes.

u'd like to take a closer look, BBSR free guided tours of the research at 10 am Wednesday year-round. The which are led by BBSR docents, gen- ist a little over an hour and take in a the laboratories and research vessels. t shop, which is open 10:30 am to 'ednesday, sells books on Bermuda's history.

R (☎ 297-1880) is west of the Swing that connects St George's and St Islands and can be reached by Biological Station Lane south from .d. You can also learn more about having a look at their website at sr.edu.

to Eat

acco Bay Beach Pavilion (☎ 297- ie concession stand at Tobacco Bay, sonably priced hot dogs and burgers is local food such as peas and rice, s and macaroni. It's open daily he summer season from roughly 3 pm.

beard's Hideout (☎ 297-1400) has a cation overlooking Achilles Bay. a bustling indoor bar that's usually with regulars and an outdoor patio ou can dine al fresco and enjoy the appetizers, the deep-fried calamari good choice. They also make a good dwich ($8.50) and have heartier ch as sirloin steak, grilled fish or tew for around $18. There's often a band playing in the evenings e week. It's open 11 am to at least aily during the tourist season but the winter.

ST DAVID'S ISLAND

Until 1934, when the first bridge was built between St David's Island and St George's Island, St David's could only be reached by boat. For the most part, it was an isolation that was cherished by its inhabitants, a substantial number of whom are of Mahican ancestry – the descendants of native North Americans taken from the colonies during British Indian raids in the early 17th century.

In 1941, most of St David's Island was turned over to the US military for the development of a naval air station and the residents, reluctant to leave St David's, were concentrated at the eastern end of the island.

In 1995, the US military returned the base lands on St David's to the Bermudian government. Large tracts of the former base still serve as Bermuda's airport, and the rest of the land is gradually being converted to civilian use. Once reserved for military personnel, Clearwater Beach, just south of the airport runway, is now a public swimming spot that's popular with island families. An adjacent area opposite the beach has been set aside for conservation as the Cooper's Island Nature Reserve, its rocky shoreline now accessible to island fishers. Although the area still feels a bit abandoned, some of the former base buildings are gaining a second life as new startup businesses.

The village of St David's, tucked into the eastern flank of the island, maintains a more timeless, unchanged character than other Bermudian communities. Most of its pastel buildings are not fancy, but they take on a picturesque quality in the late afternoon light. Certainly the town offers a glimpse of one of the least-touristed sides of Bermuda.

Gunner Point

A nice way to start an exploration of St David's Island is to drive to the end of the main road to Gunner Point, which offers a view of the nearshore islands that separate St David's from St George's.

The westernmost one, Smith's Island, is the biggest island in St George's Harbour. The eastern part of Smith's Island, as well as the entire island of Paget, which is located immediately north of Gunner Point, are government owned and set aside for preservation. In the 18th century, Smith's Island was used by whalers for boiling blubber, and Paget Island is best known as the site of the ironclad Fort Cunningham, one of the most costly forts erected in Bermuda. Unfortunately, the islands aren't readily accessible to visitors who don't have their own boats.

St David's Battery

St David's Battery, an abandoned coastal defense station, sits above Bermuda's highest sea cliffs at the easternmost point of Bermuda. In addition to fine hilltop coastal views, it has the island's most formidable guns; their rusting barrels sit like silent sentinels above the vast Atlantic. The two largest guns date to the early 1900s, reach 37 feet in length and had a shooting range of more than 7 miles.

The cliff face below contains a number of caves, but because of the steep drop they are not easily accessible. There are good water views, including one of Red Hole Bay that can be reached by walking a few minutes north past the last gun. The south side of Red Hole Bay – like St David's Battery – is encompassed within a 25-acre tract known as Great Head Park.

The quickest way to get to St David's Battery is to take Battery Rd up past the cricket grounds from Great Bay Rd. However, if you're on foot, you can also get to the battery by taking the footpath that begins at the signposted section of Great Head Park on Great Bay Rd. The path, shaded by Bermuda olivewood trees and fiddlewood, begins at the back of the parking area. Continue about 200 yards until you reach a narrow dirt road, onto which you bear right; when the track splits, bear left. En route you'll get glimpses of St David's Lighthouse, pass old military ruins and catch a few coastal views.

St David's Lighthouse

Perched atop a hill at the southeastern side of St David's, this vintage 1879 red-striped lighthouse offers a panoramic 360-degree view. Even if the lighthouse is closed often is – it's well worth mopeding u as the view can be appreciated from th foot lighthouse hill. Due to tight budg lighthouse is generally open to visitors summer only, from 10 am to noon Mon Wednesday; for current schedule inform call the park ranger's office at ☎ 236-

To get to the lighthouse, take Ligh Hill Rd south from Great Bay Rd.

Places to Eat

For a thoroughly local experience, ***Dennis's Hideaway*** *(☎ 297-0044)*, at of Cashew City Rd, a little cubbyhol overlooking Vaughan's Bay. The un tious dining room consists of a co simple tables with wooden benches, food is as fresh as it gets. Graham who has taken over the business fr father Dennis, is both fisher and co can get a fish dinner with peas and s $15, but if you pack an appetite, t treat here is to order 'the works,' an a multicourse feast that includes shar conch fritters, conch stew, mussel st chowder, shark steak, scallops and The price of $32.50 is quite reasonab you consider that most of the shellfis be imported. Hours are a bit impro call ahead.

If you prefer something more tional, the ***Black Horse Tavern*** *(☎ 29* a combination bar and restauran center of St David's village, has go and a waterside view of Great Ba are sandwiches for around $6 and dishes like shark hash or curried co rice for around $15. A house specia fish chowder, which *Bon Appétit* r rated as the best in Bermuda; a chowder with a fish sandwich and fr $11.25. It's open 11 am to at leas every day except Monday.

Runway Restaurant *(☎ 293-5 Southside Rd)*, on the northeast si airport runway, has converted th US military base's McDonald's int eatery with an varied menu. At lun are burgers and sandwiches for ar

r features a choice of Chinese dishes ian curries, served with rice: $10 for n versions and $11 for beef. It's open to 2:30 pm Monday to Saturday and 10 pm nightly.

ng There & Around

ly regular public bus to St David's is 6, which runs from the Town of St e to the village of St David's once an ntil 6:15 pm.

information on the St George's minibus, which offers an on-demand to anywhere on St David's Island, nibus Service in the Getting Around r.

ER'S TOWN

's Town, at the southwest side of Harbour, is one of the most exclusive Bermuda. Much of it is occupied by mbers-only Mid Ocean Club, which Bermuda's top-rated golf course.

e are attractive white-sand beaches, as a seaside natural rock arch, south Mid Ocean Club. These beaches, via the first right off South Rd after ean Drive, are set aside for use by nbers of the Mid Ocean Club; in , a gatekeeper limits public access to .

er's Town Rd, which runs along the peninsula east of the Mid Ocean Club, is bordered by a few dozen homes belonging to wealthy foreigners, including American billionaire Ross Perot and former Italian premier Silvio Berlusconi.

From the end of Tucker's Town Rd, you can look across a narrow strait to **Castle Island**, a nature preserve that contains the stone remains of a British fort, one of the earliest fortifications erected in the Western Hemisphere.

Nonsuch Island, to the east, is a bird sanctuary where efforts are being made to reintroduce the Bermuda petrel, or cahow, one of the most endangered birds in the world. To prepare the island for the cahow, exotic predators are being eliminated and efforts are being made to restore the island's precontact ecosystem. Not surprisingly, human access to the island is restricted, though both the Bermuda Biological Station and the Bermuda Audubon Society occasionally bring groups over; see Useful Organizations in the Facts for the Visitor chapter.

Getting There & Away

Bus No 1 connects Tucker's Town with both the City of Hamilton and Bailey's Bay. The bus goes to the Mid Ocean Club, where it turns around, but goes no farther east. The bus operates every 30 minutes from 6:45 am to 6:15 pm weekdays and 7:45 am to 5:45 pm Saturday. On Sunday the service is only once an hour from 11 am to 5 pm.

Hamilton Parish

The parish of Hamilton (not to be confused with the City of Hamilton, which is in Pembroke Parish) wraps around Harrington Sound, Bermuda's largest inland body of water.

Although Harrington Sound may have the appearance of a calm lake, it is in fact a saltwater bay, connected to the sea by a narrow inlet at the village of Flatts. Flatts, with the Bermuda Aquarium, Museum & Zoo, and Bailey's Bay, with its limestone caves, are the parish's two main visitor destinations.

Although Hamilton Parish isn't particularly known for its beaches, Shelly Bay Park, on the north shore, is a popular spot for families with children, as the waters are shallow and the park facilities include a playground.

There are some pleasant walks at Blue Hole Park and at the Bermuda Perfumery, both detailed in the Bailey's Bay section, and along the Railway Trail, detailed in the Flatts Village section. The Grotto Bay Hotel has public tennis courts and a sports shop, and Flatts is home to a h diving operation. More information o activities can be found in the Outdc tivities chapter, near the front of the

The population of Hamilton Paris proximately 4900.

Highlights

- Spend an afternoon exploring the superb Bermuda Aquarium, Museum & Zoo
- Visit Crystal Caves, with its impressive subterranean world of stalactites and stalagmites
- Walk the fragrant nature trail at the Bermuda Perfumery

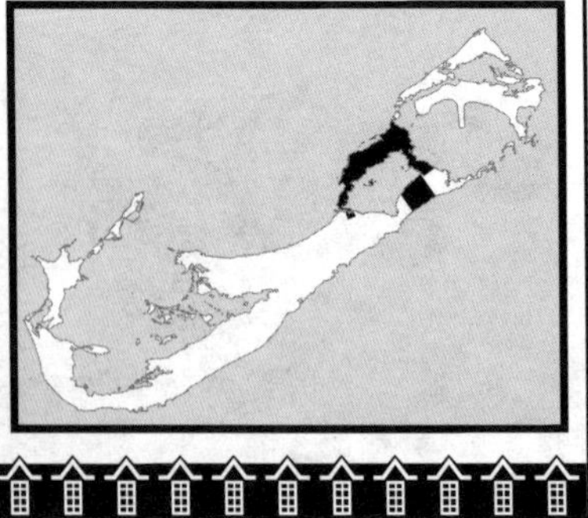

BAILEY'S BAY

Bailey's Bay, the little village at the eastern side of Hamilton Parish, has a of enjoyable short trails and an abunc caves and water-filled grottoes. The g of them, the Crystal Caves, can be vis an interesting guided tour with comr on local geology, or you can see a smaller caves by taking a hike in Bl Park. In fact, caves are so abundant not even necessary for some people their resort to see them – there are t stantial caves right on the grounds Grotto Bay Beach Hotel. One of th Cathedral Cave, even has a deep-wa that's popular with swimmers.

Entrances to all of the Bailey's Ba sights – Crystal Caves, the perfume and Blue Hole Park – are within distance of one another.

Information

The postage-stamp-size Bailey's office (☎ 293-2305), at the interse Blue Hole Hill and Wilkinson Ave, to 11:30 am and 1 to 5 pm weekday

Bermuda Perfumery

The Bermuda Perfumery (☎ 293-0 North Shore Rd, just north of the Bay post office, is a small perfum that offers free tours of its facil invites visitors to stroll around its The tours, which are available th the day and take a scant 10 mi clude an explanation of the er processes that fix the flowery scent at a little shop where visitors can sa

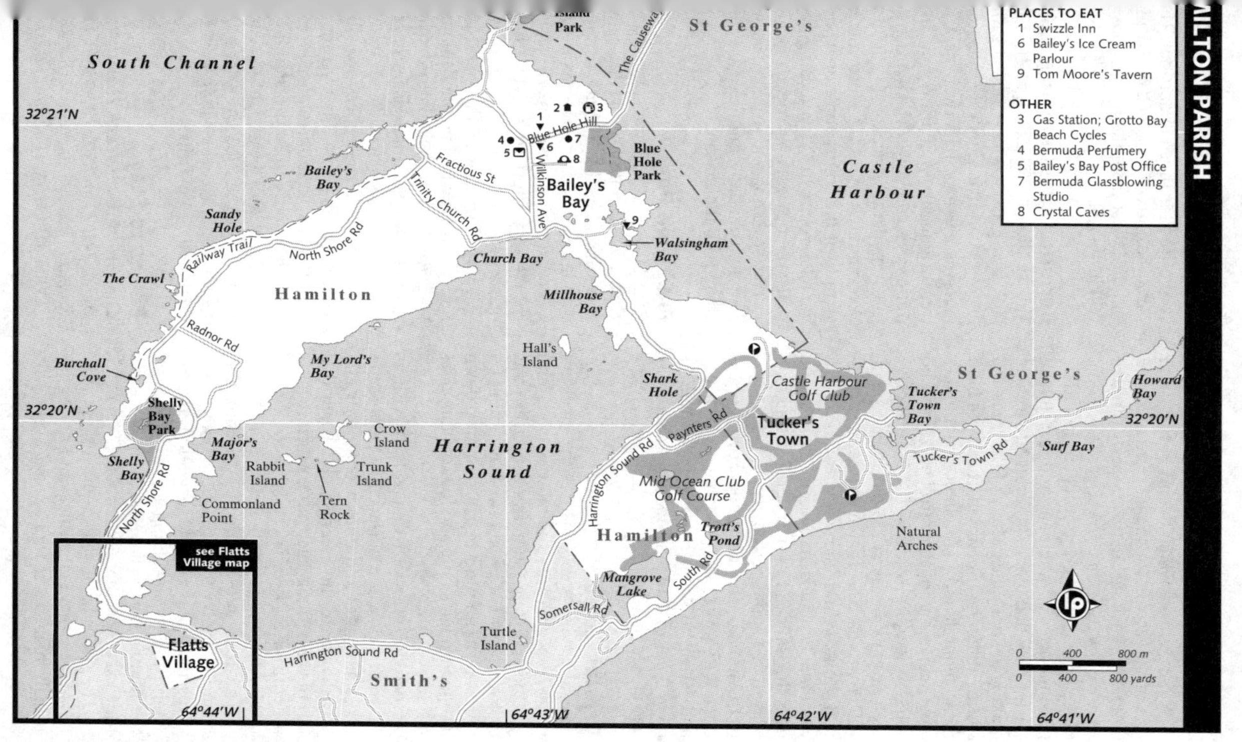

HAMILTON PARISH

purchase any of the perfumes, colognes and lotions.

A nature trail, which begins at the south side of the factory, loops one-third of a mile around the back side of the property through an area of woods and flower gardens. Some of the fragrant flowers grown here, including passionflowers, frangipani and a patch of Easter lilies that bloom in spring, are used in making the perfumes. Many of the trees and shrubs along the trail are marked with both their common and Latin names, so it makes a particularly enjoyable stroll for those who want to identify some of the flora they've seen around the island. The palmetto palm, which was used to thatch the earliest colonial homes, and the olivewood tree, a common Bermuda native, are both found near the trailhead. A free detailed trail map is available at the perfumery.

In summer, the Bermuda Perfumery is open 9:15 am to 5 pm Monday to Saturday and 10 am to 4 pm Sunday. In winter, it's open 9 am to 4:30 pm Monday to Saturday and closed Sunday.

Crystal Caves

Crystal Caves (☎ 293-0640) is the most impressive of the area's numerous caves and grottoes. This huge subterranean cavern was discovered in 1907 when two boys, intent on retrieving a stray cricket ball, shimmied down a rope through a hole and found themselves inside.

Today a series of 81 steps leads visitors 120 feet below the surface, past stalactites and stalagmites and onto a pontoon walkway that spans the greenish blue water that fills the cave floor. The water, which reaches a depth of 55 feet, is crystal clear, free of marine life and vegetation.

The tour guide provides an enjoyable commentary on the geologic origins of the caves and points out odd formations that resemble profiles, including a good likeness of the Manhattan skyline. All in all, it's a fun little excursion that takes about 20 minutes.

The site is open year-round, except for a few days around Christmas and during unusually high tides. Tours begin every half-hour from 9:30 am to 4 pm daily. Adr is $7.50 for adults, $4 for children ages 11 and free for those under four. The are at the end of Crystal Cave Rd, jus minutes' walk from the nearest bus s Wilkinson Ave.

Bermuda Glassblowing Stud

This studio (☎ 293-2234), at 16 Blu Hill, is a glassblowing workshop th duces decorative glassware, includi items as earrings, paperweights, Ch tree ornaments, miniature tree fr rines, vases and bowls. The items are site at moderate prices.

From the front of the store you ca glimpse of the craftspeople blowing the back room; for $2 you can go b watch the process up close.

The workshop and store are usua 9 am to 5 pm daily, but there are slig ations with the season.

Blue Hole Park

Blue Hole Park, off the south side Hole Hill road just before the caus an easily accessible 12-acre nature with numerous caves. The main tra follows a paved service road, passe ber of very short spur paths that marked sights.

The trail begins at the west sid reserve parking lot and almost imm leads to a bird-viewing platform ove a small pond. Two minutes farther a trail, a 40-foot side path leads to th way Cave, a fern-draped open li cavern. The main trail then passes facilities and continues east to a Bear left here to find a couple coastal caves, or bear right to reac overlooking the Blue Grotto, a pre like sunken cave. The whole walk t 20 minutes roundtrip.

Places to Stay

The ***Grotto Bay Beach Hotel*** *(☎ 800-582-3190 in the USA, ☎ 800-46 Canada, fax 293-2306, email gro 11 Blue Hole Hill, Hamilton Parish*

Bermuda's smaller resort hotels, with
oms spread around a dozen contem-
' two- and three-story buildings. The
e grounds have a couple of interesting
es and a small sandy beach with good
ing and snorkeling. Facilities include
a hot tub, four tennis courts, a fitness
and a water-sports center. The rooms
ir conditioning, TVs, phones, cof-
ers, small refrigerators, room safes,
-view verandas and either one king or
uble beds. Rates for either singles or
s without meals begin at $104 in
and $205 in summer. The hotel is
n a bus stop, making it convenient to
ous to either the City of Hamilton or
vn of St George.

s to Eat

s Ice Cream Parlour (☎ *293-9333*),
e Hole Hill opposite the Swizzle Inn,
-natural ice cream, frozen yogurt,
s, milkshakes and simple salads and
hes, all for under $5. It's open 11 am
Monday to Saturday, 11 am to 6 pm

opular ***Swizzle Inn*** (☎ *293-9300*), on
ole Hill, serves lunch from noon to
aily, with pub grub like shepherd's
gers and mash or beer-batter fish
os for around $14. Burgers or other
hes with fries average $9 and there
reasonably priced soups and salads.
er, from 6 to 10 pm nightly, entrees
om the curry of the day or a vege-
-fry for $15 to a 1lb rib-eye steak for
izzle Inn has both indoor and
dining. As its name implies, the es-
ent also lays claim to the island's
ghly touted rum swizzles – hence
tto 'Swizzle Inn, Stagger Out.' The
s open until 1 am, and in summer
ften entertainment from 9:30 pm to
t. There's also billiards, darts and
a TV.

Grotto Bay Beach Hotel (☎ *293-*
s a dining room that caters mostly
guests. Expect to pay around $15 for
akfast or lunch. At dinner, a la carte
ken and beef entrees average $20 to
$25. It's open for breakfast from 8 to 10:30 am, lunch from noon to 3 pm and dinner from 6:30 to 9 pm daily.

Tom Moore's Tavern (☎ *293-8020*), on secluded Walsingham Bay, is a perennial favorite for fine dining on the east side of the island. The restaurant occupies a historic waterfront house that dates back to 1652 and has several atmospheric dining rooms. The menu is continental with a French accent. Appetizers such as escargots, frog legs or seafood ceviche are priced around $16. Main courses, which average $33, include crispy duck in raspberry sauce, quail in puff pastry and standards such as shrimp scampi and cognac-flamed sirloin. Tom Moore's Tavern is open 7 to 9 pm nightly, and jackets are required for male diners. To get there, take Walsingham Rd off Harrington Sound Rd.

Getting There & Around

Both the northern (bus Nos 10 and 11) and the southern (bus Nos 1 and 3) bus routes around Harrington Sound converge at Bailey's Bay, making the village easy to reach on any bus traveling between the City of Hamilton and the Town of St George. At least one of these buses operates every 15 minutes from 6:45 am to 7 pm; bus No 11 provides evening service once an hour until 11:45 pm (10:45 pm on Sundays).

Mopeds can be rented at Grotto Bay Beach Cycles (☎ 293-2378), 17 Blue Hole Hill, which is at the gas station near the Grotto Bay Beach Hotel.

FLATTS VILLAGE

The village of Flatts, surrounding scenic Flatts Inlet, is home to the island's most visited attraction – the Bermuda Aquarium, Museum & Zoo.

In times past, Flatts had a reputation as a smugglers' haven, and Gibbet Island, the islet off Flatts, was once used for the execution of islanders accused of witchcraft. Today, Flatts' yacht-filled harbor shows little trace of that more sordid past. The bridge that crosses over the inlet is a good vantage point for views of the harbor and of the rapidly moving tidal waters that rush

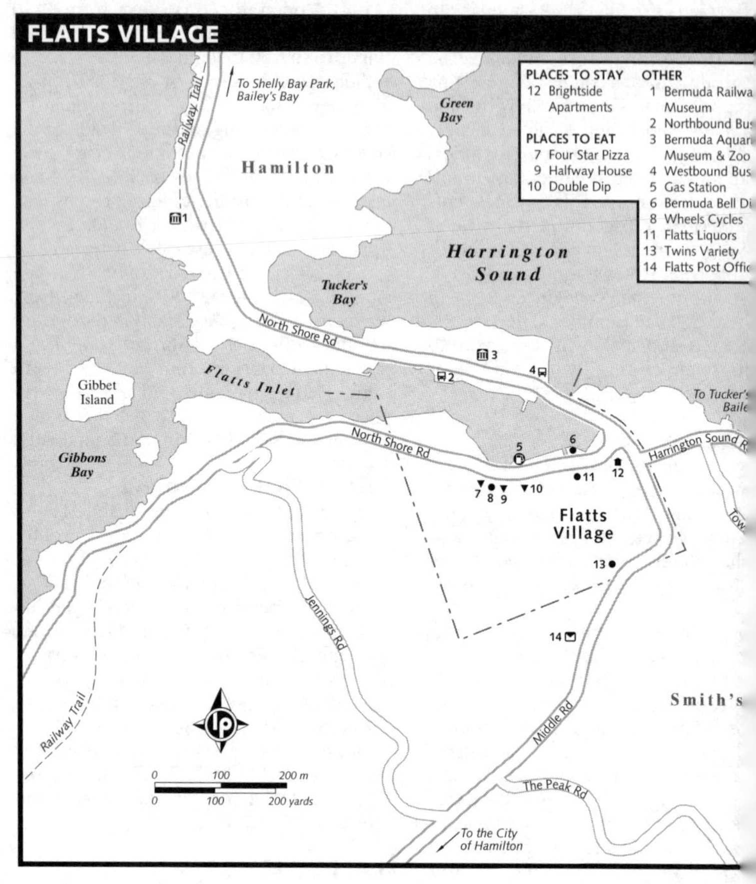

through the inlet to and from Harrington Sound.

Information

There's a Bank of Butterfield ATM outside Four Star Pizza, to the right of the front door. The Flatts post office (☎ 292-0741), 65 Middle Rd, is open 8 am to 5 pm weekdays.

Bermuda Aquarium, Museum & Zoo

The Bermuda Aquarium, Museum & Zoo (BAMZ; ☎ 293-2727) is a three-attraction site under a single roof at the nort Flatts. The aquarium dates to 1926, zoo and natural history museum we in more recent times. The facilities tinuously being upgraded and the has won international recognitio work in species preservation an efforts to increase awareness of pre vironmental issues. All in all, the s tractively presented and well worth

The **aquarium** contains two doz each arranged to show a microcosn muda's underwater ecosystem. The s

ɛent more than 200 species of fish, in-
ɹrates and corals. Be sure to pick up
ᶠ the 'Soundstiks' as you enter, which
a recorded commentary as you ap-
ı the fish tanks.

ʃ is a great place to identify some of
ɬorful tropical fish you may have seen
snorkeling or taking a glass-bottom
ruise, as the tanks have drawings and
ptions identifying their occupants.
include bright wrasses, rainbow par-
, spotted pufferfish, trumpetfish, an-
, tangs, damselfish, triggerfish and
eels, among many others.

aquarium's grand finale is at the new
0-gallon 'North Rock' tank, which
ıs a coral reef complete with purple
ıs, coral gardens and circling sharks,
ays and barracuda. The tank also dis-
Nassau groupers – once common in
da's waters but now fished to com-
ɬ extinction. The North Rock exhibit
rge that the BAMZ staffers actually
ɪt suits and dive into the tank a few
week – you can catch them swim-
ı the tank on Tuesdays, Saturdays and
's at 1 pm.

BAMZ, which is involved in sea
ɛcovery programs, also has tanks with
ɛa turtles and loggerhead turtles. An
r pool, between the aquarium and
history museum, contains harbor
ıcidentally, harbor seals are native to
ʃts of New England and Canada and
ɔund in Bermudian waters, but three
ɛals were born here at the aquarium.
want to learn more about these
mammals, staffers give a brief talk
ʃeals following their feedings, which
aily at 9 am and 1:30 and 4 pm.

ıatural history museum has simple
on Bermuda's volcanic origins and
ʃpects of its geology, including dune
e formations. It also houses 'Local
n exhibit dedicated to young chil-
th puzzles and interactive displays;
a storytelling program for children
Fridays – call ☎ 293-2727 ext 133 for
ıt schedule.

oo is small but interesting, with an
f parrots, toucans and other tropical

Witchcraft Hysteria

Bermuda was not immune from the witchcraft hysteria that swept Europe and America in the 17th century. The first death sentence imposed upon a 'witch' in Bermuda was in 1651, when a woman accused of evildoing by her neighbors was given a 'trial' in which her feet and hands were tied and she was thrown into the ocean.

In the eyes of her fellow islanders, the fact that the woman managed to float and not drown confirmed that she was indeed a witch, and she was subsequently hanged. Bermudians continued searching for witches in their midst until the hysteria ended in the 1690s.

birds, and a collection of primates such as golden lion tamarins (monkeys) and ring-tailed lemurs. Its latest addition is 'Islands of Australasia,' a nicely naturalized walk-through exhibit that lets you get eye-to-eye with wallabies, tree kangaroos, a monitor lizard and various nocturnal creatures.

There's also an invertebrate house with a children's 'touch pool' and a reptile section containing alligators and Galápagos tortoises. The Bermuda Zoo was the first to breed these giant turtles in captivity, so the tortoises you see here have offspring in North American and UK zoos.

The zoo has bred other endangered animals as well, including the nene, Hawaii's native goose, which can be seen in the aviary along with a large flock of Caribbean flamingos. Your visit helps support the zoo's work, as do purchases from its well-stocked gift shop, which sells environmentally themed T-shirts, toys, books and tapes.

The Bermuda Aquarium, Museum & Zoo is open 9 am to 5 pm daily all year, except on Christmas, with the last entry allowed at 4 pm. Admission costs $8 for adults and $4 for children ages five to 12; entry is free for children under five. The entire facility, including exhibits and restrooms, is wheelchair accessible.

Old Rattle & Shake

During the 1920s, British administrators on Bermuda decided that the island was ripe for a rail system. Locals, who were skeptical of the proposal, gave only tepid support, so the government turned to investors in England to provide the funding.

The complications in executing the project were great. People on land-scarce Bermuda didn't want to give up their property, so the railroad had to be erected largely along the coast, making it less than central. Then there were the engineering challenges: some 33 trestle bridges, half of them over water, had to be constructed along the 21 miles of track. By the time the first train left the station in 1931, the cost of the project had reached a lofty 1 million British pounds, making it one of the most expensive railways, on a per-mile basis, ever built.

The railway never caught on among islanders and quickly became a financial albatross. The reasons were numerous; the placement of the stations wasn't ideal and many people preferred to continue traveling by ferry. Still, most significant of all was the impact of WWII, which introduced the private automobile to Bermudian roads, and also made it difficult for railway operators to obtain spare parts and maintenance equipment.

By 1946, Bermuda's little railroad, which by then had been dubbed 'old rattle and shake,' was in such dire straits that the government took it over from its private owners. Passenger counts continued to drop, and on December 31, 1947, the train made its last run.

Bermuda Railway Museum

Housed in a building that once served as a railway station, this little 'museum' (☎ 293-1774), 37 North Shore Rd, has a 10-minute video presentation, a collection of period photos and a few other items relating to Bermuda's railroad, but it's largely a curiosity shop with consignment antiques such as old bottles, china, jewelry and oil lamp can also buy a reprinted map ($5) that Bermuda's former rail routes and deta history of that rail system.

The Bermuda Railway Museum is minute walk north of the Bermuda A ium, Museum & Zoo, but consider the northbound bus (just one stop), stops in front of both sites, as the r narrow and without sidewalks.

The museum is generally open 10 4 pm (to 2 pm in July and August) days; the owner lives in the house side. Admission is free, but donatio appreciated.

Railway Trail

If you're up for a hike, one section old railway trail starts, not surpri right at the grounds of the Bermud way Museum. You can follow it no for 3 miles to the east end of Ha Parish, passing the beach at Shelly B scenic coastal areas along Bailey's B further information on the trail, s Outdoor Activities chapter, near the the book.

Places to Stay

Brightside Apartments *(☎ 292-8410, 6968, email brightside@ibl.bm, PO 319, Smith's FL BX)*, on North Sh has a dozen units, some of which o picturesque Flatts Inlet. Rates in thi family-run place are the same year starting at $85 for a double room, $ cooking facilities. Fully equippe bedroom, two-bath units with kitch $160 to $230 for up to four people. A air-conditioning, ceiling fans and baths. There's a pool and a garden w trees out back. In the winter, monthl ment rentals are available for $2300

Places to Eat

Double Dip *(☎ 292-5580, 12 Nort Rd)*, in the village center, sells frozen ice cream, burgers, chicken sandwic fishcakes, all for under $5. Hours can irregular, but it's usually open noo least 5:30 pm.

nearby ***Four Star Pizza*** *(☎ 292-9111, h Shore Rd)* has 10-inch pizzas from 4-inch pizzas from $17. It's open daily 11 am (1 pm on Sunday) to 11 pm ight on weekends). You can eat in, ut or have the pizza delivered.

fway House *(☎ 295-5212, 8 North Rd)* is a friendly place with good tyle Bermudian food at honest prices. and dinner feature everything from dwiches to a hearty seafood plate with , scallops and panfried fish for $17. ocal treat, order the fishcake platter eas and rice ($7.25). On weekends lso serve breakfast with standards s an omelet with toast, bacon and juice for around $7. Halfway House th outdoor cafe tables and indoor It's open daily 11 am (8 am on week- o 10:30 pm.

most convenient place to pick up gro- s ***Twins Variety*** *(5 Middle Rd)*. You can get juice, beer, wine and spirits at ***Flatts Liquors***, on North Shore Rd in the village center.

Getting There & Around

From the City of Hamilton, bus No 3 goes to Flatts via Middle Rd, and bus Nos 10 and 11 run to Flatts via North Shore Rd. Traveling east from Flatts, bus Nos 10 and 11 continue through the north side of Hamilton Parish along the north shore, and Bus No 3 goes along the south side of Harrington Sound. All three buses go on to Bailey's Bay and the Town of St George.

At least one of these buses connects Flatts with both Hamilton and St George every 15 minutes from 6:45 am to 7 pm; bus No 11 provides evening service once an hour until 11:45 pm (10:45 pm on Sundays).

Mopeds can rented at Wheels Cycles (☎ 293-1280), on North Shore Rd in back of Four Star Pizza.

Smith's Parish

Smith's is the smallest of Bermuda's nine parishes, but it does lay claim to the highest point in Bermuda, a 259-foot hill that is, amusingly, called The Peak. This hill, on private property near the center of Smith's, is topped with a tower and visible from several points around the parish. The most scenic views in Smith's, however, are not found inland, but from the shoreline; the parish is bordered on the north and south by the ocean and on the east by Harrington Sound.

Although Smith's Parish is primarily residential, it does have a few notable sightseeing spots: the Verdmont historic house; a lovely public beach at John Smith's Bay; and Spittal Pond, Bermuda's finest nature reserve.

There are a couple of other green areas in Smith's that are set aside from development: the 7-acre Watch Hill Park near Albuoy's Point, just east of Spittal Pond on the south shore, and the 14-acre Penhurst Park, north shore. Watch Hill was once the a coastal fortification and has a nice view, and Penhurst is essentially a area that has a small dock and horse Both are used by islanders for picn but are of limited interest to most visi

The village of Flatts also falls parti Smith's, but because most of the villa Hamilton Parish, all information on F grouped together in the Hamilton chapter.

The population of Smith's Parish proximately 5400.

Highlights

- Tour the Verdmont Museum, the prized property of the Bermuda National Trust
- Enjoy a hike at Spittal Pond, a mecca for birdwatchers
- Relax on the lovely white sands of John Smith's Bay

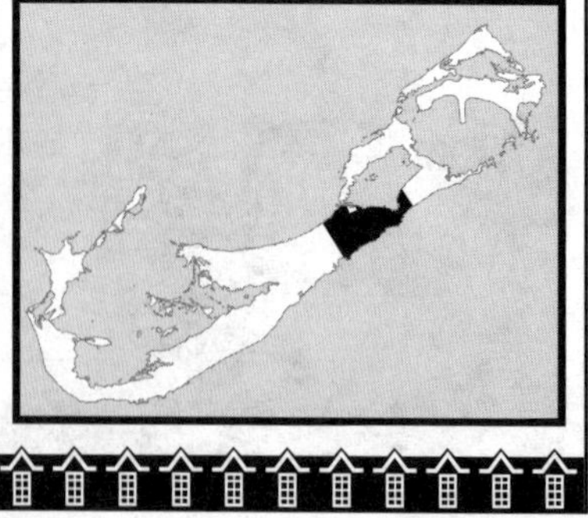

Verdmont Museum

Verdmont Museum (☎ 236-7369), o lectors Hill near its intersection with Rd, is the crown jewel of historic held by the Bermuda National Tru house, which enjoys a choice hillto was built in 1710 in a four-square Georgian style. It was once the cen 55-acre estate.

Although Verdmont was lived in was sold to the trust in 1951, its never significantly altered the prope continued to live without electri plumbing. Consequently, Verdmont its original character almost free fr modernization.

Entering the house is a bit like s back in history. It has walls made of pine captured through privateering, way of native Bermuda cedar and wood floors. Portraits of former r hang from the walls, and finely craft century furniture fills the rooms. A some of the items, including Spode and Chinese porcelain, were impo island traders, most of the furnit locally made. So much cedar was use the house that the air is still rich scent of the fragrant wood.

You'll notice there's no kitchen; tage outside the main house once s the cookhouse, which was a fairly

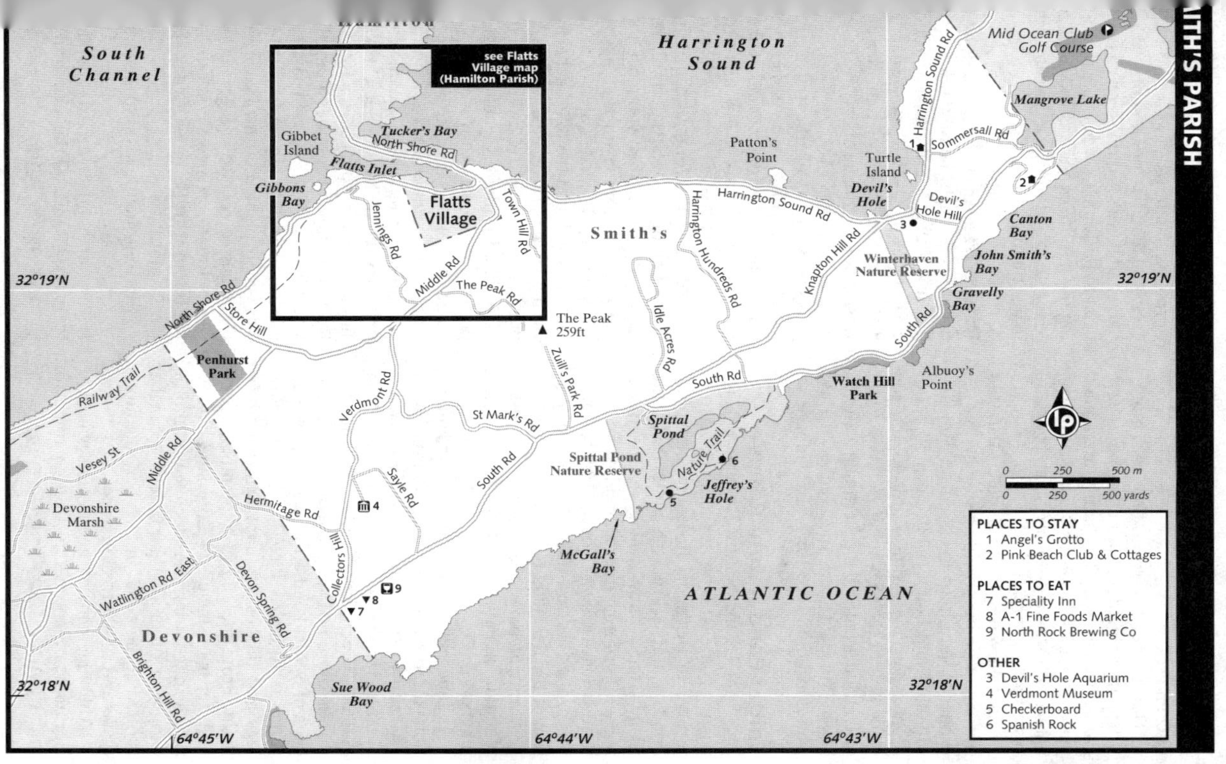
ITH'S PARISH
see Flatts Village map (Hamilton Parish)
South Channel
Harrington Sound
Mid Ocean Club Golf Course
Mangrove Lake
Gibbet Island
Tucker's Bay
North Shore Rd
Flatts Inlet
Gibbons Bay
Flatts Village
Jennings Rd
Town Hill Rd
Middle Rd
The Peak Rd
Smith's
Patton's Point
Turtle Island
Devil's Hole
Devil's Hole Hill
Harrington Sound Rd
Sommersall Rd
Harrington Hundreds Rd
Knapton Hill Rd
Winterhaven Nature Reserve
Canton Bay
John Smith's Bay
Gravelly Bay
32°19'N
Store Hill
Penhurst Park
The Peak 259ft
Idle Acres Rd
Zuill's Park Rd
South Rd
Albuoy's Point
Watch Hill Park
Railway Trail
Verdmont Rd
St Mark's Rd
Spittal Pond
Nature Trail
Spittal Pond Nature Reserve
Jeffrey's Hole
Vesey St
Devonshire Marsh
Hermitage Rd
Sayle Rd
Collectors Hill
McGall's Bay
ATLANTIC OCEAN
Watlington Rd East
Devon Spring Rd
Devonshire
Brighton Hill Rd
Sue Wood Bay
32°18'N
64°45'W
64°44'W
64°43'W
0 250 500 m
0 250 500 yards
PLACES TO STAY
1 Angel's Grotto
2 Pink Beach Club & Cottages
PLACES TO EAT
7 Speciality Inn
8 A-1 Fine Foods Market
9 North Rock Brewing Co
OTHER
3 Devil's Hole Aquarium
4 Verdmont Museum
5 Checkerboard
6 Spanish Rock

arrangement in colonial times that provided a measure of insurance from accidental kitchen fires.

The gardens surrounding the house, which are planted with flora known to have grown here in the 18th century, are a good place to look for eastern bluebirds, a colorful native bird with a distinctive blue back and russet-colored breast.

The well-versed trust volunteers that staff Verdmont enjoy providing insights on the property. Verdmont is closed on Sundays, Mondays and holidays but open 10 am to 4 pm other days. Admission is $3. Or, you could opt for the $5 combination ticket that also includes entry to the Bermuda National Trust Museum and the Tucker House Museum, both in the Town of St George.

Spittal Pond Nature Reserve

The Spittal Pond Nature Reserve, encompassing some 60 acres, is the largest nature reserve in Bermuda. It centers on Spittal Pond, a 9-acre brackish pond that's the island's finest **birdwatching** venue, attracting scores of migratory shorebirds and waterfowl. Once a favored duck-hunting locale, this property is now under the joint protection of the Bermuda National Trust and the government park system, which together maintain a nature trail for birders and hikers.

In tune with North American bird migration patterns, fall and winter offer the greatest variety of bird life. The earliest arrivals are the shorebirds, which begin appearing in August. The most abundant of the two dozen shorebird species that feed at the edge of Spittal Pond is the lesser yellowlegs, which is 10 inches long, has bright yellow legs and flashes a square white rump in flight. From the end of September, egrets and herons – including Louisiana herons, which have long slender necks and a wingspan of more than 3 feet – can be spotted at the pond. In October, migratory ducks and coots arrive in force.

Although many of the migrants winter in Bermuda, others merely stop en route to and from the Caribbean, so spring also brings migratory stopovers. In the q summer months, Spittal Pond is the d of resident mallards.

Spittal Pond is open sunrise to s daily, and there's no admission charge. want to birdwatch but not hike much, ing the park from the east side will g to the pond and some good birding va in just minutes.

Nature Trail An inviting mile-long trail runs through the Spittal Pond re passing a dairy farm, mixed wood coastal viewpoints, salt marshes and There are trailheads at both the ea west sides of the property, with p areas at each side.

It's possible to walk the trail as a lo ginning from either side. As there's r trail along the northwest side of the you'll have to walk a few minutes South Rd at the end of the 'loop,' but wise you'll be on a footpath the entir

Starting at the west-side trailhea the middle route when you reach the fence and continue on that path, leads through a wooded area of mix etation. You'll find the only cactus na Bermuda, the prickly pear, thrives i open areas here and elsewhere on th

Within 10 minutes, you'll reach posted coastal area known as the **C board**, so named because weatheri worn cross joints into the limesto here, leaving a pattern of square-sha pressions resembling a huge checke Just after that, a cattle gate leads thro fence as the path continues along th side of Spittal Pond. The trail passes a forest of casuarina, an Australian t was widely planted throughout Ber the 1950s to replace the groves o cedars lost to cedar-scale infestatio the boxed text 'Bermuda Cedar,' e the chapter.)

The trail then leads into a mars with sea lavender, salt grass and freshwater pond favored by malla teals. A right fork off the main trail short detour to **Jeffrey's Hole**, a s

rmuda Cedar

Bermuda cedar tree *(Juniperus bermudiana)*, endemic to Bermuda, was abundant on the ds when the first settlers shipwrecked in 1609. In fact, it was cedar that the settlers used to craft ships that took them to the New World. Not only did this native cedar prove suitable for shipding, it was also harvested for the construction of homes, forts and furniture. So important was cedar to the well-being of the colonists that they issued legislation to protect the trees and also awed the export of cedar timber.

he Bermuda cedar was still the most predominant tree on the island until 1942, when a scale ct was accidentally introduced and an epidemic spread like wildfire. Within a decade, more than of the island's cedar trees had succumbed to the epidemic.

iological controls, such as the release of insects that naturally prey upon the scale insect, were duced in an attempt to stop the devastation. In time, those Bermuda cedars that did survive n to develop a resistance to the scale insect. Seeds from these healthy surviving trees have intensely propagated in recent years as part of a successful community-wide campaign to the Bermuda cedar back from near extinction.

uch of the hands-on work of raising and planting the seedlings has been done by volunteers, ng from the local Rotary Club to school and garden organizations. Thanks to their efforts, g Bermuda cedars are becoming an increasingly common sight in island parks and gardens.

for an escaped slave who is said to owed away there, and then continues site of **Spanish Rock**. The original nscribed with the initials TF and the 43, is thought to have been carved by ded Spanish or Portuguese mariner.

n Spanish Rock, continue back to the rail, which offers good birding vans it passes along the southeast side of Pond. After reaching the gate, you her take a short side trail up to the de parking area or continue west he northeast side of the pond until il leads up to South Rd.

's Hole Aquarium

Hole Aquarium (☎ 293-2072), on gton Sound Rd at the east side of Parish, is not really an aquarium but a seawater-filled grotto conto Harrington Sound by natural tunr $5 ($3 for children), visitors can o the water from a wooden walkway r down at stocked sea turtles and fish circling below. It closes from r through March, but during other months it is open 9:30 am to 4:30 pm daily except holidays.

John Smith's Bay

This pretty public beach, with its broad swath of white sand, faces east and offers sheltered waters good for swimming and snorkeling. During the season there's a lifeguard, whom it's good to ask about water conditions before heading out into deeper waters, as there are occasional rip currents. Restroom facilities can be found at the south side of the beach.

John Smith's Bay is right along the side of South Rd. If you pass by at 6 am, expect to see the members of Bermuda's 'Polar Bear Club' taking their daily morning dip here.

Outdoor Activities

The best hiking and birdwatching is at Spittal Pond (see Spittal Pond Nature Reserve, earlier in this chapter). In addition, one section of the Railway Trail, which runs 1¾ miles from Devonshire Parish to the village of Flatts, passes through the north side of Smith's Parish.

Places to Stay

Angel's Grotto *(☎ 293-1986, 800-550-6288 ext 1986 in the USA and Canada, ☎ 0800-969459 ext 1986 in the UK, fax 293-4164, email ang@ibl.bm, PO Box HS 81, Smith's HS BX)* is a neat little owner-operated complex right on Harrington Sound. It has seven air-conditioned units, each with kitchen, private bath, living room, TV and phone. Prices range from $120 for a one-bedroom courtyard unit to $200 for a two-bedroom water-view apartment. There's an additional $30 charge per adult ($15 per child) for parties larger than two. It's not in a village center, but it is on the bus route.

Pink Beach Club & Cottages *(☎ 293-1666, 800-355-6161 in the USA and Canada, fax 293-8935, email info@pinkbeach.com, PO Box HM 1017, Hamilton HM DX)* is an attractive complex on the quiet south shore. Recently renovated, it has 90 units spread among two dozen low-rise pink buildings, most of which face the coast and two private sandy beaches. Each unit has air-conditioning, private bath, phone, room safe and patio. The common areas include two tennis courts, a pool, a lounge with a fireplace, a fitness club and a seafront dining room. Rates begin at $245/325 in winter/summer for two with breakfast, $285/365 with breakfast and dinner. Pink Beach Club & Cottages has a website at www.pinkbeach.com.

For information on Brightside Apartments in Flatts Village, see the Hamilton Parish chapter.

Places to Eat

All of the following places are on South Rd near its intersection with Collectors Hill.

A-1 Fine Foods Market is a full-service grocery store that's open 8 am to 10 pm Monday to Saturday and 1 to 5 pm Sunday.

The ***Speciality Inn*** *(☎ 236-3133)* has the character of a small-town diner and serves breakfast, lunch and dinner. Fish and chips, ribs and other simple dishes cost around $10, breakfast fare tends to run a few dollars less. It's open from 6 am to 10 pm Mond[ay to] Saturday.

North Rock Brewing Co *(☎ 236-[…]* about 100 yards to the east along Sout[h Rd] is a popular brewpub and restauran[t. It] has a pleasant dark-wood interior. Yo[u can] view the tanks where the brews are [made] and for $3.25, you can try four differe[nt] samples of the frothy final product. The [menu] is extensive, including appetizers su[ch as] Cajun shrimp and satay chicken as w[ell as] a variety of salads, burgers and sandw[iches] for under $10. In addition, there are [fish] and other meat dishes, such as the co[…] chicken stuffed with bananas, that [range] from around $15 at lunch to $20 at d[inner.] It's open for lunch from 11:30 am to [...] and for dinner from 6 to 10 pm; th[e bar] remains open until 1 am.

Getting There & Around

Three main roads run west to east [through] Smith's Parish: North Shore Rd alo[ng the] north coast, South Rd along the sout[h coast] and Middle Rd through the interior. [Buses] that run between the City of Hamilt[on and] the Town of St George cross Smith's [on all] three of these west-east roads.

Bus No 1 takes South Rd, stopping [near] Verdmont Museum, Spittal Pond N[ature] Reserve and John Smith's Bay. It op[erates] every 30 minutes from 6:45 am to 6[…] weekdays and from 7:45 am to 5:45 p[m Sat]urday. On Sunday the service is hourl[y from] 11 am to 5 pm.

Bus No 3 takes Middle Rd to Flat[ts and] edges along the south shore of Har[rington] Sound, operating every 30 minute[s from] 7:15 am to 6:15 pm weekdays, once [...] from 8:15 am to 6:15 pm Saturday, ar[nd] hourly from 9:15 am to 5:30 pm Sunc[ay].

Bus Nos 10 and 11 operate along [North] Shore Rd and provide service abou[t every] 15 minutes Monday to Saturday from [...] to 7 pm and then at least once an ho[ur until] 11:45 pm. Sunday service runs at lea[st] hourly from 7:45 am to 10:45 pm.

̶vonshire Parish

very center of the island, sandwiched en three parishes – Pembroke, Paget mith's – Devonshire remains one of uda's less-touristed areas, but it does a few gardens and historic sights.

on North Shore Rd, the Bermuda Na- Trust maintains the early 18th-century **tto House**, which has a few rooms with furnishings but is most interesting for itectural features: its cruciform shape elcoming-arm stairs. However, the is occupied by an elderly couple and tly has very limited opening hours; e Trust (☎ 236-6483) for information.

North Shore Rd, west of Palmetto , are two adjacent parks: The 17-acre **tto Park** is a relatively large green with water views that's popular with rs as a picnicking spot. The tiny **on Bay Park**, right at Robinson Bay, ocky shoreline.

h of Palmetto House is the **Devon- Marsh** area, part of which is under the s of the Bermuda Audubon Society. gh the wet marsh is difficult to enter, re birding possibilities along the roads that border the marsh, partic- long Vesey St.

Old Devonshire Church, at the inter- of Middle and Brighton Hill Rds, o 1716 but has been rebuilt a few nost recently following an explosion Still, it's a Devonshire landmark of nd has some 16th-century silver on

population of Devonshire Parish is mately 7500.

nation

vonshire post office (☎ 236-0281), at ge Valley Rd, is open 8 am to 5 pm ys.

Grove Garden

asant private garden, just off South osite Brighton Hill Rd, has lawns tues, lots of flowering shrubs and

Highlights

- Take a peaceful walk among native and exotic trees at the Arboretum
- Enjoy an affordable round of golf at the government-run Ocean View Golf Course
- Throw a coin into the wishing well at Palm Grove Garden

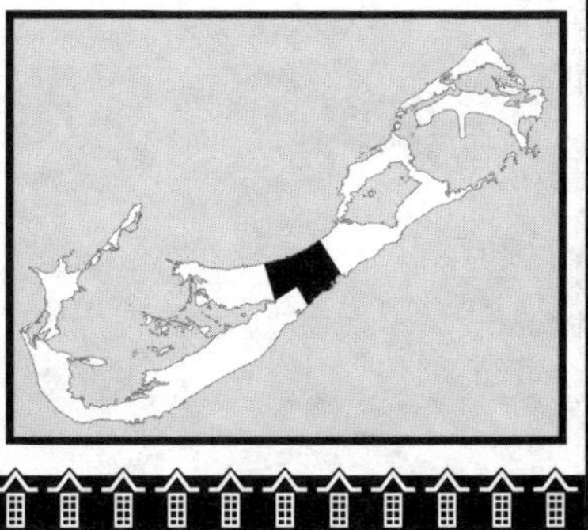

trees, tropical plants, a handsome moongate and a wishing well.

Walk up the hill, beyond cages holding a few exotic parrots and toucans, and you'll find a unique reflecting pool that contains a map of Bermuda outlined in concrete and given an element of relief with a cover of green turf.

The property is owned by one of Bermuda's more prominent families, the Gibbons, who open the garden to the public 9 am to 5 pm Monday to Thursday. Admission is free.

Devonshire Bay Park

Just 300 yards east of the Palm Grove Garden is Devonshire Bay Rd, which leads south to Devonshire Bay Park. A three-minute walk from road's end takes you to the top of a casuarina-shaded hill. This was once the site of the Devonshire Bay Battery, built in the 1860s when the US Civil War

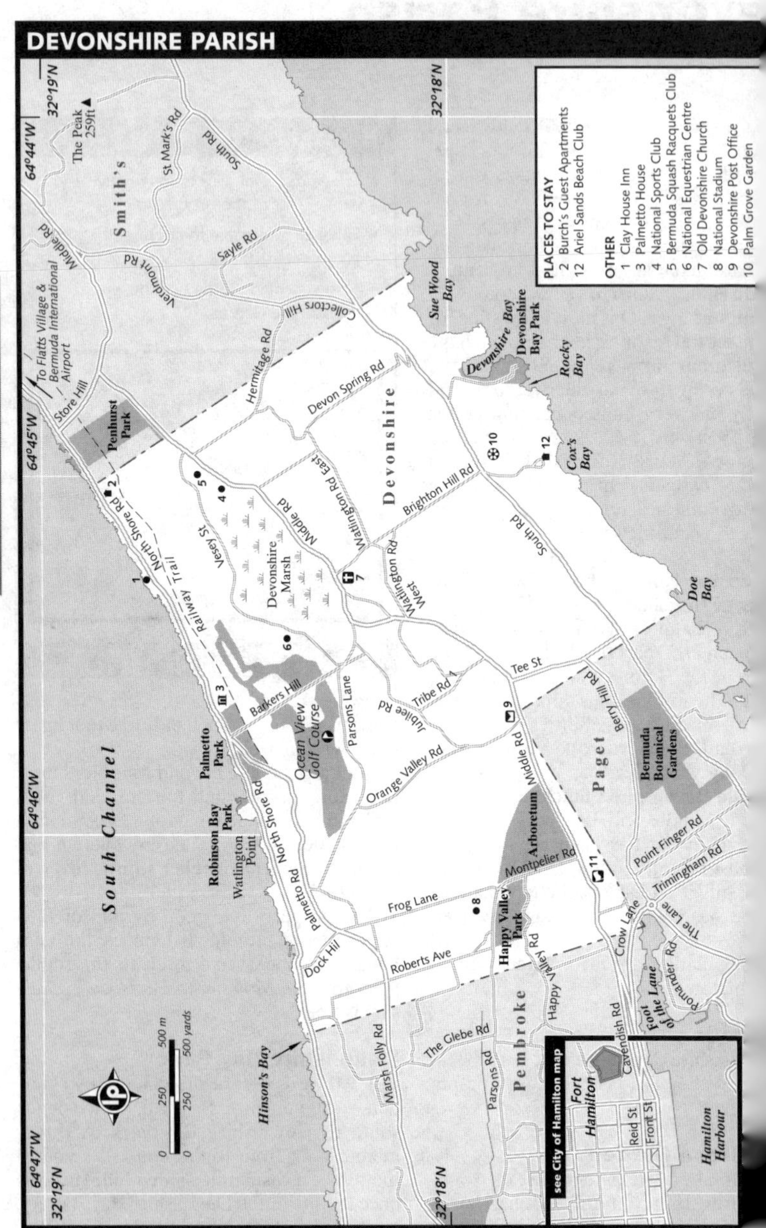

DEVONSHIRE PARISH
PLACES TO STAY
2 Burch's Guest Apartments
12 Ariel Sands Beach Club
OTHER
1 Clay House Inn
3 Palmetto House
4 National Sports Club
5 Bermuda Squash Racquets Club
6 National Equestrian Centre
7 Old Devonshire Church
8 National Stadium
9 Devonshire Post Office
10 Palm Grove Garden
South Channel
Devonshire
Smith's
Paget
Pembroke
Devonshire Marsh
Ocean View Golf Course
Penhurst Park
Palmetto Park
Robinson Bay Park
Watlington Point
Arboretum
Happy Valley Park
Bermuda Botanical Gardens
Devonshire Bay Park
Devonshire Bay
Sue Wood Bay
Rocky Bay
Cox's Bay
Doe Bay
Hinson's Bay
Hamilton Harbour
Fort Hamilton
The Peak 259ft
To Flatts Village & Bermuda International Airport
see City of Hamilton map
North Shore Rd
Railway Trail
Middle Rd
South Rd
Vesey St
Barkers Hill
Parsons Lane
Orange Valley Rd
Jubilee Rd
Tribe Rd
Tee St
Watlington Rd East
Watlington Rd West
Brighton Hill Rd
Devon Spring Rd
Hermitage Rd
Collectors Hill
Verdmont Rd
Sayle Rd
St Mark's Rd
Store Hill
Palmetto Rd
Dock Hill
Frog Lane
Roberts Ave
Montpelier Rd
Berry Hill Rd
Point Finger Rd
Trimingham Rd
Crow Lane
The Lane
Pomander Rd
Foot of the Lane
Cavendish Rd
Happy Valley Rd
The Glebe Rd
Marsh Folly Rd
Parsons Rd
Reid St
Front St
64°44'W
64°45'W
64°46'W
64°47'W
32°19'N
32°18'N
0 250 500 m
0 250 500 yards

tened tensions between the British and mericans. Remnants of the battery, y some partial walls, can still be seen, e main attractions these days are the illtop coastal view and the crashing f the Atlantic below.

park also has a little cove that's used rily by fishers to harbor their boats ean fish.

retum

2-acre property, occupying a valley at rner of Middle and Montpelier Rds, veloped into an arboretum in the late after the land was turned over to the government by the British War Dept. concept for the new arboretum was ner a collection of trees and shrubs re capable of flourishing in Bermuda. nens were brought in from countries flung as Japan, New Guinea and a, in addition to others presented by Elizabeth II from the Royal Botanic ns in Kew. The trees include conifers, fruit and nut trees, and such exotics as trees and black ebony.

aged by the Dept of Agriculture, the tum is a pleasant place that's crossed led walking paths. Visitors are free to ne grounds any day between sunrise nset.

If you enter the grounds through the Montpelier Rd entrance, you can make a pleasant 20-minute clockwise stroll that first takes you through a wildflower meadow of coreopsis, narcissus and endemic Bermudiana flowers. It then loops through the arboretum's conifer collection, which includes native Bermuda cedar and Norfolk Island pines; goes past a gazebo framed by large olive trees; and finally comes to a palm collection, which includes native Bermuda palmettos and Chinese fan palms. The walk ends by looping back to your starting point across a lawn of Bermuda grass.

rmudiana

Bermudiana Flower

One of Bermuda's few endemic flowers is the Bermudiana *(Sisyrinchium bermudiana)*, a tiny blue-purple iris with a yellow center and grasslike leaves, which resembles the blue-eyed grass of North America. It blooms from mid-April through May.

There's a bus stop on Middle Rd directly in front of the Arboretum. If you arrive by moped, there's a parking area at the south-eastern side of the Arboretum, off Montpelier Rd, at the main entrance and trailhead.

Activities

In addition to the walk through the Arboretum, if you're up for a hike, a section of the Railway Trail runs through Devonshire. It starts at the back side of Palmetto Park and continues 1¾ miles to the village of Flatts, passing Palmetto House en route and taking in coastal and inland views.

Other recreation options in Devonshire include golf at the Ocean View Golf Course and squash at the Bermuda Squash Racquets Club. For more information consult the Outdoor Activities chapter.

Places to Stay

Burch's Guest Apartments *(☎ 292-5746, 800-637-4116 in the USA, email bur@bspl.bm, 110 North Shore Rd, Devonshire FL 03)* has 10 units with kitchenettes. Although it's not central to restaurants or other tourist facilities, there is a nearby bus stop. The grounds have a little garden area with a pool. Singles/doubles cost $65/80, and there's an apartment for three people for $99. Rates are the same year-round.

Ariel Sands Beach Club *(☎ 236-1010, 800-468-6610 in the USA, fax 236-0087, email ariel@ibl.bm, PO Box HM 334, Hamilton HM BX)*, on the south shore of Devonshire is, a tranquil hotel on a private white-sand beach. Named after the magical spirit in

Shakespeare's *The Tempest*, the property is owned by the mother of actor Michael Douglas. The 47 rooms, which are spread around the grounds in a dozen buildings, have private baths, air-conditioning and, in most cases, verandas with sea views. Facilities include freshwater and saltwater pools, a guest lounge with a fireplace, three tennis courts and a bar and restaurant. Some of the guestrooms, as well as the commons building with the restaurant and lounge, are wheelchair accessible. Rates start at $220/270 in winter/summer for a double with breakfast; for another $30 per person, there's a MAP plan that includes both breakfast and dinner. Ariel Sands Beach Club maintains a website at www.arielsands.com.

Places to Eat

Caliban's *(☎ 236-1010)*, at Ariel Sands Beach Club on South Rd, has a pleasant setting, with both indoor and patio dining overlooking the beach. The a la carte menu features appetizers such as Caesar salad, smoked salmon or tuna carpaccio, and main courses include the likes of rack of lamb, sautéed jumbo shrimp or honey-roasted duck. Expect lunch, which is served from noon to 2:30 pm, to cost $15 to $25, and dinner, from 7 to 9 pm, to run closer to $40.

Entertainment

The ***Clay House Inn*** *(☎ 292-3193, 77 North Shore Rd)* is the area's main music spot. From April to October, there's a show that includes steel band and calypso music, as well as limbo dancing, on Tuesday, Wednesday and Thursday night; the cover c[…] $23 includes two drinks. On Friday an[…] urday, there's either a DJ or a ban[…] music is usually reggae or rhythm and […] and the cover charge is $5 to $10.

Ariel Sands Beach Club *(☎ 236-10[…]* South Rd, often has music from aroun[…] 11 pm, typically a solo pianist, voca[…] live band. Call for the schedule, as it […] with the season.

Spectator Sports

Because of its central location, Devo[…] Parish is home to a number of sports […] The National Stadium, on Frog Lane, […] variety of Bermuda-wide and intern[…] sporting events. At the National […] Club, on Middle Rd, rugby clubs comp[…] weekends from October to April. T[…] tional Equestrian Centre, on Vesey S[…] site of harness racing on Sunday afte[…] from January to March, as well as p[…] dressage shows.

Getting There & Around

Devonshire Parish is crossed by thre[…] roads that run west to east: South R[…] the south coast, North Shore Rd on th[…] coast and Middle Rd through the int[…]

Buses that run between the […] Hamilton and the Town of St Georg[…] Devonshire on all three of these w[…] roads. Bus No 1 operates along So[…] bus No 3 along Middle Rd and bus […] and 11 along North Shore Rd. For th[…] ule frequency, see the Getting […] section in the Smith's Parish chapter

ıget Parish

is one of the more popular parishes ›itors, not only because of its proxim- the City of Hamilton but also because ›ow Beach, the first of a string of lovely beaches that extends along Ber- 's southwest shore. The parish also has ling botanical gardens that shouldn't sed.

et has a good variety of accommoda- ·anging from moderately priced guest- ; to expensive resort hotels.

re are two main visitor areas. Most ac- odations are centered between Elbow and Paget village, the tiny commer- nter at the intersection of Middle and Rds.

parish's south shore attracts the ;oers; the north side, along Hamilton ır, is suited for those looking to get from the tourist crowd. The north Salt Kettle area, a quiet established neighborhood of older homes and well-to-do families, has a handful of small hotels with picturesque views across the harbor to the City of Hamilton.

The parish population is approximately 5100.

ılights

- ıll the Bermuda Botanical Gardens and n to identify many of the plants found ınd the island
- : Camden House, with its gracious od interior
- for yourself why Elbow Beach is a l favorite

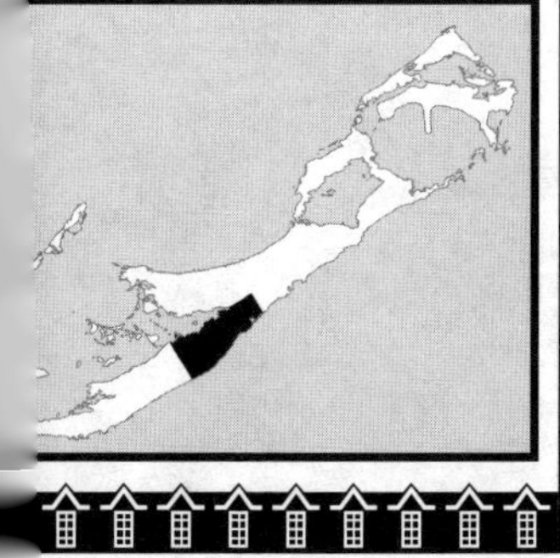

Information

Rural Hill Plaza, on South Rd about 200 yards east of Middle Rd, has a 24-hour ATM that accepts MasterCard and Visa, as well as Cirrus and Plus bankcards.

The Paget post office (☎ 236-7429), at 108 Middle Rd near its intersection with South Rd, is open 8 am to 5 pm weekdays.

King Edward VII Memorial Hospital (☎ 911 for emergencies, 236-2345 for non-emergencies), Bermuda's general hospital, is at 7 Point Finger Rd, just south of Berry Hill Rd.

Paget Pharmacy (☎ 295-3838), in the Rural Hill Plaza on South Rd, is open 8 am to 8 pm Monday to Saturday, 10 am to 6 pm Sunday.

Bermuda Botanical Gardens

The 36-acre Bermuda Botanical Gardens, bordered by South Rd and Berry Hill Rd, are the finest place in Bermuda for enjoying and identifying the island's varied flora. Originally opened in 1898, these delightful gardens encompass everything from formal plantings of roses and perennials to lofty trees and an aviary.

If you enter from the main gate on Berry Hill Rd, you'll immediately pass a cacti collection with aloes and other succulents that tolerate Bermuda's humid climate. Opposite the cacti collection is a section of conifer trees – both subtropical and temperate varieties thrive here.

Just 100 yards south of the gate is the visitor center (☎ 236-5291), open 9:30 am to 3:30 pm Tuesday to Saturday, which shows a 20-minute video presentation on the gardens (on request) and distributes a free brochure with a garden map and site

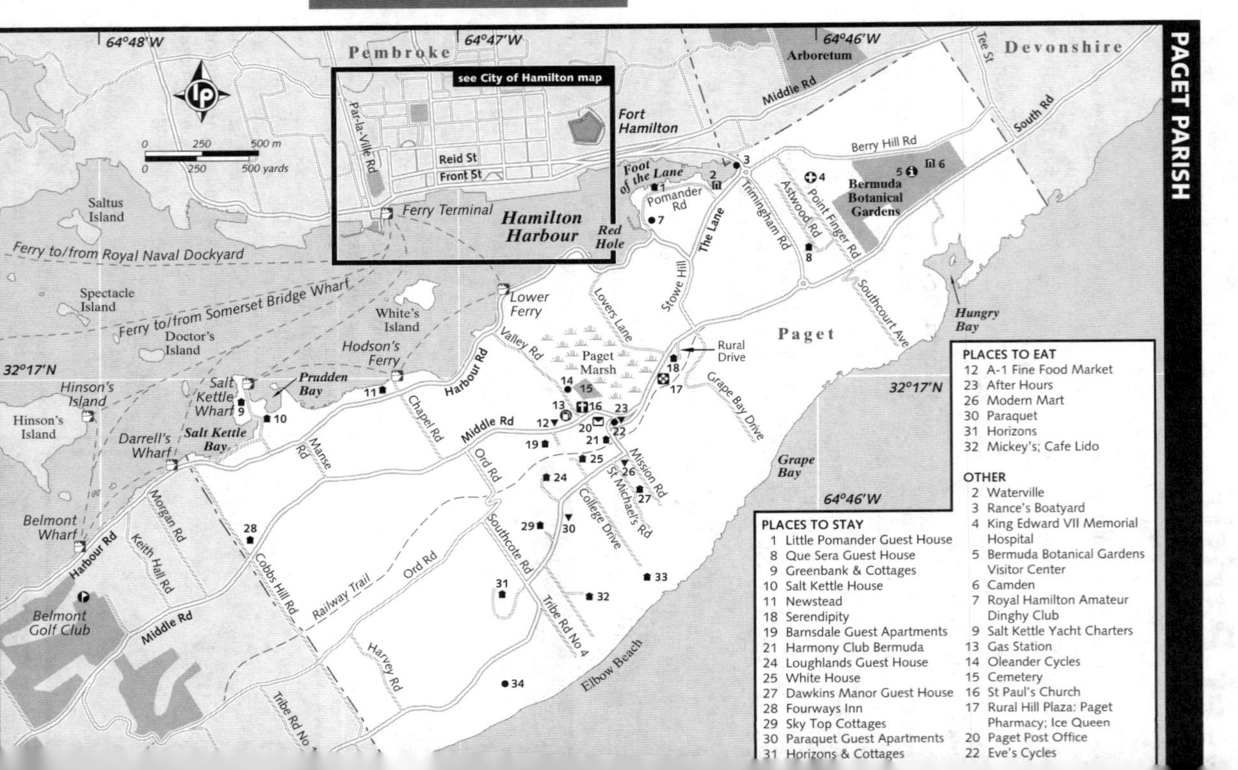
PAGET PARISH
PLACES TO EAT
12 A-1 Fine Food Market
23 After Hours
26 Modern Mart
30 Paraquet
31 Horizons
32 Mickey's; Cafe Lido
OTHER
2 Waterville
3 Rance's Boatyard
4 King Edward VII Memorial Hospital
5 Bermuda Botanical Gardens Visitor Center
6 Camden
7 Royal Hamilton Amateur Dinghy Club
9 Salt Kettle Yacht Charters
13 Gas Station
14 Oleander Cycles
15 Cemetery
16 St Paul's Church
17 Rural Hill Plaza: Paget Pharmacy; Ice Queen
20 Paget Post Office
22 Eve's Cycles
PLACES TO STAY
1 Little Pomander Guest House
8 Que Sera Guest House
9 Greenbank & Cottages
10 Salt Kettle House
11 Newstead
18 Serendipity
19 Barnsdale Guest Apartments
21 Harmony Club Bermuda
24 Loughlands Guest House
25 White House
27 Dawkins Manor Guest House
28 Fourways Inn
29 Sky Top Cottages
30 Paraquet Guest Apartments
31 Horizons & Cottages
see City of Hamilton map
Pembroke
Devonshire
Paget
64°48'W
64°47'W
64°46'W
32°17'N
0 250 500 m
0 250 500 yards
Fort Hamilton
Arboretum
Middle Rd
Tee St
South Rd
Berry Hill Rd
Bermuda Botanical Gardens
Par-la-Ville Rd
Reid St
Front St
Ferry Terminal
Hamilton Harbour
Red Hole
Foot of the Lane
Pomander Rd
The Lane
Trimingham Rd
Astwood Rd
Point Finger Rd
Southcourt Ave
Hungry Bay
Saltus Island
Ferry to/from Royal Naval Dockyard
Spectacle Island
Ferry to/from Somerset Bridge Wharf
Doctor's Island
White's Island
Lower Ferry
Stowe Hill
Lovers Lane
Valley Rd
Paget Marsh
Rural Drive
Grape Bay Drive
Grape Bay
Hodson's Ferry
Prudden Bay
Salt Kettle Wharf
Salt Kettle Bay
Hinson's Island
Darrell's Wharf
Harbour Rd
Chapel Rd
Manse Rd
Ord Rd
Mission Rd
St Michael's Rd
College Drive
Southcote Rd
Tribe Rd No 4
Belmont Wharf
Morgan Rd
Keith Hall Rd
Cobbs Hill Rd
Railway Trail
Belmont Golf Club
Harvey Rd
Elbow Beach
Tribe Rd No

ptions. The center also has restrooms gift shop that sells cold drinks, snacks ome interesting souvenirs, including al history books, coffee mugs and at-e T-shirts with floral designs.

ne of the park's highlights include a garden with native palmetto trees, a pical fruit garden, a garden for the hat features scented plants, a plumeria ion, a section of endemic and native , a ficus collection with rubber and n trees, and a flowering hibiscus gar-nere's also an orchard area with large ees, including mangoes, soursops and ida's oldest avocado tree. In addition, re greenhouses with orchids, brome-nd a variety of flowering houseplants.

in all, it's a delightful place to stroll, ere are picnic tables and benches if ant to linger longer. Because the are labeled, you can see and identify of what the gardens have to offer on wn. However, if you want more in-nto the gardens, the visitor center ree guided tours at 10:30 am Tuesday, sday and Friday.

u take a bus from Hamilton, the easi- to get to the gardens is to get off at Edward VII Memorial Hospital on nger Rd. Walk south from the hospi-take the path that begins directly op-Astwood Rd.

Bermuda Botanical Gardens are open to sunset daily, year-round. Admis-ree.

en

n, the official residence of Bermuda's , is at the northeast corner of the a Botanical Gardens. This graceful on house was built in the early 18th though its front verandas and bow s were later additions. In 1823, the was bought by the Tuckers, one of a's most prestigious families. One ccupants was Henry James Tucker, ved as the mayor of Hamilton from 1870 and started an arrowroot fac-he property.

re recent times, Camden was turned the Bermuda government to be incorporated into the botanical gardens. The house was restored in the 1970s and set aside for the premier, although in actuality it is not used as a living quarters but rather for official receptions.

Camden has a gracious interior that reflects its history and is decorated with antiques, a Waterford crystal chandelier, gilt mirrors and portraits of former premiers. The interior liberally incorporates native Bermuda cedar, which is used in the elegant staircase and wall paneling, as well as in much of the period furniture.

You don't have to wait for a formal invitation to peek inside – just stop by between noon and 2 pm on Tuesday or Friday, when Camden opens its doors to the general public. The hospitable curator enjoys talking to visitors about the history of the home, and admission is free.

Arrowroot

The rhizomes of the arrowroot plant *(Maranta arundinacea)* yield a nutritious, easily digestible starch that can be used as a thickener in gravies, puddings and other dishes. In modern times, less-expensive cornstarch has largely replaced arrowroot in the kitchen, but in days past, arrowroot was one of Bermuda's major exports.

There were two main arrowroot factories in Bermuda, one of them started by Henry James Tucker, the mayor of Hamilton in the mid-19th century. Tucker lived in Camden, a plantation house at the current Bermuda Botanical Gardens, and the arrowroot factory, where the starch was soaked from the plants and dried in the sun, was built in back of the house. The arrowroot starch exported by the Tuckers was well regarded in both England and America for its high quality.

Although arrowroot starch is no longer produced in Bermuda, Tucker's arrowroot factory still remains. These days it harbors a collection of endemic and native ferns and is one of the sights that visitors can take in at the botanical gardens.

Double Fantasy

In 1980, while John Lennon was in Bern working on compositions for an upcor album, he took a break to stroll through Bermuda Botanical Gardens. Here he spott beautiful freesia in bloom and bent dow take a closer look. The flower was lab 'Double Fantasy.' When Lennon stood u reportedly smiled and jotted down the flo name – he had found the perfect title fc new album.

Double Fantasy, Lennon's final album released shortly before his death, in 1980. the origin of the album's title surfaced, Le fans made efforts to seek out the little fl and for years the botanical gardens' stayed busy replacing the flower's ident label, which kept disappearing.

The park eventually decided to deal wi souvenir issue by printing T-shirts with a tractive 'Double Fantasy' flower desig stocking them in the visitor center gift sh

Waterville

Built around 1725, Waterville is one of the oldest buildings in Bermuda; quite suitably, it's now the headquarters of the Bermuda National Trust.

At the head of Hamilton Harbour, on The Lane just west of the roundabout, Waterville (☎ 236-6483) is open free to visitors 9 am to 5 pm weekdays. It was built by John Trimingham II, the grandson of an early Bermudian governor, and stayed in the Trimingham family for seven generations, until 1990. Over the years it was used as living quarters, a cargo storage area for the family's shipping fleet, a general store and a guesthouse (authors EB White and James Thurber were two of the better-known guests).

These days, in addition to housing the Bermuda National Trust's administrative offices, Waterville contains two rooms of antique furnishings, including a Jamaican mahogany sideboard, Staffordshire figurines, china and period portraits. There's a small rose garden located at one side of th ing and a grand 300-year-old tamari out front.

Paget Marsh

Paget Marsh, bordered on the sc South Rd and on the east by Lovers a 25-acre wetland nature reserve maintained by the Bermuda Nation and the Bermuda Audubon Society.

Despite having the appearance c hospitable overgrown swamp, the one of the least-disturbed natural Bermuda and contains the last virg of two endemic trees, the Bermuda p and the Bermuda cedar. In additio Marsh holds the full range of Be marsh habitat, including a mangrov thick with red mangrove trees t readily be identified by their hang roots. The area has survived intact because the spongy ground has human use, but also because mos ative flora has been unable to take n this wet, acidic ecosystem.

: marsh provides an unspoiled habitat merous species of birds. The wetlands ›me to the belted kingfisher, yellow-ed night heron, great egret, yellowlegs, nd sandpipers. The mangroves attract two dozen species of wintering war-the most common being the myrtle er, which feeds on the wax myrtle s found here.

000, a boardwalk was constructed into rsh, providing access for birdwatchers her visitors. The path, which is marked erpretive signs, begins at the west side vers Lane and winds through both and boggy areas.

also possible to get views into Paget from Valley Rd, as well as from South l the Railway Trail.

v Beach

Beach, which extends for more than mile, is a lovely stretch of soft beige The Elbow Beach Hotel sits at the d of the beach and claims that section guests. The rest of the beach is public, er, and can be accessed from Tribe Rd hich begins at a sharp curve on South st of the Elbow Beach Hotel.

g the closest noteworthy beach to the Hamilton, Elbow Beach attracts a of locals and visitors alike. Not only is y popular swimming and sunbathing but it's a good beach for strolling as e west side of the beach is backed by ne cliffs that provide habitat for sea-ees and birds.

w Beach has a daytime lunch wagon ices to Eat, later in this chapter) as shower and toilet facilities.

or Activities

s and motorboats can be rented at Boatyard at the head of Hamilton r. Salt Kettle Yacht Charters, at the l of the parish, provides charters and orkeling and sightseeing cruises.

: are tennis courts open to the public ons & Cottages, Newstead and Ston-Beach Hotel, and at the Pomander Gate Tennis Club, opposite the Little Pomander Guest House. See Places to Stay, below, for contact information. The tennis and squash courts at the private Coral Beach & Tennis Club are open only to members or by introduction from a member.

For long walks, there's a 2-mile section of the Railway Trail that crosses Paget. Going from west to east, the Railway Trail runs between Middle Rd and South Rd until Paget village and from there continues south of South Rd. Along the trail you'll get glimpses of old Bermudian estates, Paget Marsh and vegetable gardens where carrots and cabbages grow.

See the appropriate activity in the Outdoor Activities chapter for details on the above establishments.

Places to Stay

South Shore If you want to be near the beach, there are two resort hotels right on Elbow Beach, but most of the other south shore accommodations listed below are a 10- to 15-minute walk away.

Loughlands Guest House *(☎ 236-1253, 79 South Rd, Paget PG 03)* is a classic old guesthouse between Elbow Beach and Paget village. Most of the 25 rooms are in the main building, a Bermudian estate house with columned porches that look out upon acres of green lawn. The common areas are furnished with antiques. Guestrooms, many of which also have some antique furnishings, are equipped with coffeemakers, radios, air-conditioning and private baths. A continental breakfast with juice, cereal and pastries is included in the rate of $60/75 for singles/doubles in winter, $80/125 in summer. There are tennis courts and a pool.

Serendipity *(☎ 236-1192, fax 232-0010, 6 Rural Drive, Paget PG 06)* consists of two pleasant studio units in a free-standing cottage adjacent to the home of Judy and Albert Corday. Although it's all in one room, each unit has everything a visitor is likely to need, including a phone, TV, air-conditioning and a kitchen with stove, microwave, refrigerator and coffeemaker. One unit is furnished with two twin beds that can be made up as a king bed; the other unit has a queen bed and a sleep sofa. Each unit has a private bath. The location, set back slightly from South Rd, is a bit farther from the beach than most other Paget accommodations, but there's a pool and Elbow Beach is just a few bus stops away. The price is a bargain at $65 in January and February and $85 at other times of the year.

Barnsdale Guest Apartments *(☎ 236-0164, fax 236-4709, email barnsdale@ibl.bm, PO Box DV 628, Devonshire DV BX)*, in the village of Paget on the corner of Middle and Barnes Valley Rds, has seven studio apartments that are popular with return visitors. Two units have twin beds, and the rest have queen beds; all have TVs, phones, air-conditioning, kitchens and private baths. It's close to bus routes and a grocery store, and there's a pool on site. One potential drawback is that it's also close to the road, so light sleepers might hear traffic. Winter rates are $70/90 for singles/doubles, and summer rates are $110/130. It can be a good value if you're staying awhile, as the seventh night is free in summer; in winter every fifth night is free.

The ***White House*** *(☎/fax 236-4957, 6 Southlyn Lane, PO Box PG 235, Paget PG BX)* is a bed and breakfast with plenty of warm hospitality that's run by Odette and André Rémond, who were born in France but have lived in Bermuda for more than 40 years. Located just north of South Rd, this two-story house has three simple but pleasant guestrooms, each with air-conditioning, private bath and either two twin or one double bed. There's a nice little pool. Singles/doubles cost $90/110, continental breakfast included; discounts can be arranged for longer stays during the winter season.

Sky Top Cottages *(☎ 236-7984, fax 232-0446, email skytop@bermuda.com, PO Box PG 227, Paget PG BX)* has a lot of appeal with its peaceful hilltop location, well-maintained accommodations, friendly management and reasonable rates. The 11 units have English-style cottage decor, private baths, cable TV and cooking facilities. The cheapest is a small bedroom with a mini-refrigerator, toaster oven, microwave and coffeepot that costs $80/100 in winter/summer. Comfortable studio cottages with full kitchens cost $95/125 and spacious a ments, which have separate living roon kitchens, cost $115/145. In winter the also weekly and monthly rates availab a five-minute walk from the bus grocery store and Elbow Beach. Sky To a website at www.bermuda.com/skyto

There's a friendly family environm ***Dawkins Manor Guest House*** *(☎ 236 fax 236-7088, PO Box PG 34, Paget PC* which has eight units on a quiet side about five minutes from the beach. Al TVs, phones and air-conditioning. F cost $70/85 for singles/doubles in wint $95/120 in summer, and one-bedroom ments with kitchens cost $80/100 in and $120/140 in summer. Breakfast is cluded but can be added on for an add $7.50 per person. Some of the unit their own private entrance. There's a ming pool and common lounge; a g store is within easy walking distance.

Paraquet Guest Apartments *(☎ 23 fax 236-1665, PO Box PG 173, Pag BX)* consists of 12 units behind the Pa restaurant. The units are modern, rather straightforward. All have T conditioning, coffeemakers and ref tors. Rooms without cooking faciliti $92/122 for singles/doubles in wint $97/132 in summer. Units with a se bedroom, a living room and kitch $102/142 in winter and $112/167 in s

Stonington Beach Hotel *(☎ 23 800-447-7462 in the USA and Canad bav@triton.bercol.bm, PO Box H Hamilton HM CX)* is a 67-room reso at the east end of Elbow Beach. The are contemporary with 1st-class an including ceiling fan, cable TV, smal erator, safe, phone, two twin beds king, and a sofa bed. All rooms hav views. The hotel has a heated po tennis courts. Because it's run by s from the local college as part of th tality and culinary program, the se quite attentive – but rates are steep, at $172/192 for singles/doubles in $314/334 in summer. Full breakfast ternoon tea are included, and a din can be added at an additional cost.

PAGET PARISH

rizons & Cottages (☎ *236-0048, 800-*
)22 in the USA, fax 236-1981, 33 South
O Box PG 198, Paget PG BX) is an up-
:t cottage colony on a peaceful 25-acre
. Nine guestrooms are in the atmos-
: main house, and the other 41 are in 13
tive cottages scattered around the
ds. Each cottage has a maximum of five
oms, and most have a sitting room with
lace for common use by the guests. All
; have private baths and pleasant
many have nice hilltop views. Rates,
include breakfast and dinner, are from
52 singles/doubles in winter, $260/310
nmer. It's $25 less per person with
omitted, but that's not recommended
rizons has a good top-end restaurant.
's a pool, a nine-hole golf course and
:ennis courts. Elbow Beach is about a
inute walk away. The hotel is a mem-
the Relais et Chateaux chain.

ow Beach Hotel (☎ *236-3535, 800-*
26 in the USA, fax 236-8043, PO Box
55, Hamilton HM BX) is an upscale
hotel with a prime location on Elbow
. Although the hotel dates to 1908,
of the buildings scattered around the
: grounds are more recent additions.
sort, which contains 250 rooms and
es in all, recently underwent a $40
renovation. Facilities include a small
club, a large free-form heated pool,
courts, a pub and a couple of water-
estaurants. Rooms are comfortable,
ave one king bed or two twin beds as
s a queen sofa bed, and all have
, cable TVs, safes, air-conditioning,
bes and slippers. Rates begin at
5 in winter/summer for singles or
s. It's a member of the Rafael chain.

mony Club Bermuda (☎ *236-3500,*
-6664 in the USA, fax 236-2624, email
tions@harmonyclub.com, 109 South
get PG 03) is Bermuda's only all-
e hotel. Located inland near the
center, it has 68 rooms in a series of
: buildings of traditional Bermudian
The rooms have stylish furnishings,
offeemakers and a few friendly
like robes in the bathrooms. The
s include a swimming pool, tennis
courts, sauna and Jacuzzi. The hotel is geared for couples only and does not accept children or singles. Rates per couple, including all meals, afternoon tea, an open bar, airport transfers and use of a two-seater scooter, are $425/550 in winter/summer.

North Shore *Salt Kettle House* (☎ *236-0407, 10 Salt Kettle Rd, Paget PG 01)* is a friendly and refreshingly informal nine-room guesthouse right on the water between Prudden and Salt Kettle Bays. Rooms vary, but all have air-conditioning, private baths, access to kitchen facilities and interesting nooks and crannies. Rooms in the cottages, which are apartment-like in layout, cost $55 per person in summer, with a minimum of two guests; the largest can accommodate four people. Rooms in the historic main house, including a 'tower room' with water views in both directions, cost $85/100 for singles/doubles in summer. In winter the rates are $80/90 for singles/doubles, or $45 per person if there are more than two. A full breakfast is included. The Salt Kettle ferry stop is just a few minutes' walk away.

Greenbank & Cottages (☎ *236-3615, 800-637-4116 in the USA,* ☎ *800-267-7600 in Canada, fax 236-2427, email grebank@ibl.com, PO Box PG 201, Paget PG BX)* is comprised of an old Bermuda home and a handful of waterside cottages. All of the 11 units have air-conditioning and phones; nine have kitchens and most have water views. Each is different, but all are quite pleasant for the money. Rates in summer are $105 for a double room with continental breakfast and from $125 to $145 for the cottages with kitchens (no breakfast). There are also a couple of units that can accommodate four people for $195. Rates are about 20% lower in winter, with doubles beginning at $85. The property has a private dock and boat rentals are available; the Salt Kettle ferry dock is a minute's walk away. Greenbank & Cottages has a website at www.bermudamall.com.

Que Sera Guest House (☎ *236-1998, 28 Astwood Rd, Paget DV 04)*, near the botanical gardens, consists of two studio units at the side of the home of Richard and Harriett

PAGET PARISH

Grimes. Each unit has air-conditioning, a ceiling fan, cable TV and a private bath, as well as a little kitchen with a stove, refrigerator, microwave and coffeemaker. The units are furnished with two twin beds that can be made into a king bed, and also have a queen-size futon couch. Guests have access to a pleasant little pool, a barbecue grill and an icemaker. The year-round rate for either singles or doubles is $90. Ask about discounts for longer stays. One potential drawback is that Que Sera can be difficult to book, as it's sometimes full with repeat guests who stay for weeks at a time.

Little Pomander Guest House *(☎ 236-7635, fax 236-8332, email JohnH@ibl.bm, 16 Pomander Rd, PO Box HM 384, Hamilton HM BX)* occupies a historic home right on the water overlooking Hamilton Harbour. There are five guestrooms that have air-conditioning, cable TVs, microwaves, refrigerators and private baths. The lawn in the rear, which has lounge chairs and a barbecue grill, is a relaxing place to sit and watch the boats sail in and out of the harbor. Rates for either singles or doubles are $115 in summer and $85 in winter, with continental breakfast included.

Fourways Inn *(☎ 236-6517, 800-962-7654 in the USA, fax 236-5528, email fourways@ibl.bm, PO Box PG 294, Paget PG BX)*, at the intersection of Middle and Cobbs Hill Rds, has 10 contemporary rooms and suites in a few poolside buildings behind the exclusive Fourways restaurant. Each unit has a king-size bed, minibar, phone, kitchenette, cable TV and little extras such as bathrobes and fresh-cut flowers. The suites have spacious living rooms with queen sofa beds as well. In winter, doubles cost $150 for rooms and $190 for suites; in summer, the rooms/suites cost $230/325. A continental breakfast of bread and pastries from the inn's bakery is included in the rates.

Newstead *(☎ 236-6060, 800-468-4111 in the USA, fax 236-7454, email newstead@ibl.com, PO Box PG 196, Paget PG BX)* is a small waterfront hotel that's centered around an old manor house. It has manicured grounds, a little putting green on the front lawn, sitting rooms with Victorian furnishings, a l and lovely harbor views. Some of t rooms are in the main house but most a handful of separate buildings. Alt the decor varies, all rooms have conditioning and phones. Newstead sizable following of return guests, p larly among retirees. There are tw tennis courts and a heated pool. The ferry docks beside the hotel, making i to get to Hamilton. Year-round rates at $238/257 for singles/doubles, bre included.

Places to Eat

The ***Modern Mart*** *(104 South Rd* midsize grocery store with wine and p sections and a small deli that sells chicken ($8 for a whole one) and a few take-out foods. It's open 8 am to Monday to Saturday and 1 to 5 pm S There's another grocery store, the ***A-Food Market***, on Middle Rd near its section with Valley Rd, that has the hours and a comparable selection, hot deli foods.

Ice Queen *(☎ 236-3136)*, next to Pharmacy in the Rural Hill Plaza on Rd, has ice cream, hot dogs and beef b for around $3, gardenburgers for $5 few simple meals like chicken with c and fries for $6.50. It's open 10 am t daily and is a popular place to stop wee hours after the bars close.

Dinty's Lunch Wagon parks along Beach, at the end of Tribe Rd No 4, 1 7 pm daily in summer only. Beachgo buy soft drinks as well as inexpens dogs, fish cakes and burgers.

After Hours *(☎ 236-8563, 117 Sou* an unpretentious place at the inter of South and Middle Rds, has West items, including chicken roti sand for $9 and curry dishes with meat, bles and rice for $11 to $13. It's ope ings only, 7 pm to at least 2 am Mo Saturday.

Paraquet *(☎ 236-9742)*, on Sout few minutes' walk northeast of the Beach Hotel, is a local diner open 9:3

m daily. Until 11 am, you can get pan- French toast or eggs with bacon for juice and coffee included. At other there are sandwiches, soups and ler for under $5 and various meat and shes for $15 to $20. There's a dining but you'll strike up the best conversa- y sitting at the counter and rubbing s with the locals. The restaurant also read and a few simple pastries for ut.

key's (☎ *236-9884)*, at the Elbow Beach is that resort's most casual dining with patio dining right on the beach. and pastas cost around $15. It's also a pot to linger over a tropical drink. 's is open 11:45 am to 10:30 pm dur- summer season.

e Lido (☎ *236-9884)*, also at the Beach Hotel, is a pleasant beachside ant featuring Mediterranean food. zers like tuna carpaccio or an an- plate cost around $15. Pastas, such as ravioli or smoked salmon penne, cost $20. Other main dishes, including f the day, rack of lamb and beef ten- , average $30. Dinner is served from 9:45 pm. When making reservations, one of the waterview tables. Cafe also open for lunch, from noon to , with salads, sandwiches and pastas er $15.

zons (☎ *236-0048, 33 South Rd)*, at izons & Cottages resort, is a formal ing option with a traditional Bermu- ting, a hilltop ocean view and good and food. The fixed-price ($50), mul- menu changes daily, but expect to ench influences. You can usually from two soups, three starters and in dishes, with offerings such as una with caramelized onions or duck n polenta. Men are required to wear nd tie.

tead (☎ *236-6060, 27 Harbour Rd)* harbor views from both its formal oom and its casual patio. From 12:30 m, there are sandwiches with fries nd $10, a Greek salad with grilled for $14 and a few hot entrees for a couple of dollars more. At dinner, from 7 to 9:30 pm, the menu ranges from burgers served at the patio to elaborate seafood dishes in the dining room.

Fourways Inn (☎ *236-6517, 1 Middle Rd)*, at the Paget-Warwick parish line, is one of Bermuda's most highly regarded fine-dining spots. This highbrow restaurant, which occupies a 1727 manor house, has a formal setting and a menu that offers both traditional dishes with rich sauces and lighter contemporary fare. There are various dining rooms, as well as an outdoor courtyard with tables set around a fountain. Lunch, from noon to 3 pm, is surprisingly affordable, with sandwiches under $10, a chef's salad for $13 and a few hot dishes, such as ravioli topped with caviar or filet mignon in cognac sauce, for under $20. At dinner, from 6:30 to 9:45 pm, the menu is more extensive: starters such as lobster and mango salad or smoked salmon with asparagus average $20, and main dishes are around $30 for vegetarian offerings and $40 for steak, fish and lamb. There's a pianist nightly; men are requested to wear jackets at dinner.

Fourways Inn also has a shop out back where you can get fine pastries for take-out.

Getting There & Around

Paget Parish is crossed from west to east by three main roads: Harbour Rd along the north shore, Middle Rd in the central area and South Rd along the south shore.

There's no bus service along Harbour Rd, but that area is connected to the City of Hamilton by public ferry and sections of it are within walking distance of Middle Rd bus stops.

The two main bus routes are No 8, which runs from Hamilton to the Royal Naval Dockyard via Middle Rd, and bus No 7, which runs a similar route via South Rd. Bus No 7 is the one to take to get to Elbow Beach. Both buses operate once every 15 minutes during the day Monday to Saturday and about once every 30 minutes in the evening and on Sunday. The last No 7 bus leaves Hamilton at 9:15 pm (6 pm Sunday), and the last No 8 bus departs at 10:45 pm daily.

From the City of Hamilton, you can take bus Nos 1, 2 or 7 to get to the hospital or botanical gardens. Bus Nos 2, 7 and 8 stop at Paget village. The service along these routes is frequent, averaging once every 15 minutes throughout the day.

There are ferry terminals at Hodson's Ferry, near the Newstead hotel; at Salt Kettle Wharf, in the midst of the Salt Kettle area; and nearby at Darrell's Wharf, at the Paget-Warwick parish line. For mo
tailed information, see the Ferry sec
the Getting Around chapter.

Mopeds can be rented at Elbow
Cycle (☎ 236-9237), at the Elbow
Hotel. Mopeds can also be rented in
village at Eve's Cycles (☎ 236-624
Middle Rd, and Oleander Cycles (
5235), on Valley Rd north of St
Church.

arwick Parish

ck is the second most populated in Bermuda, with approximately 8100 :ants.

he center of the parish, on Middle Rd, quaint period church and a wetland preserve, but for most people the ht of a visit to Warwick is found along uth shore, which boasts some of da's loveliest pink-sand beaches. Coly, they offer beachgoers a splendid of options, from the quiet little coves vood Park, Jobson Cove and Chaplin the long, straight stretch of open ne at Warwick Long Bay.

ough you don't need to stay in k Parish to use the beaches, which iently are on the South Rd bus route, k would make a good base for those nt to be on the water. Warwick has no aside resorts but rather a nice collecsmaller guesthouse- and apartmentaces – some a mere stone's throw ne beach. Restaurant choices in the re limited, but most Warwick accomons are equipped with kitchens.

Highlights

- Take a leisurely walk on the expansive sands of Warwick Long Bay
- Join one of the guided horseback rides along the south shore
- Visit Astwood Park, with its romantic scenery

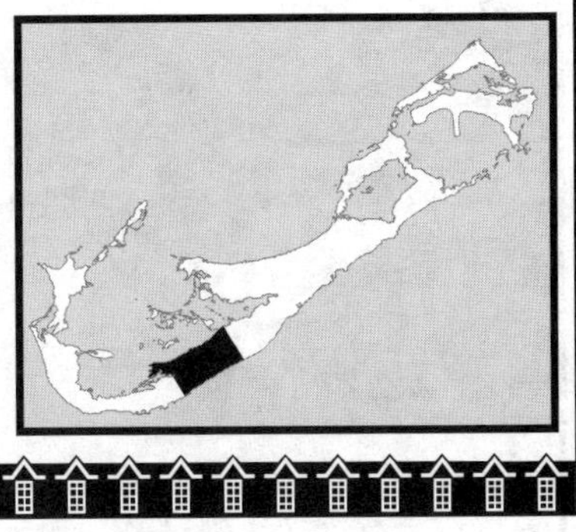

nation

rwick post office (☎ 236-4071), 70 Rd, is open 8 am to 5 pm weekdays. e's a coin laundry, Warwick Laundro- 236-5403), on Ten Pin Crescent (off Rd) just east of the bowling alley. It's am to 9 pm weekdays and 6 am to ekends.

od Park

-acre park has panoramic ocean little cove and a grassy picnic area stal knoll. Because of its scenic na- park is one of the most popular Bermuda for outdoor weddings.

ood was once earmarked as the large new resort. To make room for development, South Rd, which down to the coast here, had to first ted north. After the roadwork was ed, islanders began to have second thoughts about the desirability of another resort, and in 1984 the government negotiated the purchase of the property from the would-be developers for $2.2 million. Today, instead of leading visitors down to a megahotel, the faded asphalt of the old South Rd is the entryway into an unspoiled public park.

The beach at Astwood Park is small and rocky, but when it's calm, the nearshore rocks and reef provide snorkeling options for confident swimmers. The cliffs at the east side of the park are a favorite area for local shore fishers. In spring and fall, migratory birds can be seen among the stand of casuarina trees inland from the cliffs, as well as at the western extent of the park, where native palmetto trees and Bermuda cedars have been planted.

Astwood Park has toilets and moped parking; the entrance to the park is just west of Tribe Rd No 3.

WARWICK PARISH

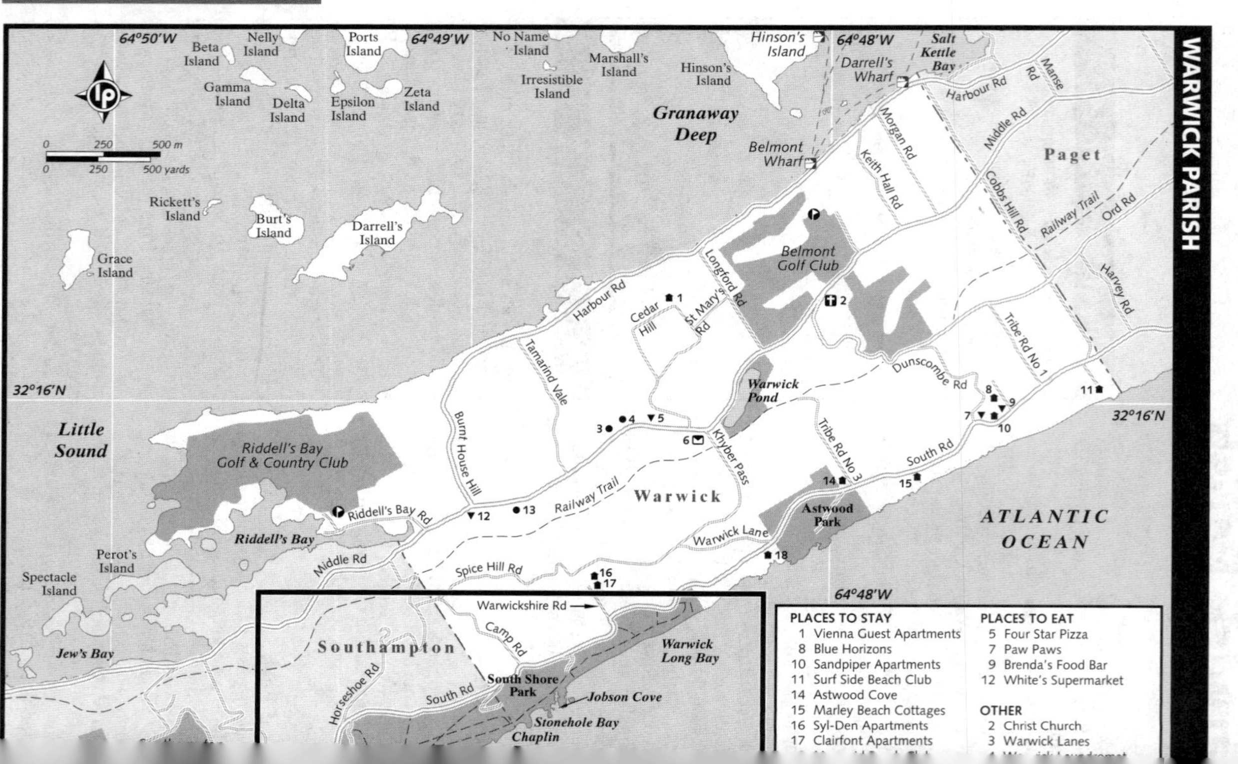

LAWSON WOOD

n cliff house

NED FRIARY

Christ Church, Warwick Parish

LAWSON WOOD

e beach, Warwick Parish

PIERCE & NEWMAN

Cannons, Royal Naval Dockyard, Sandys Parish

NED FRIARY

Gibbs Hill Lighthouse, Southampton Parish

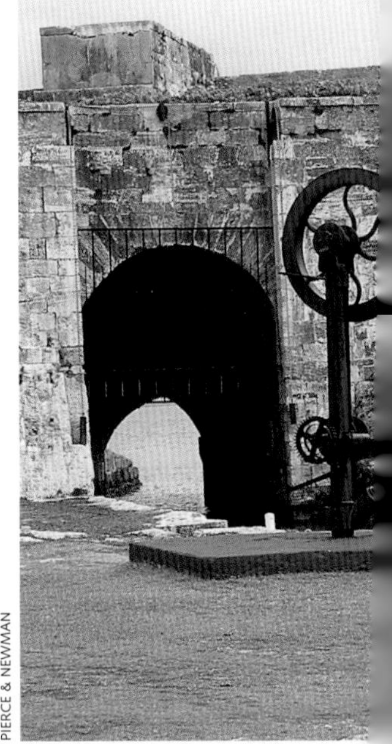

PIERCE & NEWMAN

Keep at the Maritime Museum, Sand

ick Long Bay

ck Long Bay, which forms the east-
tent of South Shore Park (see the
text), is a splendid beach of pink and
oral sands that extends unbroken for
nile, making it a fine choice for those
joy long beach strolls. Also, because
n to the ocean, it often has more surf
han the rest of South Shore Park and
a good place for bodysurfing.
e are a couple of entrances. If you
the east side of Warwick Long Bay,
nd several short footpaths that lead
e parking area down to the beach.
however, is the entrance at the west
Warwick Long Bay, as the walkway
e parking lot leads west to a rocky
ping that separates the expansive
rom a run of secluded coves and
is gives you a nice variety of tempt-
h options.
n Cove, just minutes from the west-
king lot, is the smallest of those
d has a tiny white-sand beach that's
ncircled by shoreline rocks. Because
rotected waters, Jobson Cove is
with families that have young chil-
xt is **Stonehole Bay**, which has a
each and bright turquoise waters,
adjacent **Chaplin Bay** has inviting
oves and is broader still. All are
d to one another by footpaths.

ck Pond

Pond, in the parish center about
s east of the post office, is one of
places on this side of the island for
migratory shorebirds and winter-

part of a network of shallow ponds
shes that extended east to Spittal
arwick Pond is now one of the
remaining freshwater ponds in
. Even though it's in the village
was spared the fate of many other
onds and marshes that were long
in an effort to control pesky mos-
The water level in Warwick Pond
oughout the year, as the pond is
on rainwater, and extensive mud-
during dry spells.

Because of its environmental significance, Warwick Pond was acquired in 1988 by the Bermuda National Trust and set aside as a 9-acre nature preserve. The pond can be seen from Middle Rd, which forms the preserve's northern boundary.

Christ Church

This historic church, on Middle Rd opposite the Belmont Golf Club, dates to 1719, making it one of the oldest Presbyterian churches in the Western Hemisphere. The interior has stained-glass windows and a period pulpit. Equally intriguing is the churchyard, where you'll find old gravestones, many with poignant epitaphs that provide insights into the early inhabitants of Bermuda.

Activities

Since beaches are Warwick's prime attraction, the most popular activities are water sports such as swimming, snorkeling and bodysurfing.

One of Bermuda's five diving operations, Fantasea Diving, is based at Darrell's Wharf on Warwick's north shore. Snorkel sets can be rented at Fantasea Diving, and there are snorkeling cruises departing from Darrell's Wharf and Belmont Wharf.

If you're up for a scenic hike, it's hard to beat the coastal paths that connect the lovely beaches of South Shore Park (see the boxed text). Though it's not as dynamic,

Eugene O'Neill

Famed American playwright Eugene O'Neill had a house on Harbour Rd in Warwick for a time, and it was here that he wrote *Mourning Becomes Electra, Lazarus Laughed, Strange Interlude* and *The Great God Brown*. O'Neill's daughter Oona, who married silent-film actor Charlie Chaplin, was born in Bermuda in 1925.

The book *Eugene O'Neill & Family, the Bermuda Interlude*, by Joy Bluck Waters, details the author's life on the island.

another option is the Railway Trail, which crosses the length of Warwick Parish 2 miles from west to east, running between Middle Rd and South Rd. En route, it passes on the south side of Warwick Pond and the Belmont Golf Club.

Warwick has two golf courses: the public Belmont Golf Club, at the north side of the parish, and the private Riddell's Bay Golf & Country Club, which occupies the parish's northwestern peninsula.

Spicelands Riding Centre, on Middle Rd, offers guided horseback rides. Bowling is available at Warwick Lanes, on Mid in the village center.

For further details on outdoor ac see the Outdoor Activities chapter.

Places to Stay

The family-run ***Blue Horizons*** (☎ 23 *800-637-4116 in the USA, emai bspl.bm, 93 South Rd, Warwick WK* the east side of Warwick Parish, ha dozen units, each a bit different but fortable with air-conditioning and baths. Rates are the same year-ro

South Shore Park

South Shore Park is a 1½-mile-long coastal park that encompasses some of Bermuda's beaches. The park stretches into two parishes. Its eastern boundary begins with the exp Warwick Long Bay in Warwick Parish, and the western boundary runs just beyond pictu Horseshoe Bay in Southampton Parish. In between, outcroppings of craggy rocks give w series of coves and small bays that offer protected swimming and more seclusion than the bookend beaches. A coastal trail links the beaches, making it a tidy package that's easy to e

In all, South Shore Park contains 12 sandy beaches, although a few are just postage-stan From east to west they are Warwick Long Bay, Jobson Cove, Stonehole Bay, Chaplin Bay, Beach, Angle Beach, Wafer Rocks Beach, Middle Beach, Butts Beach, Peel Rock Cove, Ho Bay and Port Royal Cove.

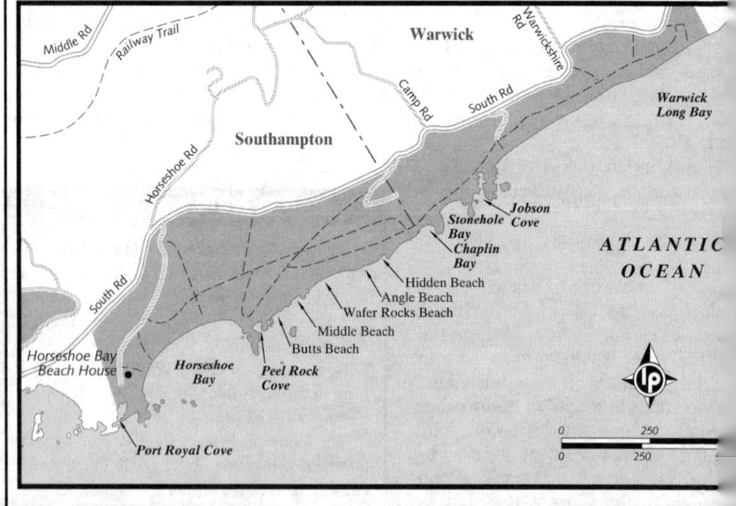

alone costs $70; one with a kitchen 90. There's also a three-room apart-ig enough for a family with a couple dren for $100. Rates are $10 less for There's a pool and snack bar. The is set back from South Rd just far to be beyond the sound of traffic.

e nearby, ***Sandpiper Apartments*** *7093, 800-637-4116 in the USA, fax 98, email san@bspl.bm, PO Box HM milton HM CX)* is a small apartment x right on South Rd. Each of the 14 is air-conditioning, two double beds, sofa bed, a private bath and a full The rate for up to two people is in winter/summer. There are also nits that have separate living rooms sleep up to four people for $145/200 r/summer. Although the complex is r the beach, there's a pool out back.

ood Cove *(☎ 236-0984, 800-637-4116 SA, fax 236-1164, email ast@bspl.bm, h Rd, Warwick WK 07)* is a recom-le apartment-style place opposite d Park. It consists of 20 modern nd suite units that are thoughtfully d and laid out. Each unit has air-ning, a phone, ceiling fan, private randa, extra sofa bed and a full that's equipped right down to the ses. The grounds have a swimming rbecue grills, a sauna (extra charge) in laundry. Rates for up to two peo-e from $84/120 in winter/summer for to $95/140 for a suite with a living or just $4 more in winter and $10 summer, you can get a 2nd-story a cathedral ceiling and a view. A es rate is available on the studios in nly. From December through Feb-re's a 30% discount on stays of one f booked directly through Astwood

en Apartments *(☎ 238-1834, 800- in the USA, fax 238-3205, email .bm, 8 Warwickshire Rd, Warwick* has five attractive units that are a ie for those who don't mind being a f blocks inland from the beach. The its are modern and comfortably l, with air-conditioning, ceiling fans, TVs, phones, kitchens and private baths. Rates for two people are $80/99 in winter/summer. There's a pool and sundeck, and the beach at Warwick Long Bay is within walking distance.

A similar deal can be found next door at the ***Clairfont Apartments*** *(☎ 238-0149, 800-637-4116 in the USA, fax 238-3503, email clairfon@ibl.bm, PO Box WK 85, Warwick WK BX)*. Its eight modern air-conditioned apartments each have a kitchen, private bath, TV and phone. Corner units are notably big, but all are comfortable and reasonably priced at $90 to $110 year-round. There's a pool on the grounds.

Vienna Guest Apartments *(☎ 236-3300, fax 236-6100, email vienna@ibl.bm, 63 Cedar Hill, Warwick WK 06)* consists of six apartments at the hilltop home of Leopold Küchler. Leopold, who manages a trading company and doubles as the Austrian honorary consul, speaks fluent German and welcomes all international visitors. Each apartment is furnished with a full kitchen, a bedroom with both a queen bed and a twin bed, and a living room with a sofa bed, TV, phone, air-conditioning and ceiling fan. The grounds have a swimming pool, sundeck and views of the Great Sound. First-floor apartments for up to two people cost $95/135 in winter/summer, upper-story apartments cost $10 more. There's a $35 charge for a third person ($20 for children under 12). Even though the location is off the beaten track, it's on a bus route. Vienna Guest Apartments maintains a website you can find at www.bermuda1.com/viennaindex.htm.

Marley Beach Cottages *(☎ 236-1143, 800-637-4116 in the USA, fax 236-1984, email mar@bspl.com, PO Box PG 278, Paget PG BX)*, on South Rd just east of Astwood Park, consists of a dozen bluffside cottages scenically set above a sandy beach. Each unit has air-conditioning, a TV, kitchen, private bath and patio. There's a heated pool and a whirlpool. Rates for doubles begin at $115 from January to mid-March, $150 during the rest of the winter season and $180 during the summer. The private white-sand beach below the cottages is available to guests.

BERMUDA DEPARTMENT OF TOURISM

Warwick Parish's pink-sand beaches are among Bermuda's best.

Surf Side Beach Club *(☎ 236-7100, 800-553-9990 in the USA, fax 236-9765, email surf@ibl.bm, PO Box WK 101, Warwick WK BX)* is a pleasant family-run place on a private beach at the southeastern edge of Warwick Parish. The 37 units, which range from studios to two-bedroom apartments, are in contemporary one- and two-story buildings spread across the 5-acre grounds. All are comfortable and come with air-conditioning, cable TV, balconies and fully equipped kitchens. It has a quiet setting but is only a few minutes' walk from the nearest bus stop. The beach offers good swimming and the facilities include a pool, fitness center, sauna, hot tub and coin laundry. Rates for studios are $125/205 in winter/summer for up to two people. Two-bedroom units cost $210/350 for up to four people. From December to March, there are discounts for longer stays, ranging fr for eight days to around 35% for a stay. Surf Side Beach Club has a w www.surfside.bm.

The ***Mermaid Beach Club*** *(☎ 2 fax 236-8784, PO Box WK 250, War BX)* is a condominium-like prope sandy cove just east of Warwick Lor was renovated in 2000, when a new added and other sections of the were upgraded. Accommodatior from hotel rooms with refrigerator bedroom suites with full kitchens. are air-conditioned and have ph oceanfront balconies or patios. heated pool and a nice little priva Room rates for doubles begin at $1 winter/summer, and a two-bedro that can sleep up to four peo $285/390.

›s to Eat

s a grocery store, ***White's Supermar-*** *2 Middle Rd)*, just west of Burnt Hill, that's open 8 am to 9 pm Mon-Saturday and 1 to 5 pm Sunday.

Middle Rd in Warwick center, you'll branch of ***Four Star Pizza*** *(☎ 232-* which offers delivery service and the ›rd variety of pizzas for dine-in or ›ıt. A 10-inch pizza with the works, meat or vegetarian, will set you back 14-inch version costs $23. It's open ›o at least 11 pm daily except Sunday, ›'s open 1 to 10 pm.

Paws *(☎ 236-7459, 87 South Rd)*, at ›ıer of Dunscombe Rd, is an informal ›ant with positive energy and good ›t lunch, from 11 am to 5 pm, there are ›hes with fries for around $8 and hot ›such as fettuccine Alfredo, from $10. ›er, from 5 to 10 pm, main dishes ave-› and include local favorites like shark Creole sauce and Paw Montespan – a ›green papaya (paw paw) dish with beef, cheese and tomato. There are ›ernational dishes, including vegetar-›a, shrimp scampi and filet mignon.

A hundred yards to the east of Paw Paws on South Rd is ***Brenda's Food Bar*** *(☎ 236-7807)*, a little snack bar with inexpensive sandwiches, burgers, fries and other simple eats. Hours are flexible, but it's usually open by 10 am.

Getting There & Around

Warwick is crossed from east to west by three main roads: Harbour Rd on the north shore, Middle Rd through the interior and South Rd along the south shore.

Bus No 8 travels along Middle Rd and bus No 7 travels along South Rd; both of the routes connect Warwick with Sandys Parish to the west and the City of Hamilton to the east. Both buses operate once every 15 minutes during the day Monday to Saturday and about once every 30 minutes in the evening and on Sunday.

There's no bus service on Harbour Rd, but there is public ferry service to the City of Hamilton from Belmont Wharf and Darrell's Wharf at the northeast side of the parish. For more detailed information, see the Ferry section in the Getting Around chapter.

Southampton Parish

Southampton Parish comprises the western elbow of Bermuda, bordered on the north by Little Sound and on the south by the Atlantic. The north side is mainly residential, and the south side is a prime visitor destination dotted by a series of bays and coves with attractive pink-sand beaches.

Bordered by Sandys Parish to the north and Warwick Parish to the east, Southampton is relatively long and thin, with a width that tapers to a mere one-third of a mile at its narrowest point. In addition to beautiful beaches, the parish has historic Gibbs Hill Lighthouse and Whale Bay Battery, and a brewery that welcomes visitors.

Southampton has the largest share of hotel rooms of any of the island's nine parishes. Two of Bermuda's largest resort hotels are on Southampton's south shore and there are a number of smaller hotels and houses, many of them located on or n waterfront.

The parish population is approxi 5900.

Highlights

- Rent a snorkel set at Church Bay to view the underwater world
- Laze the day away at picturesque Horseshoe Bay
- Chug a Wilde Hogge during a tour of the Bermuda Triangle Brewery
- Nibble on crumpets at the Gibbs Hill Lighthouse tea room

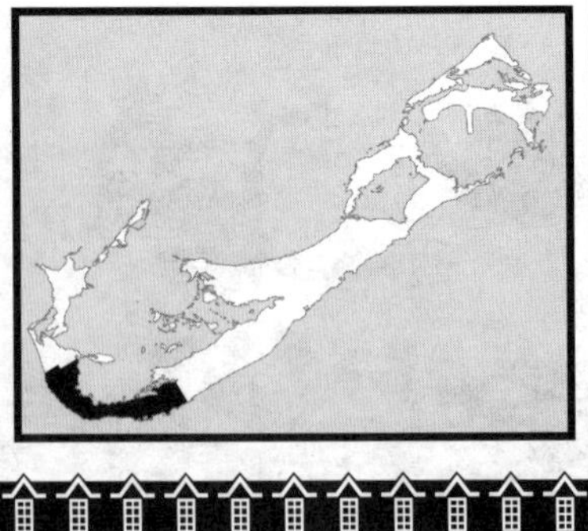

Information

The Southampton post office (☎ 238 2 Church Rd, is open 8 am to 5 pm we

Gibbs Hill Lighthouse

The Gibbs Hill Lighthouse, erected after a rash of shipwrecks along Be treacherous western shoals, is the most significant landmark, towering above its hilltop site.

Not only is it an attractive build it's unique in being the tallest cast-ir house in the world. It was one o handful of cast-iron lighthouses ere the British in the mid-18th century, most, including two surviving ones land, were only about a third as hig

The lens, which consists of co prisms, weighs 2¾ tons and is ca generating a half-million candl Using a 1000-watt electric bulb, it p a beam that can be seen up to 40 n to sea.

You can climb the eight flights of the top – some 185 steps in all – whe be rewarded with a panoramic route, you willl encounter some in shipwreck-related displays. The ligh open 9 am to 4:30 pm daily. Adm $2.50, free for children under five.

On the same grounds, opposite t way into the lighthouse, is a look been known as the Queen's View e Queen Elizabeth II paused there i admire the scenery; a plaque duly event.

The Gibbs Hill Lighthouse is house Rd, which begins just we Henry VIII restaurant on South R don't have a moped, it's about a uphill walk.

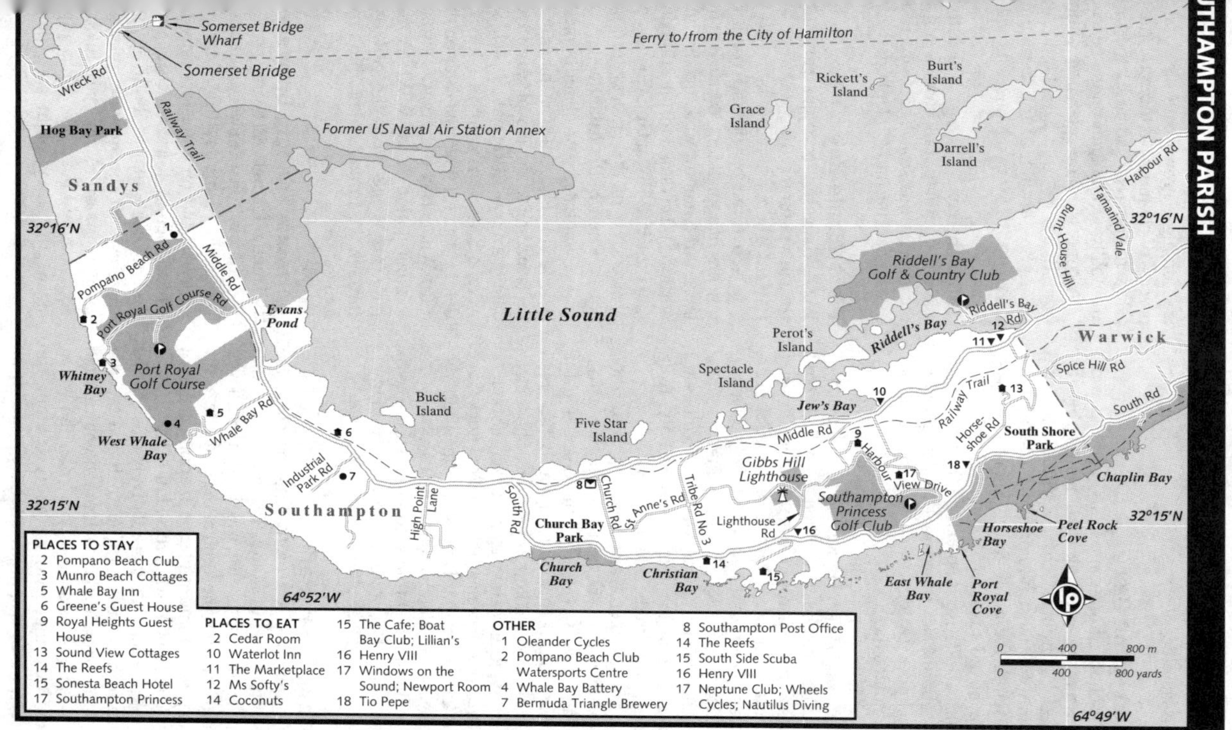
SOUTHAMPTON PARISH
PLACES TO STAY
2 Pompano Beach Club
3 Munro Beach Cottages
5 Whale Bay Inn
6 Greene's Guest House
9 Royal Heights Guest House
13 Sound View Cottages
14 The Reefs
15 Sonesta Beach Hotel
17 Southampton Princess
PLACES TO EAT
2 Cedar Room
10 Waterlot Inn
11 The Marketplace
12 Ms Softy's
14 Coconuts
15 The Cafe; Boat Bay Club; Lillian's
16 Henry VIII
17 Windows on the Sound; Newport Room
18 Tio Pepe
OTHER
1 Oleander Cycles
2 Pompano Beach Club Watersports Centre
4 Whale Bay Battery
7 Bermuda Triangle Brewery
8 Southampton Post Office
14 The Reefs
15 South Side Scuba
16 Henry VIII
17 Neptune Club; Wheels Cycles; Nautilus Diving
Ferry to/from the City of Hamilton
Somerset Bridge Wharf
Somerset Bridge
Former US Naval Air Station Annex
Little Sound
Hog Bay Park
Sandys
Southampton
Warwick
Port Royal Golf Course
Riddell's Bay Golf & Country Club
Southampton Princess Golf Club
Gibbs Hill Lighthouse
Church Bay Park
South Shore Park
Whitney Bay
West Whale Bay
Church Bay
Christian Bay
East Whale Bay
Port Royal Cove
Horseshoe Bay
Peel Rock Cove
Chaplin Bay
Jew's Bay
Riddell's Bay
Evans Pond
Burt's Island
Darrell's Island
Rickett's Island
Grace Island
Perot's Island
Spectacle Island
Five Star Island
Buck Island
Wreck Rd
Railway Trail
Middle Rd
Pompano Beach Rd
Port Royal Golf Course Rd
Whale Bay Rd
Industrial Park Rd
High Point Lane
South Rd
Church Rd
St Anne's Rd
Tribe Rd No 3
Lighthouse Rd
Harbour View Drive
Horseshoe Rd
Riddell's Bay Rd
Burnt House Hill
Tamarind Vale
Harbour Rd
Spice Hill Rd
32°16'N
32°15'N
64°52'W
64°49'W
0 400 800 m
0 400 800 yards

For information on the atmospheric lighthouse tea room, see Places to Eat later in this chapter.

Horseshoe Bay

This horseshoe-shaped bay, with its wide crescent of soft pink sand, is arguably the most beautiful beach in Bermuda. It's certainly the most popular, and it's the only beach in the entire South Shore Park (see the boxed text 'South Shore Park' in the Warwick Parish chapter) that is staffed with lifeguards. Not surprisingly, it can get quite packed with locals and tourists on a hot summer's day.

A large parking lot leads up to the Horseshoe Bay Beach House and the west end of the beach. The beach house (☎ 238-2651) has a changing room with toilet facilities and showers, a shop that rents snorkel gear, beach chairs, umbrellas and the like, and a little cafe that sells hot dogs, burgers, sandwiches and ice cream. All of the facilities are available in the tourist season only: from early April to the end of October.

You can get a nice angle on Horseshoe Bay by walking out onto the rocky outcropping at the west end of the beach. On the west side of this outcropping is the small rock-protected **Port Royal Cove**, whose clear and typically calm waters attract snorkelers. This cove, as well as the tiny **Peel Rock Cove** at the east end of Horseshoe Bay, offers relatively secluded bathing options.

The main entrance to Horseshoe Bay is on South Rd, opposite Tio Pepe restaurant, where you'll also find a bus stop.

Church Bay Park

Church Bay is a pretty little beach at the western end of South Rd. In early colonial times, a coastal fort was built here; if you walk up onto the knoll at the east side of the bay, you'll find a plaque marking the spot where the fort was erected in 1612.

The reef comes in relatively close to the shore here, making Church Bay a favorite place for snorkeling. Although you can find fish almost as soon as you enter the water, the best underwater scenery is along the reef, which is approximately 100 yards from the beach. There you'll find lots of co tropical fish, including large parrotfis feed on algae growing on the coral. process of chomping at the coral, the p fish actually create some of the san eventually accumulates on the beach.

A concessionaire sets up at Churc from 10 am to 5 pm Monday to Sa from May through October, renting kel gear ($10 for two hours) and selli drinks.

Church Bay is an easy beach to just a two-minute walk from South R the nearest bus stop. There are rest moped parking and a telephone.

West Whale Bay

West Whale Bay is a pleasant little cove in a natural setting at the end of Bay Rd. There are picnic tables on t side above the beach, and you'll f remains of a small fort, **Whale Bay Ba** mere three-minute walk up the hil northwest. This small fortification no looks the Port Royal Golf Course an a nice view of the endless turquo cobalt waters of the Atlantic.

The gun battery was built in the defend Hog Fish Cut, a channel thro reefs leading to the Royal Naval Do The battery's original 9-inch weighed 12 tons and provided defense against potential raids on th yard. Whale Bay Battery was also u lookout station during WWII. Altho guns are gone, you can still r through the former ammunition m and barracks.

Bermuda Triangle Brewery

Bermuda Triangle Brewing (☎ 2 the country's first brewery, offers f Monday to Saturday from March October, and on Saturdays only i These friendly tours, which begin and take about one hour, give lowdown on the brewing proces capping off with samples of the c four standard beers, as well as any brews that they might be exper with at the time.

Bermuda Triangle

:erms conjure up images of the paranormal the way that 'Bermuda Triangle' does.

e name is given to a triangular section of the Atlantic Ocean that's bound by Bermuda to the , Florida to the west and Puerto Rico to the south. It's thought that as many as 100 ships and s have vanished in the triangle. The mysterious disappearances in this zone, which is also n as the Devil's Triangle, date back to the mid-19th century. It wasn't until the 1970s, how- when a popular interest in UFOs and other unexplained phenomena arose, that the disap- nces drew international attention and the term Bermuda Triangle came into common use.

ıat makes the triangle unusual is that not only are the disappearances quite substantial for an f this size, but many of the vessels have gone down without so much as emitting a distress – and with no subsequent trace of the craft ever appearing. In other cases, ships have reap- d intact months after disappearing, but with no trace of the crew ever found.

largest single disappearance in the Bermuda Triangle was that of the infamous Flight 19, a of five US Navy torpedo bombers that flew out of Florida on a routine flight in December 1945 and vanished; a search plane sent in their wake also disappeared.

Various theories have been advanced to explain the disappearances, ranging from atmospheric disturbances and erratic magnetic forces to time warps and extraterrestrial kidnappings. Others just write most of it off as coincidence and the usual combination of mechanical failure, bad weather and human error.

However you look at it, the Bermuda Triangle gives those with a rich imagination plenty to work with.

to the brewery, take bus No 7 or 8, hich stop on Middle Rd near its in- n with Industrial Park Rd. The in the SAL industrial center, is yards down Industrial Park Rd on hen you see two large warehouses uth side of the road, take the road t.

r Activities

pton offers visitors a wide variety ctivities.

st side's best easy-access snorkel- Church Bay, where the nearshore ors a variety of colorful tropical fish. A concessionaire rents snorkeling gear right on the beach at Church Bay during the season.

Another snorkeling spot is Port Royal Cove at Horseshoe Bay, where snorkel rentals are also seasonally available.

Each of the big resort hotels has a dive shop: Nautilus Diving is at the Southampton Princess and South Side Scuba Watersports is at the Sonesta Beach Hotel. In addition to diving, both shops rent snorkel sets and South Side Scuba also rents kayaks. The Pompano Beach Club Watersports Centre, at the Pompano Beach Club hotel, rents kayaks, sailboats and windsurfing gear.

Hikers will find a coastal trail running from Horseshoe Bay east through South Shore Park. In addition, a section of the Railway Trail runs clear through Southampton Parish, connecting it with neighboring Sandys Parish to the northwest and Warwick Parish to the east. The Railway Trail parallels Middle Rd most of the way, offering views of Southampton's less-touristed north shore and Little Sound.

Southampton also has two 18-hole golf courses: the Southampton Princess Golf Club, at the Southampton Princess hotel, and the Port Royal Golf Course, at the north side of the parish.

There are tennis courts open to the public at the Port Royal Tennis Club (at the Port Royal Golf Course), the Sonesta Beach Hotel and the Southampton Princess.

See the appropriate activity in the Outdoor Activities chapter for details on the above establishments.

Places to Stay

Sound View Cottage *(☎ 238-0064, 9 Bowe Lane, Southampton SN 04)* is a small hilltop place in a residential neighborhood midway between Middle Rd and South Shore Park. It has three compact studio units, each with a private bath, kitchenette and air-conditioning. There's also non-cable TV that can pick up the three Bermuda stations, a swimming pool in the backyard and a patio with a barbecue. All in all, it is a good value at $ up to two adults. A child under five ca free, and an older child can stay for a tional $25. It's open from April th October only.

In the Pink

Bermuda's sand is made up of particles of coral, marine invertebrates and various shells, but it takes its distinctive light pink hue from the bodies of one particular sea creature, a member of the order Foraminifera. A marine protozoan abundant on Bermudian reefs, foraminifers have hard, tiny shells that wash up on shore after the animal within dies. These pink shell fragments provide the dominant color in what would otherwise be a confetti of bleached white coral and ivory-colored calcium carbonate shells.

Whale Bay Inn *(☎ 238-0469, fa 1224, email whalebayinn@northrock. Whaling Hill, PO Box SN 544, Southa SN BX)* is a pleasant little place peaceful location at the southern edg Port Royal Golf Course. Despite its sion, both the beach at West Whale B the bus stop on Middle Rd are withi minute walk. The five comfortably fu units each have air-conditioning, ceili cable TV, a phone, a private bath, a s bedroom, kitchen and patio. The s rates are a reasonable $85/120 for doubles; there's a $20 reduction in wi the doubles rate.

Greene's Guest House *(☎ 238-0 238-8980, 71 Middle Rd, PO Box S Southampton SN BX)* occupies a home that's situated at the north sid parish. Managed by an East India from Trinidad, it has six air-cond guestrooms with private baths, ph frigerators, coffeemakers, TVs and Guests have access to a shared ki well as a lounge. Although it's not close to the south shore's sandy there's a pool and it's on a bus rout which include a full breakfast, are for singles/doubles year-round, a you can generally negotiate a sı count in the winter if you book dir

Royal Heights Guest House *(☎ 2 fax 238-8445, 4 Crown Hill, PO Bo Southampton SN BX)*, on a hill bet Southampton Princess golf cou Middle Rd, is in a contemporary h friendly hosts and a half-dozen gu All rooms have cable TV, air-con coffeemakers, refrigerators and b Some of the rooms have connecti that can be opened for use by famil are picturesque views of the Gre from the poolside patio and from the rooms. Because of its hilltop lo best suited for guests who pla mopeds. Singles/doubles cost $1

: and $110/145 in summer, continental fast included.

nro Beach Cottages (☎ *234-1175, 800-'16 in the USA, fax 234-3528, email •@ibl.bm, PO Box SN 99, Southamp-V BX)* is comprised of nine duplex pread in an arc along low cliffs over-ıg the ocean. This quiet, secluded ex is bordered by the Port Royal Golf :, making it an ideal spot for golfers. nits are modern, with full kitchens, baths, air-conditioning, ceiling fans, ront patios, room safes, TVs and . Each has a king bed or two twin nd most also have a double sofa bed. leads down to a small, private beach tney Bay, and tennis is available Rates for one or two people are $110 er, $200 in summer; add $30 for each nal person. Munro Beach Cottages ebsite at www.munrobeach.com.

Pompano Beach Club (☎ *234-0222, '-4155 in the USA and Canada, fax 4, 36 Pompano Beach Rd, South-SB 03)* is a small upmarket hotel pleasant rooms in a handful of two-ildings. It has a private location on a cliff at the north side of the Port Golf Course. Facilities include clay courts, a heated pool and a fitness here's a small beach fronting shallow that are good for snorkeling. The have ceiling fans, air-conditioning, urnishings, king-size beds, private hones, cable TV and oceanview bal-Double rates, with breakfast and ncluded, begin at $240 in winter and summer; single rates are $40 less. nd-golf packages are also available. o Beach Club has a website at muda.com/pompano.

Reefs (☎ *238-0222, 800-742-2008 in and Canada, fax 238-8372, email @ibl.bm, 56 South Rd, Southampton* s an attractive upscale hotel on a ate beach at Christian Bay, just west nesta resort. There are 67 rooms in of terraced hillside buildings. Most ave waterview balconies and all ery tropical decor, air-conditioning, tors, room safes and phones. The grounds have two tennis courts, a shuffleboard court, a pool and a fitness center. Rates vary with the category of accommodations, beginning at $244/376 for doubles in winter/summer, including breakfast, dinner and afternoon tea. The hotel has a website at www.thereefs.com.

The ***Sonesta Beach Hotel*** (☎ *238-8122, 800-766-3728 in the USA, fax 238-8463, PO Box HM 1070, Hamilton HM EX)* is perched on a rocky outcrop that separates two protected bays, each with nice sandy beaches. The 403 rooms have the usual amenities and decor of a large resort hotel, including TVs, phones, room safes, mini-bar, air-conditioning and balconies, most with fine water views. There are six tennis courts, heated indoor and outdoor pools, a croquet lawn, a health spa (extra charge), diving facilities and shops. A shuttle bus runs around the 25-acre property and up to the public bus stop. Rates for a standard room without meals begin at $130/250 in winter/summer for either singles or doubles. Add another $15 per person for the breakfast plan or $55 for the breakfast-and-dinner plan – however, if you're not a big eater, there are cheaper options in the hotel restaurants.

The ***Southampton Princess*** (☎ *238-8000, 800-441-1414 in the USA and Canada, 020-7389-1126 in the UK, fax 238-8968, email reservations@cphotels.com, PO Box HM 1379, Hamilton HM FX)* is Bermuda's largest and most upscale resort hotel. Opened in 1972, the hotel has a quiet hilltop location amidst an 18-hole golf course. Other facilities include a fitness center, both indoor and outdoor swimming pools, 11 tennis courts, a pro shop and several restaurants. The 600 rooms and suites are pleasantly upscale with air-conditioning, cable TV, phones, room safes, waterview balconies and little extras like blow-dryers and bathrobes. Although the hotel is about a half-mile inland, its private white-sand beach – and anywhere else on the 100-acre grounds – can be reached by a complimentary shuttle. Free transport is provided to the City of Hamilton as well, where the Princess' sister hotel is located. Room rates begin at $188 for either singles or doubles in winter and $369 in summer. The resort is a member of the Fairmont chain.

Places to Eat

The cozy ***Lighthouse Tea Room*** *(☎ 238-8679)*, at the Gibbs Hill Lighthouse, has a lovely setting and view, making it a perfect spot for afternoon tea or an English-style meal. There are tempting cakes and pastries, including warm scones, toasted crumpets and currant teacakes, served with butter and jam and priced under $3. In addition, until 11:30 am, various egg breakfasts served with juice and tea or coffee are available for around $10. From 11:30 am to closing you can order light lunches such as a traditional Cornish pasty or a cheese quiche, served with salad, for around $8, as well as reasonably priced sandwiches ranging from a classic BLT to a 'Mediterranean Delight' of grilled vegetables on a rosemary bun. The tea room is open 9 am to 5 pm daily.

Ms Softy's *(☎ 238-0931, 235 Middle Rd)* is a simple local eatery offering home-style Bermudian cooking. Breakfast, which is served all day, includes French toast, pancakes and various egg dishes, most priced under $6. There are also inexpensive sandwiches, burgers, fish chowder and side dishes such as peas and rice. On Sundays, Ms Softy's serves up a traditional codfish and potatoes breakfast for $10. It's open 6 am to 10 pm Monday to Saturday and 6 am to 1 pm Sunday.

Tio Pepe *(☎ 238-1897)*, on South Rd opposite Horseshoe Bay, is an Italian restaurant with a variety of 9-inch pizzas for $11. The menu also includes lasagna, fettuccine Alfredo or other pastas for around $15, and grilled fish or steaks for $25. It's open noon to 10 pm daily. Take-out is available. At dinner there's a minimum charge of $15.75 per person.

Henry VIII *(☎ 238-1977)*, on South Rd opposite the Sonesta Beach Hotel, plays up a convivial Olde English ambiance, all burgundy and dark wood, with waitresses in Tudor-style dress. At lunch, from noon to 2:30 pm, there are sandwiches for under $10 as well as more expensive hot items, such as steak and kidney pie. The main meal here is dinner, which is served from 6 to 10 p
meat eaters will find the prime ri
Yorkshire pudding ($26.50) to be
Other similarly priced dishes may i
filet mignon, pan-fried salmon and d
orange sauce. Courses are a la carte;
additional $5.50 for soup or a simple
The restaurant also offers a good va
moderately priced wines, and the ad
pub features English lagers and Be
Triangle ale on tap.

The Sonesta Beach Hotel has a h
of dining options, the cheapest bei
Cafe in the hotel's shopping arcade
fresh-baked pastries and muffins fo
coffee for $2, as well as sandwiches, H
Dazs ice cream and frozen yogurt. T
is open 6:30 am to 10 pm daily. The
Boat Bay Club, off the lobby, is a
bistro-style place with a varied menu
cludes salads, Vietnamese spring r
fish chowder for under $10 and main
that range from tandoori vegetarian
to prime rib steak for $20 to $30. It's
to 10 pm nightly.

The Sonesta's main dinner res
Lillian's *(☎ 238-8122)*, has a N
Italian-influenced a la carte men
dishes such as spaghetti with calama
tuccini with smoked salmon and gr
paragus average $22. Other dishes, i
rack of lamb, garlic sirloin steak an
tuna in a pesto crust, average $28. A
soup or salad and another $9 for
such as steamed mussels in wine or
antipasto plate. It's open 6 to 10 pm

The ***Cedar Room*** in the Pompan
Club *(☎ 234-0222)*, at the end of F
Beach Rd, has fine dining, a supe
view and good food. At lunch ther
sandwiches, burgers, burritos and s
$8 to $11. Dinner features a five-cou
for $42, which includes a choice o
zers, a hot or chilled soup, a salad, a
of desserts and a half-dozen ma
such as beef Wellington or grilled
dress code is jackets on Tuesday,
and Saturday nights and 'smart c
other times.

Coconuts *(☎ 238-0222)*, at The Re
has a romantic seaview setting tha

rite south shore dinner spot. There's a ing prix fixe menu, with a choice of s that includes the likes of Caribbean obster tail, fish chowder, chilled strawsoup and specialty salads. The main s are creative with items such as steak with cherries, vegetarian goat cheese d black grouper with mango curry. Int cheesecake, crepes and soufflés out the desserts. The cost for the mule dinner is $49 per person. It's open 7 n nightly; reservations are required.

dows on the Sound, the main dining at the Southampton Princess hotel *-2555)*, takes its name from the dining wall of windows that look across the t lawn towards Little Sound. From 8 m daily, there's a pleasant breakfast that includes an omelet station, pan-fried fish, pastries, cereal, fresh uice and coffee. You can opt for just d items as a continental breakfast for ne full selection for $15. If you come Sunday, they add some traditional dian codfish breakfast items and the emains the same as on other days.

a jacket-and-tie dinner in the South- Princess, the ***Newport Room*** serves and continental cuisine with a nouccent. Starters such as foie gras or l salmon average $20, and main including steaks and seafood, cost $35. It's open from 7 pm nightly.

the most popular restaurant affilith the Southampton Princess is the ***t Inn*** *(☎ 238-2555)*, which is not on l grounds, but just north of the prop- Middle Rd. Located in a historic e inn, the restaurant has a pleasant view and an interesting blend of Mediterranean and Bermudian fare. include the likes of roasted salmon ild mushrooms, pistachio-crusted ops and lobster ravioli. Appetizers $15, main courses $30. Desserts, strawberry tarts and a rum-raisin cost $7.50. Waterlot Inn is open 6:30 pm for dinner; jackets and ties are l.

an pick up groceries at ***The Market-*** n Middle Rd next to Ms Softy's. The store is open 7 am to 10 pm Monday to Saturday and 1 to 5 pm Sunday.

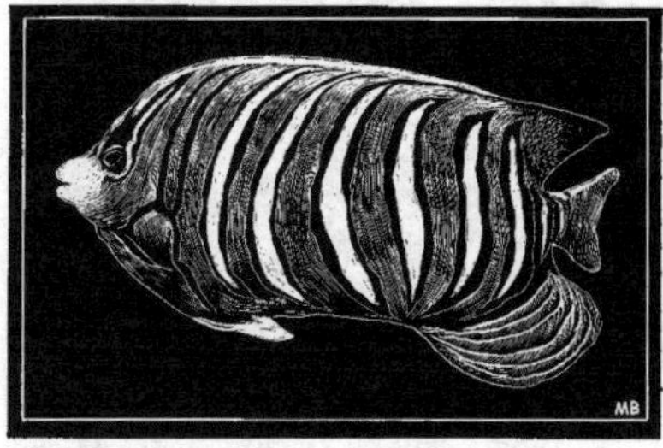

Angelfish brighten Bermuda's tranquil water.

Entertainment

The Neptune Club at the ***Southampton Princess*** *(☎ 238-8000)* has live entertainment Tuesday to Sunday nights, usually light jazz, swing or rhythm and blues. ***The Reefs*** *(☎ 238-0222)* has live music nightly, most commonly a pianist, but sometimes soca and Top 40. ***Henry VIII*** *(☎ 238-1977)* restaurant, opposite the Sonesta Beach Hotel, has entertainment most nights ranging from mellow instrumentals to calypso. If you're planning a night out, keep in mind that schedules can vary with the season, so call ahead for the latest.

Getting There & Around

Middle Rd runs along the Little Sound and is served by bus No 8, and South Rd runs along Southampton's south shore and is served by bus No 7. The service along either route is once every 15 minutes during the day and about once every 30 minutes in the evening and on Sunday.

South Rd merges with Middle Rd about midway in the parish at a spot called Barnes Corner. Note that a number of buses terminate at Barnes Corner, so if you're going any farther west, make sure you take a bus that's marked 'Dockyard' or 'Somerset.' Things are simple if you're heading east, as all No 7 and 8 buses terminate in the City of Hamilton.

Mopeds can be rented from Oleander Cycles (☎ 234-0629), on Middle Rd just north of the Port Royal Golf Course, and Wheels Cycles (☎ 238-3336), at the Southampton Princess hotel.

Sandys Parish

Sandys (pronounced 'sands'), the westernmost parish in Bermuda, is comprised of the northern part of Bermuda Island as well as Somerset Island, Watford Island, Boaz Island, Ireland Island South and Ireland Island North, all of which are connected by bridges.

The main village is Somerset, at the northern side of Somerset Island. It has its roots in colonial agriculture and retains an unabashedly local character.

Watford Island, Boaz Island and the Ireland Islands were once occupied by the British Royal Navy. Today, testimony to that past is found in the naval cemeteries that flank the road leading to the Royal Naval Dockyard.

At the southern tip of Ireland Island North is the former HMS *Malabar*, a British naval base that closed in March 1995, ending the 200-year presence of British forces in Bermuda.

Highlights

- Marvel at the world's smallest drawbridge, in Somerset Village
- Spend a day at the Royal Naval Dockyard, with its shops, galleries and excellent maritime museum
- Explore the extensive grounds of Scaur Hill Fort Park

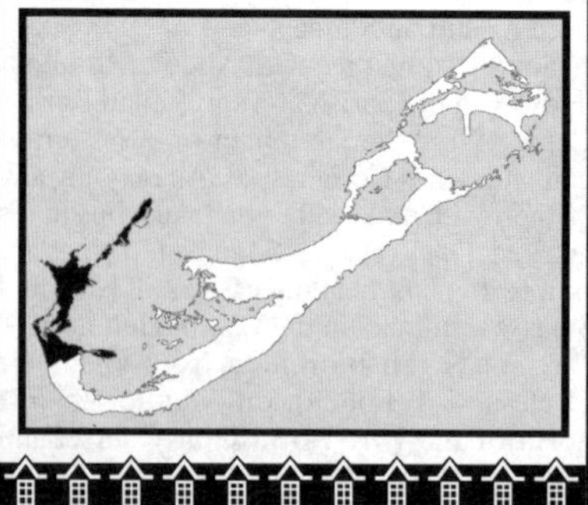

The rest of Ireland Island North is pied by the 75-acre Royal Naval Doc With its collection of 19th-century ings, this former military dockyard ar has been turned into one of Bermuda' most visitor destinations, with its own ship dock, small boat marina, ma museum, shopping center, craft ga and restaurants.

Sandys Parish is also referred Bermudians as the West End. The population is approximately 6600.

SOMERSET & AROUND

Somerset, the largest island in Sand ish, derives its name from Bermuda's ing father, Sir George Somers.

Somerset Bridge, which was built 17th century to connect Bermuda' island to Somerset Island, has as its c fame the distinction of being the smallest drawbridge. Its 30-inch spa just wide enough to allow the mast o boat to pass through as the bo between the Great Sound and Ely bour. Obviously, the sailor needs to good command and steady hand!

The heart of Somerset Island is the sleepy **Somerset Village**, abutting Mangrove Bay, where there is a small sandy beach that's popular with fishers. Unlike St George at the opposite end of Bermuda, Somerset's facilities are geared more for islanders than visitors, so it could

Munro Leaf wrote *The Sto Ferdinand* from his home in S

interesting place to poke around if ant to get off the tourist track. The prominent sight on the island is Scaur ort Park, but there are a couple of parks and nature reserves as well.

mation

nerset Village, there are branches of he Bank of Bermuda and the Bank of field on Mangrove Bay Rd, opposite merset Country Squire restaurant. ng hours for the Bank of Butterfield am to 3:30 pm weekdays (to 4:30 pm); hours for the Bank of Bermuda are n to 3 pm weekdays (to 4:30 pm on).

Mangrove Bay post office (☎ 234-3 Somerset Rd in Somerset Village, is am to 5 pm weekdays. The Somerset post office (☎ 234-0220), 1 Middle Rd south side of the Somerset Bridge, is to 11:30 am and 1 to 5 pm weekdays. dys Laundromat (☎ 238-9455), at The tplace, is open 7:30 am to about 8 pm y to Saturday and 8 am to about 5 pm ; closing hours are a bit flexible, de-g on how busy they are.

Hill Fort Park

Hill Fort is a monument to the ten-hat existed between the British and nericans in the mid-19th century. the US Civil War, the British had the defeated Confederacy, and, the fact that the victorious North erged from the war in such a battle-condition that it posed little threat ne, the British were fearful of the ity of a retaliatory US invasion of la.

in, which still had colonial ties with as well as possessions in the West ooked upon Bermuda as a forward of its naval power in the New World. uently, in 1865 the British govern-located a hefty sum for fortifying a, and in 1868 work began on Scaur rt, the most ambitious of several ojects.

Hill Fort was built at the south side rset Island, on the crest of its highest hill, with the express purpose of protecting the Royal Naval Dockyard from a land invasion. For the same reason, a deep ditch was dug from Ely's Harbour in the west to Great Harbour in the east, effectively slicing Somerset Island in two. Ramparts were built along the elevated northern side of the ditch, where platforms were installed for use by infantry men who – theoretically, at least – could mow down invading soldiers as they leaped into the ditch from the south.

So ambitious was the design of the fort that it took the better part of two decades to complete the work. By the time it was finished it was obsolete, but, considering Bermuda's history of nonexistent military confrontations, that seemed to be beside the point.

The fort was equipped with a pair of 64lb rifled muzzleloader (RML) cannons mounted on Moncrieff 'disappearing' carriages that recoiled down into recesses for reloading after firing; 5-ton counterweights then raised the carriages back to position.

In an interesting twist of fate, American troops finally did come to occupy Scaur Hill Fort, albeit by British invitation, when the 52nd Coast Artillery Battalion of the US Army took up station at the fort during WWII.

Visitors can explore the old parade grounds, march along the ditch, view the stone galleries with their cannon and rifle windows and peer into the concrete emplacements that held the disappearing RML cannons. However, true to their names, the big guns themselves have disappeared from the site.

Scaur Hill Fort is open 7:30 am to 4 pm daily. Admission is free, and on weekdays there's usually an on-site caretaker who can answer questions.

Springfield & the Gilbert Nature Reserve

This combined historic site and nature reserve, on Somerset Rd at the south side of Somerset Village, once comprised a small plantation. The manor house, known as Springfield, dates to the 17th century and was purchased by the Bermuda National

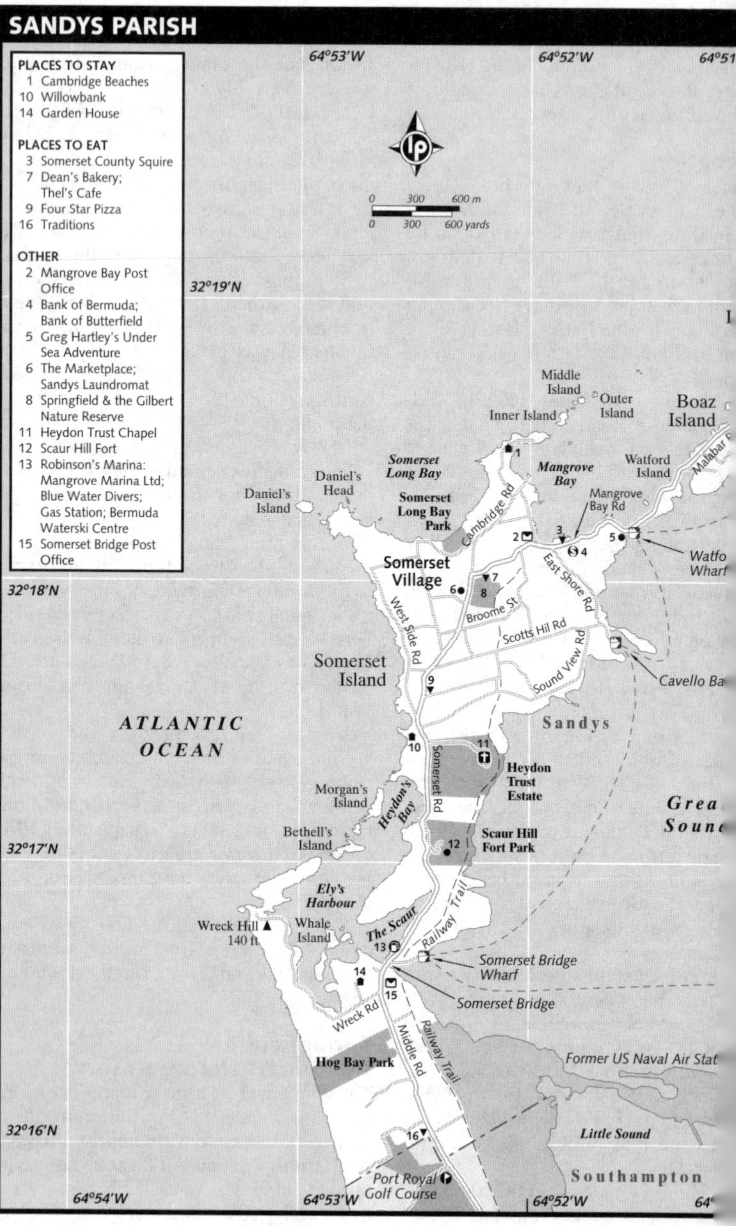
SANDYS PARISH
PLACES TO STAY
1 Cambridge Beaches
10 Willowbank
14 Garden House
PLACES TO EAT
3 Somerset County Squire
7 Dean's Bakery; Thel's Cafe
9 Four Star Pizza
16 Traditions
OTHER
2 Mangrove Bay Post Office
4 Bank of Bermuda; Bank of Butterfield
5 Greg Hartley's Under Sea Adventure
6 The Marketplace; Sandys Laundromat
8 Springfield & the Gilbert Nature Reserve
11 Heydon Trust Chapel
12 Scaur Hill Fort
13 Robinson's Marina: Mangrove Marina Ltd; Blue Water Divers; Gas Station; Bermuda Waterski Centre
15 Somerset Bridge Post Office
64°53'W
64°52'W
0 300 600 m
0 300 600 yards
32°19'N
32°18'N
32°17'N
32°16'N
64°54'W
Middle Island
Outer Island
Inner Island
Boaz Island
Watford Island
Malabar
Somerset Long Bay
Mangrove Bay
Daniel's Head
Daniel's Island
Somerset Long Bay Park
Cambridge Rd
Mangrove Bay Rd
Somerset Village
East Shore Rd
West Side Rd
Broome St
Scotts Hil Rd
Sound View Rd
Somerset Island
Cavello Bay
ATLANTIC OCEAN
Sandys
Somerset Rd
Heydon Trust Estate
Morgan's Island
Heydon's Bay
Bethell's Island
Scaur Hill Fort Park
Ely's Harbour
Wreck Hill 140 ft
Whale Island
The Scaur
Railway Trail
Somerset Bridge Wharf
Somerset Bridge
Wreck Rd
Middle Rd
Hog Bay Park
Little Sound
Port Royal Golf Course
Southampton

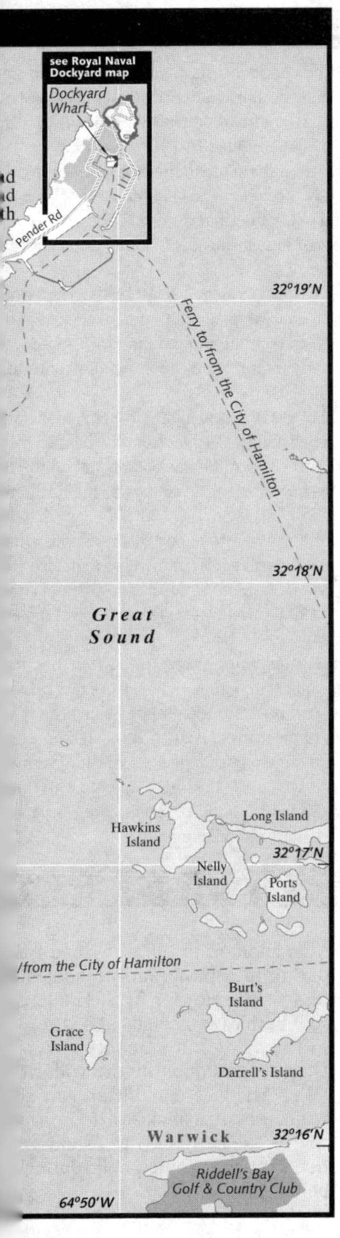

Trust in 1967. Today Springfield holds a nursery school and private apartments.

The adjacent 5-acre property, the Gilbert Nature Reserve, was purchased by the Trust in 1973 to protect its rural nature from potential development. The reserve is crossed with short footpaths that begin at the southwest side of the parking lot. The paths start in thick brush and wind past wooded areas that include mature native cedar trees as well as more recently planted cedar and palmetto trees.

Somerset Long Bay

Sandys is not endowed with the same type of glorious beaches found in neighboring parishes to its south. The main public bathing spot is **Somerset Long Bay Park**, off Cambridge Rd at the northwest side of Somerset Island. It has a sandy beach with shallow waters that are generally suitable for children; visitors will also find parking, toilets and picnic facilities.

Perhaps more interesting than the beach is the adjacent **Somerset Long Bay Nature Reserve**. A former dump site that's now owned by the Bermuda Audubon Society, this wetland habitat serves as an important nesting site for resident waterfowl and also attracts migratory birds. A trail through tall grasses at the southwest side of Somerset Long Bay Park leads into the sanctuary. Just two minutes along that trail will bring you to a good duck-viewing area. At various times of the year, you might also spot migratory herons, egrets, warblers and kingfishers, as well as resident catbirds and cardinals.

Heydon Trust Estate

The Heydon Trust Estate, along Middle Rd north of Scaur Hill Fort, is a privately held 43-acre tract of undeveloped open space. The property has banana groves, citrus orchards, gardens and wooded areas, the latter including one of the island's finest remaining stands of Bermuda cedar trees.

The centerpiece of the Heydon Trust Estate is a hilltop **chapel**, which occupies a little limestone cottage that is one of Bermuda's oldest structures, dating to the early 17th century. Inspired by its peaceful setting,

Bermuda Lights

On an island that was 'accidentally' discovered by shipwrecked castaways, it comes as no sur that marine safety has long been a major concern. Indeed, shortly after the English establishec first settlement in Bermuda, in the early 17th century, a handful of simple light beacons were se prominent hills to help guide approaching ships through Bermuda's tricky reefs.

By the 18th century, increased sea traffic had brought a sharp rise in the frequency of shipw off Bermuda. Alarmed by the situation, the British Navy erected the first lighthouse at Wreck Hi the westernmost tip of Sandys Parish. An elementary structure that burned tar as its light so the Wreck Hill Lighthouse overlooked Western Ledge Flats, a site so notorious for claiming that mariners nicknamed it 'the graveyard.'

The light's strength proved insufficient, however, and in December 1838 the French fr *L'Herminie*, a 300-foot vessel with 60 cannons and a crew of nearly 500 men, went down o reef just 4 miles west of Wreck Hill. In all, some 39 shipwrecks occurred during that decade o west side of Bermuda. In 1840, the British administration responded by appropriating funds to Bermuda's first modern lighthouse.

Situated in Southampton Parish atop 245-foot Gibbs Hill, the new lighthouse began operat May 1846. The tower, constructed of cast iron, extended a lofty 117 feet from the base to the Fired by sperm whale oil that burned from four concentric wicks, the revolving light had the c ity to reach not only the treacherous western shoals, but substantial sections of the norther southern shoals as well.

In the years that followed, attention shifted to the northeastern side of the island, whe George Somers had wrecked the *Sea Venture* some 250 years earlier and which remained be the reach of the Gibbs Hill light. In the 1870s, following a rash of shipwrecks on the reefs no St George's, Bermuda's second lighthouse, St David's Lighthouse, was built atop a hill at the e side of that parish.

This second light filled in the former blind spot. Furthermore, when viewed together, th lights cast from opposite ends of Bermuda allowed captains to gauge their ship's exact positi the decades that followed, the frequency of shipwrecks off Bermuda dropped significantly - many of the more notorious ones occurring in times of mechanical failures at the lighthouses

Both of Bermuda's 19th-century lighthouses stand largely unchanged, except for the m ization of their light mechanisms. Instead of burning whale oil, they now operate on 100(electric bulbs, which cast beams 40 miles out to sea. Bermuda's lighthouses also serve as lanc for airplane pilots, who can spot the lights from more than 100 miles away.

an interdenominational Christian organization has been using the cottage as a chapel since 1974.

Visitors are free to take a look at the chapel, which is used for informal sunrise and afternoon prayer services. Opposite the chapel is a lookout point with a vista of the Great Sound. If you look straight out you'll get a bird's-eye view of Tucker's Peninsula, which once served as home to the US Naval Air Station Annex.

In addition to the views and tra during the spring and autumn mi seasons the Heydon Trust Estate is spot for birdwatching.

The road into the property, Drive, begins opposite the Willowb tel on Middle Rd and leads east al yards, where it makes a loop aro chapel. The Heydon Trust Estate is c free of charge to the public during hours.

Bay Park

3ay Park, at the south side of Sandys, is f Bermuda's newest public parks, its 38 comprised of property purchased from adjoining estates.

: three estates had kept the land in a ıl state, free of 20th-century develop- consequently, the park is a repository ts for Bermuda's rural past and holds relics dating to the early colonial per- ɪring that period, Sandys and nearby ampton Parish held a substantial er of Bermuda's farms; Hog Bay Park orates a block of that original agri- al land. In the early 1990s, before the ty was opened as a public park, re- ers from the College of William and n Williamsburg, Virginia, uncovered a r of artifacts and identified some of es of former sites. The sites include a sed for the production of lime; the nts of servants' quarters; and the re- of a buttery, a small structure used for orage in pre-refrigeration days.

Bay Park, which extends from Rd to the Atlantic Ocean, can be a ice to explore for those who enjoy g about old house sites and the like. around the property are fallow fields ce grew tobacco and cassava, aban- cottages, a lime kiln and some mature of native trees. The path begins at the e parking area at the northeast cor- he park and can be followed all the wn to the bay, where hikers will be ed with a fine coastal view.

or Activities

ve Marina Ltd, at Robinson's Marina erset Bridge, rents kayaks, canoes, oats, snorkel sets and fishing gear. ater Divers, which also operates out nson's Marina, arranges diving, and acent Bermuda Waterski Centre s waterskiing. Greg Hartley's Under enture conducts helmet-diving trips : Watford Bridge dock.

i-mile stretch of the Railway Trail m Southampton Parish to Somerset The section on Somerset Island is open to both hikers and motorbikes and is a scenic route, with views of the Great Sound along the way. En route, the Railway Trail passes the eastern sides of Scaur Hill Fort Park, the Heydon Trust Estate and the Gilbert Nature Reserve, offering hikers some nice diversions.

See the appropriate activity in the Outdoor Activities chapter for details on the above establishments.

Places to Stay

Garden House *(☎ 234-1435, fax 234-3006, 4 Middle Rd, Somerset Bridge, Sandys SB 01)* is an old Bermuda home with a handful of rental units in a quiet setting just south of Somerset Bridge. Accommodations include a studio unit with private bath and kitchen, as well as a one-bedroom one-bath cottage and a two-bedroom two-bath cottage, both with living rooms, kitchens and private baths. All units have phones, TVs and VCRs. The owner's Doberman handles security on this quiet 2-acre estate, which contains a pool and fruit trees. Rates are $100/105 in winter/summer for the studio, $115/120 for the one-bedroom cottage and $215/245 for the two-bedroom cottage. These rates include up to two people in the smaller units and four people in the two-bedroom cottage.

Willowbank *(☎ 234-1616, 800-752-8493 in the USA, ☎ 800-463-8444 in Canada, email reservations@willowbank.bm, PO Box MA 296, Sandys MA BX)* is a 65-unit complex on the beach southwest of Somerset Village. This is a nondenominational Christian hotel with an alcohol-free environment that caters to families. There are some religious services, mainly a morning Bible study and evening hymn sessions, but they are optional. Accommodations, which are in a dozen low-rise buildings spread around the 6-acre grounds, are comfortable enough but basic. Rooms have private baths but no TVs or phones. Singles begin at $116/144 in winter/summer and doubles begin at $186/228. Breakfast and dinner are included in the rates. There's a coffee shop that serves soup and sandwiches at lunchtime, and the grounds have two tennis courts and a heated pool.

***Cambridge Beaches** (☎ 234-0331, 800-468-7300 in the USA, ☎ 800-463-5990 in Canada, fax 234-3352, email cambeach@ibl.bm, Somerset MA 02)* is an exclusive cottage community spread out along a 25-acre peninsula at the northernmost point of Somerset Island. It's bordered by sandy beaches and has its own marina that offers guests a complimentary shuttle to Hamilton. All 81 of the units have air-conditioning and private baths; most also have waterview terraces. Rates for singles begin at $250/390 in winter/summer, doubles at $280/420, breakfast and dinner included. An array of activities is available for guests, ranging from lawn croquet and tennis to deep-sea fishing. In addition to the ground's five private beaches, there are a couple of pools and a health spa. The resort has a website at www.cambridgebeaches.com.

Places to Eat

The village of Somerset is not a dining destination per se, but there are several places where you can grab a quick bite if you are wandering around the area at mealtime.

On Somerset Rd, northeast of Springfield & the Gilbert Nature Reserve, you'll find two local eateries. ***Dean's Bakery** (☎ 234-2918)* has the usual bakery items, as well as inexpensive sandwiches and meat pies; it's open 6:30 am to 6 pm Monday to Saturday. The nearby ***Thel's Cafe** (☎ 234-1767, 19 Somerset Rd)* features simple fare, including omelets ($7.50) served all day. There are also lunch and dinner plates, such as fried chicken with macaroni, for around $10. Thel's is open 6 am to 9:30 pm daily (to 11:30 pm Friday and Saturday).

The ***Somerset Country Squire** (☎ 234-0105, 10 Mangrove Bay Rd)*, a basement pub in the village center, has sandwiches for around $8 and curry of the day or steak and kidney pie for double that. At dinner, seafood and steak dishes are priced from $20. In summer, you can opt to sit at the outdoor patio that overlooks Mangrove Bay. Meals are available 11:30 am to 4 pm and 6:30 to 10 pm daily.

***Four Star Pizza** (☎ 234-2626, 65 Somerset Rd)*, south of Somerset Village, charges $11 for a 10-inch cheese pizza or $16 fo loaded with toppings. It's open 11 am least 11 pm daily except Sunday, whe open 1 to 10 pm.

At the very southern end of the p opposite the gate to the former US Air Station Annex, is ***Traditions** (☎ 3770, 2 Middle Rd)*, a friendly neighbo restaurant with affordable prices. It various breakfast options, including French toast or pancakes served with juice and coffee for $7.50. At lunc dinner the menu ranges from sandw gardenburgers and hamburgers for a $4 to a combination steak and se platter for $16. Traditions is open 7 9 pm Monday to Saturday.

You can pick up groceries at ***The M place***, on Somerset Rd opposite Spri & the Gilbert Nature Reserve. The s open 7 am to 10 pm Monday to Satu to 5 pm Sunday.

Getting There & Around

The main road through Sandys is M Rd, which changes its name to Somer as it crosses Somerset Bridge, to Ma Bay Rd as it passes the village of So and to Malabar Rd as it continues the Royal Naval Dockyard.

Bus Bus Nos 7 and 8 operate along th road. When you're boarding in the Hamilton, take note of the desti marked on the front of the bus, as s these buses only go as far as Barnes in Southampton Parish; others stop i erset Village and still others go on Royal Naval Dockyard. Service b Hamilton and Somerset Village ru every 15 minutes during the day an once every 30 minutes in the eveni the last bus at 11:45 pm (10:45 pm S

Ferry The Somerset/Dockyard rou vides service between the City of H and Sandys Parish, with stops at th Naval Dockyard, Boaz Island, W Bridge, Cavello Bay and Somerset The order of stops varies with the so check the schedule beforeha

ule is most frequent on weekdays and frequent on Sunday. For more detailed nation, see the Ferry section in the ng Around chapter, near the front of ook.

AL NAVAL DOCKYARD

the American Revolution in 1776, the n, who were no longer able to use ports former American colonies, needed a dockyard facility and resupply depot ad the capacity to repair naval vessels so serve as a midway station between Scotia and the British West Indies.

serve this purpose, hilly Ireland Island, western tip of Bermuda, was ear- d to become a new 'Gibraltar of the The location was selected because it deepwater cove, a huge sheltered an- ge and commanding land and sea of all approaches. Surveys and draw- y military architects and engineers ndertaken and construction began in

h of the back-breaking work was out by convicts who were brought ritain and quartered in 'prison ships': ermanently docked hulks with un- bly crowded conditions and wretched ion. Outbreaks of diseases, including fever, claimed hundreds of prisoners. nearly 10,000 convicts were sent to da between 1814 and 1863 to work on ckyard and related projects.

main elements of the Georgian-style, ne-block Dockyard fort were com- in the 1820s, but construction on uildings, including many of the mag- continued until the 1860s.

of the Royal Naval Dockyard's first operations took place while the fort under construction: during the War , a British fleet set sail from the rd in August 1814 on the infamous it sacked and burned Washington, the years that followed, the Dock- t only kept tabs on American activi- the Atlantic, but also on French rs in the West Indies.

e 20th century, the Royal Naval rd served as a North Atlantic base during WWI and WWII and was used briefly by NATO during the postwar period. Still, with the collapse of the British Empire, activities at the Dockyard base tapered off. Strapped for cash, the British Admiralty decided it no longer needed the remote outpost and in 1951 the Royal Naval Dockyard was closed and the property abandoned.

Since then, the Dockyard's buildings have been renovated and given a second life. The Bermuda Maritime Museum occupies the buildings in the former Keep. The Cooperage, where barrels were made, is now the site of an atmospheric pub, a movie theater and the Bermuda Craft Market. The attractive twin-towered naval administration building on the waterfront has been turned into a shopping center, called the Clocktower Mall.

Most people visit the Royal Naval Dockyard to have lunch at one of the restaurants, browse for souvenirs at the crafts shops or shop at the Clocktower Mall. In addition to the Bermuda Maritime Museum, you can pleasantly pass an hour or two simply strolling about the rest of the Dockyard grounds. For those who care to explore the underwater world as well, there is the Bermuda Snorkel Park, where masks and snorkels can be rented.

There's no admission charge to the Royal Naval Dockyard, except for entry into the Bermuda Maritime Museum and the Bermuda Snorkel Park.

Information

There's a small Visitors Service Bureau (☎ 234-3824) in the old Cooperage where you can get brochures and general tourist information. It also sells one-day and three-day bus passes. It's open 9 am to 5 pm Sunday to Friday, though hours are sometimes reduced slightly in winter.

The Bank of Bermuda, west of the tourist office on Dockyard Terrace, is open 9 am to 3 pm Monday to Thursday, 11 am to 4:30 pm Friday and 11 am to 1 pm Saturday. It has an ATM that's accessible at other times.

The tourist office sells phone cards in $10 to $25 denominations. There are pay phones at a number of points around the Dockyard,

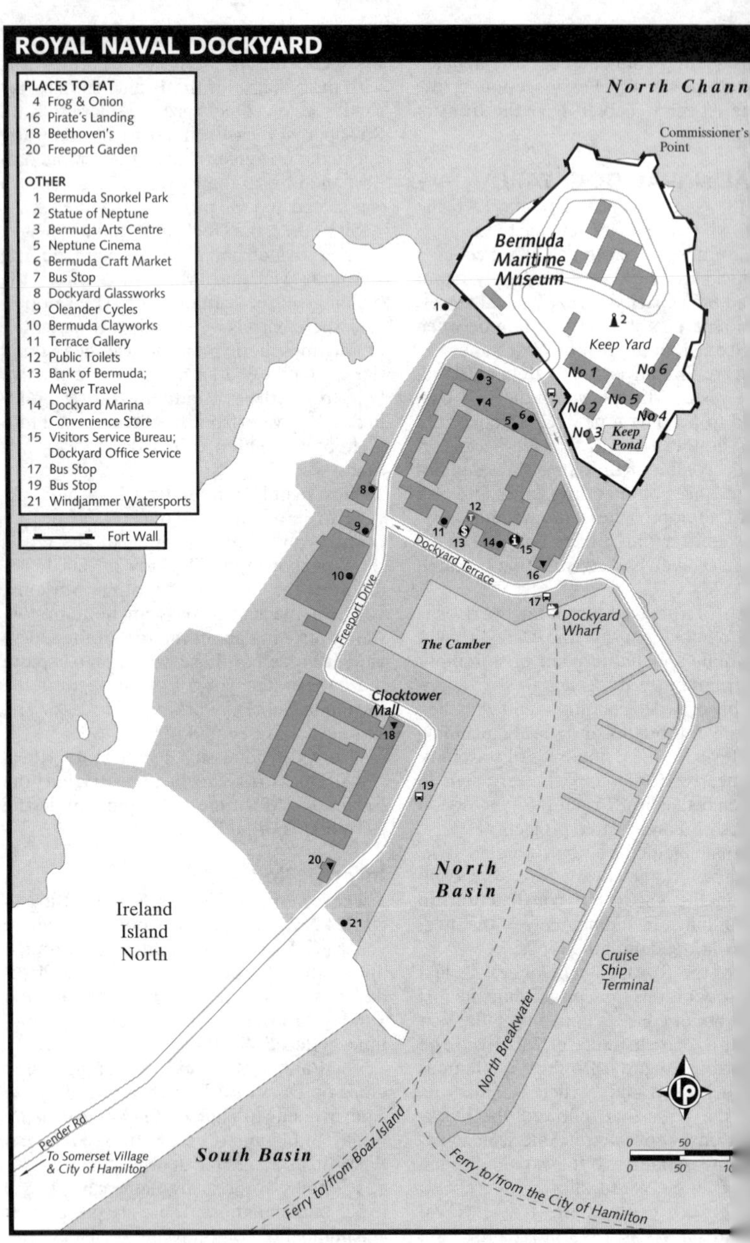
ROYAL NAVAL DOCKYARD
PLACES TO EAT
4 Frog & Onion
16 Pirate's Landing
18 Beethoven's
20 Freeport Garden
OTHER
1 Bermuda Snorkel Park
2 Statue of Neptune
3 Bermuda Arts Centre
5 Neptune Cinema
6 Bermuda Craft Market
7 Bus Stop
8 Dockyard Glassworks
9 Oleander Cycles
10 Bermuda Clayworks
11 Terrace Gallery
12 Public Toilets
13 Bank of Bermuda; Meyer Travel
14 Dockyard Marina Convenience Store
15 Visitors Service Bureau; Dockyard Office Service
17 Bus Stop
19 Bus Stop
21 Windjammer Watersports
Fort Wall
North Chann
Commissioner's Point
Bermuda Maritime Museum
Keep Yard
No 1
No 2
No 3
No 4
No 5
No 6
Keep Pond
Dockyard Terrace
Freeport Drive
Dockyard Wharf
The Camber
Clocktower Mall
North Basin
Cruise Ship Terminal
North Breakwater
Ireland Island North
Pender Rd
To Somerset Village & City of Hamilton
South Basin
Ferry to/from Boaz Island
Ferry to/from the City of Hamilton

ding the cruise ship terminal and the :tower Mall.

ere's a travel agency, Meyer Travel 4-2992), on the 2nd floor of the build- at houses the Bank of Bermuda.

e Dockyard Marina Convenience Store, ent to the tourist office and open 8 am om daily, sells soda, beer and snacks lso carries simple snorkeling gear.

nuda Maritime Museum

uda's most significant historic mu- the Bermuda Maritime Museum, was urated by Queen Elizabeth II in 1975. useum occupies the Dockyard's 6-acre which retains its original fortress cha- , separated from the rest of the Dock- y a moat. Indeed, to enter the gate of eep today you must still walk across oat footbridge.

ny of the exhibits are in ordnance ngs, the high-vaulted brick ceilings of were once stacked with munitions; days, each building contains displays erent themes.

lding No 1, known as the Queen's Ex- n Hall, has exhibits on the naval ties en Canada and Bermuda, displays on g and navigation, and model ships, in- ; one of the *Deliverance* and others of adian-built two-masted schooners. ote of the bitumen (tar) floor in this ne bitumen, which came from Pitch n Trinidad, was spread on the floor to t sparking when barrels were rolled it. Nearly 5000 barrels of gunpowder tored in Building No 1. In the event tumen alone didn't handle the situa- e limestone walls were constructed a eet thick in the hopes of minimizing e from a potential explosion.

back, Building No 2 is the former House, erected in 1837 to temporar- e munitions unloaded from ships re being repaired in the Dockyard. t houses a fascinating collection of s recovered from shipwrecks, includ- es of pewter and pottery from the *ture*, as well as silver and gold coins, d jewelry that was recovered from ntury Spanish shipwrecks.

NED FRIARY

Another version of this replica of the *Deliverance* can be seen at the Bermuda Maritime Museum.

Building No 3, to the immediate south, contains a collection of Bermuda bills and coins, including specimens of the island's unique hog money. Building No 4, at the southeast corner, has period maps and other items from the early explorers who came to Bermuda and the New World.

Building No 5, the Forster Cooper Building, is a former cooperage that made the all-essential barrels that were once used to store virtually everything from ale to gunpowder. Now the building houses exhibits on shipbuilding and the history of the Dockyard; a separate entrance leads to an interesting collection of more than 1000 antique bottles.

The largest collection of items can be found in Building No 6, the Boatloft, at the east side of the Keep Yard. There you'll find an extensive display on Bermuda dinghies, 14-foot boats made of Bermuda cedar and driven by oversized sails. In addition to a completely fitted dinghy and other related exhibits, there's also a children's room with some interactive displays and play stations featuring maritime themes.

Beyond the indoor exhibits, visitors can also wander around the Keep Pond; view the oversized statue of Neptune, which stands in the Keep Yard; and walk through the gate to the upper grounds, where sheep graze.

At the upper grounds you can walk along the lofty fortress walls, which are still dotted with old cannons, and enjoy fine views of the surrounding coast. In this same area, at the highest point on the museum's grounds, you'll find the Commissioner's House, the substantial former home of the Royal Naval Dockyard commissioner. After years of neglect, this multistory stone house, which dates to 1823, has just undergone a thorough renovation and will now be used to host banquets and other special events.

The museum is open 10 am (9:30 am in summer) to 5 pm daily, with the last entry allowed at 4:30 pm. Admission is $7.50 for adults, $6 for senior citizens, $3 for children ages five to 18, and free for children under five.

Bermuda Snorkel Park

The Bermuda Snorkel Park (☎ 234-1006), at the northwest side of the Royal Naval Dockyard, has a shallow lagoon, a small sandy beach and a nearshore reef that offers decent snorkeling.

Located directly under the towering walls of the Bermuda Maritime Museum, the water contains a handful of colonial-era cannons that were probably shoved over the fortress walls when they proved defective. The park installs buoys to identify the cannon locations, but they don't maintain them, so you may have to ask the attendant for directions. Those who don a mask can also expect to see a few dozen varieties of tropical fish, including colorful butterfly fish, turquoise wrasses and large coral-chopping parrotfish. One caveat: although the beach usually appears clean, the area was formerly a landfill and heavy storms can expose some of the buried fill, temporarily trashing the shoreline.

For $2 visitors can go in and use the b
or for $17.50 rent a snorkel, mask, fin
buoyancy vest for the day. If you only w
spend a short time in the water, you ca
rent the gear for just one hour at $10.
are showers and changing rooms on sit

The snorkel park is open only duri
peak tourist season, from May th
October. The hours are from 9:30 am to
daily.

Places to Eat

If you're up for a frozen yogurt or ice c
the Clocktower Mall has a ***Häagen-D***
cream shop, where a small scoop will s
back just $2.50.

Frog & Onion *(☎ 234-2900)*, which
its name from its two owners, one
and one Bermudian, has a period p
mosphere and easily rates as the Dock
most popular dining spot. At lunch th
specialty salads or a variety of sand
for around $10. You'll also find all th
pub standards, including fish and
meat pies and bangers and mash at
ate prices. In addition, there's a full
menu with the likes of grilled tuna or
lamb for $19 to $24. Lunch is serve
11:30 am (noon on Sunday) to 4 p
dinner from 6 to around 9:30 pm;
stays open until midnight. It's clo
Monday in winter.

If you prefer someplace a bit chea
Pirate's Landing *(☎ 234-5151)*, a caf
site the ferry dock, has simple lunch
cluding burgers or salads for around
a daily pasta special for $9. Betwee
7 pm there's an $18 early-bird me
offers your choice of pasta, soup
and dessert with coffee; otherwise
entrees range from $13 for pasta to
steak. It's open 11:30 am to 4 pm f
and 6 to 10 pm for dinner.

Freeport Garden *(☎ 234-1692, 1*
Rd), opposite the south side of the
tower Mall, is an unpretentious re
that serves up a BLT or hamburg
complete with fries and coleslaw for
also has pasta dishes and garlic bre
$12 and local favorites such as curry
or fish and chips for a few dolla

ɔort Garden is open 11:30 am to 6 pm ay to Wednesday and from 11:30 am to n Thursday to Saturday.

e Dockyard's newest restaurant, *oven's (☎ 234-5009)*, in the Clocktower is owned and managed by a pair of chefs. It offers an eclectic menu that les appetizers such as Scottish smoked n, tuna carpaccio or tempura snails for d $15, and main dishes like teriyaki breast or Angus steak in port wine for around $25. It's open for lunch 11:30 am to 3 pm daily, year-round. r is available in the summer season to 9 pm Thursday to Saturday.

rtainment

rog & Onion (☎ 234-2900) has pool , and during the cruise ship season s DJ music on Wednesday nights.

Neptune Cinema (☎ 234-2923), op- the Frog & Onion, shows first-run ood movies.

ping

erage Area The Bermuda Craft t (☎ 434-3208), 4 Freeport Rd, has an ve selection of handicrafts made by rtists. There are various stalls selling ately priced jewelry, pottery, water- stained glass, candles, hand-printed and similar items that could make ouvenirs. It's open 10 am to 5 pm

Bermuda Arts Centre (☎ 234-2809), north side of the craft market, sells y local artists in a variety of media g paintings, sculpture, pottery, wood- batiks, prints and notecards. Five ave permanent studios in the center, g one that specializes in quilted wall s and another who sculpts with fra- tive Bermuda cedar. It's open 10 am daily.

iew Terrace Gallery (☎ 234-0701), 5 rd Terrace, also has an artist-in- e program with studios and a gallery t's open 10 am to 5 pm daily.

ockyard Glassworks (☎ 234-4216), port Drive, you can watch glass- at work and purchase the final product. There are plates and bowls, mostly priced from $35 to $100, as well as cheaper Bermuda tree frog and snail figurines ($12), wind chimes and knickknacks. If you want to buy a locally made souvenir, be sure to look at the labels carefully as some of the lower priced items are imported. It's open 10 am to 5 pm daily, but there are no glassblowing demonstrations on Monday and Friday.

You also can watch potters at work at the Bermuda Clayworks (☎ 234-5116), on Freeport Drive, where skilled artisans create the pottery that's sold on site. Many of the pieces have attractive island-themed designs, ranging from dolphins and ocean patterns to the more abstract. Mugs cost around $20, and vases are priced from around $50. It's open 9 am to 5 pm daily.

Clocktower Mall The Clocktower Mall contains an array of shops and galleries. It's open 9:30 am to 5 pm weekdays, 10 am to 5 pm Saturday and 11 am to 5 pm Sunday.

The Michael Swan Gallery has a variety of gift items including pastel prints of Bermuda scenes, with some nice choices from around $50. The Carole Holding Studio also has island-themed watercolors. Ships Inn Book Gallery specializes in used books on Bermuda, including rare and antique tomes. Calypso carries stylish women's clothing, leather bags and jewelry. Davidson's of Bermuda has T-shirts and other casual wear. Makin Waves specializes

What Time Is It?

At first glance, it might seem redundant that the Clocktower Mall, which once served as an administration building, has two separate 100-foot-high clocktowers. If you look closer, you'll notice that the clocks on the two towers read differently – but that's by design, not error. As with everything else in the Dockyard, the clocks had a practical purpose related to the sea: one was installed to show the actual time, the other to indicate the time of high tide.

in beach items such as sunglasses, sunblock, sun hats, T-shirts and sandals. Dockyard Linens sells tea towels and placemats with Bermuda designs.

The Clocktower Mall also has branches of a couple of Hamilton's leading stores, including AS Cooper & Sons, which has everything from fashionable clothing and perfume to Waterford crystal and Wedgwood porcelain. Crisson has a wide collection of watches, ranging from high-end brands like Rolex and Cartier to moderately priced items made by Seiko and Casio; it also carries expensive imported jewelry and gemstones as well as Bermudian-themed pendants and bracelets with sea turtles, seashells and similar designs.

Also in the mall is Dockyard Wines & Spirits, which has a small collection of wines and spirits and can deliver duty-free liquor to your ship.

Getting There & Around

Bus No 7, which travels via the south shore, leaves the Royal Naval Dockyard for the City of Hamilton at 20 and 50 minutes past the hour, and bus No 8, which travels to Hamilton via Middle Rd, leaves the Dockyard at five and 35 minutes past the hour. On weekdays, buses operate on this schedule from 6:35 am to 6:35 pm, after which there are a few staggered night buses, th leaving the Dockyard at 11:50 pm. On day the schedule is slightly lighte there's no bus service from the Doc after 6:35 pm.

If you pick up a No 7 or 8 bus in H ton, make sure it reads 'Dockyard,' as buses continue that far. Travel time on bus route averages about an hour be Hamilton and the Dockyard.

The ferry between Hamilton an Royal Naval Dockyard makes an inte alternative to the bus; you might w take the ferry one way and the bus the

The ferry runs 11 times a day on days. It takes between 30 and 75 minu pending on whether you catch a nonsto or one that stops at various places in S Parish en route. Boats are slightly le quent on Saturday and half as frequ Sunday. For more details, see the section in the Getting Around chapte

During the tourist season, Ol Cycles (☎ 234-2764) rents mopeds west side of the Royal Naval Dockya

The Bermuda Train Company (5972) offers a motorized shuttle aro Royal Naval Dockyard for $2 a ri signed to resemble a miniature tra shuttle follows the main roads arou Dockyard continuously throughout

cknowledgments

NKS

to the following intrepid readers who used the first edition of Bermuda and wrote in with comments and advice:

Orr, Fiona Campbell, Jean Whittaker, Joris Van Dele, Laura Lee, Manuel Joe Fumagger, ne Friesen, Mary E Moore, Mike Walmsley, Nicky & Phil Viner, Rich Schwerdt, Richelle F Roy Little

Guides by Region

Lonely Planet is known worldwide for publishing practical, reliab no-nonsense travel information in our guides and on our web si Lonely Planet list covers just about every accessible part of the Currently there are fifteen series: travel guides, Shoestrings, Cond Phrasebooks, Read This First, Healthy Travel, Walking guides, Cycling guides, Pisces Diving & Sno guides, City Maps, Travel Atlases, Out to Eat, World Food, Journeys travel literature and Pictori

---

AFRICA Africa on a shoestring • Africa – the South • Arabic (Egyptian) phrasebook • Arabic (Mo phrasebook • Cairo • Cape Town • Cape Town city map • Central Africa • East Africa • Egypt • Egyp atlas • Ethiopian (Amharic) phrasebook • The Gambia & Senegal • Healthy Travel Africa • Kenya • Keny atlas • Malawi, Mozambique & Zambia • Morocco • North Africa • Read This First Africa • South Africa, & Swaziland • South Africa, Lesotho & Swaziland travel atlas • Swahili phrasebook • Tanzania, Zar Pemba • Trekking in East Africa • Tunisia • West Africa • Zimbabwe, Botswana & Namibia • Zim Botswana & Namibia travel atlas • World Food Morocco

Travel Literature: The Rainbird: A Central African Journey • Songs to an African Sunset: A Zimbabwe • Mali Blues: Traveling to an African Beat

AUSTRALIA & THE PACIFIC Auckland • Australia • Australian phrasebook • Bushwalking in Australia walking in Papua New Guinea • Fiji • Fijian phrasebook • Healthy Travel Australia, NZ and the Pacific • of Australia's Great Barrier Reef • Melbourne • Melbourne city map • Micronesia • New Caledonia • Ne Wales & the ACT • New Zealand • Northern Territory • Outback Australia • Out to Eat – Melbourn to Eat – Sydney • Papua New Guinea • Pidgin phrasebook • Queensland • Rarotonga & the Cook Samoa • Solomon Islands • South Australia • South Pacific • South Pacific Languages phrasebook • S Sydney city map • Sydney condensed • Tahiti & French Polynesia • Tasmania • Tonga • Tramping Zealand • Vanuatu • Victoria • Western Australia

Travel Literature: Islands in the Clouds • Kiwi Tracks: A New Zealand Journey • Sean & David's Long

CENTRAL AMERICA & THE CARIBBEAN Bahamas, Turks & Caicos • Bermuda • Central America o string • Costa Rica • Cuba • Dominican Republic & Haiti • Eastern Caribbean • Guatemala, Belize & La Ruta Maya • Jamaica • Mexico • Mexico City • Panama • Puerto Rico • Read This First Central America • World Food Mexico • Yucatán

Travel Literature: Green Dreams: Travels in Central America

EUROPE Amsterdam • Amsterdam city map • Andalucía • Austria • Baltic States phrasebook • Ba Berlin • Berlin city map• Britain • British phrasebook • Brussels, Bruges & Antwerp • Budapest city map Islands • Central Europe • Central Europe phrasebook • Corfu & Ionians • Corsica • Crete • Crete c • Croatia • Cyprus • Czech & Slovak Republics • Denmark • Dublin • Eastern Europe • Eastern Europ book • Edinburgh • Estonia, Latvia & Lithuania • Europe on a shoestring • Finland • Florence • France phrasebook • Germany • German phrasebook • Greece • Greek Islands • Greek phrasebook • H Iceland, Greenland & the Faroe Islands • Istanbul city map • Ireland • Italian phrasebook • Italy • Lisbon • London • London city map • London condensed • Mediterranean Europe • Mediterranea phrasebook • Munich • Norway • Paris • Paris city map • Paris condensed • Poland • Portugal • phrasebook • Portugal travel atlas • Prague • Prague city map • Provence & the Côte d'Azur • Read Europe • Romania & Moldova • Rome • Russia, Ukraine & Belarus • Russian phrasebook • Scand Baltic Europe • Scandinavian Europe phrasebook • Scotland • Slovenia • Spain • Spanish phrasebo tersburg • Switzerland • Trekking in Spain • Ukrainian phrasebook • Venice • Vienna • Walking i Walking in Ireland • Walking in Italy • Walking in Spain • Walking in Switzerland • Western Europe Europe phrasebook • World Food Italy • World Food Spain

Travel Literature: The Olive Grove: Travels in Greece

Mail Order

Lonely Planet products are distributed worldwide. They are also available by mail order from Lonely Planet, so if you have difficulty finding a title please write to us. North and South American residents should write to 150 Linden St, Oakland, CA 94607, USA; European frican residents should write to 10a Spring Place, London, NW5 3BH; and residents of other ies to PO Box 617, Hawthorn, Victoria 3122, Australia.

N SUBCONTINENT Bangladesh • Bengali phrasebook • Bhutan • Delhi • Goa • Hindi/Urdu phrasebook • India & Bangladesh travel atlas • Indian Himalaya • Karakoram Highway • Kerala • Mumbai • Nepal • Nepali ook • Pakistan • Rajasthan • Read This First: Asia & India • South India • Sri Lanka • Sri Lanka phrasebook ng in the Indian Himalaya • Trekking in the Karakoram & Hindukush • Trekking in the Nepal Himalaya
iterature: In Rajasthan • Shopping for Buddhas • The Age of Kali

DS OF THE INDIAN OCEAN Madagascar & Comoros • Maldives • Mauritius, Réunion & Seychelles

.E EAST & CENTRAL ASIA Bahrain, Kuwait & Qatar • Central Asia • Central Asia phrasebook • Dubai w phrasebook • Iran • Israel & the Palestinian Territories • Israel & the Palestinian Territories travel atlas ul • Istanbul city map • Istanbul to Cairo on a shoestring • Jerusalem • Jerusalem city map • Jordan • Syria & Lebanon travel atlas • Lebanon • Middle East • Oman & the United Arab Emirates • Syria • • Turkey travel atlas • Turkish phrasebook •Yemen
iterature: The Gates of Damascus • Kingdom of the Film Stars: Journey into Jordan • Black on Black: isited

AMERICA Alaska • Backpacking in Alaska • Baja California • Boston • California & Nevada • Calindensed • Canada • Chicago • Chicago city map • Deep South • Florida • Hawaii • Las Vegas • Los • Miami • New England • New Orleans • New York City • New York city map • New York condensed ork, New Jersey & Pennsylvania • Oahu • Pacific Northwest USA • Puerto Rico • Rocky Mountain San Francisco • San Francisco city map • Seattle • Southwest USA • Texas • USA • USA phrasebook uver • Washington, DC & the Capital Region • Washington, DC city map
terature: Drive Thru America

-EAST ASIA Beijing • Cantonese phrasebook • China • Hong Kong • Hong Kong city map • Hong acau & Guangzhou • Japan • Japanese phrasebook • Japanese audio pack • Korea • Korean phrase-yoto • Mandarin phrasebook • Mongolia • Mongolian phrasebook • North-East Asia on a shoestring • South-West China • Taiwan • Tibet • Tibetan phrasebook • Tokyo
terature: Lost Japan • In Xanadu

AMERICA Argentina, Uruguay & Paraguay • Bolivia • Brazil • Brazilian phrasebook • Buenos Aires Easter Island • Chile & Easter Island travel atlas • Colombia • Ecuador & the Galapagos Islands • Healthy ntral & South America • Latin American Spanish phrasebook • Peru • Quechua phrasebook • Rio de Rio de Janeiro city map • South America on a shoestring • Trekking in the Patagonian Andes • Venezuela
terature: Full Circle: A South American Journey

EAST ASIA Bali & Lombok • Bangkok • Bangkok city map • Burmese phrasebook • Cambodia • Hanoi Travel Asia & India • Hill Tribes phrasebook • Ho Chi Minh City • Indonesia • Indonesia's Eastern ndonesian phrasebook • Indonesian audio pack • Jakarta • Java • Laos • Lao phrasebook • Laos travel alay phrasebook • Malaysia, Singapore & Brunei • Myanmar (Burma) • Philippines • Pilipino (Tagalog) ok • Read This First Asia & India • Singapore • South-East Asia on a shoestring • South-East Asia phrase-hailand • Thailand's Islands & Beaches • Thailand travel atlas • Thai phrasebook • Thai audio pack • • Vietnamese phrasebook • Vietnam travel atlas • World Food Thailand • World Food Vietnam

AILABLE: Antarctica • The Arctic • Brief Encounters: Stories of Love, Sex & Travel • Chasing Rick-onely Planet Unpacked • Not the Only Planet: Travel Stories from Science Fiction • Sacred India • h Children • Traveller's Tales

LONELY PLANET

You already know that Lonely Planet produces more than this guidebook, but you might not be aware of the other products we on this region. Here is a selection of titles which you may want to c out as well:

Diving & Snorkeling Bermuda
ISBN 0 86442 573 2
US$15.95 • UK£9.99 • 120FF

Bahamas, Turks & Caicos
ISBN 1 86450 199 5
US$19.99 • UK£12.99 • 149FF

Jamaica
ISBN 0 86442 780 8
US$17.95 • UK£11.99 • 140FF

Puerto Rico
ISBN 0 86442 552 X
US$15.95 • UK£9.99 • 120FF

Available wherever books are sold.

ONELY PLANET

THE ROAD

vel Guides explore cities, regions and countries and supplies information transport, restaurant and accommodation, regardless of your budget. y come with reliable, easy-to-use maps, practical advice, cultural and orical facts and a run down on attractions both on and off the beaten k. There are over 200 titles in this classic series covering nearly every ntry in the world.

Lonely Planet Upgrades extend the shelf lives of existing travel guides by detailing any changes that may affect travel in a region since the book has been published. Upgrades can be downloaded on **www.lonelyplanet.com/upgrades**

velers with more time than money, **Shoestring** guides offer dependrst-hand information with hundreds of detailed maps, plus insider stretching money as far as possible. Covering entire continents in ases, the six-volume shoestring guides have been known as 'back-' bibles' for over 25 years.

discerning short-term visitor, **Condensed** guides highlight the best ation has to offer in a full-color pocket-sized format designed for ccess. From top sights and walking tours to opinionated reviews of o eat, stay, shop and have fun.

c lets travelers use their Palm™ or Visor™ handheld computers to em through a city's highlights with quick tips on transport, history, life, major sights and shopping and entertainment options. It can ckly search and sort hundreds of reviews of hotels, restaurants and ons and pinpoint the place on scrollable street maps. CitySync can nloaded from www.citysync.com

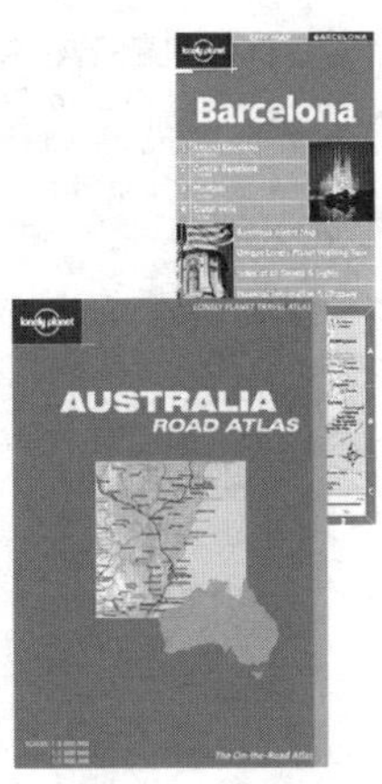

S & ATLASES

Planet's **City Maps** feature downtown and metropolitan maps as ransit routes, and walking tours. The maps come complete with an streets, a listing of sights and a plastic coat for extra durability.

lases are an essential navigation tool for serious travelers. Crossed with the guidebooks, they also feature distance and climate nd a complete site index.

LONELY PLANET

ESSENTIALS

Read This First books help new travelers to hit the road with confidence. These invaluable pre-departure guides give step-by-step advice on preparing for a trip, budgeting, arranging a visa, planning an itinerary and staying safe while still getting off the beaten track.

Healthy Travel pocket guides offer a regional run down on disease hot spots and practical advice on pre-departure health measures, staying well on the road and what to do in emergency situations. The guides come with a user-friendly design and helpful diagrams and tables.

Lonely Planet's **Phrasebooks** cover the essential words and phrases travelers may need when they're strangers in a strange land. It comes in a pocket-sized format with color tabs for quick reference, extensive vocabulary lists, easy-to-follow pronunciation keys and two-way dictionaries.

Lonely Planet's **Travel Journal** is a lightweight but sturdy travel diary for jotting down all those on the road observations and significant travel moments. It comes with a handy time zone wheel, world maps and useful travel information.

Lonely Planet's eKno is an all-in-one communication service developed especially for travelers, with low-cost international calls, free email and voicemail so that you can keep in touch while on the road. Check it out on **www.ekno.lonelyplanet.com**

FOOD & RESTAURANT GUIDES

Lonely Planet's **Out to Eat** guides recommend the brightest and best places to eat and drink in the top international cities. These gourmet companions are arranged by neighborhood, packed with dependable maps, garnished with scene-setting photos and served with quirky features.

For people who live to eat, drink and travel, **World Food** guides are full of lavish photos good enough to eat. They come packed with details on regional cuisine, guides to local markets and produce, sumptuous recipes, useful phrases for shopping and dining, and a comprehensive culinary dictionary.

TDOOR GUIDES

those who believe the best way to see the world is on foot, Lonely et's **Walking Guides** detail everything from family strolls to difficult , with 'when to go and how to do it' advice supplemented by reliable s and essential travel information.

ing Guides map a destination's best bike tours, long and short, in day-lay detail. They contain all the information a cyclist needs, including ce on bike maintenance, places to eat and stay, innovative maps with iled cues to the rides and elevation charts.

Watching Wildlife series is perfect for travelers who want authorita- information but don't want to tote a field guide. Packed with advice where, when and how to view a region's wildlife, each title features tos of over 300 species and contains engaging comments and insights local flora and fauna.

h underwater color photos throughout, **Pisces Books** explore the best diving and snorkeling areas. Each book contains listings of div- ices and dive resorts and detailed information on depth, visibility, of dives and a round up of the marine life you're likely to see your mask.

OFF THE ROAD

Journeys, the travel literature series written by renowned travel authors, capture the spirit of a place or illuminate a culture with a journalist's attention to detail and a novelistic flair for words. These are tales to soak up while you're actually on the road or dip into as an at-home armchair indulgence.

The new range of lavishly illustrated **Pictorial** books is just the ticket for both travelers and dreamers. Off-beat tales and vivid photographs bring the adventure of travel to your doorstep long before the journey begins and long after it is over.

The Lonely Planet **Videos** encourage the same independent tough-minded approach as the guideboks. Currently airing throughout the world, this award-winning series features innovative footage and an all-original soundtrack.

Yes, we know, work is tough, so do a little bit of desk side-dreaming with the spiral bound Lonely Planet **Diary,** the tear away page-a-day **Day to Day Calendar** or any Lonely Planet **Wall Calendar,** filled with great photos from around the world.

TRAVELERS NETWORK

Lonely Planet online, Lonely Planet's award-winning web site has insider information on hundreds of destinations from Amsterdam to Zimbabwe complete with interactive maps and relevant links. The site also offers the latest travel news, recent reports from travelers on the road, guidebook upgrades, a travel links site, an online book buying option and a lively traveler's bulletin board. It can be viewed at www.lonelyplanet.com or AOL keyword: lp

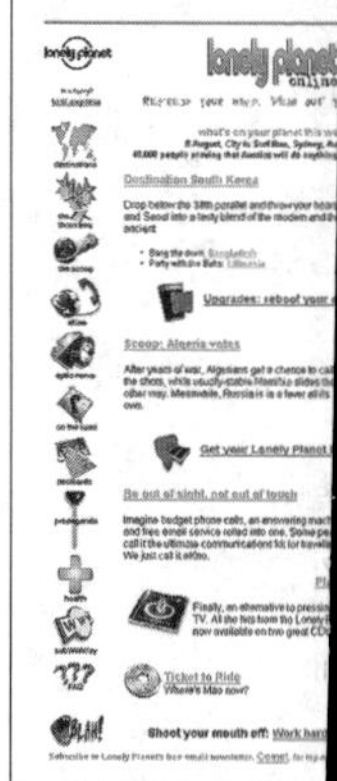

Planet Talk is the quarterly print newsletter full of gossip, advice, anecdotes and author articles. It provides an antidote to the being-at-home blues and lets you plan and dream for the next trip. Contact the nearest Lonely Planet office for your free copy.

Comet, the free Lonely Planet newsletter, comes via email once a month. It's loaded with travel news, advice, dispatches from authors, travel competitions and letters from readers. To subscribe, click on the Comet subscription link on the front page of the web site.

dex

Bold indicates maps.

C

Bold indicates maps.

ed Text

MAP LEGEND

Note: Not all symbols displayed above appear in this book.

LONELY PLANET OFFICES

Australia
PO Box 617, Hawthorn 3122, Victoria
☎ 03 9819 1877 fax 03 9819 6459
email talk2us@lonelyplanet.com.au

USA
150 Linden Street, Oakland, California 94607
☎ 510 893 8555, TOLL FREE 800 275 8555
fax 510 893 8572
email info@lonelyplanet.com

UK
10A Spring Place, London NW5 3BH
☎ 020 7428 4800 fax 020 7428 4828
email go@lonelyplanet.co.uk

France
1 rue du Dahomey, 75011 Paris
☎ 01 55 25 33 00 fax 01 55 25 33 01
www.lonelyplanet.fr

World Wide Web: www.lonelyplanet.com *or* AOL keyword: lp
Lonely Planet Images: lpi@lonelyplanet.com.au